Volume

Rectangular solid

$V = \ell wh$

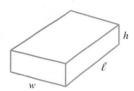

Cone

$$V = \frac{1}{3}\pi r^2 h$$

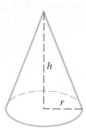

Cube

$V = e^3$

Sphere

$$V = \frac{4}{3}\pi r^3$$

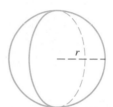

Cylinder

$V = \pi r^2 h$

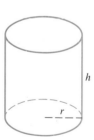

Pyramids

$$V = \frac{1}{3}(\text{area of base})(\text{height})$$

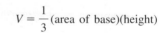

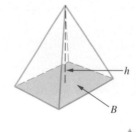

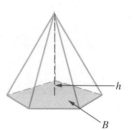

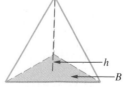

The challenge of climbing a mountain is matched by
the reward of achievement. So it is with many
human activities, perhaps especially learning
math. As the mountain climber perseveres to
reach a goal, so can the student of
Fundamentals of Mathematics.

Instructor's Annotated Edition

Fundamentals
of
Mathematics

Sixth Edition

Jack Barker

James Rogers

James Van Dyke

Portland Community College

SAUNDERS COLLEGE PUBLISHING

Harcourt Brace College Publishers

Fort Worth   Philadelphia   San Diego   New York   Orlando   Austin
San Antonio   Toronto   Montreal   London   Sydney   Tokyo

To our wives:

Mary Barker
Elinore Rogers
Carol Van Dyke

Some material in this work previously appeared in *Fundamentals of Mathematics, Fifth Edition,* copyright © 1991, 1987, 1983, 1979, 1975 by Saunders College Publishing. All rights reserved.

Text Typeface: Times Roman
Compositor: York Graphic Services
Acquisitions Editor: Deirdre Lynch
Developmental Editor: Laurie Golson
Photo Research: Lori Eby, Picture Developmental Editor
Managing Editor: Carol Field
Project Editor: Maureen Iannuzzi
Copy Editor: Colleen Cranney
Manager of Art and Design: Carol Bleistine
Art Director: Anne Muldrow
Art Assistant: Sue Kinney
Text Designer: Rebecca Lemna
Cover Designer: Rebecca Lemna
Text Artwork: Grafacon, Inc.
Layout Artist: York Graphic Services
Director of EDP: Tim Frelick
Production Manager: Carol Florence
Marketing Manager: Monica Wilson

Cover Credit: Mike Powell/© Tony Stone Worldwide

Printed in the United States of America

Instructor's Annotated Edition Fundamentals of Mathematics, Sixth Edition

ISBN: 0-03-010853-5

Library of Congress Catalog Card Number: 94-067076

4567890123   032   10 987654321

CONTENTS

TO THE STUDENT

Fundamentals of Mathematics will help you review basic concepts of mathematics so that you are prepared for proficiency exams or for further college mathematics courses, like basic algebra.

The Challenge and the Reward

Learning mathematics may be challenging, but it is also rewarding: As an adult, you know the many ways we use mathematics in daily modern life — from balancing a checkbook to negotiating a car deal. Not a day goes by that you aren't using math skills. The better your skills, the easier modern life becomes.

The System for Success

Like any challenging activity, succeeding in mathematics happens when you set a goal and make a commitment. It happens when you adopt a system, a routine, for achieving your goal. For instance, if you want to learn karate, you set a goal and make a commitment. You arrange your life so that you can practice regularly, doing the exercises your karate instructor recommends, working hard, and focusing on your goal.

Fundamentals of Mathematics encourages your system for success in two important ways. First, the opening pages for each chapter describe a **mathematics study system** that has proven effective for thousands of students. You may want to read all these opening pages before starting your course, and then refer to them regularly as you go along. Part of the system includes techniques for overcoming the anxiety you may feel about mathematics. Additional study resources are suggested in Appendix B.

Second, each section of *Fundamentals of Mathematics* is organized around a **mathematics learning system.** Each section begins with a short list of objectives — your "mini-goals" for success — and an example of how meeting the objectives can be useful in the real world. Next are the new words you will encounter in the section, because mathematics is a language, and learning the language allows you to learn the skills and concepts of mathematics. Following the vocabulary is the how and why for each objective — explaining the skills and the concepts you need to learn to meet the objective. Key skills and concepts are highlighted in boxes.

Examples for the objective, showing how to use the skills and concepts, are provided next. Paired with each example is a "warm up" problem, with space for you to practice right away what you are learning. Answers for the warm ups are printed on the bottom of the page. Each section concludes with a diverse collection of exercises.

To give you a better idea of how to use the learning system in *Fundamentals of Mathematics,* read the flow chart on the next page. Then go with the flow!

Your Learning System for Success, Chapter by Chapter

Study each section of the chapter.	
Read the Objectives to set your "mini-goals" for the section.	You'll recognize most objectives in highlighted skill boxes later on in the section.
Read the Application to see how the objectives apply to the real world.	The application is marked with the symbol 🌐. This symbol appears again in an example later on, showing how the application problem is solved.
Read the Vocabulary so that you recognize the new words coming up in the section.	You can refer to the vocabulary any time you need to — when you study for the chapter test, for example.
Achieve each objective for the section.	
Read How and Why for the objective. Read slowly, trying to understand the concepts and the skills.	Take special note of **highlighted skills and concepts**, in boxes. Most skill boxes relate directly to an objective. The steps given in a skill box are those you'll see again in examples.
	The **Caution** label alerts you to common mistakes you'll want to avoid.
Study the **Examples** for the objective. If you aren't sure you understand the solutions, reread the How and Why.	Take special note of the common **Directions** and **Strategy** for examples. Try to see the pattern: similar problem, similar strategy. Strategies for examples closely correspond to the highlighted skill boxes, and therefore to the objectives.
	Solutions for the examples are detailed, step-by-step, and annotated with brief explanations.
Try the **Warm ups** paired with the examples. Each warm up is very similar to its paired example.	**Answers** for warm ups are given at the bottom of the page, so you can check your understanding of the paired example immediately.
	Workspace for warm ups is provided right on the page, so you can write and read without breaking your focus.
Go to the next objective or	

Try the **Exercises** for the section. If you have trouble, return to the paired examples and warm ups.

Answers for all odd-numbered exercises are in the back of the book. Exercises are paired, odd with even, so that if you are working the odd exercises correctly, you should be able to work the even exercises correctly, too.

Exercises come in categories. **Categories A, B, and C** are basic skills of progressive difficulty. You should be able to work category A mentally, and your instructor may allow you to use a calculator to work category C.

You'll want to work problems in the **Applications** category, and you may want to try problems in the **Challenge** category. Don't skip the **State Your Understanding** category (because when you can say it, you can do it!) or the **Maintain Your Skills** category (because you'll need to keep doing it!).

Use the **Support Materials** that accompany the book.

If your school has a computer lab or video resources, get additional help from **MathCue™ Interactive Software** or the collection of **videotapes** that accompany the book. You might also consider getting the **Student's Solutions Manual.**

Go to the next section
or

Try the **Concept Review** for the chapter to help you prepare for the chapter test. If you have trouble, go back and review the content.

Answers for all Concept Review questions are in the back of the book. These are true-false questions. False statements need to be rewritten so that they are true.

Take the **Test** for the chapter, timing yourself just as though it were a classroom test. If you do well, then congratulations! Your system for success worked!

Answers for all test questions are in the back of the book, keyed to objectives so that you'll know whether you've reached your ''mini-goals'' (and, if you haven't, which objectives to study again).

Support Materials   An excellent collection of support materials for *Fundamentals of Mathematics* is available to you. In printed, electronic, and video formats, these materials can be an important part of your system for success.

Student's Solutions Manual   Detailed, annotated, step-by-step solutions are provided for every other odd-numbered exercise in the section exercise sets and for every exercise in the Chapter Concept Reviews and Chapter Tests.

Videotapes   An outstanding section-by-section video review features on-location segments to illustrate applications. Each tape covers one chapter, with roughly 15 minutes per section. Experienced video teacher Loretta Palmer from Utah Valley State College reviews examples from the book and explains key concepts, weaving into the presentation real-life footage, movie clips, and interviews with diverse, real-world users of mathematics. Study skills and math anxiety are covered as well.

MathCue™ Interactive Software   Available in IBM and Macintosh formats, *Math-Cue™ Interactive Software* helps you learn, review, and practice skills, discover and explore concepts, and pinpoint and correct weak areas of understanding. *MathCue™* is designed by George W. Bergeman of Northern Virginia Community College and comprises a variety of interactive tools:

Tailored to every section of the book, **MathCue™ Tutorial** gives you problems to solve and tutors you with annotated, step-by-step solutions, each step shown one at a time. *Tutorial* keeps track of your progress and you can check your progress at any time. You can back up to review missed problems or print out your scores. If you miss problems, *Tutorial* tells you which section in the book you should look at again.

MathCue™ Practice helps you focus on solving particular types of problems. From a collection of sample problems, you choose which types and how many of each type you want to practice. If you want, you can get immediate feedback after you work each problem, or you can work in test mode, getting feedback only when you end your practice session. When you start a new session, *Practice* remembers which problem types you have worked on previously, or you can choose other types. *Practice* scores your performance for each problem type, referring you to specific places in the book if you need more help. *Practice* also saves your scores from session to session.

Based on an expert system (a branch of artificial intelligence), **MathCue™ Solution Finder** lets you pose your own problems and get annotated, step-by-step solutions in return. *Solution Finder* tracks your progress, tells you which sections in the book to refer to when appropriate, and prints your scores.

Also available, though only to your instructor, are a collection of tests for each chapter of the book. You might ask your instructor to give you a copy of a chapter test *before* you begin the chapter. Answers for the test include a reference to specific objectives. If your answer is not correct, you will know which objectives to focus especially hard on when you study the chapter.

Standardized Tests   If you are studying *Fundamentals of Mathematics* to prepare for the California Mathematical Skills (ELM) exam, the Texas Academic Skills Program (TASP) exam, or the Florida College Level Academic Skills Test (CLAST), you may find the tables on the following pages helpful. The tables correspond topics covered on the standardized tests with sections or chapters of the book.

CLAST Skills and Their Locations in the Book

Skill	Location in Book
1A1a Add and subtract rational numbers	Sections 3.6–3.9
1A1b Multiply and divide rational numbers	Sections 3.3, 3.4
1A2a Add and subtract rational numbers in decimal form	Sections 4.4, 4.5
1A2b Multiply and divide rational numbers in decimal form	Sections 4.6–4.9
1A3 Calculate percent increase and decrease	Section 6.8
2A1 Recognize the meaning of exponents	Sections 1.7, 2.3, 2.5
2A2 Recognize the role of the base number in determining place value in the base-ten numeration system and in systems that are patterned after it	Sections 1.1, 1.2, 4.1
2A3 Identify equivalent forms of positive rational numbers	Sections 6.2–6.6
2A4 Determine the order relation between magnitudes	Sections 1.2, 3.5, 4.2
4A1 Solve real-world problems which do not require the use of variables and which do not require the use of percent.	Chapters 1, 2, 3, 4, 5
4A2 Solve real-world problems that require the use of percent	Section 6.8
4A3 Solve problems that involve the structure and logic of arithmetic	Throughout
1B1 Round measurements to the nearest given unit of the measuring device	Section 4.3
1B2a Calculate distances	Section 7.4
1B2b Calculate area	Sections 7.5, 7.6
1B2c Calculate volume	Section 7.7
2B2 Classify simple plane figures by recognizing their properties	Chapter 7
3B1 Infer formulas for measuring geometric figures	Chapter 7
3B2 Identify applicable formulas for computing measures of geometric figures	Chapter 7
4B1 Solve real-world problems involving perimeter, area, and volume of geometric figures	Sections 7.4–7.7
1C1a Add and subtract real numbers	Sections 8.2, 8.3
1C1b Multiply and divide real numbers	Sections 8.4, 8.5
1C2 Apply the order of operations agreement to computations involving numbers and variables	Section 8.6
1C4 Solve linear equations and inequalities	Sections 1.4, 1.6, 1.8, 3.4, 3.9, 4.5, 4.8, 4.10, 8.7
1C5 Use given formulas to compute results when geometric measurements are not involved	Throughout
2C3 Recognize statements and conditions of proportionality and variation	Chapter 5
1D1 Identify information contained in a bar, line, and circle graph	Section 6.9
4D1 Interpret real-world data from tables and charts	Section 6.10

ELM Skills and Their Locations in the Book

Skill	Location in Book
Whole numbers and their operations	Chapter 1
Fractions and their operations	Chapter 3
Decimals and their operations	Chapter 4
Exponentiation and square roots	Sections 1.7, 2.3, 2.5
Fraction–decimal conversion	Sections 4.2, 4.9
Applications (averages, percents)	Sections 1.9, 3.10, 4.10, 6.8
Ratio, proportion, and variance	Chapter 5
Reading data from graphs and charts	Sections 6.9, 6.10
Perimeters and areas of triangles, squares, rectangles, and parallelograms	Sections 7.4–7.6
Circumferences and areas of circles	Sections 7.5, 7.6
Volumes of cubes, cylinders, rectangular solids, and spheres	Section 7.7

TASP Skills and Their Locations in the Book

Skill	Location in Book
Use number concepts and computation skills	Throughout
Solve word problems involving integers, fractions, or decimals (including percents, ratios, and proportions)	Chapters 3–6, 8
Solve one- and two-variable equations	Sections 1.4, 1.6, 1.8, 3.4, 3.9, 4.5, 4.8, 4.10, 8.7
Solve problems involving geometric figures	Chapter 7

TO THE INSTRUCTOR

Fundamentals of Mathematics, 6th edition, is a worktext for college students who need to review the basic skills and concepts of arithmetic in order to pass competency or placement exams, or prepare for courses such as business mathematics or elementary algebra. The text is accompanied by a complete system of ancillaries in a variety of media, affording great flexibility for individual instructors and students.

A Textbook for Adult Students

Though the mathematical content of *Fundamentals of Mathematics* is elementary, students using the text are most often mature adults, bringing with them to the course adult attitudes and experiences and a broad range of abilities. Teaching elementary content to these students, therefore, is effective when it accounts for their distinct and diverse adult needs. As you read about and examine the features of *Fundamentals of Mathematics* and its ancillaries, you will see how they especially meet these three needs of your students:

Students must establish good study habits and overcome math anxiety.

Students must see connections between mathematics and the modern, day-to-day world of adult activities.

Students must be paced and challenged according to their individual level of understanding.

A Textbook for Many Course Formats

Fundamentals of Mathematics is suitable for individual study or for a variety of course formats: lab, both supervised and self-paced; lecture; group; or combined formats. For a lecture-based course, for example, each section is designed to be covered in a standard 50-minute class. The lecture can be interrupted periodically so that students individually can work the warm up exercises, or work in small groups on the group activities. In a self-paced lab course, warm up exercises give students a chance to practice while they learn, and get immediate feedback since warm up answers are printed on the bottom of each page.

Using the text's ancillaries, instructors and students have even more options available to them. Computer users, for example, can take advantage of complete electronic tutorial and testing systems, fully coordinated with the text. A detailed description of each print, video, and computer ancillary is found on page xii.

Teaching Methodology

As you peruse the 6th edition of *Fundamentals of Mathematics,* you will see distinctive format and pedagogy, reflecting these aspects of teaching methodology:

Teaching by objective Each section focuses on a short list of objectives, stated at the beginning of the section. The objectives correspond to the sequence of exposition and tie together other pedagogy, including the highlighted content, the examples, and the exercises.

Teaching by application An opening application, marked by the symbol 🌐, is featured at the beginning of each section and is solved as an example within the section. Other applications also may appear as examples, and exercise sets most often include a collection of applications. Applications cover a diverse range of fields, demonstrating the utility of the content in business and science and in daily life as well.

Stressing language New words for each section are explained in the vocabulary segment that precedes the exposition. Exercise sets include questions requiring verbal responses.

Stressing skill, concept, and problem solving   Each section covers concepts *and* skills, fully explained and demonstrated in the exposition for each objective. Carefully constructed examples for each objective are connected by a common strategy that reinforces both the skill and the underlying concepts. Skills are not treated as isolated feats of memorization but as the practical result of conceptual understanding: Skills are strategies for solving related problems. Students learn to see the connections among problems and their common solutions.

Topics and Sequence

Chapter 1 begins with the numeration system including the concepts of place value, word name, expanded form, rounding, and inequality; so the student will have a thorough understanding of the concepts of "number" prior to performing operations. The basic operations of addition, subtraction, multiplication, and division of whole numbers are reviewed. The student is introduced to estimating when doing different operations. The ability to estimate gives one a feeling of assurance with respect to whether or not the problem has been done correctly. Following Section 1.4, we introduce the concept of solving equations with whole-number solutions. This Getting Ready for Algebra section is followed by others immediately after Sections 1.6, 1.8, and throughout the text to help the student prepare for the study of algebra. Exponents and powers of ten are examined so that they can be used in the order of operations with whole numbers and for writing the prime factors of a whole number in Chapter 2. The chapter finishes with order of operations and average. Order of operations shows the importance of rules in finding the correct answers and is an important step in the study of mathematics. Average is applied to real-life situations.

Chapter 2 starts with the divisibility tests which will be helpful in prime factoring a number and in reducing fractions. Whole number classifications of multiples, divisors, factors, primes, and composites follow and give the student needed practice with multiplication and division. The chapter finishes with prime factorization and least common multiple, two concepts that will play an important role in the chapter on fractions.

Chapter 3 begins with a discussion of the meaning of a fraction, using shaded-unit regions and rulers to model the concept. This visual presentation backs the mathematical concept. Operations on fractions and mixed numbers are covered. Building and reducing fractions utilize the concepts and skills acquired in Chapter 2. In adding fractions, the concept of least common denominator flows from the Chapter 2 presentation of least common multiple. The chapter concludes with a presentation of the order of operations and average. Getting Ready for Algebra topics follow Sections 3.4 and 3.9.

Chapter 4 covers decimals, following an approach parallel to the presentation of whole numbers. The concepts of place value, word names, expanded form, rounding, and inequality are extended to decimals. The basic operations are covered. A special section on multiplying and dividing by powers of ten is included and uses the exponent skills developed in Chapter 1. Conversions between fractions and decimals are given to show the relationship between the two ways of writing a rational number. The fact that not all fractions have an exact decimal representation demonstrates the need for fractions and the practical use of rounding. The chapter ends with a review of the order of operations and average. Getting Ready for Algebra topics follow Sections 4.5, 4.8, and 4.10.

Chapter 5 discusses ratios, rates, and proportions. Each of these concepts leads to useful applications of mathematics to practical situations. The student is introduced to the formal process of translating from a written statement of facts to a mathematical statement that can be solved. This skill is reinforced in the next two chapters. Solving a proportion is related to solving an equation in algebra.

Chapter 6 presents percent as a useful way of describing a numerical comparison. Students practice changing from percents to decimals to fractions so that they can see the relationship of percent to the different numbers. Students become skilled at expressing a number in any one of the forms. Solutions of percent problems are covered using either ratios or the formula $R\%$ of $A = B$. The formula $R\%$ of $A = B$ is presented in the form of a triangle for quick recall. A special section on applications is included that contains business, environmental issues, and other topics. The chapter ends with sections on graphs and charts and tables. Students are given the chance to draw conclusions from visual displays and to construct similar displays. Information is extracted from charts using material commonly seen in magazines and newspapers.

Chapter 7 covers both English and metric measurements. Conversions within one system and between the systems are investigated. The metric system gives a student a skill that can be used in science courses and, increasingly, in everyday activities. Measurement is applied to geometric figures covering perimeter, area, and volume. Compound figures are used for area and volume.

Chapter 8 expands the number system to include signed numbers. Operations on signed numbers include absolute value, opposites, addition, subtraction, multiplication, and division. Order of operations and the solution of equations with signed numbers conclude the chapter. This chapter together with previous sections on Getting Ready for Algebra serve as a bridge for the student's future study of algebra.

Special Content

Special content focuses on study skills and math anxiety, calculators, and simple algebraic equations.

Good Advice for Studying begins each chapter. Written by the instructor/counselor team of Dorette Long and Sylvia Thomas, Rogue Community College, these essays address the unique study problems that students of *Fundamentals of Mathematics* experience. Students learn not only general study skills, but study skills specific to mathematics and to the pedagogy and ancillaries of *Fundamentals of Mathematics*. Special techniques are described to overcome the pervasive problem of math anxiety.

Accompanying each essay is a photo of people engaged in a rewarding, though challenging, activity — from long-distance running to preparing haute cuisine. Captions for the photos reinforce goal-setting, consistency, positive attitude, and other techniques described in the essays.

Though one essay begins each chapter, students may profit by reading all the essays at once, then returning to them as the need arises. A fuller description of how to learn from these essays appears in To the Student.

Calculator examples, marked by the symbol ▦, demonstrate how to use a scientific calculator, though the use of a calculator is left to the discretion of the instructor. Nowhere is the use of a calculator required.

In addition to the specially marked examples, Category C exercises for each section may provide calculator drill. Appendix 1 reviews the basics of operating a standard scientific calculator.

Getting Ready for Algebra segments follow sections 1.4, 1.6, 1.8, 3.4, 3.9, 4.5, 4.8, and 4.10, where operations lend themselves to solving simple algebraic equations. Though completely optional, each Getting Ready for Algebra segment includes its own exposition, examples and warm ups, and exercises. Instructors can cover these segments as part of the normal curriculum or assign them to individual students showing readiness.

Students' photos are sprinkled throughout the text. Featured are math students from across the country, and some of the winners of the Barker/Rogers/Van Dyke Problem Posing Project. These winning students wrote original applications of developmental mathematics. (For more information about the project, see the *Instructor's Manual*.)

Special Pedagogy

The pedagogical system of *Fundamentals of Mathematics* meets two important criteria: coordinated purpose and consistency of presentation.

Each section begins with numbered **Objectives,** followed by a relevant **Application** and definitions of new **Vocabulary** to be encountered in the section. Following the vocabulary, **How and Why** segments, numbered to correspond to the objectives, explain and demonstrate concepts and skills. Throughout the How and Why segments, **skill boxes** clearly identify and outline skills in step-by-step form. Skill box titles closely correspond to the objectives. Also throughout the How and Why segments, **concept boxes** highlight important properties, formulas, and theoretical facts underlying the skills. Concept boxes are often summaries of related material. Following each How and Why segment are **Examples and Warm Ups.** Each example is paired with a warm up, with workspace provided. Answers for warm ups are given at the bottom of the page, affording immediate feedback.

Examples similar to one another are linked by a common **Direction** and a common **Strategy** for solution. Directions and strategies are closely related to the skill boxes. Examples include detailed annotations, showing how the strategy is specifically applied. Connecting examples by a common solution helps students recognize the similarity of problems and their solutions, despite their specific differences. In this way, students may improve their problem-solving skills.

Both in the How and Why segments and in the examples, **Caution** remarks help to avert common mistakes.

Exercises, Reviews, Tests

Thorough, varied, properly paced, and well chosen exercises are a hallmark of *Fundamentals of Mathematics*. Exercise sets are provided at the end of each section and at the end of each chapter. Necessary workspace is provided for all exercises, and each exercise set can be torn out and handed in without disturbing any other part of the book.

Section Exercises   Exercises for each section are paired so that each odd-numbered exercise has an even-numbered exercise that is equivalent in type and difficulty. Since answers for odd-numbered section exercises are in the back of the book, students can use odd-numbered exercises for practice, and instructors can assign even-numbered exercises for homework.

Section exercises are categorized to satisfy teaching and learning purposes. Exercises for estimation/mental, pencil and paper, application, and calculator skills are provided, as well as opportunities for students to challenge their abilities and to master communication and group problem solving.

Category A exercises are those that students should be able to solve mentally, without paper and pencil and without a calculator. Mentally working problems improves students' estimating abilities. **Category B** exercises and **Category C** exercises are similar except for the level of difficulty: All students should be able to master category B, while category C contains more difficult exercises. At the discretion of the instructor, category C exercises may also provide calculator practice and reinforce the need for estimating.

Application exercises comprise a great variety, drawn from business, health, environment, consumer, and science fields. Both professional and daily-life uses of mathematics are encountered.

State Your Understanding exercises require a verbal response, usually no more than two or three sentences. These exercises are suitable for group discussion as well as individual assignment.

Challenge exercises stretch the content and are more demanding, both computationally and conceptually.

Group Activity exercises offer specific opportunities for small groups of students to work together to solve problems. While each student needs to develop independent problem solving ability, group problem solving challenges students to communicate effectively and learn from each other.

Maintain Your Skills exercises continually reinforce mastery of skills and concepts from previous sections. The reinforced section is referenced so students can return to the section as needed.

Chapter Exercises   At the conclusion of each chapter are two sets of exercises, one designed to focus on understanding concepts, the other on mastering skills and preparing for the classroom exam. Answers for all chapter exercises are in the back of the book.

Chapter Concept Review exercises require students to judge whether a statement is true or false and, if false, to rewrite the sentence to make it true. Students evaluate their understanding of concepts and also gain experience using the vocabulary of mathematics.

Chapter Test exercises follow the Concept Review. Written to imitate a 50-minute exam, each Chapter Test covers all the chapter content. Students can use the Chapter Test as a self-test before the classroom test. Answers to test items, in the back of the book, reference the relevant section objective.

Ancillaries

Three major media — print, electronic, and video — are utilized in the Barker/Rogers/Van Dyke ancillary package. Coordinated use of the ancillaries greatly increases the effectiveness and flexibility of the text, both for the instructor and the student.

Instructor's Manual   Instructor-appropriate solutions are provided for every other odd-numbered exercise and all even-numbered exercises in the section exercise sets. Solutions for all other exercises are provided in the *Student Solutions Manual* (see next page). The *Instructor's Manual* also contains essays on teaching problem solving, teaching estimation, incorporating writing into the curriculum, using group activities, and integrating technology.

The *Instructor's Manual* concludes with a description of the Barker/Rogers/Van Dyke Problem Posing Project, designed by Phyllis Leonard of Chemeketa Community College. The purpose of the project is to encourage students to identify situations, particularly from their own lives, that involve mathematical concepts, and to work in groups to pose, and solve, problems. As part of the project, Saunders College Publishing sponsored a contest among students in the fall of 1993. Students who submitted the best problems were awarded money to defray the costs of textbooks. Winning problems are printed in the *Instructor's Manual*.

Prepared Tests   In ready-to-duplicate form, six tests for each chapter and six final exams are provided. Half the tests are free-response; half are multiple-choice. One third of the tests are easier (the ratio of easier, average, and harder items is 40/50/10); one third of the tests are average (the ratio is 25/50/25), and one third of the tests are harder (the ratio is 10/50/40). Each test includes skill, concept, and application test items in a 70/15/15 ratio. Answer keys are provided, and each answer references a section objective.

ExaMaster+[tm]   A flexible, powerful testing system, *ExaMaster+*[tm] offers teachers a wide range of integrated testing options and features:

Using **ExaMaster+**[tm] **Computer Testbank,** in either IBM or Macintosh format, teachers can select, edit, or create not only test items but algorithms for test items as well. Using algorithms, teachers can generate virtually an unlimited number of test items. For each chapter, 200 test items are provided, each of which can be selected with or without multiple-choice distractors. Teachers can select test items according to a variety of other criteria, including section, objective, focus (skill, concept, or application), and difficulty (easier, medium, or harder). Teachers can scramble the order of test items, administer tests on-line, and print objective-referenced answer keys. Teachers can use *ExaMaster+*™ to create extra practice worksheets as well. *ExaMaster+*™ also includes full-function gradebook and graphing features.

In printed form, **ExaMaster+™ Printed Testbank** arranges *ExaMaster+*™ data-bank test items by chapter, section, objective, focus, and difficulty. Answers are displayed with each test item.

Using **ExaMaster+™ RequesTest™,** teachers can select *ExaMaster+*™ test items, or specify criteria for test items, then call the Saunders Software Support Department (1-800-447-9457) who will generate, print, and mail or fax the *ExaMaster+*™ test within 48 hours.

Student's Solutions Manual   Detailed, annotated, step-by-step solutions are provided for every other odd-numbered exercise in the section exercise sets and for every exercise in the Concept Reviews and Tests.

Videotapes   An outstanding section-by-section video review features on-location segments to illustrate applications. Each tape covers one chapter, with roughly 15 minutes per section. Experienced video teacher Loretta Palmer from Utah Valley State College reviews examples from the book and explains key concepts, weaving into the presentation real-life footage, movie clips, and interviews with diverse, real-world users of mathematics. Study skills and math anxiety are covered as well.

MathCue™ Interactive Software   Available in IBM and Macintosh formats, *MathCue*™ *Interactive Software* for students affords opportunities for learning, reviewing, and practicing skills, discovering and exploring concepts, and pinpointing and correcting weak areas of understanding. *MathCue*™ is designed by George W. Bergeman of Northern Virginia Community College and comprises a variety of interactive tools:

Tailored to every section of the book, **MathCue™ Tutorial** presents students with problems to solve and tutors students by displaying annotated, step-by-step solutions. Students may view partial solutions to get started on a problem, see a continuous record of progress, and back up to review missed problems. Student scores can also be printed.

Based on an expert system, **MathCue™ Solution Finder** lets students pose their own problems and get annotated, step-by-step solutions in return. *Solution Finder* tracks student progress, refers students to specific sections in the book when appropriate, and prints student scores.

An algorithm-based software, **MathCue™ Practice** allows students to generate large numbers of practice problems keyed to problem types from each section of the book. *Practice* scores students' performance, and saves students' scores session to session.

Changes in the Sixth Edition

Instructors who have used previous editions of *Fundamentals of Mathematics* will see changes in format, pedagogy, exercises, and the sectioning of content. The primary focus of revision has been to improve the pedagogy, broaden the variety of applications, shorten the book without compromising important content, and give renewed emphasis to the teaching and learning methods espoused by the National Council of Teachers of Mathematics.

Changes in Content   The text has been reduced from 71 to 62 sections by combining sections 3.1–2, 3.4–5, 3.7–8, 3.9–10, 4.1–2, 4.3–4, 6.8–9, and 7.1–2, and by deleting section 7.9 on reasoning. For instructors who want to include reasoning in their course, this material is available through custom publishing. The text has been further reduced by deleting Appendix V covering plain geometry, which also is still available through custom publishing.

Chapter 2 Primes and Multiples now begins with Divisibility Tests rather than with Multiples. Chapter 3 Fractions and Mixed Numbers now includes calculator examples, where appropriate. Section 5.1 Ratio and Rate now distinguishes more clearly between ratio and rate. Section 6.7 Solving Percent Problems now includes three methods, rather than two, for solving percent problems.

New to the sixth edition are the chapter-opening essays Good Advice for Studying (see "Special Content," previously).

Changes in Exercises, Reviews, and Tests   A greater distinction is made in the level of difficulty for Categories A, B, and C exercises. Category D exercises are now more meaningfully labeled as Application exercises, and their variety, realism, and relevance have been improved. New categories of section exercises are now included: State Your Understanding, Challenge, and Group Activity (see "Exercises, Reviews, Tests"). Chapter Pre-Tests have been eliminated, and chapter Tests now more closely resemble a 50-minute test. Test questions no longer reference section objectives; instead these references are given with the answers in the back of the book.

Changes in Format and Pedagogy   In the fifth edition, a section contained one How and Why, followed by one set of Model Problem Solving examples. In the sixth edition, a section may contain more than one How and Why, each one numbered to correspond to a numbered objective, and each followed by its own set of examples and warm ups. The main reason for these changes is to more closely connect objectives, exposition, and examples.

In the fifth edition, examples and warm ups were paired vertically. In the sixth edition, examples and warm ups are paired horizontally: examples in one column, warm ups in another. The main reason for this change is to use space more efficiently, and to keep the flow of examples going.

In the fifth edition, each example had a separate direction, even when the preceding example had the same direction. In the sixth edition, several examples may share a common, general direction, much the same way section exercises may share a common, general direction. Furthermore, examples sharing a common direction also share a common strategy for solution. The main reason for these changes is to help students recognize the similarity of problems and their solutions, despite their specific differences. In this way, students may improve their problem-solving skills.

In the fifth edition, highlighted material was labeled as Rule, Property, Procedure, Formula, and Caution, but was otherwise untitled. In the sixth, only the Caution label remains. For all other highlighted material, the label has been replaced by a title reflecting content. The main reasons for these changes are to highlight material more meaningfully, and to eliminate the sometimes arbitrary distinction between property, rule, and so on.

Step-by-step skills, for example, are consistently titled as To Add Fractions, To Multiply Whole Numbers, and so on, often repeating the objective statement. Further, steps are consistently repeated in the strategy for the related examples. In this way, strong connections are made between objectives, skills, and solving common problems.

ACKNOWLEDGEMENTS

The authors appreciate the continuing enthusiastic support of their wives, Mary Barker, Elinore Rogers, and Carol Van Dyke, who made the completion of this work possible. Lily O'Rielly of Portland Community College is commended for her excellent contribution in updating the exercise sets. We also thank our colleagues for their help and suggestions for the improvement of the text. Many thanks go to our editor, Deirdre Lynch, and Laurie Golson, our developmental editor, for their input and suggestions for the revision. We also appreciate the work of Maureen Iannuzzi of Saunders and Linda Tarman of York Graphic Services for their help in preparing the text for publication.

Thanks also go to the reviewers for their excellent contributions to the development of this and prior editions of the text:

Willie Artis, *Central Piedmont Community College*
James Bennett, *Eastfield College*
Tim Cavanaugh, *University of Northern Colorado*
Laurence Chernoff, *Miami-Dade Community College*
Lee Dell'Isola, *Walters State Community College*
Linda Desue, *Edison State Community College*
Louise Ettline, *Trident Technical College*
Roy D. Frysinger, *Harrisburg Area Community College*
Roberta Hinkle Gansman, *Guilford Technical Community College*
Bill Hajdukiewica, *Miami-Dade Community College-North*
Virginia Hamilton, *Shawnee State University*
Calvin Holt, *Paul D. Camp Community College*
Jean L. Holton, *Tidewater Community College*
Elizabeth Koball, *Tidewater Community College*
Robert Langston, *Tarrant County Junior College*
Paul Wayne Lee, *St. Philip's College*
Virginia Licato, *Camden County College*
Peggy Lumpkin, *Wallace State College*
Shelba Mormon, *North Lake College*
Frederic Norwood, *William Paterson College*
Lily O'Rielly, *Portland Community College*
Julienne K. Pendleton, *Brookhaven College*
Roy Pearson, *St. Louis Community College at Florissant Valley*
David Price, *Tarrant County Junior College*
Greg St. George, *University of Montana*
Michele A. Sassone, *Bergen Community College*
Ned J. Schillow, *Lehigh County Community College*
Ara B. Sullenberger, *Tarrant County Junior College*
Mary Jane Smith, *Tidewater Community College*
Phyllis Steinmann, *Scottsdale Community College*
Lenore Vest, *Lower Columbia College*
Priscilla Wake, *San Jacinto College*
Cora S. West, *Florida Community College at Jacksonville-Kent Campus*
Juanita Woods, *Chattanooga State Technical College*

Special thanks to Kathy Butts-Bernunzio of Portland Community College and Cheryl Roberts of Northern Virginia Community College for their accuracy review of the entire book. We also thank the following people for their excellent work on the ancillaries that accompany the book:

Oiyin Pauline Chow, Harrisburg Area Community College (*Instructor's Manual* and *Student's Solutions Manual*)

Joan Van Glabek, Edison Community College — Collier Campus (*ExaMaster+^{tm} Printed Testbank* and *Prepared Tests*)

George Bergeman, Northern Virginia Community College (*MathCue^{tm} Interactive Software*)

Loretta Palmer, Utah Valley State College (*Videotapes*)

JACK BARKER
JAMES ROGERS
JAMES VAN DYKE
PORTLAND, OREGON
SEPTEMBER 1994

HIGHLIGHTS OF
Fundamentals of Mathematics

CHAPTER **6**

Percent

Dedicated practice with the tools of the trade achieves masterful results for this woodcarver. In business and science, the tools of the trade are mathematical skills: Practice leads to mastery, mastery to achievement. (Tony Stone Images)

Dealing with Math Anxiety

Each chapter begins with an inspiring photo and caption to reinforce the message that life offers many challenges, and that every challenge — including math — has its rewards.

Each chapter begins, too, with *Good Advice for Studying*. As a collection, these essays constitute a complete study system geared especially for the Barker/Rogers/VanDyke series and for math-anxious adults.

An appendix offers more resources for learning good study skills and conquering math anxiety.

---

2   CHAPTER I   WHOLE NUMBERS

GOOD ADVICE FOR STUDYING

Strategies for Success

Are you afraid of math? Do you panic on tests or "blank out" and forget what you have studied, only to recall the material after the test? Then you are just like many other students. In fact, research studies estimate that as many as 50% of you have some degree of math anxiety.

What is math anxiety? It is a learned fear response to math that causes disruptive, debilitating reactions to tests. It can be so encompassing that it becomes a dread of doing *anything* that involves numbers. Although some anxiety at test time is beneficial — it can motivate and energize you, for example — numerous studies show that too much anxiety results in poorer test scores. Besides performing poorly on tests, you may be distracted by worrisome thoughts, and be unable to concentrate and recall what you've learned. You may also set unrealistic performance standards for yourself and imagine catastrophic consequences of your failure to be successful in math. Your physical signs could be muscle tightness, upset stomach, sweating, headache, shortness of breath, shaking, or rapid heartbeat..

The good news is that anxiety is a learned behavior and therefore can be unlearned. If you want to stop feeling anxious, the choice is up to you. You can choose to learn behaviors that are more useful to achieve success in math. Proven methods for managing math anxiety will be explained in more detail in the following chapters. You can learn and choose the ways that work best for you.

To achieve success, you can focus on two broad strategies: First, you can study math in ways *proven* to be effective in learning mathematics and taking tests. Second, you can learn to physically and mentally *relax*, to manage your anxious feelings and to think rationally and positively. Make a time commitment to practice relaxation techniques, study math, and record your thought patterns. A commitment of one or two hours a day may be necessary in the beginning. Remember, it took time to learn your present study habits and to be anxious. It will take time to unlearn these behaviors. After you become proficient with these methods, you can devote less time to them.

Begin now to learn your strategies for success. If, during studying or testing, you notice yourself becoming tense and your breathing becomes shallow, follow this simple coping strategy. Say to yourself: "I'm in control. Relax and take a deep breath." Breathe deeply and properly by relaxing your stomach muscle (that's right, you have permission to let your stomach protrude!) and inhaling so that air reaches the bottom of your lungs. Hold the air in for a few seconds, then slowly exhale, pulling your stomach muscle in as you exhale. This easy exercise not only strengthens your stomach muscle, but gives your body and brain the oxygen you need to perform free from physical stress and anxiety.

Next, be sure you have read To the Student on page ix. This will help you to understand the authors' organization or "game plan" for your math experience in this course.

At the beginning of each chapter you will find more Good Advice for Studying that will help you to study and take tests more effectively, and to manage your anxiety. You may want to read ahead so that you can improve even more quickly. Good luck!

Teaching by Objective

① Each section begins with a list of numbered objectives, students' goals for the sections.

② How and Why segments are numbered to correspond to the objectives.

③ Skill boxes and example sets correspond to objectives, too.

When chapter test answers are given in the back of the book, objectives are referenced. Test answers in the instructor's *Prepared Tests*, *Printed Testbank*, and *Computer Testbank* are keyed to objectives as well.

Teaching by Application

④ Each section highlights an application, illustrating how meeting the objectives is useful in the real world.

⑤ Later in the section, the application is solved. Notice the globe icon is used in both places.

Many other applications are presented and solved as examples throughout the book. Exercise sets, too, include a wide variety of applications drawn from business, health and environmental studies, social and physical sciences, and daily life.

Stressing Language

⑥ Each section introduces and defines new vocabulary that students will encounter.

Exercise sets for each section (see page xxviii) include State Your Understanding questions, requiring verbal responses, and Group Activities, giving students opportunities to practice using the language of math correctly and effectively.

At the end of each chapter, a Concept Review (see page xxxi) asks students to recognize true statements and rewrite false statements to make them true.

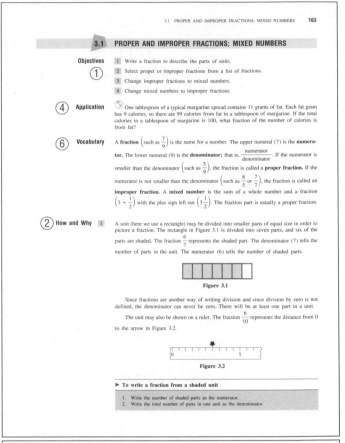

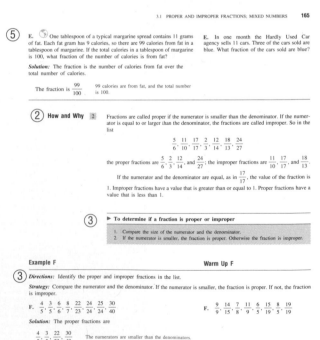

168 CHAPTER 3 FRACTIONS AND MIXED NUMBERS

The shortcut uses multiplication and addition:

$$1\frac{3}{7} = \frac{7 \cdot 1 + 3}{7} = \frac{7 + 3}{7} = \frac{10}{7}$$

▶ **To change a mixed number to an improper fraction**

(1)
1. Multiply the denominator times the whole number.
2. Add the numerator to the product in step 1.
3. Place the sum from step 2 over the denominator.

Examples J–L   **Warm Ups J–L**

Directions: Change each mixed number to an improper fraction.

(3) *Strategy:* Multiply the whole number by the denominator. Add the numerator. Write the sum over the denominator.

J. $2\frac{4}{5}$ J. $3\frac{5}{6}$ (4)

Solution:

$2\frac{4}{5} = \frac{2(5) + 4}{5}$ Multiply the whole number by the denominator, add the product to the numerator, and place the sum over the denominator.

$\quad = \frac{14}{5}$

K. $4\frac{5}{9}$ K. $5\frac{5}{8}$

Solution:

$4\frac{5}{9} = \frac{4(9) + 5}{9}$ Multiply the whole number by the denominator, add the product to the numerator, and place the sum over the denominator.

$\quad = \frac{41}{9}$

L. 7   L. 8

Solution: First, rewrite the whole number as a mixed number. Use the fraction $\frac{0}{1}$.

$7 = 7\frac{0}{1} = \frac{7(1) + 0}{1}$ Note: Any fraction that equals 0 could be used.

$\quad = \frac{7}{1}$

(5) Answers to warm ups: J. $\frac{23}{6}$ K. $\frac{45}{8}$ L. $\frac{8}{1}$

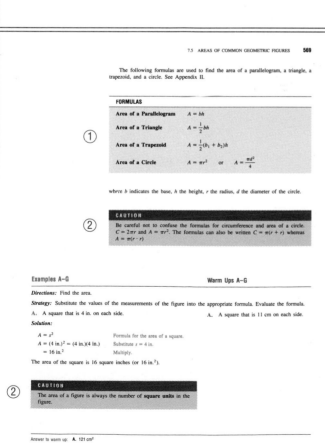

7.5 AREAS OF COMMON GEOMETRIC FIGURES   **569**

The following formulas are used to find the area of a parallelogram, a triangle, a trapezoid, and a circle. See Appendix II.

FORMULAS

(1)

Area of a Parallelogram	$A = bh$
Area of a Triangle	$A = \frac{1}{2}bh$
Area of a Trapezoid	$A = \frac{1}{2}(b_1 + b_2)h$
Area of a Circle	$A = \pi r^2$ or $A = \frac{\pi d^2}{4}$

where b indicates the base, h the height, r the radius, d the diameter of the circle.

(2) **CAUTION**
Be careful not to confuse the formulas for circumference and area of a circle. $C = 2\pi r$ and $A = \pi r^2$. The formulas can also be written $C = \pi(r + r)$ whereas $A = \pi(r \cdot r)$.

Examples A–G   **Warm Ups A–G**

Directions: Find the area.

Strategy: Substitute the values of the measurements of the figure into the appropriate formula. Evaluate the formula.

A. A square that is 4 in. on each side.   A. A square that is 11 cm on each side.

Solution:

$A = s^2$ Formula for the area of a square.
$A = (4 \text{ in.})^2 = (4 \text{ in.})(4 \text{ in.})$ Substitute $s = 4$ in.
$\quad = 16 \text{ in.}^2$ Multiply.

The area of the square is 16 square inches (or 16 in.²).

(2) **CAUTION**
The area of a figure is always the number of **square units** in the figure.

Answer to warm up: A. 121 cm²

Stressing Skill, Concept, and Problem-Solving

(1) How and Why segments discuss skills and concepts. Skill boxes are step-by-step; concept boxes highlight properties, formulas, and theoretical facts.

(2) Caution boxes alert students to common errors. Caution boxes appear in How and Why segments and example sets.

(3) Each example set emphasizes how one Strategy is used to solve similar problems. Skills are treated as strategies for solving related problems. Students learn to see the connections among problems and their common solutions.

(4) Warm ups paired to examples give students a chance to practice problem solving as they learn. Strategies connect Warm ups to the examples.

(5) Answers for Warm ups appear at the bottom of the page, affording immediate feedback and reinforcement.

Providing Thorough and Graded Exercises

Exercises for each section are categorized to satisfy specific teaching and learning purposes. Exercises are also paired, odd with even. Answers for odd-numbered exercises are in the back of the book.

① Category A is appropriate for estimation and mental exercises.

② Category B contains skills exercises that all students should be able to work.

③ Category C contains more difficult skill exercises. These exercises may be suitable for practice using a scientific calculator.

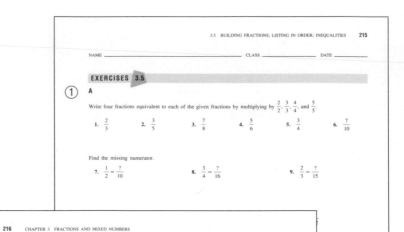

3.5 BUILDING FRACTIONS; LISTING IN ORDER; INEQUALITIES   215

NAME _____   CLASS _____   DATE _____

EXERCISES 3.5

① **A**

Write four fractions equivalent to each of the given fractions by multiplying by $\frac{2}{2}$, $\frac{3}{3}$, $\frac{4}{4}$, and $\frac{5}{5}$.

1. $\frac{2}{3}$ 2. $\frac{3}{5}$ 3. $\frac{7}{8}$ 4. $\frac{5}{6}$ 5. $\frac{3}{4}$ 6. $\frac{7}{10}$

Find the missing numerator.

7. $\frac{1}{2} = \frac{?}{10}$ 8. $\frac{3}{4} = \frac{?}{16}$ 9. $\frac{2}{3} = \frac{?}{15}$

216   CHAPTER 3 FRACTIONS AND MIXED NUMBERS

22. $\frac{1}{2}, \frac{3}{5}, \frac{7}{10}$ 23. $\frac{1}{2}, \frac{3}{8}, \frac{1}{3}$ 24. $\frac{2}{3}, \frac{8}{15}, \frac{3}{5}$

Are the following statements true or false?

25. $\frac{1}{4} < \frac{3}{4}$ 26. $\frac{5}{9} > \frac{7}{9}$ 27. $\frac{11}{16} > \frac{7}{8}$ 28. $\frac{9}{16} < \frac{5}{8}$

② **B**

Write four fractions equivalent to each of the given fractions by multiplying by $\frac{2}{2}$, $\frac{3}{3}$, $\frac{4}{4}$, and $\frac{5}{5}$.

29. $\frac{4}{10}$ 30. $\frac{3}{9}$ 31. $\frac{7}{3}$ 32. $\frac{6}{5}$

Find the missing numerator.

33. $\frac{3}{4} = \frac{?}{36}$ 34. $\frac{2}{3} = \frac{?}{24}$ 35. $\frac{1}{5} = \frac{?}{75}$

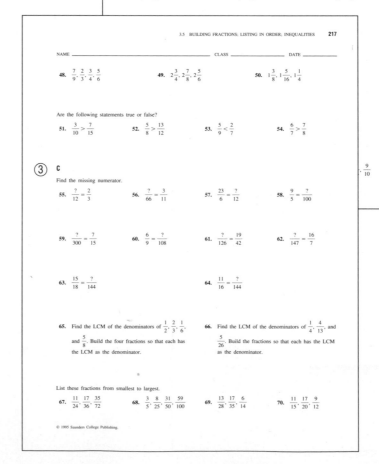

3.5 BUILDING FRACTIONS; LISTING IN ORDER; INEQUALITIES   217

NAME _____   CLASS _____   DATE _____

48. $\frac{7}{9}, \frac{2}{3}, \frac{3}{4}, \frac{5}{6}$ 49. $2\frac{3}{4}, 2\frac{7}{8}, 2\frac{5}{6}$ 50. $1\frac{3}{8}, 1\frac{5}{16}, 1\frac{1}{4}$

Are the following statements true or false?

51. $\frac{3}{10} > \frac{7}{15}$ 52. $\frac{5}{8} > \frac{13}{12}$ 53. $\frac{5}{9} < \frac{2}{7}$ 54. $\frac{6}{7} > \frac{7}{8}$

③ **C**

Find the missing numerator.

55. $\frac{?}{12} = \frac{2}{3}$ 56. $\frac{?}{66} = \frac{3}{11}$ 57. $\frac{23}{6} = \frac{?}{12}$ 58. $\frac{9}{5} = \frac{?}{100}$

59. $\frac{?}{300} = \frac{7}{15}$ 60. $\frac{6}{9} = \frac{?}{108}$ 61. $\frac{?}{126} = \frac{19}{42}$ 62. $\frac{?}{147} = \frac{16}{7}$

63. $\frac{15}{18} = \frac{?}{144}$ 64. $\frac{11}{16} = \frac{?}{144}$

65. Find the LCM of the denominators of $\frac{1}{2}, \frac{2}{3}, \frac{1}{6}$, and $\frac{5}{8}$. Build the four fractions so that each has the LCM as the denominator.

66. Find the LCM of the denominators of $\frac{1}{4}, \frac{4}{13}$, and $\frac{5}{26}$. Build the fractions so that each has the LCM as the denominator.

List these fractions from smallest to largest.

67. $\frac{11}{24}, \frac{17}{36}, \frac{35}{72}$ 68. $\frac{3}{5}, \frac{8}{25}, \frac{31}{50}, \frac{59}{100}$ 69. $\frac{13}{28}, \frac{17}{35}, \frac{6}{14}$ 70. $\frac{11}{15}, \frac{17}{20}, \frac{9}{12}$

3.10 ORDER OF OPERATIONS; AVERAGE **273**

NAME _____ CLASS _____ DATE _____

① **59.** Coho Inc. packs a variety carton of canned seafood. Each carton contains three $3\frac{1}{2}$-oz cans of smoked sturgeon, five $6\frac{3}{4}$-oz cans of tuna, four $5\frac{1}{2}$-oz cans of salmon, and four $10\frac{1}{2}$-oz cans of sardines. How many ounces of seafood are in the carton? If the carton sells for $52, to the nearest cent, what is the average cost per ounce?

60. In a walk for charity seven people walk $2\frac{7}{8}$ miles, six people walk $3\frac{4}{5}$ miles, nine people walk $4\frac{1}{4}$ miles, and five people walk $5\frac{3}{4}$ miles. What are the total miles walked? If the charity raises $2355, to the nearest dollar, what is the average amount raised per mile?

61. Tom Peterson's Appliances buys 48 television sets for $14,976. They sell one third of the sets for $450 each, one fourth for $462, and five twelfths for $482. What is the profit from the sale of the sets?

62. A 1575-acre farm is subdivided and sold. Three fifths of the farm sells for $245 an acre, one third of the farm sells for $375 an acre, and the rest sells for $610 an acre. What is the total sale price for the farm?

② **State Your Understanding**

63. Is the following exercise worked correctly? If not, why not?

$$6\frac{12}{25} - 3\frac{1}{5} + 2\left(1\frac{1}{2}\right)^2$$
$$\frac{162}{25} - \frac{16}{5} + 2\left(\frac{3}{2}\right)^2$$
$$\frac{162}{25} - \frac{16}{5} + (3)^2$$
$$\frac{162}{25} - \frac{16}{5} + 9$$
$$\frac{162}{25} - \frac{80}{25} + \frac{225}{25}$$
$$\frac{82}{25} + \frac{225}{25}$$
$$\frac{310}{25} = \frac{62}{5} = 12\frac{2}{5}$$

64. Must the average of a group of numbers be larger than the smallest number and smaller than the largest number? Why?

© 1995 Saunders College Publishing.

274 CHAPTER 3 FRACTIONS AND MIXED NUMBERS

③ **Challenge**

Perform the indicated operations.

65. $2\frac{5}{8}\left(4\frac{1}{5} - 3\frac{5}{6}\right) \div 2\frac{1}{2}\left(3\frac{1}{7} + 2\frac{1}{5}\right)$

66. $1\frac{2}{5}\left(5\frac{1}{5} - 4\frac{3}{4}\right)^2 \div 4\frac{1}{2}\left(3\frac{1}{7} - 2\frac{1}{3}\right)^2$

67. The Acme Fish Company pays $1500 per ton for crab. Jerry catches $3\frac{2}{5}$ tons, his brother Joshua catches $1\frac{1}{2}$ times as many as Jerry. Their sister, Salicita, catches $\frac{7}{8}$ the amount that Joshua does. What is the total amount paid to the three people by Acme Fish Company (to the nearest dollar)?

④ **Group Activity**

68. Prepare for the chapter exam by having each member take the Chapter Test. Check the answers and if any are incorrect, work with the people who made the mistakes to be sure that they understand the error so that they can avoid similar mistakes in the future.

⑤ **Maintain Your Skills (Sections 2.5, 3.3, 3.6, 3.7)**

Divide.

69. $\frac{7}{9} \div \frac{16}{3}$

70. $\frac{7}{3} \div \frac{14}{5}$

71. $\frac{25}{32} \div \frac{15}{36}$

72. $\frac{25}{36} \div \frac{15}{32}$

Multiply.

73. $\frac{15}{28} \cdot \frac{21}{45} \cdot \frac{20}{35}$

74. $\frac{9}{15} \cdot \frac{21}{28} \cdot \frac{35}{6}$

75. Prime factor 650.

76. Prime factor 975.

77. A coffee table is made of a piece of maple that is $\frac{3}{4}$ inch thick, a piece of chipboard that is $\frac{3}{8}$ inch thick, and a veneer that is $\frac{1}{8}$ inch thick. How thick is the table top?

78. A woman works a five-day week for the following hours: $6\frac{3}{4}$ hours, $7\frac{1}{3}$ hours, $6\frac{2}{3}$ hours, $9\frac{3}{4}$ hours, and $7\frac{1}{2}$ hours. How many hours does she work for the week? What is her pay if the rate is $5\frac{1}{2}$ per hour?

① Applications are given in every section. Science, industry, business, and everyday-life applications are covered.

② State Your Understanding exercises give opportunities for students to use the language of math effectively and accurately.

③ Challenge exercises stretch the content and are suitable for the better student.

④ Group Activity exercises are suitable for small groups of students working together and learning from each other. These exercises may require outside research.

⑤ Maintain Your Skill exercises reinforce previously covered material.

Getting Ready for Algebra

Optional sections throughout the text begin to connect arithmetic with algebra.

Each Getting Ready for Algebra follows the pattern of a typical section, including objectives, application, How and Why, vocabulary when appropriate, skill, concept, and caution boxes, and example and exercise sets.

① Example sets for Getting Ready for Algebra include Strategies and Warm ups.

② Exercise sets for Getting Ready for Algebra cover skills and applications.

GETTING READY FOR ALGEBRA   **205**

GETTING READY FOR ALGEBRA

Objective   Solve an equation of the form $\frac{ax}{b} = \frac{c}{d}$, where a, b, c, and d are whole numbers.

Application   One third of all the mileage put on a private car is from commuting to work. If Nancy averages 510 miles per month in commuting to work, how many miles does she put on her car in a month?

How and Why   We have previously solved equations in which variables (letters) were either multiplied or divided by whole numbers. We performed the inverse operations to solve for the variable. To eliminate multiplication, we divided by the number being multiplied. To eliminate division, we multiplied by the number that is the divisor. Now we solve some equations in which variables are multiplied by fractions. Recall from Chapter 1 that if a number is multiplied times a variable, there is usually no multiplication sign between them. That is, $2x$ is understood to mean 2 times x, and $\frac{2}{3}x$ means $\frac{2}{3}$ times x. However, we usually do not write $\frac{2}{3}x$. Instead, we write this as $\frac{2x}{3}$. We can do this because

$$\frac{2}{3}x = \frac{2}{3} \cdot x = \frac{2}{3} \cdot \frac{x}{1} = \frac{2x}{3}$$

Therefore, we will write $\frac{2}{3}x$ as $\frac{2x}{3}$. Remember, however, for convenience we may use either of these forms. Recall that $\frac{2x}{3}$ means 2 times x with that product divided by 3.

▶ **To solve an equation of the form $\frac{ax}{b} = \frac{c}{d}$**

1. Multiply both sides of the equation by b to eliminate the division on the left side.
2. Divide both sides by a to isolate the variable.

Examples A–C   **Warm Ups A–C**

Directions: Solve.

① *Strategy:* Multiply both sides by the denominator of the fraction containing the variable. Solve as before.

A. $\frac{3x}{4} = 2$ A. $\frac{7x}{8} = 14$

Solution:

$4\left(\frac{3x}{4}\right) = 4(2)$ To eliminate the division, multiply both sides by 4.

$3x = 8$ Simplify.

$\frac{3x}{3} = \frac{8}{3}$ To eliminate the multiplication, divide both sides by 3.

$x = \frac{8}{3}$

GETTING READY FOR ALGEBRA   **207**

NAME _____   CLASS _____   DATE _____

EXERCISES

Solve.

②
1. $\frac{2x}{3} = \frac{1}{2}$ 2. $\frac{2x}{5} = \frac{2}{3}$ 3. $\frac{3y}{4} = \frac{4}{5}$ 4. $\frac{7y}{8} = \frac{5}{6}$

5. $\frac{4z}{5} = \frac{3}{4}$ 6. $\frac{5z}{4} = \frac{8}{9}$ 7. $\frac{17}{9} = \frac{8x}{9}$ 8. $\frac{29}{10} = \frac{9x}{5}$

9. $\frac{7a}{4} = \frac{5}{2}$ 10. $\frac{15a}{4} = \frac{24}{5}$ 11. $\frac{47}{4} = \frac{47b}{6}$ 12. $\frac{13}{3} = \frac{52b}{9}$

13. $\frac{41z}{6} = \frac{41}{3}$ 14. $\frac{9b}{23} = \frac{23}{3}$ 15. $\frac{2a}{15} = \frac{11}{4}$ 16. $\frac{119x}{12} = \frac{119}{8}$

② **Applications**

17. Garth walks $\frac{1}{3}$ of the distance from his home to school. If he walks $\frac{1}{2}$ mile, what is the distance from his home to school?

18. Mark cuts a board into nine pieces of equal length. If each piece is $1\frac{4}{9}$ feet long, what is the length of the board?

NAME _____ CLASS _____ DATE _____

① **CHAPTER 5   Concept Review**

Check your understanding of the language of basic mathematics. Tell whether each of the following statements is True (always true) or False (not always true). For those statements that you judge to be false, revise them to make them true.

1. A ratio is a comparison of two fractions.

2. A proportion is a comparison of two ratios.

3. The cross products of a proportion are always equal.

4. Five people is an example of a measurement.

5. To determine whether a proportion is true or false, the ratios must have the same units.

6. To solve a proportion one needs to find the replacement for the missing number that will make the proportion true.

Use the following information to answer questions 7–10 as being True or False.

If a fir tree that is 18 ft tall casts a shadow of 17 ft, how tall is a tree that casts a shadow of 25 ft?

7. The following chart can be used to solve the given problem.

	First Tree	Second Tree
Height	17	18
Shadow	x	25

8. The following chart can be used to solve the given problem.

	First Tree	Second Tree
Shadow	17	25
Height	18	x

© 1995 Saunders College Publishing.

NAME _____ CLASS _____ DATE _____

② **CHAPTER 5   Test**

1. Write a ratio to compare 12 pounds to 15 pounds.

2. On a test Ken answered 24 of 30 questions correctly. At the same rate, how many would he answer correctly if there were 100 questions on a test?

3. Solve the proportion: $\frac{2.4}{8} = \frac{0.36}{w}$.

4. Is the following proportion true or false?
$$\frac{16}{34} = \frac{24}{51}$$

5. Is the following proportion true or false?
$$\frac{9 \text{ inches}}{2 \text{ feet}} = \frac{6 \text{ inches}}{16 \text{ inches}}$$

6. Solve the proportion: $\frac{13}{36} = \frac{y}{18}$.

7. If Mary is paid $49.14 for 7 hours of work, how much should she expect to earn for 12 hours of work?

8. Write a ratio to compare six hours to three days and reduce. (Compare in hours.)

9. There is a canned food sale at the supermarket. A case of 24 cans of peas is priced at $19.68. What is the price of 10 cans of peas?

10. If 40 pounds of beef contains 7 pounds of bones, how many pounds of bones may be expected in 100 pounds of beef?

11. Solve the proportion: $\frac{0.3}{0.9} = \frac{0.8}{x}$.

12. A charter fishing boat has been catching an average of 3 salmon for every 4 people they take fishing. At that rate, how many fish will they catch if over a period of time they take a total of 32 people fishing?

© 1995 Saunders College Publishing.

Concluding the Chapter

① The Chapter Concept Review asks students to judge whether statements are true or false, and to rewrite false statements so that they are true. Students test their understanding of concepts and also perfect their use of mathematical language. All answers are given in the back of the book.

② The Chapter Test imitates a 50-minute classroom exam. Answers for the Chapter Test are in the back of the book. Each answer references an objective so that students can efficiently strengthen areas of weakness.

Other chapter tests are available to instructors in the *Prepared Tests* ancillary and in the ExaMaster Computer Testbank and Printed Testbank.

Whole Numbers

For crew racers, the reward of cooperative strength is graceful power. Working in a group to solve math problems can produce powerful results, too. (©Gary Benson/AllStock, Inc.)

GOOD ADVICE FOR STUDYING

Strategies for Success

Are you afraid of math? Do you panic on tests or "blank out" and forget what you have studied, only to recall the material after the test? Then you are just like many other students. In fact, research studies estimate that as many as 50% of you have some degree of math anxiety.

What is math anxiety? It is a learned fear response to math that causes disruptive, debilitating reactions to tests. It can be so encompassing that it becomes a dread of doing *anything* that involves numbers. Although some anxiety at test time is beneficial — it can motivate and energize you, for example — numerous studies show that too much anxiety results in poorer test scores. Besides performing poorly on tests, you may be distracted by worrisome thoughts, and be unable to concentrate and recall what you've learned. You may also set unrealistic performance standards for yourself and imagine catastrophic consequences of your failure to be successful in math. Your physical signs could be muscle tightness, upset stomach, sweating, headache, shortness of breath, shaking, or rapid heartbeat.

The good news is that anxiety is a learned behavior and therefore can be unlearned. If you want to stop feeling anxious, the choice is up to you. You can choose to learn behaviors that are more useful to achieve success in math. Proven methods for managing math anxiety will be explained in more detail in the following chapters. You can learn and choose the ways that work best for you.

To achieve success, you can focus on two broad strategies: First, you can study math in ways *proven* to be effective in learning mathematics and taking tests. Second, you can learn to physically and mentally *relax,* to manage your anxious feelings and to think rationally and positively. Make a time commitment to practice relaxation techniques, study math, and record your thought patterns. A commitment of one or two hours a day may be necessary in the beginning. Remember, it took time to learn your present study habits and to be anxious. It will take time to unlearn these behaviors. After you become proficient with these methods, you can devote less time to them.

Begin now to learn your strategies for success. If, during studying or testing, you notice yourself becoming tense and your breathing becomes shallow, follow this simple coping strategy. Say to yourself: "I'm in control. Relax and take a deep breath." Breathe deeply and properly by relaxing your stomach muscle (that's right, you have permission to let your stomach protrude!) and inhaling so that air reaches the bottom of your lungs. Hold the air in for a few seconds, then slowly exhale, pulling your stomach muscle in as you exhale. This easy exercise not only strengthens your stomach muscle, but gives your body and brain the oxygen you need to perform free from physical stress and anxiety.

Next, be sure you have read To the Student on page ix. This will help you to understand the authors' organization or "game plan" for your math experience in this course.

At the beginning of each chapter you will find more Good Advice for Studying that will help you to study and take tests more effectively, and to manage your anxiety. You may want to read ahead so that you can improve even more quickly. Good luck!

1.1 PLACE VALUE AND WORD NAMES

Objectives

1 Determine the place value of a digit in a whole number.

2 Identify the digit that has a given place value in a whole number.

3 Write the place-value name of a whole number given its word name.

4 Write the word name of a whole number given its place-value name.

Application

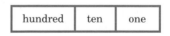 The Peach Tree Lumber Company purchases the timber on Erica Haley's property for $39,350. What word name will the finance officer, Henry Peete, write on the check?

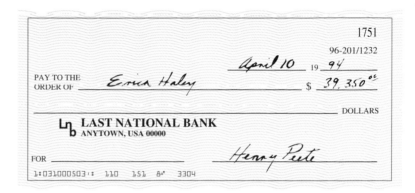

Vocabulary

The **digits** are 0, 1, 2, 3, 4, 5, 6, 7, 8, and 9. The **natural numbers** or **counting numbers** are 1, 2, 3, 4, 5, 6, and so on. The **whole numbers** are 0, 1, 2, 3, 4, 5, and so on.

To write numbers larger than 9 the digits are written in positions having **place values.** In 125, 1 is in the position having place value hundred; 2 is in the position having place value ten; and 5 is in the position having place value one. When the name of a number is written using digits and place values it is called the **place-value name.**

Word names are spoken or written words that name a number. The word name for 125 is one hundred twenty-five.

How and Why

1

2

In our number system (called the Hindu-Arabic system), digits and commas are the only symbols used to write whole numbers. This system is also called a base-ten (decimal) system. From right to left, the first three place-value names are one, ten, and hundred. (See Fig. 1.1.)

hundred	ten	one

Figure 1.1

In 573, the digit 3 has place value one   (1)
the digit 7 has place value ten   (10)
the digit 5 has place value hundred (100)
so 573 is 5 hundreds + 7 tens + 3 ones.

Continuing to the left, the digits are grouped in threes. (See Fig. 1.2.) The first five groups are (from right to left) unit, thousand, million, billion, and trillion. The group on the far left may have one, two, or three digits. All other groups *must* have three digits. In each group the names are the same.

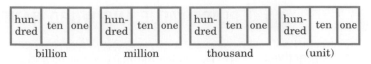

Figure 1.2

The place value of any position is one, ten, or hundred, followed by the group name.

Figure 1.3

In Figure 1.3,

Digit	Place Value
2	ten (10)
8	one thousand (1,000)
7	hundred thousand (100,000)
3	ten million (10,000,000)
5	one billion (1,000,000,000)
6	hundred billion (100,000,000,000)

Examples A–D   ## Warm Ups A–D

Directions: Determine the place value of a digit.

Strategy: Use Figure 1.2 to identify the digit's group and position in the group.

A. The digits 2, 4, and 5 in 23,465.   **A.** The digits 3, 6, and 7 in 175,306.

Solution:

2 has place value ten thousand (10,000).	2 is in the tens position in the thousands group.
4 has place value hundred (100).	4 is in the hundreds position in the units group.
5 has place value one (1).	5 is in the ones position in the units group.

B. The digits 4, 6, and 3 in 546,213.   **B.** The digits 4, 5, and 9 in 1,934,056.

Solution:

4 has place value ten thousand.	4 is in the tens position in the thousands group.
6 has place value thousand.	6 is in the ones position in the thousands group.
3 has place value one.	3 is in the ones position in the units group.

Answers to warm ups: **A.** 3 has place value hundred (100); 6 has place value one (1); 7 has place value ten thousand (10,000).   **B.** 4 has place value thousand (1000); 5 has place value ten (10); 9 has place value hundred thousand (100,000).

Directions: Identify the digit in a given position.

Strategy: Identify the group and the position within the group.

C. The ten thousands place in 835,601.

Solution:

835 is the thousands group.	The second group is the thousands group.
The digit is 3.	The tens position is in the middle of the group.

C. The hundreds place in 835,601.

D. The hundred billions place in 234,567,892,000.

Solution:

234 is the billions group.	The fourth group is the billions group.
The digit is 2.	The hundreds place is the place on the left.

D. The hundred thousands place in 234,567,892.

How and Why 3 4

Numbers written using digits and place values are called place-value names. We will see how to write these using word names.

Consider the number 1,321,208.

Place-Value Name	1	321	208
Word Name for Group	one	three hundred twenty-one	two hundred eight
Group Name	million	thousand	(unit)

Word name: One million, three hundred twenty-one thousand, two hundred eight.

▶ **To write the word name for a whole number given its place-value name**

1. Begin with the group on the left and write the word name for the group followed by the group name.
2. Repeat step one until all groups have been named. Do not write the group name "unit."

CAUTION

Do not use the word "and" when reading or writing a whole number.

Although most people would know you mean 573 when you say "five hundred and seventy-three," it is not correct to read or write 573 with "and."

To write the place-value name from the word name we write the digits that represent the name for the group and insert a comma for the group name. So the place-value name for

"Two hundred twenty-five thousand, three hundred ten"

is

225,310

▶ **To write the place-value name of a whole number given its word name**

1. Write the digits that represent the place-value name of the group beginning on the left.
2. Insert a comma for the group name.

Examples E–G   **Warm Ups E–G**

Directions: Write the word name.

Strategy: Starting on the left write the word name for the group followed by the group name. Repeat this process until all groups are named.

E. 17,698,453   **E.** 6,455,091

Solution:

17,	Place-value name.
Seventeen	Word name for group.
million,	Group name.
698	Place-value name.
six hundred ninety-eight	Word name for group.
thousand,	Group name.
453	Place-value name.
four hundred fifty-three	Word name for group.

CAUTION

The group name "units" is not written.

The word name is seventeen million, six hundred ninety-eight thousand, four hundred fifty-three.

Answer to warm up: **E.** Six million, four hundred fifty-five thousand, ninety-one

F. 🌐 The Peach Tree Lumber Company purchases the timber on Erica Haley's property for $39,350. What word name will the finance officer, Henry Peete, write on the check?

F. The Peach Tree Lumber Company buys a second plot of timber from Ms. Haley for $14,840. What word name does the finance officer write on the check?

Solution:

```
                                              1751
                                          96-201/1232
                          April 10   19 94
PAY TO THE
ORDER OF   Erica Haley              $  39,350 00

Thirty-nine thousand, three hundred fifty        DOLLARS

     ⌐┐ LAST NATIONAL BANK
     └┘  ANYTOWN, USA 00000

FOR _____      Henry Peete

⑁031000503⑁  110  151  8⑁  3304
```

To write the word name for $39,350, write: Thirty-nine thousand, three hundred fifty. (The group name "units" is *not* written.)

Directions: Write the place-value name.

Strategy: Identify the place-value name for the group and replace the group name with a comma.

G. Two million, thirty-seven thousand, five hundred sixty-four.

G. Thirty-two million, twenty-seven thousand, nine hundred ten.

Solution:

2,	Millions group.
037,	Thousands group. (Note that a zero is added on the left to fill out the three digits in the group.)
564	Units group.

The place-value name is 2,037,564.

Answers to warm ups: **F.** Fourteen thousand, eight hundred forty   **G.** 32,027,910

NAME _____ CLASS _____ DATE _____

EXERCISES 1.1

A

Determine the place value of the digit 8.

1. 83
ten

2. 268
unit or one

3. 43,892
hundred

4. 85,690
ten thousand

5. 18,345
thousand

Write the word name.

6. 620
six hundred twenty

7. 621
six hundred twenty-one

8. 602
six hundred two

9. 6021
six thousand, twenty-one

10. 6201
six thousand,
two hundred one

Write the place-value name.

11. Three thousand two hundred
3200

12. Three hundred twenty
320

13. Five hundred twenty-one
521

14. Thirty-eight
38

15. Two thousand six
2006

16. Two hundred six
206

B

Determine the place value of the digit 5.

17. 336,510
hundred

18. 145,361
thousand

19. 513,084
hundred thousand

20. 644,258   ten

21. 57,932
ten thousand

22. 395,622
thousand

Write the word name.

23. 34,910
thirty-four thousand,
nine hundred ten

24. 34,901
thirty-four thousand,
nine hundred one

25. 3491
three thousand,
four hundred ninety-one

26. 34,091
thirty-four thousand,
ninety-one

Use the graph for Exercises 27–28. The graph shows the population of the Portland area as compared to the population of the state of Oregon.

27. Write the word name for the population in the Portland area.   one million, two hundred thirty-five
thousand, nine hundred fifty-six

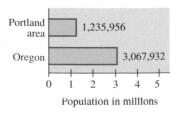

Population in millions

28. Write the word name for the population in the state of Oregon.   three million, sixty seven thousand, nine
hundred thirty-two

29. What digit is in the hundreds place in 67,799?
7

30. What digit is in the tens place in 45,932?   3

31. What digit is in the ten thousands place in 478,943?   7

32. What digit is in the thousands place in 378,925?
8

Write the place-value name.

33. Three hundred fifty-one thousand, six   351,006

34. Forty-five thousand, eighty-two   45,082

35. Two hundred thirty thousand, four hundred twenty-nine   230,429

36. Seven hundred three thousand, one hundred nine
703,109

37. Six thousand, five hundred ninety-seven   6597

38. Seven hundred fifty-six thousand, three hundred forty-two   756,342

Determine the place value of the digit 9.

39. 92,456,821
ten million

40. 34,987,446
hundred thousand

41. 789,002,344
million

42. 2,895,763,210
ten million

43. 4,985,112,740
hundred million

44. 19,032,467,821
billion

Write the word name.

45. 603,630,063
six hundred three million, six hundred thirty thousand, sixty-three

46. 8,321,456,789
eight billion, three hundred twenty-one million, four hundred fifty-six thousand, seven hundred eighty-nine

47. 40,040,400
forty million, forty thousand, four hundred

48. 30,303,030
thirty million, three hundred three thousand, thirty

49. 4,589,324
four million, five hundred eighty-nine thousand, three hundred twenty-four

50. 4,509,340,001
four billion, five hundred nine million, three hundred forty thousand, one

51. What digit is in the hundred thousands place in 3,468,923?   4

52. What digit is in the millions place in 34,680,234,000?   0

53. What digit is in the ten thousands place in 14,668,394,220?   9

54. What digit is in the ten millions place in 56,789,002,331?   8

Write the place-value name.

55. Five hundred sixty-one million, seventy-two thousand, one   561,072,001

56. Nine million, nine thousand, nine hundred nine
9,009,909

57. Fifteen billion, twenty-five million, two hundred thousand, two   15,025,200,002

58. One hundred fifteen billion, three hundred million, four hundred thousand, sixty-five   115,300,400,065

NAME _____ CLASS _____ DATE _____

Applications

59. Sue decides to have a "math-costume" party. She sends everyone invitations with this number on it: 568,234,709. She asks Ellis to dress as the digit in the hundreds place. What costume does Ellis need?
7

60. Elena wants to go to Sue's party (see Exercise 59) as a 6. What place does she represent?   ten million

61. Freddye buys a new Grand Cherokee for $26,995 and writes a check to pay for it. What word name does she need to write on the check?   twenty-six thousand, nine hundred ninety-five

62. Omar buys a used Dodge Dynasty for $7,988 and writes a check to pay for it. What word name does he need to write on the check?   seven thousand, nine hundred eighty-eight

63. Red Lion Inns earned $92,745,000 in 1992. Stockholders receive $1000 for every million dollars earned. What amount was paid to the stockholders in 1992? $92,000

64. During the first quarter of 1993, Red Lion Inns earned $23,039,000. What was the stockholders' share of the quarterly earnings (see Exercise 63)?
$23,000

65. The U.S. Fish and Wildlife Department estimates the salmon runs could be as high as 154,320 fish by 1997 on the Rogue River if new management practices are used in logging along the river. Write the word name for the number of fish.
one hundred fifty-four thousand, three hundred twenty

66. Ducks Unlimited estimated that 389,500 ducks spent the winter at the Klamath Falls refuge. Write the word name for the number of ducks.
three hundred eighty-nine thousand, five hundred

67. Portland Community College receives a bid of ten million, six hundred thirty-four thousand, seven hundred fifty dollars for a new library. Write the place-value name for the bid. $10,634,750

68. Officials for Power Ball, an interstate lottery game, estimate the prize money for the next drawing to be thirty-one million, six hundred fifty thousand dollars. Write the place-value name for the prize.
$31,650,000

State Your Understanding

69. Explain why base-ten is a good name for our number system.

70. Explain why the digit 7 has two values associated with it in 175,892 and tell what the values are.

Challenge

71. What is the place value of the digit 4 in 3,456,709,230,000?   hundred billion

72. Write the word name for 3,456,709,230,000.
three trillion, four hundred fifty-six billion, seven hundred nine million, two hundred thirty thousand

73. Write the word name for 50,050,050,050,000.
fifty trillion, fifty billion, fifty million, fifty thousand

Group Activity

74. Each digit in the number 5,456,827 represents a value such that when these values are added up the sum is the original number. Find the value that each digit represents. How did you get the value?

1.2 EXPANDED FORM; ROUNDING; INEQUALITIES

Objectives

1 Write the expanded form of a whole number from its place-value name.

2 Write the place-value name of a whole number from its expanded form.

3 Tell whether an inequality involving two whole numbers is true or false.

4 Round a whole number.

Application

Mary Kay buys a new Honda Accord for $14,745. To the nearest hundred dollars, how much does she pay for the car?

Vocabulary

The **value of a digit** or the **digit value** is the product of the digit and its place value. In 3246, the value of the digit 3 is 3 × 1000, or 3000.

The **expanded form** of a whole number is the indicated sum of the digit values.

The symbols for **less than, <,** and **greater than, >,** are used to express a relationship between two numbers that are not equal.

To **round** a whole number is to give an approximate value. 987 ≈ 990. The symbol ≈ means approximately equal to.

How and Why

1

2

The value of a digit is found by multiplying the digit by its place value. So in 45,678 the digit values are

$$4 \times 10,000 = 40,000, \qquad 5 \times 1000 = 5000$$
$$6 \times 100 = 600, \qquad 7 \times 10 = 70, \qquad \text{and} \qquad 8 \times 1 = 8$$

The digit values are used to express a whole number in expanded form. The expanded form is useful in gaining an understanding of computation with whole numbers.

▶ **To write the expanded form of a whole number from its place-value name**

1. Find the digit value for each digit by multiplying that digit by its place value.
2. Write the indicated sum of the digit values.

The place-value name of a whole number written in expanded form can be found by adding the digit values. So, 30,000 + 4000 + 700 + 10 + 2 = 34,712.

▶ **To write the place-value name of a whole number from its expanded form**

Find the sum of the digit values.

Examples A–E   **Warm Ups A–E**

Directions: Write the expanded form from the place-value name.

Strategy: Find the digit value of each digit by multiplying that digit times its place value, and then write the indicated sum of the digit values.

A. 768   A. 935

Solution:

$7 \times 100 = 700$	The digit value of 7.
$6 \times 10 = 60$	The digit value of 6.
$8 \times 1 = 8$	The digit value of 8.
$700 + 60 + 8$	The sum of the digit values.

or

7 hundreds + 6 tens + 8 ones	Instead of the digit values use the digit and the word name for its place value.

B. 8491

Solution:

$8000 + 400 + 90 + 1$

B. 7395

C. 45,625

Solution:

$40,000 + 5000 + 600 + 20 + 5$

C. 64,732

Directions: Write the place-value name from the expanded form.

Strategy: Find the sum of the digit values.

D. $60,000 + 4000 + 900 + 30 + 7$

Solution:

64,937   Add.

D. $70,000 + 2000 + 400 + 50 + 9$

E. $50,000 + 9000 + 0 + 20 + 9$

Solution:

59,029

E. $60,000 + 0 + 700 + 10 + 4$

How and Why 3   If two whole numbers are not equal, then one is either *less than* or *greater than* the other. Look at this number line (or ruler):

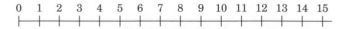

Numbers to the right of a given number are greater than the number (the measure is larger), so

$8 > 5$	8 is greater than 5
$7 > 1$	7 is greater than 1
$14 > 12$	14 is greater than 12
$15 > 0$	15 is greater than 0

Numbers to the left of any given number are less than the given number (the measure is smaller), so

---

Answers to warm ups: **A.** 900 + 30 + 5 or 9 hundreds + 3 tens + 5 ones   **B.** 7000 + 300 + 90 + 5   **C.** 60,000 + 4000 + 700 + 30 + 2
D. 72,459   **E.** 60,714

$$2 < 6 \qquad \text{2 is less than 6}$$
$$7 < 10 \qquad \text{7 is less than 10}$$
$$5 < 9 \qquad \text{5 is less than 9}$$
$$11 < 13 \qquad \text{11 is less than 13}$$

For larger numbers, imagine the number line extended as far as you like. Note that the symbols $<$ and $>$ always point to the smaller number, so

$$109 < 405 \qquad \text{109 is less than 405}$$
$$34 > 25 \qquad \text{34 is greater than 25}$$
$$1009 > 1007 \qquad \text{1009 is greater than 1007}$$

Inequality statements can be true or false. For instance, $6 > 10$ is false because 6 is to the left of 10 on the number line. Also, $5 < 11$ is true because 5 is to the left of 11 on the number line.

Examples F–H	Warm Ups F–H

Directions: True or false.

Strategy: Draw or visualize a number line and see if the inequality symbol is pointing to the number on the left.

F. $495 > 501$ | **F.** $299 > 411$

Solution: False; 495 is to the left of 501 on a number line, so the symbol is not pointing to the smaller number.

G. $564 < 567$ | **G.** $2388 < 2500$

Solution: True; 564 is to the left of 567 on a number line. The symbol is pointing to the smaller number.

H. $12,578 > 10,405$ | **H.** $24,532 > 26,976$

Solution: True.

How and Why   4   We can use the number line to see how whole numbers are rounded. Suppose we want to round 27 to the nearest ten. Looking at the number line,

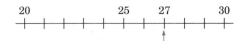

we see the arrow under 27 is closer to 30 than to 20. We say that 27 rounds to 30.

To round 34,568 to the nearest thousand without a number line, draw an arrow under the digit in the *rounding place,* which in this case is the thousands place.

$$34,568$$
$$\uparrow$$

Since the digit to the right of the rounding place has a digit value of 500, which is half of 1000, 34,568 is at least halfway to 35,000. Whenever the number we are rounding is halfway or closer to the larger number we choose the larger number. So

$$34,568 \approx 35,000 \qquad \text{34,568 is closer to 35,000 than to 34,000}$$

Answers to warm ups: **F.** False   **G.** True   **H.** False

▶ **To round a whole number to a given rounding place**

1. Identify the digit in the rounding place (the given place) by drawing an arrow under it.
2. If the digit to the right of the rounding place is five or greater, round up by adding one to the digit in the rounding place. If the digit to the right of the rounding place is less than five, round down by keeping the digit in the rounding place.
3. Replace each digit to the right of the rounding place with zero.

With practice you can eliminate the arrow in identifying the rounding place and do it mentally.

Examples I–K	**Warm Ups I–K**

Directions: Round to the given place.

Strategy: Use an arrow to identify the digit in the rounding place, the given place. If the digit to the right of the rounding place is five or greater, round up; if the digit to the right is four or less, round down.

I. 23,549; hundred

Solution:

23,549   Draw an arrow under the digit in the hundreds place; 5.
  ↑
23,549   Since the digit to the right is 4, keep the 5.
  ↑
23,500   Replace each digit to the right of the rounding place with 0.

I. 27,389; thousand

J. 137,589; thousand

Solution:

137,589   Draw an arrow under the digit in the thousands place; 7.
    ↑
137,589   Since the digit to the right is 5, round up by adding 1 to 7.
    ↑
138,000   Replace each digit to the right of the rounding place with 0.

J. 167,844; ten thousand

> **CAUTION**
>
> Don't forget to replace all digits to the right of the arrow with zeros.

K. 🌐 Mary Kay buys a new Honda Accord for $14,745. How much does she pay for the car, to the nearest hundred dollars?

Solution:

14,745   Identify the digit in the hundreds place.
  ↑
14,700   The digit to its right is 4, so round down.

To the nearest hundred dollars, Mary Kay pays $14,700 for the Honda.

K. The budget of a local community college is $36,419,850, but it is reported to the newspaper to the nearest ten thousand dollars. What budget is reported?

Answers to warm ups: **I.** 27,000   **J.** 170,000   **K.** $36,420,000

NAME _____ CLASS _____ DATE _____

EXERCISES 1.2

A

Write the expanded form from the place-value name.

1. 901
900 + 0 + 1

2. 416
400 + 10 + 6

3. 5007
5000 + 0 + 0 + 7

4. 7050
7000 + 0 + 50 + 0

5. 321
300 + 20 + 1

6. 7258
7000 + 200 + 50 + 8

Write the place-value name from the expanded form.

7. 900 + 50 + 1   951

8. 400 + 30 + 3   433

9. 40,000 + 5000 + 300 + 80 + 9   45,389

10. 50,000 + 0 + 300 + 20 + 7   50,327

True or false.

11. 16 < 19   True

12. 5 > 12   False

13. 67 > 49   True

14. 35 < 42   True

15. 37 < 29   False

16. 56 > 52   True

Round to the given place.

17. 511 (ten)   510

18. 457 (hundred)   500

19. 2753 (ten)   2750

20. 5350 (hundred)   5400

21. 582 (hundred)   600

22. 4173 (ten)   4170

B

Write the expanded form from the place-value name.

23. 70,003
70,000 + 0 + 0 + 0 + 3

24. 50,325
50,000 + 0 + 300 + 20 + 5

25. 70,307
70,000 + 0 + 300 + 0 + 7

26. 54,934
50,000 + 4000 + 900 + 30 + 4

27. 502,065
500,000 + 0 + 2000 + 0 + 60 + 5

28. 530,208
500,000 + 30,000 + 0 + 200 + 0 + 8

Write the place-value name from the expanded form.

29. 80,000 + 4000 + 300 + 20 + 8   84,328

30. 20,000 + 6000 + 200 + 0 + 2   26,202

31. 40,000 + 5000 + 300 + 20 + 5   45,325

32. 90,000 + 6000 + 0 + 0 + 7   96,007

33. 5 ten thousands + 4 thousands + 3 hundreds + 6 tens + 5 ones   54,365

C

A survey of car sales in Wisconsin shows the following distribution of sales among these dealers.

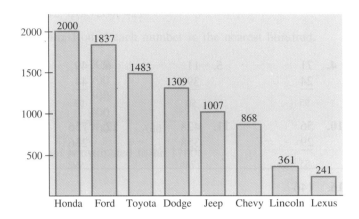

41. What is the total number of Fords, Toyotas, and Lexuses sold?   3561

42. What is the total number of Chevys, Lincolns, Dodges, and Hondas sold?   4538

43. What is the total number of Hondas, Jeeps, Chevys, and Lincolns sold?   4236

44. What is the total number of Dodges, Fords, Lincolns, Toyotas, and Lexuses sold?   5231

45. What is the total number sold of the three best-selling cars?   5320

46. What is the total number of cars sold?   9106

Estimate the sum and then add.

47. 34,675
   3,201
  57,832
     72
90,000; 95,780

48.   345
  4,678
    69
 76,458
80,000; 81,550

49. 10,765
   321
  4,752
 54,786
  4,675
60,000; 75,299

50.   5,783
   992
 21,653
  6,321
 32,710
70,000; 67,459

51. 34 + 1008 + 549 + 1456
3000; 3047

52. 973 + 32 + 156 + 4678
6000; 5839

53. 12 + 8270 + 4083 + 16,756
30,000; 29,121

54. 37 + 1859 + 5937 + 32,164
40,000; 39,997

NAME _____ CLASS _____ DATE _____

55. 23,706 + 34 + 7561 + 9346 + 236
40,000; 40,883

56. 96 + 783 + 3678 + 12,555 + 8999
20,000; 26,111

Applications

57. The biologist at the Bonneville fish ladder counted the following number of coho salmon during a one-week period: Monday, 895; Tuesday, 675; Wednesday, 124; Thursday, 1056; Friday, 308; Saturday, 312; and Sunday, 219. How many salmon went through the ladder that week?   3589 salmon

58. A new-car dealership has the following sales in a given week: Monday, $36,750; Tuesday, $46,780; Wednesday, $21,995; Thursday, $35,900; Friday, $67,950; Saturday, $212,752; and Sunday, $345,720. What are the gross sales for the week?
$767,847

59. Attendance at three consecutive Super Bowls is 78,943, 85,782, and 103,456. What is the total attendance at the three games?   268,181

60. A recent survey of unemployed people in a Northeast city found 3567 Caucasians, 678 Afro-Americans, 324 Hispanics, 381 Asians, and 82 others. How many are unemployed in this city?
5032

61. The Mendosa family has the following payments to make each month: rent, $630; car, $210; TV, $28; washer and dryer, $63; insurance, $112. What is the total of these payments each month? $1043

62. Five rooms of a house contain lamps that have the following wattages: kitchen, 200 W; dining room, 125 W; bathroom, 75 W; living room, 250 W; and bedroom, 75 W. What is the total wattage of the lamps?   725 W

63. The Wildlife Department organizes a count of seagulls at eight beach sites along the West Coast. The counts are as follows: Oceanside, 213; Seaside, 341; Parkview, 102; Yachats, 97; Monterey, 308; Seaview, 56; Long Beach, 412; and Netarts, 217. According to the count, how many seagulls are on these beaches? Round to the nearest ten.
1750 seagulls

64. Lea sold five houses last month for the following prices: $123,675, $457,000, $89,050, $312,885, and $210,560. What is the total value of her sales? Round to the nearest hundred dollars. $1,193,200

© 1995 Saunders College Publishing.

65. Mitchell puts the following number of miles on his car in a six-month period: 354, 1003, 534, 175, 322, 421. Find the total number of miles driven. If the car should be serviced after it has been driven 3000 miles, does it need service now?   2809 miles; no

66. John Cagney works for $325 a week plus commissions. If his commissions for the week are $115, $78, $91, $217, and $72, what are his total earnings for the week? $898

State Your Understanding

67. Explain to an 8-year-old child that 8 + 7 = 15.

68. When you add 36 and 48 you must "carry 1" to the tens column. Explain what "carrying 1" means.

Challenge

69. Add the following numbers, round the sum to the nearest hundred, and write the word name for the rounded sum: one hundred sixty; eighty thousand, three hundred twelve; four hundred seventy-two thousand, nine hundred fifty-two; and one hundred forty-seven thousand, five hundred twenty-three.
seven hundred thousand, nine hundred

70. Add the following numbers, round the sum to the nearest ten thousand, and write the word name for the rounded sum: one million, eight hundred thirteen thousand, four hundred sixty-one; four hundred twenty-eight thousand, two hundred fifty-one; twelve million, seven hundred nineteen thousand, nine; and four million, fifty-two thousand, nine hundred.   nineteen million, ten thousand

71. Peter sells three Honda Civics for $14,385 each, four Accords for $17,435 each, and two Acuras for $26,548 each. What is his total dollar sales for the nine cars? $165,991

Group Activity

72. Add and round to the nearest hundred:

$$
\begin{array}{r}
14{,}657 \\
3{,}766 \\
123{,}900 \\
569 \\
54{,}861 \\
346{,}780 \\
\hline
\end{array}
$$

Now round each addend to the nearest hundred and then add. Discuss why the answers are different. Be prepared to explain why this happens.

| 1.4 | **SUBTRACTING WHOLE NUMBERS** |

Objectives

1 Subtract whole numbers.

2 Estimate the difference of two whole numbers.

Application

🌐 Nina Carretta receives an electricity bill that shows that 1572 kilowatt-hours (KWH) of energy have been used. If 682 KWH were used for lighting and appliances and the rest for hot water, how many KWH were used for heating water?

Vocabulary

The symbol for subtraction is "$-$" and is read "minus." The result obtained from subtracting is called the **difference.**

How and Why 1

Subtraction can be thought of as finding the missing addend in an addition exercise. For instance, $9 - 5 = ?$ asks $5 + ? = 9$. Since $5 + 4 = 9$, we know that $9 - 5 = 4$. Similarly, $47 - 15 = ?$ asks $15 + ? = 47$. Since $15 + 32 = 47$, we know that $47 - 15 = 32$.

For larger numbers, such as $274 - 162$, we take advantage of the column form and expanded notation to find the missing addend in each column.

$$
\begin{array}{l}
274 = 2 \text{ hundreds} + 7 \text{ tens} + 4 \text{ ones} \\
\underline{162 = 1 \text{ hundred } + 6 \text{ tens} + 2 \text{ ones}} \\
 1 \text{ hundred } + 1 \text{ ten } + 2 \text{ ones} = 112
\end{array}
$$

Check by adding:

$$
\begin{array}{r}
162 \\
\underline{112} \\
274
\end{array}
$$

So, $274 - 162 = 112$.

When using the column form it is possible that subtraction in a given column cannot be done. For instance, $453 - 238 = ?$

$$
\begin{array}{l}
453 = 4 \text{ hundreds} + 5 \text{ tens} + 3 \text{ ones} \\
\underline{238 = 2 \text{ hundreds} + 3 \text{ tens} + 8 \text{ ones}}
\end{array}
$$

We cannot subtract 8 ones from 3 ones, $8 + ? = 3$, so we must rename by borrowing one of the tens from the 5 tens (1 ten = 10 ones) and add this to the 3 ones.

$$
\begin{array}{l}
453 = 4 \text{ hundreds} + 4 \text{ tens} + 13 \text{ ones} \\
\underline{238 = 2 \text{ hundreds} + 3 \text{ tens} + 8 \text{ ones}} \\
 2 \text{ hundreds} + 1 \text{ ten } + 5 \text{ ones} = 215
\end{array}
$$

Check by adding:

$$
\begin{array}{r}
238 \\
\underline{215} \\
453
\end{array}
$$

So, $453 - 238 = 215$. The examples show a shortcut for borrowing.

▶ **To subtract whole numbers**

1. Write the whole numbers in columns so the places are lined up.
2. Subtract each column, starting with the ones place and moving left.
3. When the digits in a column cannot be subtracted, borrow 1 from the next column and rename by adding 10 to the upper digit in the current column and then subtract.

Examples A–F   **Warm Ups A–F**

Directions: Subtract.

Strategy: Write the numbers in columns, making sure to line up the places. Subtract the columns from right to left. If the subtraction in any column cannot be done, borrow one from the next column and rename by adding ten to the upper digit in the current column and then subtract.

A. 75 − 32   **A.** 96 − 53

Solution: Write the numbers in columns, lining up the places.

```
  75      Subtract the ones column: 5 − 2 = 3
  32      Subtract the tens column: 7 − 3 = 4
  ──
  43
```

CHECK: Add.

```
  32
  43
  ──
  75
```

So, 75 − 32 = 43.

B. 42 − 29   **B.** 64 − 48

Solution: Write the numbers in columns, lining up the places.

```
 3 12      Since 9 ones cannot be subtracted from 2 ones, we borrow 1 ten
  4 2      from the 4 tens. Since 1 ten = 10 ones, add the 10 ones to the 2
  2 9      ones for a total of 12 ones. The renaming is shown above each
  ───      column.
  1 3
```

CHECK: Add.

```
  29
  13
  ──
  42
```

So, 42 − 29 = 13.

C. 752 − 295   **C.** 567 − 398

Solution: We must rename in two columns.

```
 6 14      Starting on the left, we borrow 1 ten (10 ones) from the tens
   4 12    to rename the ones (10 + 2 = 12).
 7 5 2     Now borrow 1 hundred (10 tens) from the hundreds column
 2 9 5     to rename the tens (10 + 4 = 14).
 ─────
 4 5 7
```

CHECK: Add.

```
  295
  457
  ───
  752
```

So, 752 − 295 = 457.

Answers to warm ups: **A.** 43   **B.** 16   **C.** 169

D. 2500 − 689

D. 4600 − 1343

Solution:

$$\begin{array}{r} {\scriptstyle 9} \\ {\scriptstyle 4\ 10\ 10} \\ 2\ 5\ 0\ 0 \\ \underline{6\ 8\ 9} \\ \end{array}$$

We cannot subtract in the ones column, and since there are 0 tens we cannot borrow from the tens column. Instead, we go to the hundreds column and borrow 1 hundred (10 tens).

$$\begin{array}{r} {\scriptstyle 1\ 14\ \ 9} \\ {\scriptstyle 4\ 10\ 10} \\ 2\ 5\ 0\ 0 \\ \underline{6\ 8\ 9} \\ 1\ 8\ 1\ 1 \end{array}$$

Now borrow a ten to make 10 ones. We can now subtract in the ones and tens columns but not in the hundreds column, so we must borrow to subtract in the hundreds column.

CHECK: Add.

$$\begin{array}{r} 689 \\ \underline{1811} \\ 2500 \end{array}$$

So, 2500 − 689 = 1811.

E. 3582 − 2785

E. 5677 − 3529

Solution:

ENTER | 3582 | − | 2785 | = |

DISPLAY   3582. 3582. 2785. 797.

The difference is 797.

F. Nina Carretta receives an electricity bill that shows that 1572 kilowatt-hours (KWH) of energy have been used. If 682 KWH were used for lighting and appliances and the rest for hot water, how many KWH were used for heating water?

F. Nina also pays the water and garbage bills for the next three months. She pays a total of $125. If the water bill is $48, how much is the garbage bill?

Solution: To find the number of KWH used for heating water, subtract the number of KWH used for lighting and appliances from the total used.

$$\begin{array}{r} 1572 \\ \underline{682} \\ 890 \end{array}$$

Nina used 890 KWH for heating water.

Answers to warm ups: **D.** 3257   **E.** 2148   **F.** $77

How and Why [2]   The difference of two whole numbers can be estimated by rounding each number to the largest place in the two numbers and then subtracting these rounded numbers. For instance,

$$
\begin{array}{rl}
6110 & 6000 \\
\underline{4392} & \underline{4000} \\
& 2000
\end{array}
$$

The largest place is thousand, so round each number to the nearest thousand and subtract.

The estimate of the difference is 2000. One use of the estimate is to see if the difference is correct. If the actual difference is not close to 2000, you should check the subtraction. In this case the actual difference is 1718, which is close to the estimate.

▶ **To estimate the difference of two whole numbers**

1. Round each number to the largest place in either number.
2. Subtract the rounded numbers.

Examples G–H   **Warm Ups G–H**

Directions: Estimate the difference and subtract.

Strategy: Round each number to the largest place in either number. Subtract the rounded numbers to find the estimate. Subtract the original numbers.

G.   687 and 364   G.   744 and 572

Solution: Round each number to the nearest hundred.

$$
\begin{array}{rl}
687 & 700 \\
\underline{364} & \underline{400} \\
& 300 \qquad \text{Subtract.}
\end{array}
$$

$$
\begin{array}{r}
687 \\
\underline{364} \\
323 \qquad \text{Subtract.}
\end{array}
$$

The difference is estimated to be 300; it is 323.

H.   63,590 and 14,350   H.   73,555 and 26,956

Solution: Round each number to the nearest ten thousand.

$$
\begin{array}{rl}
63{,}590 & 60{,}000 \\
\underline{14{,}350} & \underline{10{,}000} \\
& 50{,}000 \qquad \text{Subtract.}
\end{array}
$$

$$
\begin{array}{r}
63{,}590 \\
\underline{14{,}350} \\
49{,}240 \qquad \text{Subtract.}
\end{array}
$$

The difference is estimated to be 50,000; it is 49,240.

Answers to warm ups: **G.** 100; 172   **H.** 40,000; 46,599

NAME _____ CLASS _____ DATE _____

EXERCISES 1.4

A

Subtract.

1. 24
　　 13
　　 11

2. 17
　　 　6
　　 11

3. 45
　　 21
　　 24

4. 18
　　 12
　　 　6

5. 27
　　 15
　　 12

6. 26
　　 23
　　 　3

7. 45
　　 34
　　 11

8. 43
　　 22
　　 21

9. 76
　　 42
　　 34

10. 84
　　 63
　　 21

11. 72
　　 34
　　 38

12. 35
　　 19
　　 16

13. 64
　　 48
　　 16

14. 65
　　 37
　　 28

15. 70
　　 46
　　 24

16. 90
　　 72
　　 18

17. 45 − 19   26

18. 54 − 28   26

19. 102 − 63   39

20. 110 − 76   34

B

Subtract.

21. 423
　　 121
　　 302

22. 567
　　 253
　　 314

23. 258
　　 139
　　 119

24. 431
　　 217
　　 214

25. 759
　　 478
　　 281

26. 387
　　 194
　　 193

27. 488
　　 　99
　　 389

28. 376
　　 　87
　　 289

29. 476
　　 　80
　　 396

30. 745
　　 　70
　　 675

Estimate the difference and subtract.

31. 875
　　 406
　　 500; 469

32. 455
　　 207
　　 300; 248

33. 509
　　 234
　　 300; 275

34. 802
　　 341
　　 500; 461

35. 405
　　 368
　　 0; 37

36. 702
　　 457
　　 200; 245

37. 500
　　 428
　　 100; 72

38. 700
　　 233
　　 500; 467

39. 673 − 462   200; 211

40. 963 − 758   200; 205

© 1995 Saunders College Publishing.

C

A survey of car sales in Wisconsin shows the following distribution of sales among these dealers.

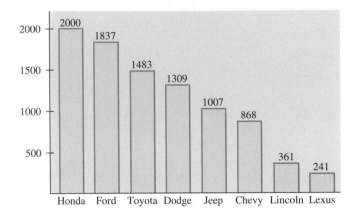

41. How many more Hondas are sold than Fords?
163

42. How many more Toyotas are sold than Jeeps?
476

43. How many fewer Chevys are sold than Dodges?
441

44. How many fewer Lincolns are sold than Fords?
1476

45. How many more Jeeps are sold than Lexuses?
766

46. How many more Fords are sold than Dodges?
528

Estimate the difference and subtract.

47.	3478	**48.**	6589	**49.**	3671	**50.**	8934
	2764		1756		846		963
0; 714		5000; 4833		3000; 2825		8000; 7971	

51.	36,897	**52.**	56,244	**53.**	70,000	**54.**	30,000
	21,734		23,133		45,732		12,779
20,000; 15,163		40,000; 33,111		20,000; 24,268		20,000; 17,221	

55. 9845 − 5467
5000; 4378

56. 7634 − 4281
4000; 3353

57. 73,921 − 56,833
10,000; 17,088

58. 54,633 − 49,007
0; 5626

59. 203,855 − 175,622
0; 28,233

60. 432,856 − 376,666
0; 56,190

NAME _____ CLASS _____ DATE _____

Applications

61. If there are 103,550 seats available for the Super Bowl and all but 15,788 are sold, how many seats have been sold for the game?   87,762 seats

62. A forester counted 23,679 trees that are ready for harvest on a certain acreage. If the Forestry Service rules that 8543 mature trees must be left on the acreage, how many trees can be harvested? 15,136 trees

63. A casting of aluminum weighs 93 lb. The same casting of iron weighs 287 lb. How much more does the iron casting weigh?   194 lb

64. The new sewer line being installed in downtown Memphis will handle 345,760 gallons of refuse per minute. The old line handled 178,550 gallons per minute. How many more gallons per minute will the new line handle?   167,210 gallons

65. A community college receives two bids for the construction of its new library, $6,874,230 and $6,456,990. How much is saved by awarding the contract to the lower bid? $417,240

66. The population of Marysville was 85,987 in 1990 and it has grown to 121,465 in 1995. How many additional people live in Marysville in 1995? 35,478 people

67. The Cleer Glass Company had $34,875 in their checking account. If the treasurer of the company writes checks totaling $12,853, how much is left in the account? $22,022

68. Rich has $4565 in his checking account. He writes a check for two thousand three hundred forty-seven dollars. How much does he have left in his account? $2218

69. The Acme warehouse has 456,893 cases of peas at the beginning of the month. During the month they ship out the following number of cases: week one, 5680; week two, 10,560; week three, 23,900; and week four, 9456. How many cases, to the nearest hundred, are left in the warehouse?   407,300 cases

70. Fong's Grocery owes a supplier $25,875. During the month Fong's makes payments of $460, $983, $565, and $10,730. How much does Fong's still owe, to the nearest hundred dollars? $13,100

State Your Understanding

71. Explain to an 8-year-old child why $15 - 9 = 6$.

72. When subtracting $34 - 19$, you must "borrow" one from the three. What is meant by borrowing one?

Challenge

73. How much greater is three hundred million, three hundred thousand, three than forty million, forty thousand, forty? Write the word name for the difference.   two hundred sixty million, two hundred fifty-nine thousand, nine hundred sixty-three

74. How much greater is seven million, two hundred forty-seven thousand, one hundred ninety-five than two million, eight hundred four thousand, fifty-three? Write the word name for the difference.   four million, four hundred forty-three thousand, one hundred forty-two

75. The payroll at a local small business is $65,825 per month. If five employees each earn $4560 per month, eight employees each earn $3670 per month, and three employees each earn $1950 per month, how much does the one remaining employee earn per month? $7815

Group Activity

76. If Ramon delivers 112 loaves of bread to each store on his delivery route, how many stores are on the route if he delivers a total of 4368 loaves? (*Hint:* Subtract 112 loaves for each stop from the total number of loaves.) What operation does this perform? Make up three more examples and demonstrate them in class.

GETTING READY FOR ALGEBRA

Objective   Solve an equation of the form $x + a = b$ or $x - a = b$, where a, b, and x are whole numbers.

Application   The selling price of a pair of shoes is $67. If the markup on the shoes is $23, what is the cost to the store? Cost + markup = selling price.

Vocabulary   An **equation** is a statement about numbers that says that two expressions are equal. Letters, called **variables** or **unknowns,** are often used to represent numbers.

How and Why   Examples of equations are

$$8 = 8 \qquad 12 = 12 \qquad 100 = 100 \qquad 20 + 5 = 25 \qquad 49 - 9 = 40$$

When variables are used, an equation can look like this:

$$x = 2 \qquad x = 5 \qquad y = 12 \qquad x + 3 = 10 \qquad y - 7 = 13$$

This kind of equation will only be true when the letter is replaced by a specific number. For example,

$x = 2$ is true only when x is replaced by 2.

$x = 5$ is true only when x is replaced by 5.

$y = 12$ is true only when y is replaced by 12.

$x + 3 = 10$ is true only when x is replaced by 7, so that $7 + 3 = 10$.

$y - 7 = 13$ is true only when y is replaced by 20, so that $20 - 7 = 13$.

The numbers that make equations true are called *solutions.* Solutions of equations such as $x - 4 = 7$ can be found by trial and error, but let's develop a more practical way.

Addition and subtraction are inverse or opposite operations. For example, if 12 is added to a number and then 12 is subtracted from that sum, the difference is the original number.

As a specific example, add 11 to 15: $15 + 11 = 26$; the sum is 26. If 11 is subtracted from that sum, $26 - 11$, the result is 15, which was the original number.

We will use this idea to solve the following equation:

$x + 15 = 19$	15 is added to the number represented by x.
$x + 15 - 15 = 19 - 15$	To remove the addition and have only x on the left side of the equal sign, we subtract 15. To keep a true equation, we must subtract 15 from both sides.
$x = 4$	This equation will be true when x is replaced by 4.

To check, replace x in the original equation with 4 and see if the result is a true statement:

$$x + 15 = 19$$
$$4 + 15 = 19$$
$$19 = 19 \qquad \text{The statement is true, so the solution is 4.}$$

K.   45, 261, and 315   **K.**   89, 267, and 125

Solution:

$(45)(261)(315) = (50)(300)(300)$ Round each number to its
                                      largest place.

$\qquad\qquad\quad = 4,500,000$ Multiply.

$(45)(261)(315) = 3,699,675$ Product found using a
                                calculator.

The product is estimated to be 4,500,000 and is 3,699,675.

NAME _____ CLASS _____ DATE _____

EXERCISES 1.5

A

Multiply.

1. 31
   4
   ̄ ̄
   124

2. 43
   3
   ̄ ̄
   129

3. 22
   4
   ̄ ̄
   88

4. 13
   3
   ̄ ̄
   39

5. 27
   4
   ̄ ̄
   108

6. 72
   6
   ̄ ̄
   432

7. 63
   7
   ̄ ̄
   441

8. 82
   8
   ̄ ̄
   656

9. $9 \cdot 32$
   288

10. $7 \cdot 33$
   231

11. 9(45)
   405

12. 3(78)
   234

13. (34)(0)
   0

14. (0)923
   0

15. 70
   30
   ̄ ̄
   2100

16. 30
   40
   ̄ ̄
   1200

17. 56
   50
   ̄ ̄
   2800

18. 93
   60
   ̄ ̄
   5580

19. 117
   8
   ̄ ̄
   936

20. 212
   7
   ̄ ̄
   1484

B

Multiply.

21. (8)(17)(0)(8)
   0

22. (17)(5)(3)(0)(2)
   0

23. 232
   8
   ̄ ̄
   1856

24. 612
   5
   ̄ ̄
   3060

25. 706
   6
   ̄ ̄
   4236

26. 403
   7
   ̄ ̄
   2821

27. 4050
   8
   ̄ ̄
   32,400

28. (6090)(3)
   18,270

29. (46)(23)
   1058

30. (58)(81)
   4698

Estimate the product and multiply.

31. 378
   16
   ̄ ̄
8000; 6048

32. 673
   23
   ̄ ̄
14,000; 15,479

33. 700
   84
   ̄ ̄
56,000; 58,800

34. 400
   74
   ̄ ̄
28,000; 29,600

35. 544
   40
   ̄ ̄
20,000; 21,760

36. 277
      70
21,000; 19,390

37. 412
      300
120,000; 123,600

38. 567
      600
360,000; 340,200

39. 703
      67
49,000; 47,101

40. 509
      58
30,000; 29,522

C

Multiply.

41. 567
      34
  19,278

42. 743
      56
  41,608

43. 874
      87
  76,038

44. 889
      52
  46,228

45. 646
      245
  158,270

46. 328
      322
  105,616

47. 67(5007)
335,469

48. 92(7002)
644,184

49. 57(4554)
259,578

50. 73(7227)
527,571

Estimate the product and multiply.

51. (407)(4076)
1,600,000; 1,658,932

52. (607)(3075)
1,800,000; 1,866,525

53. (712)(1451)
700,000; 1,033,112

54. (633)(2361)
1,200,000; 1,494,513

55. (5007)(503)
2,500,000; 2,518,521

56. (6004)(405)
2,400,000; 2,431,620

57. (24)(45)(36)
40,000; 38,880

58. (32)(71)(82)
168,000; 186,304

59. (14)(38)(65)
28,000; 34,580

60. (19)(49)(51)
50,000; 47,481

NAME _____   CLASS _____ DATE _____

Applications

61. During the first week of the Rotary Rose Sale 235 dozen roses are sold. It is estimated that a total of 18 times that number will be sold during the sale. What is the estimated number of dozens of roses that will be sold?   4230 dozen

62. The Good Food Grocery Store orders 564 cases of fruit cocktail. If each case costs $18, what is the total cost of the fruit cocktail? $10,152

63. Salmon counted at the Bonneville fish ladder average 134 fish per day during a 17-day period. How many salmon are counted during the 17-day period?   2278 salmon

64. During 1995 the population of Washington County grew at a pace of 1563 people per month. What was the total growth in population during 1995?   18,756 people

65. A certain bacteria culture triples its size every hour. If the culture has a count of 375 at 10 A.M., what will the count be at 2 P.M. the same day?
30,375 bacteria

66. The starling population of the United States doubles every three years. If the current population of these birds is estimated to be 1,750,300, what will the population be in nine years?   14,002,400 starlings

67. The water consumption in Hebo averages 320,450 gallons per day. How many gallons of water are consumed in a 31-day month, rounded to the nearest thousand gallons?   9,934,000 gallons

68. The property tax on homes in Mt. Pedro averages $1312 per home. What is the total tax collected from 7850 homes, rounded to the nearest ten thousand dollars? $10,300,000

69. Janet orders four hundred fifty radios for sale in her discount store. If she pays $78 per radio, what do the radios cost her? $35,100

70. Janet sells the radios (see Exercise 69) for $105 each. How many dollars does she raise from selling all the radios? What is her profit from the sale of the radios? $47,250; $12,150

State Your Understanding

71. Explain to an 8-year-old child that 3(8) = 24.

72. When 74 is multiplied by 8 we carry 3 to the tens column. Explain why this is necessary.

Challenge

73. Find the product of twenty-four thousand, fifty-five and two hundred thirteen thousand, two hundred seventy-six. Write the word name for the product.   five billion, one hundred thirty million, three hundred fifty-four thousand, one hundred eighty

74. Find the product of two million, five thousand, sixteen and three hundred thirty-four thousand, two hundred. Write the word name for the product.   six hundred seventy billion, seventy-six million, three hundred forty-seven thousand, two hundred

75. Jose harvests 75 bushels of grain per acre from his 11,575 acres of grain. If Jose can sell the grain for $27 a bushel, what is the crop worth, to the nearest thousand dollars? $23,439,000

Group Activity

76. Multiply the following numbers by 10: 23, 56, 789, 214, and 1345. Now multiply each of the above numbers by 100 and 1000. What do you observe?

1.6 DIVIDING WHOLE NUMBERS

Objectives

1. Divide whole numbers.
2. Estimate the quotient of whole numbers.

Application

The Belgium Bulb Company packs six hyacinth bulbs per package for shipping to the United States. How many packages can be made from 8724 bulbs?

Vocabulary

In $8 \div 2 = 4$, 8 is called the **dividend,** 2 the **divisor,** and 4 the **quotient.** A division problem is written

$$8 \div 2 \quad \text{or} \quad 2\overline{)8} \quad \text{or} \quad \frac{8}{2}$$

The expression $75 \div 8$ does not have a whole number quotient. It can be written $8\overline{)75} = 9$ remainder 3. In this case, 9 is commonly called the quotient (actually, 9 is only a partial quotient), and 3 is called the **remainder.**

How and Why   1

To divide $96 \div 24 = ?$ (read "96 divided by 24") is to ask what number times the second number equals the first:

$$96 \div 24 = ? \quad \text{asks} \quad 24 \times ? = 96$$

Quotient   Missing Factor

In $96 \div 24 = ?$, we can find the missing factor by repeatedly subtracting 24 from 96:

$$
\begin{array}{r}
96 \\
24 \\
\hline
72 \\
24 \\
\hline
48 \\
24 \\
\hline
24 \\
24 \\
\hline
0
\end{array}
$$

Four subtractions, so $96 \div 24 = 4$.

More quickly, we can guess the number of 24's and subtract from 96:

$$
\begin{array}{r}
24\overline{)96} \\
48 \\
\hline
48 \\
48 \\
\hline
0
\end{array}
\quad
\begin{array}{l}
\text{2 twenty-fours} \\
\\
\underline{\text{2 twenty-fours}} \\
4
\end{array}
\qquad \text{or} \qquad
\begin{array}{r}
24\overline{)96} \\
72 \\
\hline
24 \\
24 \\
\hline
0
\end{array}
\quad
\begin{array}{l}
\text{3 twenty-fours} \\
\\
\underline{\text{1 twenty-four}} \\
4
\end{array}
$$

$$
\text{or} \qquad
\begin{array}{r}
24\overline{)96} \\
96 \\
\hline
0
\end{array}
\quad
\begin{array}{l}
\underline{\text{4 twenty-fours}} \\
4
\end{array}
$$

In each case, $96 \div 24 = 4$.

Brian Clampitt, West Valley College in Saratoga, CA, is a fulltime student who also runs an after-school recreation program at Trace Elementary School. Brian was a winner of the Barker/Rogers/Van Dyke problem-posing contest. His math teacher was Anya Kroth.

This process works regardless of the size of the numbers. If the divisor is considerably smaller than the dividend, you will want to guess a rather large number.

$$
\begin{array}{r|l}
36\overline{)7308} & \\
\underline{3600} & 100 \\
3708 & \\
\underline{3600} & 100 \\
108 & \\
\underline{108} & \underline{3} \\
0 & 203
\end{array}
\qquad \text{so} \qquad 7308 \div 36 = 203
$$

All division problems can be done by this method. However, the process can be shortened by finding the number of groups, starting with the largest place value on the left, in the dividend, and then working toward the right. Study the following example. Note that the answer is written above the problem for convenience.

$23\overline{)17135}$ We will work from left to right. Notice that 23 does not divide 1, and 23 does not divide 17.

$$
\begin{array}{r}
745 \\
23\overline{)17135} \\
\underline{161} \\
103 \\
\underline{92} \\
115 \\
\underline{115} \\
0
\end{array}
$$

However, 23 will divide 171 seven times (remember that 171 is really 17,100, so 23 divides it 700 times). Place the 7 in the hundreds column above the 1.

Now multiply 7 times 23: (7)(23) = 161. Remember that 161 is really 16,100. We do not show the zeros because the placement of the 161 under the 171 keeps the place values lined up. Subtract. Bring down the next digit (3).

Now, 23 divides 103 four times (remember that 103 is really 1030, so 23 divides it 40 times), so a 4 goes in the tens column in the answer.
Now multiply 4 times 23, (4)(23) = 92, and subtract from 103. Bring down the next digit (5).

Finally, 23 divides 115 five times, so a 5 goes in the ones column in the answer. Now multiply 5 times 23, (5)(23) = 115, and subtract. Since the difference is zero, the division is complete.

CHECK:
$$
\begin{array}{r}
745 \\
\underline{\times\ 23} \\
2235 \\
\underline{1490} \\
17135
\end{array}
$$

Check by multiplying the answer times the divisor.

The answer (quotient) is 745.

Not all division problems "come out even" (have a zero remainder). In

$$
\begin{array}{r}
3 \\
12\overline{)41} \\
\underline{36} \\
5
\end{array}
$$

we see that 41 contains 3 twelves and 5 toward the next group of twelve. The answer is written as 3 remainder 5. The word "remainder" is abbreviated "R," and then the result is:

3 R 5

A check can be made by finding (12)(3) and adding the remainder:

$$
\begin{array}{r}
12 \\
\underline{3} \\
36 \\
\underline{5} \\
41
\end{array}
$$

▶ **To divide two whole numbers**

1. Divide the divisor into the first group of digits on the left in the dividend that it will divide.
2. Place the partial quotient above the last digit in the group of numbers and multiply times the divisor. Place the product under the group of digits used in the dividend.
3. Subtract.
4. Bring down the next digit on the right and divide the result by the divisor. Continue the process until all digits on the right have been used.
5. If the final subtraction is not 0, write the quotient using the remainder: partial quotient R remainder.

Recall that $45 \div 0 = ?$ asks what number times 0 is 45: $0 \times ? = 45$. By the zero-product property we know that $0 \times ? = 0$, so it cannot equal 45.

CAUTION

Division by zero is not defined. It is an operation that cannot be performed.

When dividing by a single-digit number the division can be done mentally using "short division."

$$3\overline{)1269} \qquad 423$$

Divide 3 into 12. Write the answer, 4, under the 2 in the dividend. Now divide the 6 by 3 and write the answer, 2, under the 6. Finally divide the 9 by 3 and write the answer, 3, under the 9.

The quotient is 423.

If the "mental" division does not come out even each remainder is used in the next division.

$$3\overline{)1358} \qquad 452 \text{ R } 2$$

$13 \div 3 = 4$ R 1. Write the 4 under the 3 in the dividend. Now form a new number using the remainder 1 and the next digit 5, 15. Divide 3 into 15. Write the answer, 5, under the 5 in the dividend. Since there is no remainder, divide the next digit, 8, by 3. The result is 2 R 2. Write this under the 8.

The quotient is 452 R 2.

Examples A–I	**Warm Ups A–I**

Directions: Divide.

Strategy: Divide using the four-step process. Use short division for single-digit divisors. Remember to include the remainder, if any, in the quotient.

A. 7)4207

A. 9)5436

Solution: Since there is a single-digit divisor we will use short division.

    7)4207   7 divides 42 six times.
      601   7 divides 0 zero times.
                  7 divides 7 one time.

CAUTION

A zero must be placed in the dividend so that the 6 and the 1 have the correct place values.

The quotient is 601.

B. 8)3345

B. 6)1345

Solution: Since there is a single-digit divisor we will use short division.

    8)3345   33 ÷ 8 = 4 R 1
      418 R 1   14 ÷ 8 = 1 R 6
                  65 ÷ 8 = 8 R 1

The quotient is 418 R 1.

C. $20{,}150 \div 25$

C. $18{,}252 \div 36$

Solution: With a two-digit divisor we will use long division.

```
        806
  25)20150
      200
      ‾‾‾
       15
        0
      ‾‾‾
      150
      150
      ‾‾‾
        0
```

25 does not divide 2 or 20 but divides 201 eight times: $(8)(25) = 200$. Write the 8 above the 1 (hundreds column) in the answer. Subtract and bring down the next digit, 5.

25 does not divide 15, so place a 0 in the tens column of the answer (above the 5). Multiply and subtract. Bring down the next digit, 0.

25 divides 150 six times: $(6)(25) = 150$. Place the 6 above the 0 (ones column) in the answer. Multiply and subtract.

Answers to warm ups: **A.** 604   **B.** 224 R 1   **C.** 507

D. 20,440 ÷ 365

D. 35,334 ÷ 453

Solution: With a three-digit divisor we will use long division.

$$
\begin{array}{r}
56 \\
365\overline{)20440} \\
1825 \\
\hline
2190 \\
2190 \\
\hline
0
\end{array}
$$

365 does not divide 2.
365 does not divide 20.
365 does not divide 204.
365 divides 2044 fives times: (5)(365) = 1825.
365 divides 2190 six times: (6)(365) = 2190.

E. 120 ÷ 27

E. 3049 ÷ 39

Solution: Use long division.

$$
\begin{array}{r}
4\ R\ 12 \\
27\overline{)120} \\
108 \\
\hline
12
\end{array}
$$

12 is a remainder because it does not contain a single group of 27.

CHECK:

$$
\begin{array}{r}
27 \\
4 \\
\hline
108 \\
12 \\
\hline
120
\end{array}
$$

To check, multiply the divisor by the partial quotient and add the remainder.

F. 1697 ÷ 55

F. 45,931 ÷ 17

Solution: Use long division.

$$
\begin{array}{r}
30\ R\ 47 \\
55\overline{)1697} \\
1650 \\
\hline
47
\end{array}
$$

CHECK:

$$
\begin{array}{r}
55 \\
30 \\
\hline
1650 \\
47 \\
\hline
1697
\end{array}
$$

G. 47,432 ÷ 56

G. 7488 ÷ 78

Solution:

| ENTER | 47432 | ÷ | 56 | = |

DISPLAY   47432. 47432. 56. 847.

The quotient is 847.

Answers to warm ups: **D.** 78   **E.** 78 R 7   **F.** 2701 R 14   **G.** 96

H. 🖩 $37\overline{)6483}$ **H.** $306\overline{)43947}$

Solution:

ENTER | 6483 | | ÷ | | 37 | | = |

DISPLAY   6483. 6483. 37. 175.2162

The partial quotient is 175. We need to find the remainder.

$$\frac{175 \text{ R ?}}{37\overline{)6483}}$$

To find the remainder, first find the product of 37 and 175.

ENTER | 37 | | × | | 175 | | = |

DISPLAY   37. 37. 175. 6475.

Now subtract this product from the original dividend to get the remainder.

ENTER | 6483 | | − | | 6475 | | = |

DISPLAY   6483. 6483. 6475. 8.

The answer is 175 R 8.

I. 🌐 The Belgium Bulb Company packs six hyacinth bulbs per package for shipment to the United States. How many packages can be made from 8724 bulbs?

I. The Belgium Bulb Company packs 18 daffodil bulbs per package for shipment. How many packages can be made from 51,750 bulbs?

Solution: To find the number of packages divide the number of bulbs by the number of bulbs per package. Use short division.

$$\frac{6\overline{)8724}}{1454}$$

CHECK:

$$\begin{array}{r} 1454 \\ \underline{6} \\ 8724 \end{array}$$

The Belgium Bulb Company can make 1454 packages.

How and Why   **2**   The quotient of two whole numbers can be estimated by rounding each number to its largest place and then dividing the rounded numbers. For instance,

$27\overline{)6345}$ $30\overline{)6000}$ Round each number to its largest place.

$$\begin{array}{r} 200 \\ 30\overline{)6000} \\ \underline{6000} \end{array}$$ Divide.

Answers to warm ups: **H.** 143 R 189   **I.** 2875 packages

The estimate of the quotient is 200. One use of the estimate is to see if the quotient is correct. If the actual quotient is not close to 200, you should check the division. In this case the actual quotient is 235, which is close to the estimate.

The estimated quotient will not always come out even. When this happens, round the first partial quotient and use it for first entry in the whole number quotient. For instance,

$$741\overline{)340678} \qquad 700\overline{)300000}$$

Round each number to its largest place.

$$\begin{array}{r} 400 \\ 700\overline{)300000} \end{array}$$

Divide 3000 by 700 for the first partial quotient.
Since $4(700) = 2800$ and $5(700) = 3500$, we choose the closer value, 4.

The estimated quotient is 400.

▶ **To estimate the quotient of two whole numbers**

1. Round each number to its largest place.
2. Divide the rounded numbers.
3. If the first partial quotient has a remainder, choose the digit that will give the closer value when multiplied by the divisor. Write zeros to complete the estimated division.

Examples J–K   **Warm Ups J–K**

Directions: Estimate the quotient and divide.

Strategy: Round each number to its largest place. Divide the rounded numbers. Choose the closer value after the initial division if necessary. Divide the original numbers.

J. 687 and 34   **J.** 434 and 57

Solution: Round each number to its largest place and divide.

$$34\overline{)687} \qquad 30\overline{)700}$$

$$\begin{array}{r} 20 \\ 30\overline{)700} \end{array}$$

Divide. Since the initial division does not come out even, choose 2 as $2(30) = 60$ is closer to 70 than $3(30) = 90$.

$$\begin{array}{r} 20 \\ 34\overline{)687} \\ \underline{68} \\ 7 \\ \underline{0} \\ 7 \end{array}$$

20 R 7

The quotient is estimated to be 20 and is 20 R 7.

Answer to warm up: **J.** 7; 7 R 35

K.   63,590 and 158   **K.**   78,555 and 416

Solution: Round each number to its largest place and divide.

$158\overline{)63{,}590}$ $200\overline{)60{,}000}$

                   $\dfrac{300}{200\overline{)60{,}000}}$ Divide.

$\dfrac{402}{158\overline{)63{,}590}}$ 402 R 74

$\dfrac{63\ 2}{39}$

$\dfrac{0}{390}$

$\dfrac{316}{74}$

The quotient is estimated to be 300 and is 402 R 74.

NAME _____ CLASS _____ DATE _____

EXERCISES 1.6

A

Divide.

1. $7\overline{)84}$ 12

2. $8\overline{)64}$ 8

3. $9\overline{)36}$ 4

4. $5\overline{)35}$ 7

5. $17\overline{)17}$ 1

6. $30\overline{)90}$ 3

7. $7\overline{)497}$ 71

8. $4\overline{)168}$ 42

9. $5\overline{)305}$ 61

10. $8\overline{)168}$ 21

11. $13\overline{)2600}$ 200

12. $17\overline{)3400}$ 200

13. $23\overline{)51}$ 2 R 5

14. $31\overline{)65}$ 2 R 3

15. $30\overline{)97}$ 3 R 7

16. $40\overline{)89}$ 2 R 9

17. $135 \div 9$ 15

18. $192 \div 6$ 32

19. $510 \div 17$ 30

20. $720 \div 18$ 40

B

Divide.

21. $8\overline{)896}$ 112

22. $9\overline{)378}$ 42

23. $7\overline{)2996}$ 428

24. $6\overline{)1422}$ 237

25. $4\overline{)12,208}$ 3052

26. $6\overline{)12,324}$ 2054

27. $2472 \div 12$ 206

28. $4263 \div 21$ 203

29. $837 \div 21$ 39 R 18

30. $896 \div 32$ 28

31. $(62)(?) = 3596$ 58

32. $(?)(73) = 2555$ 35

33. $1053 \div 27$ 39

34. $2788 \div 34$ 82

Estimate the quotient and divide.

35. $43\overline{)675}$
20; 15 R 30

36. $28\overline{)456}$
20; 16 R 8

37. $36\overline{)85,607}$
2000; 2377 R 35

38. $64\overline{)87,903}$
2000; 1373 R 31

39. 17)45,677
3000; 2686 R 15

40. 19)54,875
3000; 2888 R 3

41. 78)3467
40; 44 R 35

42. 94)6791
80; 72 R 23

43. 57)46,113
800; 809

44. 65)20,020
300; 308

C

Divide.

45. 234)11,934   51

46. 322)24,472   76

47. 142)17,750   125

48. 193)41,495   215

49. 417)40,032   96

50. 512)43,008   84

Estimate the quotient and divide.

51. 103)59,602
600; 578 R 68

52. 123)67,891
700; 551 R 118

53. 234)124,875
500; 533 R 153

54. 321)289,067
1000; 900 R 167

55. 436)780,854
2000; 1790 R 414

56. 356)560,999
2000; 1575 R 299

57. 708)218,772
300; 309

58. 604)185,428
300; 307

59. 337,326 ÷ 627
500; 538

60. 153,295 ÷ 713
300; 215

NAME _____ CLASS _____ DATE _____

Applications

61. The Belgium Bulb Company has 295,476 bulbs. If they ship them for sale in packages of 12, how many packages can they make?   24,623 packages

62. The Belgium Bulb Company has 552,224 hyacinth bulbs. If they are shipped in packages of 8 bulbs, how many packages will they have?
69,028 packages

63. A forestry survey finds 1664 trees ready to harvest on a 13-acre plot. On the average, how many trees are ready to harvest per acre?   128 trees

64. Rosebud Lumber Company replants 5696 seedling fir trees on a 16-acre plot of logged-over land. What is the average number of seedlings planted per acre?   356 seedlings

65. The estate of Ken Barker totals $347,875. It is to be shared equally by his five nephews. How much will each nephew receive? $69,575

66. Eight co-owners of the Alley Cat dress shop share equally in the proceeds when the business is sold. If the business sells for $229,928, how much will each receive? $28,741

67. The Nippon Electronics firm assembles radios for export to the United States. Each radio is constructed using 14 resistors. How many radios can be assembled using the 32,278 resistors in stock? How many resistors are left over?
2305 radios; 8 resistors

68. The Nippon Electronics firm in Exercise 67 assembles a second radio containing 17 resistors. Using the 32,278 resistors in stock, how many of these radios can be assembled? How many resistors are left over?   1898 radios; 12 resistors

69. It takes the Morris Packing Plant eight hours to process 12 tons of lima beans. How long does it take the plant to process 780 tons of lima beans?   520 hours

70. It takes the Pacific Packing Plant six hours to process four tons of Dungeness crab. How long does it take the plant to process 392 tons of Dungeness crab?   588 hours

State Your Understanding

71. Explain to an 8-year-old child why 45 ÷ 9 = 5.

72. Explain the concept of a remainder.

Challenge

73. Two 7-member teams bet on the point total difference for a basketball series between the Lakers and the Clippers. The winning team gets $5 per point. The series had the following scores: Lakers 112, Clippers 93; Clippers 98, Lakers 92; Lakers 134, Clippers 102; Lakers 127, Clippers 102; and Clippers 101, Lakers 94. If the winnings are to be split evenly among the team members, how much will each receive? $45

74. The Belgium Bulb Company has 171,000 tulip bulbs to market. Eight bulbs are put in a package when shipping to the United States and sold for $3 per package. Twelve bulbs are put in a package when shipping to France and sold for $5 per package. In which country will the Belgium Bulb Company get the greatest gross return? What is the difference in gross receipts?   France; $7125

Group Activity

75. Perform the following divisions:

23,000,000 ÷ 10	140,000,000 ÷ 10
23,000,000 ÷ 100	140,000,000 ÷ 100
23,000,000 ÷ 1000	140,000,000 ÷ 1000
23,000,000 ÷ 10,000	140,000,000 ÷ 10,000
23,000,000 ÷ 100,000	140,000,000 ÷ 100,000

Can you devise a rule for dividing by 10, 100, 1000, 10,000, and 100,000?

GETTING READY FOR ALGEBRA

Objective   Solve an equation of the form $ax = b$ or $\dfrac{x}{a} = b$, where x, a, and b are whole numbers.

Application   What is the width (w) of a rectangular lot in a subdivision if the length (ℓ) is 125 feet and the area (A) is 9375 square feet? Use the formula $A = \ell w$.

How and Why   1   In Section 1.4 the equations involved the inverse operations addition and subtraction. Multiplication and division are also inverse operations. We can use this idea to solve equations containing those operations.

For example, if 4 is multiplied by 2, $4 \cdot 2 = 8$, the product is 8. If the product is divided by 2, $8 \div 2$, the result is 4, the original number. In the same manner, if 12 is divided by 3, $12 \div 3 = 4$, the quotient is 4. If the quotient is multiplied by 3, $4 \cdot 3$, the result is 12, the original number. We use this idea to solve equations in which the variable is either multiplied or divided by a number.

When a variable is multiplied or divided by a number, the multiplication symbols ($\cdot$ or $\times$) and the division symbol ($\div$) normally are not written. We write $3x$ for three times x and $\dfrac{x}{3}$ for x divided by 3.

Consider the following:

$$3x = 9$$

$$\frac{3x}{3} = \frac{9}{3} \qquad \text{Division will eliminate multiplication.}$$

or $\qquad\qquad x = 3$

If x in the original equation is replaced by 3, we have

$$3x = 9$$
$$3 \cdot 3 = 9$$
$$9 = 9, \text{ which is a true statement.}$$

Therefore, the solution is 3.

If the variable is divided by a number,

$$\frac{x}{5} = 20$$

$$5 \cdot \frac{x}{5} = 5 \cdot 20 \qquad \text{Multiplication will eliminate division.}$$

Thus, $\qquad\qquad x = 100$

If x in the original equation is replaced by 100, we have

$$\frac{100}{5} = 20$$

$$20 = 20, \text{ which is a true statement.}$$

Therefore, the solution is 100.

▶ **To solve an equation using multiplication or division**

1. Divide both sides by the same number to isolate the variable, or
2. Multiply both sides by the same number to isolate the variable.
3. Check the solution by substituting it for the variable in the original equation.

Examples A–E   **Warm Ups A–E**

Directions: Solve and check.

Strategy: Isolate the variable by multiplying or dividing both sides of the equation by the same number. Check the solution by substituting it for the variable in the original equation.

A. $2x = 12$ **A.** $3y = 15$

Solution:

$2x = 12$

$\dfrac{2x}{2} = \dfrac{12}{2}$ Isolate the variable by dividing both sides of the equation by 2.

$x = 6$ Simplify.

CHECK:

$2x = 12$

$2(6) = 12$ Substitute 6 for x in the original equation.

$12 = 12$ The statement is true.

The solution is $x = 6$.

B. $\dfrac{x}{5} = 4$ **B.** $\dfrac{a}{6} = 7$

Solution:

$\dfrac{x}{5} = 4$

$5 \cdot \dfrac{x}{5} = 5(4)$ Isolate the variable by multiplying both sides by 5.

$x = 20$ Simplify.

CHECK:

$\dfrac{x}{5} = 4$

$\dfrac{20}{5} = 4$ Substitute 20 for x in the original equation.

$4 = 4$ The statement is true.

The solution is $x = 20$.

C. $\dfrac{b}{2} = 9$ **C.** $\dfrac{c}{3} = 12$

Solution:

$\dfrac{b}{2} = 9$

$2 \cdot \dfrac{b}{2} = 2(9)$ Isolate the variable by multiplying both sides of the equation by 2.

$b = 18$ Simplify.

Answers to warm ups: **A.** $y = 5$ **B.** $a = 42$

CHECK:

$$\frac{b}{2} = 9$$

$$\frac{18}{2} = 9 \qquad \text{Substitute 18 for } b \text{ in the original equation.}$$

$$9 = 9 \qquad \text{The statement is true.}$$

The solution is $b = 18$.

D. $\quad 3y = 12$

D. $\quad 5z = 35$

Solution:

$$3y = 12$$

$$\frac{3y}{3} = \frac{12}{3} \qquad \text{Isolate the variable by dividing both sides of the equation by 3.}$$

$$y = 4 \qquad \text{Simplify.}$$

CHECK:

$$3y = 12$$

$$3(4) = 12 \qquad \text{Substitute 4 for } y \text{ in the original equation.}$$

$$12 = 12 \qquad \text{The statement is true.}$$

The solution is $y = 4$.

E.  What is the width (w) of a rectangular lot in a subdivision if the length (ℓ) is 125 feet and the area (A) is 9375 square feet? Use the formula $A = \ell w$.

Solution: To find the width of the lot, substitute the area, $A = 9375$, and the length, $\ell = 125$, into the formula and solve.

$$A = \ell w$$

$$9375 = 125w \qquad A = 9375, \ \ell = 125.$$

$$\frac{9375}{125} = \frac{125w}{125} \qquad \text{Divide both sides by 125.}$$

$$75 = w$$

E. What is the length (ℓ) of a second lot in the subdivision if the width (w) is 90 feet and the area (A) is 10,350 square feet? Use the formula $A = \ell w$.

Answers to warm ups: **C.** $c = 36$ **D.** $z = 7$

CHECK: If the width is 75 feet and the length is 125 feet, is the area 9375 square feet?

$A = (125 \text{ ft})(75 \text{ ft}) = 9375 \text{ sq ft}$ True

The width of the lot is 75 feet.

NAME _____ CLASS _____ DATE _____

EXERCISES

Solve and check.

1. $3x = 15$ $x = 5$

2. $\dfrac{z}{4} = 5$ $z = 20$

3. $\dfrac{c}{3} = 6$ $c = 18$

4. $5x = 30$ $x = 6$

5. $12x = 48$ $x = 4$

6. $\dfrac{y}{8} = 12$ $y = 96$

7. $\dfrac{b}{8} = 15$ $b = 120$

8. $15a = 135$ $a = 9$

9. $12x = 144$ $x = 12$

10. $\dfrac{x}{14} = 12$ $x = 168$

11. $\dfrac{y}{13} = 24$ $y = 312$

12. $23c = 184$ $c = 8$

13. $27x = 648$ $x = 24$

14. $\dfrac{a}{32} = 1536$ $a = 49{,}152$

15. $\dfrac{b}{29} = 1566$ $b = 45{,}414$

16. $63z = 2457$ $z = 39$

17. $80 = 16x$ $5 = x$

18. $288 = 9y$ $32 = y$

19. $71 = \dfrac{w}{18}$ $1278 = w$

20. $57 = \dfrac{c}{23}$ $1311 = c$

Applications

21. Find the width of a rectangular garden plot that has a length of 35 feet and an area of 595 square feet. Use the formula $A = \ell w$.   17 ft

22. Find the length of a room that has an area of 391 square feet and a width of 17 feet.   23 ft

23. Crab, at the dock, sells for $2 per pound. A fisherman sells his catch and receives $4680. How many pounds of crab does he sell?   2340 lb

24. Felicia earns $7 an hour. Last week she earned $231. How many hours did she work last week?
33 hours

1.7 **EXPONENTS AND POWERS OF TEN**

Objectives

1 Find the value of an expression written with an exponent.

2 Multiply or divide a whole number by a power of ten.

Application

A recent fund-raising campaign raised an average of $123 per donor. How much was raised if there were 10,000 (10^4) donors?

Vocabulary

Whole number **exponents** greater than one show how many times a number is used as a factor:

$$8 = 2 \cdot 2 \cdot 2 = 2^3 \qquad (10)(10)(10)(10)(10) = 10^5$$

Exponents

A **power of ten** is the value obtained when ten is written with an exponent. The expression 10^5 is read "ten to the fifth power." Exponents of 2 and 3 are often read **"squared"** and **"cubed."**

How and Why 1

Whole number exponents greater than one are used to write repeated multiplications in shorter form. For example, $3^4 = 3 \cdot 3 \cdot 3 \cdot 3$. The value of 3^4 is 81 since $3 \cdot 3 \cdot 3 \cdot 3 = 81$, and 81 is sometimes referred to as the fourth power of three:

$$\text{Base} \to 3^{\overset{\text{Exponent}}{\downarrow 4}} = 81 \leftarrow \text{Value}$$

If one is used as the exponent, the number named is equal to the base. That is, $7^1 = 7$. If zero is used as the exponent, the number named is one (unless the base is zero). That is, $7^0 = 1$.

▶ **To find the value of an expression with an exponent**

1. Identify the exponent.
2. If the exponent is zero and the base number is not zero, the value is one.
3. If the exponent is one, the value is the base number.
4. If the exponent is larger than one, use the base as a factor as many times as shown by the exponent and multiply.

Examples A–C   **Warm Ups A–C**

Directions: Find the value.

Strategy: Identify the exponent. If it is zero the value is one. If it is one the value is the base number. If it is greater than one, use it to tell how many times the base is used as a factor and then multiply.

A. 2^3 **A.** 4^2

Solution:

$2(2)(2) = 8$ The exponent tells us to use the base 2 as a factor 3 times.

Answer to warm up: **A.** 16

B. 17^1

B. 9^0

Solution:

17   The exponent is 1, so the value is the base number.

C. 10^7

C. 3^5

Solution:

10(10)(10)(10)(10)(10)   The exponent is greater than one so the
base 10 is used as a factor seven times.

10,000,000   Multiply.

D. 9^4

D. 6^5

Solution:

ENTER    9 x^y 4 =

DISPLAY   9.   9.   4.   6561.

So $9^4 = 6561$.

How and Why   2   It is particularly easy to multiply or divide a whole number by a power of ten. Consider the following and their products when multiplied by ten.

$$5 \times 10 = 50 \qquad 7 \times 10 = 70 \qquad 3 \times 10 = 30$$

Each product is the single digit with a zero written on the right.

If the whole number is not a single-digit number (larger than nine), the place value of every digit becomes ten times larger when the number is multiplied by ten.

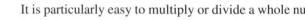

$$24 \times 10 = 2 \text{ tens} + 4 \text{ ones}$$
$$\underline{\qquad\qquad\qquad 10}$$
$$2 \text{ hundreds} + 4 \text{ tens} \qquad \text{since ten} \times \text{ten} = \text{hundred}$$
$$\text{and one} \times \text{ten} = \text{ten}$$
$$= 240$$

So, to multiply by ten, we need to merely write a zero on the right of the whole number. If a whole number is multiplied by ten more than once, a zero is written on the right for each ten. So,

$$24 \times 10^4 = 240,000 \qquad \text{Four zeros are written on the right, one for each 10.}$$

Since division is the inverse of multiplication, dividing by ten will eliminate the last zero on the right of a whole number. So,

$$240,000 \div 10 = 24,000 \qquad \text{Eliminate the final zero on the right.}$$

If we divide by ten more than once, one zero is eliminated for each 10. So,

$$240,000 \div 10^3 = 240 \qquad \text{Eliminate three zeros.}$$

Answers to warm ups: **B.** 1   **C.** 243   **D.** 7776

▶ **To multiply a whole number by a power of ten**

1. Identify the exponent of ten.
2. Write as many zeros to the right of the whole number as the exponent of ten.

▶ **To divide a whole number by a power of ten**

1. Identify the exponent of ten.
2. Eliminate the same number of zeros on the left of the whole number as the exponent of ten.

Using powers of ten we have yet another method of writing a whole number in expanded form.

$$2345 = 2000 + 300 + 40 + 5$$
$$= 2 \text{ thousands} + 3 \text{ hundreds} + 4 \text{ tens} + 5 \text{ ones}$$
$$= 2 \cdot 10^3 + 3 \cdot 10^2 + 4 \cdot 10^1 + 5 \cdot 10^0$$

Examples E–I   **Warm Ups E–I**

Directions: Multiply or divide.

Strategy: Identify the exponent of ten. For multiplication, write the same number of zeros on the right of the whole number as the exponent of ten. For division, eliminate the same number of zeros on the right of the whole number as the exponent of ten.

E. $12{,}748 \times 10^5$ E. 1699×10^8

Solution:

$12{,}748 \times 10^5 = 1{,}274{,}800{,}000$ The exponent of 10 is 5.
To multiply, write 5 zeros on the
right of the whole number.

F. 346×10^2 F. 57×10^4

Solution:

$346 \times 10^2 = 34{,}600$ The exponent of 10 is 2. To multiply, write 2
zeros on the right of the whole number.

G. $\dfrac{975{,}000}{10^2}$ G. $\dfrac{1{,}860{,}000}{10^4}$

Solution:

$\dfrac{975{,}000}{10^2} = 9750$ The exponent of 10 is 2. To divide, eliminate 2
zeros on the right of the whole number.

Answers to warm ups: **E.** 169,900,000,000   **F.** 570,000   **G.** 186

1.8	**ORDER OF OPERATIONS**

Objective

Perform any combination of operations on whole numbers.

Application

The Lend A Helping Hand Association prepares two types of food baskets for distribution to the needy. The family pack contains nine cans of vegetables and the elderly pack contains four cans of vegetables. How many cans of vegetables are needed for 125 family packs and 50 elderly packs?

How and Why

Without a rule, it is possible to interpret $2 \cdot 3 + 4$ two ways:

$$2 \cdot 3 + 4 = 6 + 4 \qquad \text{Multiply first.}$$
$$= 10 \qquad \text{Then add.}$$
$$2 \cdot 3 + 4 = 2 \cdot 7 \qquad \text{Add first.}$$
$$= 14 \qquad \text{Then multiply.}$$

In order to decide which answer to use, it is agreed to multiply first. So,

$$2 \cdot 3 + 4 = 10$$

A computation agreement as to which operation is performed first when two or more operations are involved is necessary so that people, calculators, and computers get the same result.

▶ **To evaluate an expression with more than one operation follow these steps.**

Step 1. PARENTHESES — Do the operations within grouping symbols first (parentheses, fraction bar, etc.), in the order given in steps 2, 3, and 4.

Step 2. EXPONENTS — Do the operations indicated by exponents.

Step 3. MULTIPLY and DIVIDE — Do only multiplication and division as they appear from left to right.

Step 4. ADD and SUBTRACT — Do addition and subtraction as they appear from left to right.

So we see that

$$8 - 10 \div 2 = 8 - 5 \qquad \text{Divide first.}$$
$$= 3 \qquad \text{Then subtract.}$$
$$(6 - 4)(6) = (2)(6) \qquad \text{Subtract in parentheses first.}$$
$$= 12 \qquad \text{Then multiply.}$$
$$16 - 2^4 = 16 - 16 \qquad \text{Find the value of the power first.}$$
$$= 0 \qquad \text{Then subtract.}$$

Other exercises involving all of the operations are shown in the examples.

Examples A–I   **Warm Ups A–I**

Directions: Perform the indicated operations.

Strategy: The operations are done in this order: operations inside parentheses first, exponents next, then multiplication and division, and finally, addition and subtraction.

A. $7 \cdot 9 + 6 \cdot 2$ **A.** $4 \cdot 3 + 6 \cdot 5$

Solution:

$$7 \cdot 9 + 6 \cdot 2 = 63 + 12 \qquad \text{Multiply first.}$$
$$= 75 \qquad \text{Add.}$$

B. $25 - 6 \div 3 + 8 \cdot 4$ **B.** $4 \cdot 18 - 9 \div 3 + 6 \cdot 2$

Solution:

$$25 - 6 \div 3 + 8 \cdot 4 = 25 - 2 + 32 \qquad \text{Divide and multiply.}$$
$$= 55 \qquad \text{Subtract and add.}$$

C. $17 - 5 + 3^2$ **C.** $4 \cdot 22 - 5^2 + 3 \cdot 4$

Solution:

$$17 - 5 + 3^2 = 17 - 5 + 9 \qquad \text{Do exponents first.}$$
$$= 21 \qquad \text{Subtract and add.}$$

D. $5 \cdot 9 + 9 - 6(7 + 1)$ **D.** $24 - 6 + 6 - 3(5 - 3)$

Solution:

$$5 \cdot 9 + 9 - 6(7 + 1) = 5 \cdot 9 + 9 - 6(8) \qquad \text{Add in parentheses first.}$$
$$= 45 + 9 - 48 \qquad \text{Multiply.}$$
$$= 6 \qquad \text{Add and subtract.}$$

E. $3 \cdot 4^3 - 8 \cdot 3^2 + 11$ **E.** $5 \cdot 2^3 - 2 \cdot 4^2 + 25 - 7 \cdot 3$

Solution:

$$3 \cdot 4^3 - 8 \cdot 3^2 + 11 = 3 \cdot 64 - 8 \cdot 9 + 11 \qquad \text{Do exponents first.}$$
$$= 192 - 72 + 11 \qquad \text{Multiply.}$$
$$= 131 \qquad \text{Subtract and add.}$$

F. $(2^2 + 2 \cdot 3)^2 + 3^2$ **F.** $(3^3 - 4 \cdot 2)^2 + 5^2$

Solution: First do the operations in the parentheses following the proper order.

$$(2^2 + 2 \cdot 3)^2 + 3^2 = (4 + 2 \cdot 3)^2 + 3^2 \qquad \text{Do the exponent.}$$
$$= (4 + 6)^2 + 3^2 \qquad \text{Multiply.}$$
$$= (10)^2 + 3^2 \qquad \text{Add.}$$

Answers to warm ups: **A.** 42   **B.** 81   **C.** 75   **D.** 18   **E.** 12

CHECK:

$$\frac{y}{5} + 4$$

$$\frac{5}{5} + 4$$

$$1 + 4$$

$$5$$

The soluti

Now that the operations inside the parentheses are complete, continue using the order of operations.

$$= 100 + 9 \qquad \text{Do the exponents.}$$
$$= 109 \qquad \text{Add.}$$

G. $8(3 \cdot 4 - 6) \div 6 - 3$

Solution: Do the operations in parentheses first.

$$
\begin{aligned}
8(3 \cdot 4 - 6) \div 6 - 3 &= 8(12 - 6) \div 6 - 3 \qquad &\text{Multiply.} \\
&= 8(6) \div 6 - 3 \qquad &\text{Subtract.} \\
&= 48 \div 6 - 3 \qquad &\text{Multiply.} \\
&= 8 - 3 \qquad &\text{Divide.} \\
&= 5 \qquad &\text{Subtract.}
\end{aligned}
$$

G. $6(5 \cdot 4 - 8 \cdot 2) \div 8 + 4$

C. $\dfrac{z}{2} - 6$

Solution:

$$\frac{z}{2} -$$

$$\frac{z}{2} - 6 +$$

$$2\left(\frac{z}{2}\right)$$

H.   ⌨ $8 + 6 \cdot 5 \div 3$

Solution:

ENTER	8	+	6	×	5	÷	3	=

DISPLAY   8.   8.   6.   6.   5.   30.   3.   18.

The answer is 18.

H. $13 + 9 \cdot 20 \div 12$

CHECK:

$$\frac{z}{2} - 6 =$$

$$\frac{20}{2} - 6 =$$

$$10 - 6 =$$

$$4 =$$

The solution

I.   🌐 The Lend A Helping Hand Association prepares two types of food baskets for distribution to the needy. The family pack contains nine cans of vegetables and the elderly pack contains four cans of vegetables. How many cans of vegetables are needed for 125 family packs and 50 elderly packs?

Solution: To find the number of cans of vegetables needed for the packs, multiply the number of packs by the number of cans per pack. Then add the two amounts.

$$
\begin{aligned}
125(9) + 50(4) &= 1125 + 200 \qquad &\text{Multiply.} \\
&= 1325 \qquad &\text{Add.}
\end{aligned}
$$

The Lend A Helping Hand Association needs 1325 cans of vegetables.

I.   The Fruit-of-the-Month Club prepares two types of boxes for shipment. Box A contains six apples and Box B contains ten apples. How many apples are needed for 96 orders of Box A and 82 orders of Box B?

D. $3b + 4 =$

Solution:

$$3b + 4$$
$$3b + 4 - 4$$

$$3b$$
$$\frac{3b}{3}$$

$$b$$

Answers to warm u

19. Rana is paid $40 per day plus $8 per artificial flower arrangement she designs and completes. How many arrangements did she complete if she earned $88 for the day? Use the formula $S = B + PN$, where S is the total salary earned, B is the base pay for the day, P is the pay per unit, and N is the number of units completed.   6 arrangements

20. Rana's sister works at a drapery firm where the pay is $50 per day plus $12 per unit completed. How many units did she complete if she earned $122 for the day?   6 units

Examples

Directions

Strategy:
sides by th

A. $2x -$

Solution:

$2x$
$2x - 7$

CHECK:

$2x - 7$
$2(8) - 7$

$16 - 7$
9

The solution

___

B. $\dfrac{y}{5} + 4 =$

Solution:

$\dfrac{y}{5} + $

$\dfrac{y}{5} + 4 - $

$\dfrac{y}{5}$

$5\left(\dfrac{y}{5}\right)$

y

___

1.9   AVERAGE

Objective   Find the average of a group of numbers.

Application   In order to help Pete lose weight, the dietician has him record his caloric intake for a week. He records the following: Monday, 3165; Tuesday, 1795; Wednesday, 1500; Thursday, 2615; Friday, 1407; Saturday, 1850; and Sunday, 1913. What is Pete's average caloric intake per day?

Vocabulary   The **average** or **arithmetic mean** of a group of numbers is the number such that the sum of the group of numbers and the sum if each member of the group is replaced by the number (average) is the same. For instance, the average of 3, 7, and 8 is 6 because $3 + 7 + 8 = 6 + 6 + 6 = 18$.

How and Why   The average or arithmetic mean of a group of numbers is used in statistics. It is one of the ways used to measure central tendency. The average of a group of numbers is found by adding the members of the group and dividing the sum by the number of members in the group. The average of 7, 11, and 15 is

$$(7 + 11 + 15) \div 3 = 33 \div 3 = 11$$

The "central" number or average does not need to be one of the members of the group. The average of 23, 32, 45, and 56 is

$$(23 + 32 + 45 + 56) \div 4 = 156 \div 4 = 39$$

▶ **To find the average of a group of whole numbers**

1. Add the numbers.
2. Divide the sum by the number of numbers in the group.

Examples A–F   **Warm Ups A–F**

Directions: Find the average.

Strategy: Add the numbers in the group. Divide the sum by the number of numbers in the group.

A.   39 and 47   **A.**   49 and 83

Solution:

$39 + 47 = 86$ Add the numbers in the group.

$86 \div 2 = 43$ Divide the sum by the number of numbers in the group.

The average is 43.

Answer to warm up: **A.** 66

NAME _____ CLASS _____ DATE _____

EXERCISES 1.9

A

Find the average.

1. 3, 7   5

2. 7, 11   9

3. 8, 10   9

4. 9, 13   11

5. 3, 11   7

6. 15, 19   17

7. 8, 14, 17   13

8. 9, 11, 13   11

9. 9, 13, 17   13

10. 8, 11, 17   12

11. 5, 9, 13   9

12. 21, 26, 28   25

13. 3, 5, 7, 9   6

14. 5, 5, 9, 9   7

15. 2, 4, 5, 5   4

16. 4, 5, 6, 9   6

17. 10, 14, 26, 30   20

18. 10, 22, 18, 19, 46   23

B

Find the average.

19. 8, 11, 12, 17   12

20. 4, 7, 8, 10, 16   9

21. 15, 30, 39   28

22. 16, 46, 55   39

23. 14, 18, 30, 42   26

24. 11, 34, 41, 62   37

NAME _____   _____ CLASS _____ DATE _____

CHAPTER 1 Test

1. Add: 206 + 3982 + 16 + 145 + 9 + 2731
   7089 [1.3-1]

2. Round to the nearest ten thousand: 693,856,639
   693,860,000 [1.2-4]

3. Multiply: (370)(48)
   17,760 [1.5-1]

4. Find the average of 2344, 461, and 1944.
   1583 [1.9]

5. Divide: $85\overline{)6715}$
   79 [1.6-1]

6. Divide: 20,196 ÷ 66
   306 [1.6-1]

7. Write the word name for 4205.
   Four thousand, two hundred five [1.1-4]

8. Round to the nearest hundred: 5642
   5600 [1.2-4]

9. Write the place-value name for three hundred nine thousand, nine hundred sixty-three.
   309,963 [1.1-3]

10. Write the word name for 120,355.
    One hundred twenty thousand, three hundred fifty-five [1.1-4]

11. Multiply: 13×10^2
    1300 [1.7-2]

12. Write the place value name for 40,000 + 3000 + 600 + 80 + 1.
    43,681 [1.2-2]

13. Add: 337
             8
            25
           874
          2283
          3527 [1.3-1]

14. Divide: $176\overline{)62,197}$
    353 R 69 [1.6-1]

15. Subtract: 8277
              3047
              5230 [1.4-1]

16. Find the value of 4^4.
    256 [1.7-1]

17. Add: $382 + 77 + 5280 + 9$
5748 [1.3-1]

18. Write 937 in expanded form.
$900 + 30 + 7$ [1.2-1]

19. Multiply: $(498)(976)$
486,048 [1.5-1]

20. Divide: $3{,}006{,}000{,}000 \div 10^3$
3,006,000 [1.7-2]

21. Divide: $98\overline{)20{,}482}$
209 [1.6-1]

22. Subtract: $19{,}864 - 2876$
16,988 [1.4-1]

23. Find the average of 274, 682, 1924, 361, and 1294.
907 [1.9]

24. Perform the indicated operations:
$18 \div 3 + 3 \cdot 5 - 1$
20 [1.8]

25. State whether the following is true or false:
$299 > 312$
False [1.2-3]

26. Write the place value of the digit 4 in 34,388.
Thousand [1.1-1]

27. Divide: $234\overline{)20{,}845}$
89 R 19 [1.6-1]

28. Pete owes $4015 on his beach lot. After making payments of $212, $125, and $305, how much does he still owe on the lot?
$3373 [1.8]

29. A farmer delivers 87 tote boxes of cucumbers. If each box contains 874 pounds of cucumbers, how many pounds of cucumbers did the farmer deliver? (Round to the nearest thousand pounds.)
76,000 lb [1.2-4, 1.5-1]

30. A walnut grower sold 11,580 50-pound sacks of nuts. Of these, 5450 sacks were sold at $15 per sack and the rest were sold at $13 per sack. What was the total income from the two sales?
$161,440 [1.8]

Primes and Multiples

Physical challenges build endurance, one day at a time. So do mathematical challenges. The key is consistent, progressive effort. (Charles Gupton/ Tony Stone Images)

Maintain Your Skills (1.3, 1.4, 1.5, 1.6)

68. Find the sum of 78, 1823, 503, 3, 1007, and 28.
3442

69. Find the sum of 33,485, 8298, 29, and 2092.
43,904

70. Find the difference of 10,023 and 5987.   4036

71. Find the difference of 21,003 and 9875.   11,128

72. Find the difference of 10,000 and 8923.   1077

73. Find the product of 22, 32, and 9.   6336

74. Find the product of 209 and 12.   2508

75. Find the product of 297 and 98.   29,106

76. The Grow-em Good vegetable farm has a total of 12 vehicles that use diesel fuel. The storage tank that contains the supply of diesel fuel holds a total of 2500 gallons. If 18 gallons are pumped into each of the 12 vehicles per day (average) from the tank, how many full days will the tank last? How many gallons remain in the tank?   11 days; 124 gallons remain

77. The local Pay and Take grocery has a sale on tomato soup. To be sure that they have an ample supply, they buy 12 cases of tomato soup, each containing 48 cans. If the store sells an average of 42 cans per day, how many days will the 12 cases last? How many cans of soup are left?
13 days; 30 cans remain

2.3 DIVISORS AND FACTORS

Objectives

1 Write a whole number as the product of two factors in all possible ways.

2 List all of the factors (divisors) of a whole number.

Application

A television station has 130 minutes of programming to fill. In what ways can the time be scheduled if each program must last a whole number of minutes and if each schedule must include programs all the same length?

Vocabulary

If a first number is a multiple of a second number, we say the second is a **factor** of the first. Thus 6 is a factor of 24 since $4 \cdot 6$ is 24.

Recall that $16^2 = 16 \cdot 16 = 256$, so the **square** of 16 is 256.

When two or more numbers are multiplied, each number is a factor. Therefore, if a first number is a factor of a second number, it is also a **divisor** of the second number.

How and Why 1

To write 250 as a product of two factors in all possible ways, we could use trial and error. However, dividing 250 by all the smaller numbers would take too long. The following steps take less time.

1. List all the counting numbers from 1 to the first number whose square is larger than 250. Since $15 \times 15 = 225$ and $16 \times 16 = 256$, we stop at 16.

1	6	11	16
2	7	12	
3	8	13	
4	9	14	
5	10	15	

We can stop at 16 since 250 divided by any number larger than 16 gives a quotient that is less than 16. But all the possible factors less than 16 are already in the chart.

2. Divide each of the listed counting numbers into 250. If it divides evenly, write the factors. If not, cross out the number.

1 · 250	6̸	1̸1̸	1̸6̸
2 · 125	7̸	1̸2̸	
3̸	8̸	1̸3̸	
4̸	9̸	1̸4̸	
5 · 50	10 · 25	1̸5̸	

These steps give us a list of all the two-factor products. Hence 250 written as a product of two factors in all possible ways is

$$1 \cdot 250 \qquad 2 \cdot 125 \qquad 5 \cdot 50 \qquad 10 \cdot 25$$

▶ **To use the square method to write a whole number as the product of two factors in all possible ways**

1. List all the counting numbers from one to the first number whose square is larger than the whole number.
2. For each number on the list, test whether the number is a divisor of the whole number.
3. If the number isn't a divisor, cross it off the list.
4. If the number is a divisor, write the indicated product of two factors. The first factor is the tested number; the second factor is the quotient of the number and the tested number.

D.   68   **D.**   82

Solution:

$1 \cdot 68$	$\not{5}$	$\not{9}$
$2 \cdot 34$	6	
$\not{3}$	$\not{7}$	
$4 \cdot 17$	$\not{8}$	

Stop at 9 since $9^2 = 81$. This gives us all of the pairs of factors whose product is 68.

$\downarrow$
$1 \cdot 68$
$2 \cdot 34$
$4 \cdot 17$

List the pairs vertically and read as the arrows indicate. There are a total of six factors.

In order, all of the factors of 68 are 1, 2, 4, 17, 34, and 68.

E.   29   **E.**   37

Solution:

$1 \cdot 29$	$\not{4}$
$\not{2}$	$\not{5}$
$\not{3}$	$\not{6}$

Stop at 6 since $6^2 = 36$.

The list of factors is 1 and 29.

Answers to warm ups: **D.** 1, 2, 41, 82   **E.** 1, 37

NAME _____ _____ CLASS _____ DATE _____

EXERCISES 2.3

A

List all of the factors (divisors) of the whole number.

1. 16
1, 2, 4, 8, 16

2. 18
1, 2, 3, 6, 9, 18

3. 23
1, 23

4. 45
1, 3, 5, 9, 15, 45

5. 36
1, 2, 3, 4, 6, 9,
12, 18, 36

6. 30
1, 2, 3, 5, 6, 10, 15, 30

7. 28
1, 2, 4, 7, 14, 28

8. 60
1, 2, 3, 4, 5, 6, 10, 12,
15, 30, 60

9. 65
1, 5, 13, 65

10. 48
1, 2, 3, 4, 6, 8, 12,
16, 24, 48

Write the whole number as the product of two factors in all possible ways.

11. 18
$1 \cdot 18; 2 \cdot 9; 3 \cdot 6$

12. 32
$1 \cdot 32; 2 \cdot 16; 4 \cdot 8$

13. 24
$1 \cdot 24; 2 \cdot 12; 3 \cdot 8; 4 \cdot 6$

14. 36
$1 \cdot 36; 2 \cdot 18; 3 \cdot 12;$
$4 \cdot 9; 6 \cdot 6$

15. 31
$1 \cdot 31$

16. 28
$1 \cdot 28; 2 \cdot 14; 4 \cdot 7$

17. 50
$1 \cdot 50; 2 \cdot 25; 5 \cdot 10$

18. 42
$1 \cdot 42; 2 \cdot 21; 3 \cdot 14;$
$6 \cdot 7$

19. 37
$1 \cdot 37$

20. 41
$1 \cdot 41$

B

List all of the factors (divisors) of the whole number.

21. 72
1, 2, 3, 4, 6, 8, 9, 12,
18, 24, 36, 72

22. 76
1, 2, 4, 19, 38, 76

23. 92
1, 2, 4, 23, 46, 92

24. 90
1, 2, 3, 5, 6, 9, 10, 15,
18, 30, 45, 90

25. 102
1, 2, 3, 6, 17, 34,
51, 102

26. 112
1, 2, 4, 7, 8, 14, 16,
28, 56, 112

27. 122
1, 2, 61, 122

28. 132
1, 2, 3, 4, 6, 11, 12,
22, 33, 44, 66, 132

29. 142
1, 2, 71, 142

30. 152
1, 2, 4, 8, 19,
38, 76, 152

Write each whole number as the product of two factors in all possible ways.

31. 98
$1 \cdot 98; 2 \cdot 49; 7 \cdot 14$

32. 100
$1 \cdot 100; 2 \cdot 50; 4 \cdot 25;$
$5 \cdot 20; 10 \cdot 10$

33. 104
$1 \cdot 104; 2 \cdot 52; 4 \cdot 26;$
$8 \cdot 13$

34. 114
$1 \cdot 114; 2 \cdot 57; 3 \cdot 38;$
$6 \cdot 19$

35. 105
$1 \cdot 105; 3 \cdot 35;$
$5 \cdot 21; 7 \cdot 15$

Group Activity

64. In 1990 each American consumed approximately 42 gallons of soft drinks, 25 gallons of milk, and 40 gallons of alcoholic beverages. Determine the number of ounces of milk, soft drinks, and alcoholic beverages each member of your group consumes in one week. Multiply this amount by 52 to get the annual consumption. Divide by 128 to determine the number of gallons per category, per person. Determine a group average for each category. Compare this with the 1990 national average in a chart or graph.

Maintain Your Skills (Sections 1.5, 1.6, 1.9)

Multiply.

65. 49(51)   2499   **66.** 69(403)   27,807   **67.** 88(432)   38,016   **68.** 307(502)   154,114

Divide.

69. 78)2418   31   **70.** 82)24,682   301   **71.** 401)9664   24 R 40   **72.** 401)160,805   401 R 4

73. How many speakers can be wired from a spool of wire containing 1000 feet if each speaker requires 24 feet of wire? How much wire is left?

41 speakers; 16 feet left

74. A consumer magazine tested 15 brands of tires to determine the number of miles traveled before the tread was gone. The results are in the chart below.

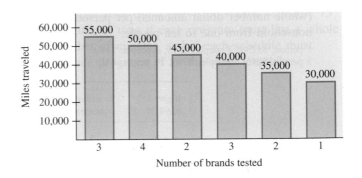

What was the average mileage of the 15 brands?

45,000 miles

2.4 PRIMES AND COMPOSITES

Objective Determine whether a whole number is prime or composite.

Application Janna won a math contest at her school. One of the questions in the contest was, "Is 234,423 prime or composite?" What should she have answered?

Vocabulary A **prime number** is a whole number greater than one with exactly two different factors (divisors). **Composite numbers** are whole numbers greater than one with more than two different factors (divisors).

How and Why The whole numbers zero (0) and one (1) are neither prime nor composite. Two (2) is a prime number ($2 = 2 \cdot 1$), since two and one are the only factors of two. Three (3) is a prime number, since one and three are the only factors of three. Four (4) is a composite number ($4 = 4 \cdot 1$ and $4 = 2 \cdot 2$), since it has more than two factors.

To tell whether a number is prime or composite, list its factors or divisors in a chart like those in Section 2.3. For instance, the charts for 299 and 307 are

$$
\begin{array}{llll}
1 \cdot 299 & \cancel{6} & \cancel{11} & \\
2 & 7 & \cancel{12} & \\
\cancel{3} & 8 & 13 \cdot 23 & \text{We stop here since 299 has} \\
\cancel{4} & \cancel{9} & & \text{at least four factors.} \\
\cancel{5} & \cancel{10} & &
\end{array}
$$

Therefore, 299 is a composite number.

$$
\begin{array}{llll}
1 \cdot 307 & \cancel{6} & \cancel{11} & \cancel{16} \\
2 & 7 & \cancel{12} & \cancel{17} \\
\cancel{3} & 8 & \cancel{13} & \cancel{18} \quad \text{Stop here since } 18 \cdot 18 = 324. \\
\cancel{4} & \cancel{9} & \cancel{14} & \\
\cancel{5} & \cancel{10} & \cancel{15} &
\end{array}
$$

We see that 307 has exactly two factors (1 and 307), so 307 is a prime number.

All primes up to a given number may be found by a method called the Sieve of Eratosthenes. Eratosthenes (born ca. 230 B.C.) is remembered for both the prime sieve and his method for measuring the circumference of the earth. The accuracy of his measurement, compared with modern methods, is within 50 miles, or six-tenths of one percent.

To use the famous Sieve to find the primes up to 30, list the numbers 2 to 30.

$$
\begin{array}{llllll}
2 & 3 & \cancel{4} & 5 & \cancel{6} & 7 \\
\cancel{8} & 9 & \cancel{10} & 11 & \cancel{12} & 13 \\
\cancel{14} & 15 & \cancel{16} & 17 & \cancel{18} & 19 \\
20 & 21 & \cancel{22} & 23 & \cancel{24} & 25 \\
\cancel{26} & 27 & \cancel{28} & 29 & \cancel{30} &
\end{array}
$$

All multiples of 2, except 2, are not prime, so they are crossed off.

$$
\begin{array}{llllll}
2 & 3 & \cancel{4} & 5 & \cancel{6} & 7 \\
\cancel{8} & \boxed{9} & \cancel{10} & 11 & \cancel{12} & 13 \\
\cancel{14} & \boxed{15} & \cancel{16} & 17 & \cancel{18} & 19 \\
20 & \boxed{21} & \cancel{22} & 23 & \cancel{24} & 25 \\
\cancel{26} & \boxed{27} & \cancel{28} & 29 & \cancel{30} &
\end{array}
$$

All remaining multiples of 3, except 3, are not prime, so they are crossed off.

2	3	4̸	5	6̸	7
8̸	9̸	1̸0̸	11	1̸2̸	13
1̸4̸	1̸5̸	1̸6̸	17	1̸8̸	19
2̸0̸	2̸1̸	2̸2̸	23	2̸4̸	25
2̸6̸	2̸7̸	2̸8̸	29	3̸0̸	

All remaining multiples of 5, except 5, are not prime, so they are crossed off.

The multiples of the other numbers, except themselves, have been crossed off. We need to test divisors only up to the first number whose square ($6 \cdot 6 = 36$) is larger than 30. So, the primes less than 30 are 2, 3, 5, 7, 11, 13, 17, 19, 23, and 29.

From the preceding Sieve we see that we can shorten the factor chart by omitting all the numbers except those that are prime. For instance, is 371 prime or composite?

$1 \cdot 371$	11
2̸	13
3̸	17
5̸	19
	23 $23^2 = 529$
$7 \cdot 53$	Stop here, since we do not need all factors.

Since $7 \cdot 53 = 371$, 371 is composite. (It has *at least* four factors: 1, 7, 53, and 371). We know that a number is prime if no smaller prime divides it evenly (see Example D).

Keep the divisibility tests for 2, 3, and 5 in mind since they are prime numbers.

▶ **To tell whether a number is prime or composite (0 and 1 are neither prime nor composite)**

1. List 1 and all prime numbers whose square is less than the number.
2. Test each to determine if they divide the number.
   a. If the number has exactly two divisors (factors), it is prime.
   b. If the number has more than two divisors (factors), it is composite.

Examples A–F

Warm Ups A–F

Directions: Tell whether the number is prime or composite.

Strategy: List 1 and all possible prime factors of the given number and test to see whether any divide the number. If only two divide the number, it is prime.

A. 101

A. 71

Solution: List 1 and the prime numbers that are 11 or less.

$1 \cdot 101$	5̸
2̸	7̸
3̸	1̸1̸

The numbers 2, 3, and 5 can be crossed out using the divisibility tests. We stop at 11 since $11^2 > 101$.

We see that there are exactly two factors; therefore, 101 is prime.

Answer to warm up: **A.** Prime

B. 143

B. 119

Solution: List 1 and the prime numbers that are 13 or less.

    1 · 143   7̸
    2̸   11 · 13
    3̸   13   Stop at 13 since $13^2 > 143$.
    5̸

We stop testing at 11 since we see that 143 has more than two factors. Therefore 143 is a composite number.

C. 247

C. 323

Solution: List 1 and the prime numbers that are 17 or less.

    1 · 247   7̸
    2̸   1̸1̸
    3̸   13 · 19
    5̸   17   Stop at 17 since $17^2 > 247$.

We stop testing at 13 since we see that 247 has more than two factors. Therefore 247 is a composite number.

D. 457

D. 547

Solution: List 1 and the prime numbers that are 23 or less.

    1 · 457   7̸   1̸9̸
    2̸   1̸1̸   2̸3̸   Stop at 23 since $23^2 > 457$.
    3̸   1̸3̸
    5̸   1̸7̸

After testing all of the prime numbers in the list, we determine that 457 is a prime number since it has exactly two factors.

E. 123,455

E. 341,121

Solution:

  123,455 is divisible by 5   The ones-place digit is 5.

Since 123,455 is divisible by 5, it has more than two factors and is composite.

Answers to warm ups: **B.** Composite   **C.** Composite   **D.** Prime   **E.** Composite

F. 🌐 Janna won a math contest at her school. One of the questions in the contest was "Is 234,423 prime or composite?" What should she have answered?

F. Janna was also asked "Is 234,425 prime or composite?" What should she have answered?

Solution: Test the number for divisibility by prime numbers.

234,423 is not divisible by 2 The ones-place digit is 3.

234,423 is divisible by 3 $2 + 3 + 4 + 4 + 2 + 3$ or 18 is divisible by 3.

Since 234,423 is divisible by 3, it has more than two factors and Janna should have answered "Composite."

EXERCISES 2.4

A

Tell whether the number is prime or composite.

1. 8
Composite

2. 4
Composite

3. 7
Prime

4. 11
Prime

5. 12
Composite

6. 14
Composite

7. 19
Prime

8. 21
Composite

9. 22
Composite

10. 31
Prime

11. 29
Prime

12. 23
Prime

13. 24
Composite

14. 28
Composite

15. 37
Prime

16. 41
Prime

17. 26
Composite

18. 36
Composite

19. 43
Prime

20. 47
Prime

21. 40
Composite

22. 44
Composite

B

Tell whether the number is prime or composite.

23. 48
Composite

24. 51
Composite

25. 61
Prime

26. 59
Prime

27. 88
Composite

28. 81
Composite

29. 83
Prime

30. 87
Composite

31. 91
Composite

32. 93
Composite

33. 97
Prime

34. 99
Composite

35.

39.

43.

C   l

Tell   t

47.   f

          -

          ł

          s

          b

51.

55.   A
          p

App

59.

          Si
          fa

61.   —
          Ans

Challenge

72. Find the LCM of 144, 180, and 240.
720

73. Find the LCM of 128, 256, and 192.
768

74. Find the LCM of 1728, 960, and 864.
8640

75. Find the LCM of 1800, 1500, and 1200.
18,000

Group Activity

76. Determine the low temperature for any city on the first of every month last year. Find the least common multiple for the first of January, April, July, and October. Do the same for the first of February, May, August, and November. Do the same for the first of March, June, September, and December. Compare these three common multiples.

Maintain Your Skills (Sections 1.8, 1.9, 2.3)

77. List all of the factors of 375.
1, 3, 5, 15, 25, 75, 125, 375

78. List all of the factors of 275.
1, 5, 11, 25, 55, 275

79. List all of the divisors of 488.
1, 2, 4, 8, 61, 122, 244, 488

80. List all of the divisors of 480.
1, 2, 3, 4, 5, 6, 8, 10, 12, 15, 16, 20, 24, 30, 32, 40, 48, 60, 80, 96, 120, 160, 240, 480

81. Is 8008 divisible by 56?
Yes

82. Is 8008 divisible by 143?
Yes

83. Is 8008 divisible by 11?
Yes

84. A marketing researcher checked the weekly attendance at 14 theaters. The results are shown in the following table:

Number of Theaters	Attendance
1	900
2	1000
2	1200
3	1300
2	1400
2	1600
1	1800
1	1900

85. The Sav-Mor Department Store has made a profit on appliances of $112 so far this week. If their profit on each appliance is $7, how many more appliances must they sell so that the profit for the entire week will be more than $170?   At least nine

What was the average attendance at the 14 theaters?   1350 people

NAME _____ CLASS _____ DATE _____

CHAPTER 2   Concept Review

Check your understanding of the language of basic mathematics. Tell whether each of the following statements is True (always true) or False (not always true). For those statements that you judge to be false, revise them to make them true.

1. Every multiple of 6 ends with the digit 6.   False: Not all multiples of 6 end with the digit 6. For example, 12 is a multiple of 6. [2.1-2]

2. Every multiple of 10 ends with the digit 0.
True [2.1-2]

3. Every multiple of 13 is divisible by 13.
True [2.2-2]

4. Every multiple of 7 is the product of 7 and some natural number.   True [2.2-2]

5. Every whole number, except the number 1, has at least two different factors.   True [2.2-2]

6. Every factor of 200 is also a divisor of 200.
True [2.2-2]

7. Every multiple of 200 is also a factor of 200.
False: Only one multiple of 200 is also a factor of 200 — itself. [2.1-1]

8. The square of 200 is 100.   False: The square of 200 is 40,000. One half of 200 is 100. [2.4]

9. Every natural number ending in 4 is divisible by 4.
False: Not all natural numbers ending in 4 are divisible by 4; for example, 54 is not divisible by 4. [2.1-1]

10. Every natural number ending in 6 is divisible by 2.
True [2.2-2]

11. Every natural number ending in 9 is divisible by 3.
False: Not all natural numbers ending in 9 are divisible by 3. For example 19 is not divisible by 3. [2.1-1]

12. The number 123,321,231 is divisible by 3.
True [2.1-1]

13. The number 123,321,234 is divisible by 4.   False: The number 123,321,234 is *not* divisible by 4. It is divisible by 2, 3, and 6. [2.1-1]

14. The number 123,321,235 is divisible by 5.
True [2.1-1]

15. All prime numbers are odd.   False: Two is the only prime number that is not odd. [2.4]

16. Every composite number ends in 1, 3, 7, or 9.
False: Not all composite numbers end in 1, 3, 7, or 9. All even numbers larger than 2 are composite as are all numbers larger than 5 that end in 5. [2.4]

17. Every composite number has four or more factors.
False: Every composite number has three or more factors. [2.4]

18. Every prime number has exactly two multiples.
False: Every prime number has exactly two factors. [2.4]

19. It is possible for a composite number to have exactly three divisors.   True [2.4]

20. All of the prime factors of a natural number are smaller than the number.   False: All of the prime factors of a composite number are smaller than the number. [2.4]

21. The least common multiple (LCM) of three different prime numbers is the product of the three numbers.   True [2.6]

22. Some natural numbers have exactly five different prime factors.   True [2.5]

CHAPTER 3

Fractions and Mixed Numbers

Challenges come in many forms. For the competitor in a race, or the math-anxious student, success comes through perseverance and positive attitude. (Lori Adamski Peek/ Tony Stone Images)

The shortcut uses multiplication and addition:

$$1\frac{3}{7} = \frac{7 \cdot 1 + 3}{7} = \frac{7 + 3}{7} = \frac{10}{7}$$

▶ **To change a mixed number to an improper fraction**

1. Multiply the denominator times the whole number.
2. Add the numerator to the product in step 1.
3. Place the sum from step 2 over the denominator.

Examples J–L   **Warm Ups J–L**

Directions: Change each mixed number to an improper fraction.

Strategy: Multiply the whole number by the denominator. Add the numerator. Write the sum over the denominator.

J. $2\frac{4}{5}$ **J.** $3\frac{5}{6}$

Solution:

$$2\frac{4}{5} = \frac{2(5) + 4}{5}$$ Multiply the whole number by the denominator, add the product to the numerator, and place the sum over the denominator.

$$= \frac{14}{5}$$

K. $4\frac{5}{9}$ **K.** $5\frac{5}{8}$

Solution:

$$4\frac{5}{9} = \frac{4(9) + 5}{9}$$ Multiply the whole number by the denominator, add the product to the numerator, and place the sum over the denominator.

$$= \frac{41}{9}$$

L. 7   **L.** 8

Solution: First, rewrite the whole number as a mixed number. Use the fraction $\frac{0}{1}$.

$$7 = 7\frac{0}{1} = \frac{7(1) + 0}{1}$$ Note: Any fraction that equals 0 could be used.

$$= \frac{7}{1}$$

Answers to warm ups: **J.** $\frac{23}{6}$ **K.** $\frac{45}{8}$ **L.** $\frac{8}{1}$

NAME _____ CLASS _____ DATE _____

EXERCISES 3.1

A

Identify the proper and improper fractions from the list.

1. $\dfrac{3}{7}, \dfrac{4}{7}, \dfrac{5}{7}, \dfrac{6}{7}, \dfrac{7}{7}, \dfrac{8}{7}, \dfrac{9}{7}$

Proper fractions: $\dfrac{3}{7}, \dfrac{4}{7}, \dfrac{5}{7}, \dfrac{6}{7}$

Improper fractions: $\dfrac{7}{7}, \dfrac{8}{7}, \dfrac{9}{7}$

2. $\dfrac{5}{6}, \dfrac{8}{7}, \dfrac{14}{15}, \dfrac{16}{18}, \dfrac{17}{17}, \dfrac{23}{25}$

Proper fractions: $\dfrac{5}{6}, \dfrac{14}{15}, \dfrac{16}{18}, \dfrac{23}{25}$

Improper fractions: $\dfrac{8}{7}, \dfrac{17}{17}$

3. $\dfrac{7}{13}, \dfrac{8}{15}, \dfrac{10}{13}, \dfrac{11}{15}, \dfrac{12}{23}$

Proper fractions: $\dfrac{7}{13}, \dfrac{8}{15}, \dfrac{10}{13}, \dfrac{11}{15}, \dfrac{12}{23}$

Improper fractions: none

4. $\dfrac{9}{11}, \dfrac{9}{10}, \dfrac{9}{9}, \dfrac{9}{8}, \dfrac{9}{7}$

Proper fractions: $\dfrac{9}{11}, \dfrac{9}{10}$

Improper fractions: $\dfrac{9}{9}, \dfrac{9}{8}, \dfrac{9}{7}$

5. $\dfrac{7}{4}, \dfrac{10}{11}, \dfrac{13}{13}, \dfrac{20}{19}, \dfrac{3}{5}$

Proper fractions: $\dfrac{10}{11}, \dfrac{3}{5}$

Improper fractions: $\dfrac{7}{4}, \dfrac{13}{13}, \dfrac{20}{19}$

6. $\dfrac{6}{11}, \dfrac{10}{8}, \dfrac{11}{6}, \dfrac{10}{12}, \dfrac{9}{9}$

Proper fractions: $\dfrac{6}{11}, \dfrac{10}{12}$

Improper fractions: $\dfrac{10}{8}, \dfrac{11}{6}, \dfrac{9}{9}$

Write the fraction represented by the figure.

7. 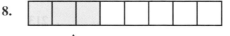 $\dfrac{5}{8}$

8. 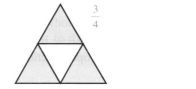 $\dfrac{3}{8}$

9. 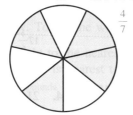 $\dfrac{4}{7}$

10. $\dfrac{3}{4}$

11. $\dfrac{4}{5}$

12. $\dfrac{7}{8}$

Change the improper fraction to a mixed number.

13. $\dfrac{19}{4}$ $4\dfrac{3}{4}$ **14.** $\dfrac{19}{5}$ $3\dfrac{4}{5}$ **15.** $\dfrac{11}{2}$ $5\dfrac{1}{2}$ **16.** $\dfrac{14}{5}$ $2\dfrac{4}{5}$ **17.** $\dfrac{21}{4}$ $5\dfrac{1}{4}$ **18.** $\dfrac{7}{2}$ $3\dfrac{1}{2}$

Change the mixed number to an improper fraction.

19. $5\dfrac{4}{7}$ $\dfrac{39}{7}$ **20.** $4\dfrac{3}{8}$ $\dfrac{35}{8}$ **21.** 12 $\dfrac{12}{1}$ **22.** 13 $\dfrac{13}{1}$ **23.** $7\dfrac{3}{4}$ $\dfrac{31}{4}$ **24.** $6\dfrac{5}{6}$ $\dfrac{41}{6}$

G. ▦ $\dfrac{493}{551}$ G. $\dfrac{703}{851}$

Solution:

ENTER	[493] [a^{b/c}] [551] [=]
DISPLAY	493. 493⌐. 493⌐551. 17⌐19.

$\dfrac{493}{551} = \dfrac{17}{19}$

H. 🌐 Morris washes cars on Saturday to earn extra money. On a certain Saturday he has 12 cars to wash. After he has washed 8 of them, what fraction of the total has he washed? Reduce the fraction to lowest terms.

Solution: Form the fraction: $\dfrac{\text{number of cars washed}}{\text{total number of cars}}$.

$\dfrac{8}{12}$ Eight cars are washed.
              The total number of cars.

$\dfrac{8}{12} = \dfrac{2 \cdot \overset{1}{\cancel{4}}}{3 \cdot \underset{1}{\cancel{4}}} = \dfrac{2}{3}$ Reduce.

Morris has washed $\dfrac{2}{3}$ of the cars.

H. If in Example H Morris washes only 4 cars, what fraction of the total are washed?

NAME _____   _____ CLASS _____ DATE _____

EXERCISES 3.2

A

Reduce to lowest terms.

1. $\dfrac{6}{12}$ $\frac{1}{2}$ 2. $\dfrac{6}{15}$ $\frac{2}{5}$ 3. $\dfrac{6}{9}$ $\frac{2}{3}$ 4. $\dfrac{8}{12}$ $\frac{2}{3}$ 5. $\dfrac{10}{25}$ $\frac{2}{5}$ 6. $\dfrac{16}{18}$ $\frac{8}{9}$

7. $\dfrac{30}{50}$ $\frac{3}{5}$ 8. $\dfrac{40}{70}$ $\frac{4}{7}$ 9. $\dfrac{12}{16}$ $\frac{3}{4}$ 10. $\dfrac{18}{24}$ $\frac{3}{4}$ 11. $\dfrac{12}{20}$ $\frac{3}{5}$ 12. $\dfrac{20}{22}$ $\frac{10}{11}$

13. $\dfrac{32}{40}$ $\frac{4}{5}$ 14. $\dfrac{30}{40}$ $\frac{3}{4}$ 15. $\dfrac{60}{36}$ $\frac{5}{3}$ 16. $\dfrac{55}{22}$ $\frac{5}{2}$ 17. $\dfrac{14}{18}$ $\frac{7}{9}$ 18. $\dfrac{28}{36}$ $\frac{7}{9}$

19. $\dfrac{21}{35}$ $\frac{3}{5}$ 20. $\dfrac{25}{45}$ $\frac{5}{9}$ 21. $\dfrac{20}{5}$ 4 22. $\dfrac{40}{4}$ 10

B

23. $\dfrac{63}{27}$ $\frac{7}{3}$ 24. $\dfrac{60}{35}$ $\frac{12}{7}$ 25. $\dfrac{14}{42}$ $\frac{1}{3}$ 26. $\dfrac{30}{45}$ $\frac{2}{3}$ 27. $\dfrac{12}{36}$ $\frac{1}{3}$ 28. $\dfrac{20}{36}$ $\frac{5}{9}$

29. $\dfrac{27}{36}$ $\frac{3}{4}$ 30. $\dfrac{32}{36}$ $\frac{8}{9}$ 31. $\dfrac{29}{36}$ $\frac{29}{36}$ 32. $\dfrac{23}{36}$ $\frac{23}{36}$ 33. $\dfrac{50}{75}$ $\frac{2}{3}$ 34. $\dfrac{30}{75}$ $\frac{2}{5}$

35. $\dfrac{55}{75}$ $\frac{11}{15}$ 36. $\dfrac{15}{75}$ $\frac{1}{5}$ 37. $\dfrac{600}{800}$ $\frac{3}{4}$ 38. $\dfrac{500}{900}$ $\frac{5}{9}$ 39. $\dfrac{45}{80}$ $\frac{9}{16}$ 40. $\dfrac{65}{80}$ $\frac{13}{16}$

41. $\dfrac{72}{96}$ $\frac{3}{4}$ 42. $\dfrac{88}{92}$ $\frac{22}{23}$ 43. $\dfrac{72}{12}$ 6 44. $\dfrac{96}{16}$ 6

C

45. $\dfrac{75}{125}$ $\frac{3}{5}$ 46. $\dfrac{64}{120}$ $\frac{8}{15}$ 47. $\dfrac{96}{126}$ $\frac{16}{21}$ 48. $\dfrac{72}{100}$ $\frac{18}{25}$ 49. $\dfrac{99}{132}$ $\frac{3}{4}$ 50. $\dfrac{84}{120}$ $\frac{7}{10}$

Maintain Your Skills (Sections 1.3, 1.4, 1.6, 2.5)

81. How much less than 5982 is 4076?

1906

82. How much more is 9312 than 599?

8713

83. Find the difference of 5111 and 2899.

2212

84. Subtract 791 from 10,000.

9209

85. Find the sum of 1091, 789, 879, 52, 9, and 63.

2883

86. Find the total of 60,234, 5160, 407, 20, 32,412, and 78.   98,311

87. Prime factor 320.

$2 \cdot 2 \cdot 2 \cdot 2 \cdot 2 \cdot 2 \cdot 5$ or $2^6 \cdot 5$

88. Prime factor 374.

$2 \cdot 11 \cdot 17$

89. How many bricks, each weighing 4 pounds, will it take to weigh 6000 pounds?   1500 bricks

90. Trudy has to read all of her psychology text before the final week of the term. If the text is 980 pages long and Trudy does not want to read during weekends, how many pages must she read each day, on the average, to read the text before the start of the final week? Assume that the semester is 15 weeks long.   14 pages

3.3 MULTIPLYING AND DIVIDING FRACTIONS

Objectives

  1 Multiply fractions.

  2 Find the reciprocal of a number.

  3 Divide fractions.

Application

During one year, $\dfrac{7}{8}$ of all the cars sold by Trust-em Used Cars had automatic transmissions. Of the cars sold with automatic transmissions, $\dfrac{1}{70}$ had to be repaired before they were sold. What fraction of the cars sold had automatic transmissions and had to be repaired?

Vocabulary

A **product** is the answer to a multiplication problem. If two fractions have a product of 1, either fraction is called the **reciprocal** of the other. For example, $\dfrac{2}{3}$ is the reciprocal of $\dfrac{3}{2}$.

How and Why **1**

What is $\dfrac{1}{2}$ of $\dfrac{1}{3}$ or $\dfrac{1}{2} \cdot \dfrac{1}{3} = ?$ See Figure 3.4. The rectangle is divided into three parts. One part, $\dfrac{1}{3}$, is shaded blue. To find $\dfrac{1}{2}$ of the shaded third, divide each of the thirds into two parts (halves). Figure 3.5 shows the rectangle divided into six parts. So, $\dfrac{1}{2}$ of the shaded third is $\dfrac{1}{6}$ of the rectangle, which is shaded orange:

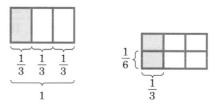

Figure 3.4   **Figure 3.5**

$$\frac{1}{2} \text{ of } \frac{1}{3} = \frac{1}{2} \cdot \frac{1}{3} = \frac{1}{6} = \frac{\text{number of parts shaded orange}}{\text{total number of parts}}$$

What is $\dfrac{1}{4}$ of $\dfrac{3}{4}$? $\left(\dfrac{1}{4} \cdot \dfrac{3}{4} = ? \right)$ In Figure 3.6 the rectangle has been divided into four parts, and $\dfrac{3}{4}$ is represented by the parts that are shaded blue. To find $\dfrac{1}{4}$ of the $\dfrac{3}{4}$, divide each of the fourths into four parts. The rectangle is now divided into 16 parts, so that $\dfrac{1}{4}$ of each of the three original fourths is shaded orange and represents $\dfrac{3}{16}$. (See Fig. 3.7.)

$$\frac{1}{4} \text{ of } \frac{3}{4} = \frac{1}{4} \cdot \frac{3}{4} = \frac{3}{16}$$

E. $\dfrac{20}{30} \cdot \dfrac{15}{88}$

E. $\dfrac{32}{45} \cdot \dfrac{35}{24}$

Solution: Prime factor the numbers because there are so many common factors it is not easy to see all of them.

$$\dfrac{20}{30} \cdot \dfrac{15}{88} = \dfrac{2 \cdot 2 \cdot 5}{2 \cdot 3 \cdot 5} \cdot \dfrac{3 \cdot 5}{2 \cdot 2 \cdot 2 \cdot 11}$$

$$= \dfrac{\cancel{2} \cdot \cancel{2} \cdot \cancel{5}}{\cancel{2} \cdot \cancel{3} \cdot \cancel{5}} \cdot \dfrac{\cancel{3} \cdot 5}{\cancel{2} \cdot 2 \cdot 2 \cdot 11}$$

$$= \dfrac{5}{44}$$

F. $\dfrac{16}{75} \cdot \dfrac{45}{56}$

F. $\dfrac{18}{35} \cdot \dfrac{28}{45}$

Solution:

ENTER	16	$a^{b/c}$	75	$\times$
DISPLAY	16.	16⌋.	16⌋75.	16⌋75.
ENTER	45	$a^{b/c}$	56	$=$
DISPLAY	45.	45⌋.	45⌋56.	6⌋35.

So $\dfrac{16}{75} \cdot \dfrac{45}{56} = \dfrac{6}{35}$.

G. During one year, $\dfrac{7}{8}$ of all the cars sold by Trust-em Used Cars had automatic transmissions. Of the cars sold with automatic transmissions, $\dfrac{1}{70}$ had to be repaired before they were sold. What fraction of the cars sold had automatic transmissions and had to be repaired?

Solution: Multiply the part of the cars with automatic transmissions by the part with transmissions that had to be repaired.

$$\dfrac{7}{8} \cdot \dfrac{1}{70} = \dfrac{\overset{1}{\cancel{7}}}{8} \cdot \dfrac{1}{\underset{10}{\cancel{70}}} = \dfrac{1}{80}$$

So $\dfrac{1}{80}$ of the total cars sold had automatic transmissions and had to be repaired.

G. During one year $\dfrac{2}{3}$ of all the tires sold by the Tire Factory were highway tread tires. If $\dfrac{1}{40}$ of the highway treads had to be repaired, what fraction of the tires sold had to be repaired?

Answers to warm ups: **E.** $\dfrac{28}{27}$ or $1\dfrac{1}{27}$ **F.** $\dfrac{8}{25}$ **G.** $\dfrac{1}{60}$

How and Why 2   Finding a reciprocal is often called "inverting" a fraction. For instance, the reciprocal of $\frac{3}{7}$ is $\frac{7}{3}$. We check by showing that the product is 1.

$$\frac{3}{7} \cdot \frac{7}{3} = \frac{21}{21} = 1$$

▶ **To find the reciprocal of a fraction**

Interchange the numerator and the denominator.

The reciprocal of whole numbers or mixed numbers can be found by first writing them as improper fractions. The reciprocal of 32 $\left(32 = \frac{32}{1}\right)$ is $\frac{1}{32}$ and the reciprocal of $4\frac{1}{5}$ $\left(4\frac{1}{5} = \frac{21}{5}\right)$ is $\frac{5}{21}$.

CAUTION

The number zero, 0, does not have a reciprocal.

Examples H–I   **Warm Ups H–I**

Directions: Find the reciprocal.

Strategy: Interchange the numerator and the denominator, or "invert" the fraction.

H. $\frac{7}{10}$ **H.** $\frac{8}{11}$

Solution:

The reciprocal of $\frac{7}{10}$ is $\frac{10}{7}$.   Exchange the numerator and the denominator.

CHECK: $\frac{7}{10} \cdot \frac{10}{7} = \frac{70}{70} = 1$

I. $1\frac{4}{9}$ **I.** $1\frac{5}{6}$

Solution: First write $1\frac{4}{9}$ as an improper fraction.

$1\frac{4}{9} = \frac{13}{9}$

Answer to warm up: **H.** $\frac{11}{8}$ or $1\frac{3}{8}$

The reciprocal of $\dfrac{13}{9}$ is $\dfrac{9}{13}$.   Invert the fraction.

CHECK: $\dfrac{13}{9} \cdot \dfrac{9}{13} = \dfrac{117}{117} = 1$

How and Why ⬚3

It is pointed out in Chapter 1 that division is the inverse of multiplication. That is, the answer to a division problem is the number that is multiplied times the divisor (second number), which will give the first number as an answer. Another way of thinking of division is to ask, "How many groups of a certain size are contained in a number?"

	Think	*Answer*
$6 \div 2$	How many twos in six?	3
$\dfrac{4}{5} \div \dfrac{1}{10}$	How many one-tenths in four-fifths?	See Figure 3.8.

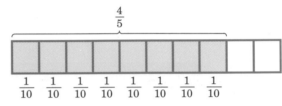

Figure 3.8

In Figure 3.8 we see that there are eight one-tenths in four-fifths. Therefore, we can say

$$\frac{4}{5} \div \frac{1}{10} = 8$$

Since $8 \cdot \dfrac{1}{10} = \dfrac{8}{10} = \dfrac{4}{5}$, we know that the answer is correct.

The answer can also be obtained from the fractions by multiplying $\dfrac{4}{5}$ by the reciprocal of $\dfrac{1}{10}$.

$$\frac{4}{5} \div \frac{1}{10} = \frac{4}{5} \cdot \frac{10}{1} = \frac{40}{5} = 8$$

▶ **To divide fractions**

Multiply the first fraction by the reciprocal of the divisor; that is, invert and multiply.

CAUTION

Do not reduce the fractions before changing the division to multiplication; that is, invert before reducing.

Answer to warm up: I. $\dfrac{6}{11}$

Examples J–N

Directions: Divide. Reduce to lowest terms.

Strategy: Multiply by the reciprocal of the divisor.

J. $\dfrac{7}{23} \div \dfrac{16}{23}$

J. $\dfrac{11}{19} \div \dfrac{15}{19}$

Solution:

$$\dfrac{7}{23} \div \dfrac{16}{23} = \dfrac{7}{23} \cdot \dfrac{23}{16} \qquad \text{Multiply by the reciprocal of the divisor.}$$

$$= \dfrac{7}{16}$$

K. $\dfrac{8}{3} \div \dfrac{4}{5}$

K. $\dfrac{9}{2} \div \dfrac{6}{5}$

Solution:

$$\dfrac{8}{3} \div \dfrac{4}{5} = \dfrac{\overset{2}{8}}{3} \cdot \dfrac{5}{\underset{1}{4}} \qquad \text{Invert the divisor and multiply.}$$

$$= \dfrac{10}{3} \text{ or } 3\dfrac{1}{3}$$

L. $\dfrac{1}{12} \div \dfrac{3}{5}$

L. $\dfrac{5}{11} \div \dfrac{2}{3}$

Solution:

$$\dfrac{1}{12} \div \dfrac{3}{5} = \dfrac{1}{12} \cdot \dfrac{5}{3} \qquad \text{Invert the divisor and multiply.}$$

$$= \dfrac{5}{36}$$

M. 🖩 $\dfrac{8}{63} \div \dfrac{24}{77}$

M. $\dfrac{9}{64} \div \dfrac{27}{80}$

Solution:

ENTER	8	a^{b/c}	63	÷	
DISPLAY	8.	8⌐.	8⌐63.	8⌐63.	

ENTER	24	a^{b/c}	77	=	
DISPLAY	24.	24⌐.	24⌐77.	11⌐27.	

So $\dfrac{8}{63} \div \dfrac{24}{77} = \dfrac{11}{27}$.

N. ⊕ If the distance a nut moves on a bolt with one turn is $\dfrac{3}{16}$ inch, how many turns will it take to move the nut $\dfrac{3}{4}$ inch?

N. If in Example N the distance the nut moves on the bolt with one turn is $\dfrac{3}{32}$ inch, how many turns will it take to move the nut $\dfrac{3}{4}$ inch?

Solution: To find the number of turns needed to move the nut the required distance, divide the required distance by the distance the nut moves in one turn.

$$\frac{3}{4} \div \frac{3}{16} = \frac{\cancel{3}}{\underset{1}{4}} \cdot \frac{\overset{4}{\cancel{16}}}{\cancel{3}} = 4 \qquad \text{Invert the divisor and multiply.}$$

It takes 4 turns to move the nut $\dfrac{3}{4}$ inch.

NAME _____ CLASS _____ DATE _____

EXERCISES 3.3

A

Multiply. Reduce to lowest terms.

1. $\dfrac{1}{5} \cdot \dfrac{2}{5}$ $\quad \frac{2}{25}$ **2.** $\dfrac{7}{8} \cdot \dfrac{1}{6}$ $\quad \frac{7}{48}$ **3.** $\dfrac{3}{5} \cdot \dfrac{6}{11}$ $\quad \frac{18}{55}$ **4.** $\dfrac{3}{2} \cdot \dfrac{5}{14}$ $\quad \frac{15}{28}$ **5.** $\dfrac{5}{4} \cdot \dfrac{7}{10}$ $\quad \frac{7}{8}$

6. $\dfrac{2}{3} \cdot \dfrac{3}{8}$ $\quad \frac{1}{4}$ **7.** $\dfrac{5}{8} \cdot \dfrac{4}{15}$ $\quad \frac{1}{6}$ **8.** $\dfrac{15}{20} \cdot \dfrac{8}{12}$ $\quad \frac{1}{2}$ **9.** $\dfrac{5}{24} \cdot \dfrac{8}{10}$ $\quad \frac{1}{6}$ **10.** $\dfrac{4}{9} \cdot \dfrac{3}{8}$ $\quad \frac{1}{6}$

11. $\dfrac{9}{12} \cdot \dfrac{10}{15}$ $\quad \frac{1}{2}$ **12.** $\dfrac{7}{9} \cdot \dfrac{3}{14}$ $\quad \frac{1}{6}$ **13.** $8 \cdot \dfrac{25}{40}$ $\quad 5$ **14.** $\dfrac{25}{36} \cdot 18$ $\quad \frac{25}{2}$

Find the reciprocal.

15. $\dfrac{3}{8}$ $\quad \frac{8}{3}$ **16.** $\dfrac{5}{11}$ $\quad \frac{11}{5}$ **17.** 5 $\quad \frac{1}{5}$ **18.** 0 $\quad$ None   **19.** $4\dfrac{1}{2}$ $\quad \frac{2}{9}$ **20.** $5\dfrac{2}{3}$ $\quad \frac{3}{17}$

Divide. Reduce to lowest terms.

21. $\dfrac{3}{7} \div \dfrac{4}{9}$ $\quad \frac{27}{28}$ **22.** $\dfrac{9}{8} \div \dfrac{5}{7}$ $\quad \frac{63}{40}$ **23.** $\dfrac{7}{20} \div \dfrac{14}{15}$ $\quad \frac{3}{8}$ **24.** $\dfrac{8}{13} \div \dfrac{2}{13}$ $\quad 4$ **25.** $\dfrac{8}{9} \div \dfrac{8}{3}$ $\quad \frac{1}{3}$

26. $\dfrac{5}{6} \div \dfrac{5}{3}$ $\quad \frac{1}{2}$ **27.** $\dfrac{6}{33} \div \dfrac{3}{11}$ $\quad \frac{2}{3}$ **28.** $\dfrac{8}{12} \div \dfrac{5}{12}$ $\quad \frac{8}{5}$ **29.** $\dfrac{12}{16} \div \dfrac{3}{4}$ $\quad 1$ **30.** $\dfrac{24}{36} \div \dfrac{8}{9}$ $\quad \frac{3}{4}$

B

Multiply. Reduce to lowest terms.

31. $\dfrac{4}{6} \cdot \dfrac{9}{30} \cdot \dfrac{10}{6}$ $\quad \frac{1}{3}$ **32.** $\dfrac{2}{3} \cdot \dfrac{4}{15} \cdot \dfrac{18}{7}$ $\quad \frac{16}{35}$ **33.** $7 \cdot \dfrac{1}{4} \cdot \dfrac{8}{21}$ $\quad \frac{2}{3}$

34. $\dfrac{21}{2} \cdot 8 \cdot \dfrac{1}{7}$ $\quad 12$ **35.** $\dfrac{21}{5} \cdot \dfrac{5}{4} \cdot \dfrac{4}{21}$ $\quad 1$ **36.** $\dfrac{24}{30} \cdot \dfrac{3}{8} \cdot \dfrac{4}{9}$ $\quad \frac{2}{15}$

83. If the head of a pin is $\frac{1}{20}$ inch wide, how many pinheads will it take to form a line $\frac{4}{5}$ inch long?   16 pins

84. Exact Electronics manufactures copper wire with a diameter of $\frac{5}{32}$ inch. How many turns of the wire will fill the first level on a spool of width $\frac{45}{32}$ inch?   9 turns

85. An article is priced to sell for $96 at the Aquarium Gift Store. It is sale-priced at $\frac{1}{3}$ off. What is its sale price? $64

86. The National Zoo has T-shirts that regularly sell for $30. The shirts are marked $\frac{1}{5}$ off during the Labor Day sale. What is the sale price of a T-shirt? $24

87. As part of her job at a pet store, Becky feeds each gerbil $\frac{1}{8}$ cup of seeds each day. If the seeds come in packages of $\frac{5}{4}$ cups, how many gerbils can be fed from one package?   10 gerbils

88. The Green Thumb Nursery advises that when planting spinach you should use $\frac{1}{16}$ cup of seed for a 50-foot row. How many rows can be planted using $\frac{7}{8}$ cup of seed?   14 rows

89. A building materials outlet is stocking up on $\frac{3}{4}$-inch plywood for a sale. They order 200 sheets of the plywood. How high will the sheets reach whey they are stacked?   150 inches

90. A paper stock measures $\frac{1}{90}$ inch thick per sheet. How thick is a pile of 300 sheets? $\frac{10}{3}$ inches or $3\frac{1}{3}$ inches

91. A snail can crawl $\frac{5}{8}$ inch in one minute. How long will it take the snail to cover three inches? $\frac{24}{5}$ minutes or $4\frac{4}{5}$ minutes

92. The distance a nut moves on a bolt with one turn is $\frac{3}{16}$ inch. How many turns are needed to make the nut move two inches? $\frac{32}{3}$ turns or $10\frac{2}{3}$ turns

NAME _____ CLASS _____ DATE _____

93. Underinflation of car tires can waste up to $\dfrac{1}{20}$ of a car's fuel by increasing the "rolling resistance." If Martin uses 820 gallons of gas in a year, how many gallons could potentially be saved by proper tire inflation?   41 gallons

State Your Understanding

94. Explain why $\dfrac{1}{2} \cdot \dfrac{1}{4} = \dfrac{1}{8}$.

95. Explain why $\dfrac{1}{2} \div \dfrac{1}{4} = 2$.

Challenge

Perform the indicated operations.

96. $\left(\dfrac{81}{75} \cdot \dfrac{96}{99} \cdot \dfrac{55}{125}\right) \div \dfrac{128}{250}$ $\dfrac{9}{10}$

97. $\left(\dfrac{39}{980} \cdot \dfrac{300}{312} \cdot \dfrac{560}{720} \cdot \dfrac{240}{450}\right) \div \dfrac{275}{350}$ $\dfrac{2}{99}$

98. The In-n-Out Grocery has a standard work week of 40 hours. Jane works $\dfrac{3}{4}$ of a standard week, Jose works $\dfrac{5}{8}$ of a standard week, Aria works $\dfrac{9}{8}$ of a standard week, and Bill works $\dfrac{6}{5}$ of a standard week. How many hours did each employee work? In-n-Out pays an average salary of $7 an hour. What is the week's payroll for the above four employees?

Jane, 30 hours; Jose, 25 hours; Aria, 45 hours; Bill, 48 hours; $1036

B. $\left(3\frac{3}{4}\right)\left(2\frac{2}{5}\right)$

B. $\left(2\frac{2}{3}\right)\left(2\frac{1}{4}\right)$

Solution:

$$\left(3\frac{3}{4}\right)\left(2\frac{2}{5}\right) = \frac{15}{4} \cdot \frac{12}{5}$$

$$= \frac{\overset{3}{\cancel{15}}}{\underset{1}{\cancel{4}}} \cdot \frac{\overset{3}{\cancel{12}}}{\underset{1}{\cancel{5}}} \qquad \text{Reduce.}$$

$$= \frac{9}{1} = 9 \qquad \text{Multiply and write as a whole number.}$$

C. $6\left(\frac{3}{4}\right)\left(2\frac{1}{3}\right)$

C. $4\left(3\frac{3}{5}\right)\left(\frac{5}{9}\right)$

Solution:

$$6\left(\frac{3}{4}\right)\left(2\frac{1}{3}\right) = \frac{\overset{3}{\cancel{6}}}{1} \cdot \frac{\overset{1}{\cancel{3}}}{\underset{2}{\cancel{4}}} \cdot \frac{7}{\underset{1}{\cancel{3}}}$$

$$= \frac{21}{2} = 10\frac{1}{2} \qquad \text{Multiply and write as a mixed number.}$$

D. ▦ $4\frac{2}{3}\left(8\frac{5}{6}\right)$

D. $5\frac{3}{8}\left(6\frac{1}{2}\right)$

Solution:

ENTER	4	a^b/c	2	a^b/c	3	×
DISPLAY	4.	4⌐.	4⌐2.	4⌐2⌐.	4⌐2⌐3.	4⌐2⌐3.

ENTER	8	a^b/c	5	a^b/c	6	=
DISPLAY	8.	8⌐.	8⌐5.	8⌐5⌐.	8⌐5⌐6.	41⌐2⌐9.

So $4\frac{2}{3}\left(8\frac{5}{6}\right) = 41\frac{2}{9}$.

How and Why   2   Division of mixed numbers is also done by changing to improper fractions first.

$$\left(5\frac{1}{4}\right) \div \left(2\frac{4}{7}\right) = \left(\frac{21}{4}\right) \div \left(\frac{18}{7}\right) \qquad \text{Change to improper fractions.}$$

$$= \left(\frac{21}{4}\right)\left(\frac{7}{18}\right) \qquad \text{Multiply by the reciprocal of the divisor.}$$

$$= \frac{147}{72} = 2\frac{3}{72} \qquad \text{Multiply and write as a mixed number.}$$

$$= 2\frac{1}{24} \qquad \text{Reduce.}$$

Answers to warm ups: **B.** 6   **C.** 8   **D.** $34\frac{15}{16}$

▶ **To divide whole numbers and/or mixed numbers**

1. Change them to improper fractions.
2. Divide.

Examples E–I   **Warm Ups E–I**

Directions: Divide. Write as a mixed number.

Strategy: Change the mixed numbers and whole numbers to improper fractions. Divide and reduce to lowest terms. Write the answer as a mixed number.

E. $3\dfrac{1}{3} \div 6\dfrac{7}{8}$

E. $4\dfrac{5}{6} \div 2\dfrac{11}{12}$

Solution:

$$3\dfrac{1}{3} \div 6\dfrac{7}{8} = \dfrac{10}{3} \div \dfrac{55}{8} \qquad 3\dfrac{1}{3} = \dfrac{10}{3} \text{ and } 6\dfrac{7}{8} = \dfrac{55}{8}.$$

$$= \dfrac{\overset{2}{\cancel{10}}}{3} \cdot \dfrac{8}{\underset{11}{\cancel{55}}} \qquad \text{Invert the divisor and multiply.}$$

$$= \dfrac{16}{33}$$

F. $12\dfrac{3}{16} \div 21\dfrac{3}{5}$

F. $15\dfrac{5}{8} \div 12\dfrac{1}{2}$

Solution:

$$12\dfrac{3}{16} \div 21\dfrac{3}{5} = \dfrac{195}{16} \div \dfrac{108}{5}$$

$$= \dfrac{\overset{65}{\cancel{195}}}{16} \cdot \dfrac{5}{\underset{36}{\cancel{108}}} \qquad \text{Invert the divisor and multiply.}$$

$$= \dfrac{325}{576}$$

G. $4 \div 3\dfrac{1}{3}$

G. $8\dfrac{5}{6} \div 5$

Solution:

$$4 \div 3\dfrac{1}{3} = \dfrac{4}{1} \div \dfrac{10}{3}$$

29. $\left(2\frac{5}{8}\right)\left(1\frac{1}{6}\right)$ $3\frac{1}{16}$ **30.** $\left(4\frac{2}{5}\right)\left(1\frac{3}{8}\right)$ $6\frac{1}{20}$ **31.** $\left(7\frac{3}{4}\right)\left(\frac{2}{3}\right)(0)$ 0 **32.** $\left(3\frac{5}{9}\right)\left(6\frac{3}{8}\right)(0)$ 0

33. $\left(3\frac{1}{3}\right)(6)\left(3\frac{3}{4}\right)$ 75 **34.** $\left(4\frac{1}{5}\right)(5)\left(2\frac{7}{9}\right)$ $58\frac{1}{3}$ **35.** $\left(3\frac{2}{3}\right)\left(\frac{15}{22}\right)\left(7\frac{1}{2}\right)$ $18\frac{3}{4}$ **36.** $\left(4\frac{3}{4}\right)\left(3\frac{1}{5}\right)\left(5\frac{5}{8}\right)$ $85\frac{1}{2}$

Divide. Write as a mixed number if possible.

37. $3\frac{1}{5} \div 1\frac{1}{5}$ $2\frac{2}{3}$ **38.** $3\frac{2}{3} \div 2\frac{2}{3}$ $1\frac{3}{8}$ **39.** $1\frac{5}{9} \div 9\frac{1}{3}$ $\frac{1}{6}$ **40.** $5\frac{3}{5} \div 2\frac{4}{5}$ 2

41. $\frac{7}{8} \div 3\frac{3}{4}$ $\frac{7}{30}$ **42.** $\frac{11}{15} \div 2\frac{4}{5}$ $\frac{11}{42}$ **43.** $6\frac{2}{3} \div 10$ $\frac{2}{3}$ **44.** $5\frac{3}{7} \div 19$ $\frac{2}{7}$

45. $3\frac{2}{3} \div \frac{1}{5}$ $18\frac{1}{3}$ **46.** $8\frac{3}{4} \div 2\frac{1}{3}$ $3\frac{3}{4}$ **47.** $3\frac{3}{4} \div \frac{7}{15}$ $8\frac{1}{28}$ **48.** $5\frac{5}{6} \div \frac{20}{9}$ $2\frac{5}{8}$

C

Multiply. Write as a mixed number if possible.

49. $\left(4\frac{1}{5}\right)\left(1\frac{1}{3}\right)\left(6\frac{2}{7}\right)$ $35\frac{1}{5}$ **50.** $\left(12\frac{1}{4}\right)\left(1\frac{1}{7}\right)\left(2\frac{1}{3}\right)$ $32\frac{2}{3}$ **51.** $(14)\left(6\frac{1}{2}\right)\left(1\frac{2}{13}\right)$ 105

NAME _____ CLASS _____ DATE _____

52. $(12)\left(1\frac{4}{15}\right)\left(6\frac{1}{4}\right)$ 95

53. $\left(5\frac{2}{3}\right)\left(1\frac{1}{2}\right)\left(8\frac{3}{17}\right)$ $69\frac{1}{2}$

54. $\left(8\frac{1}{3}\right)\left(6\frac{3}{5}\right)\left(2\frac{1}{2}\right)$ $137\frac{1}{2}$

55. $\left(5\frac{1}{3}\right)\left(2\frac{3}{14}\right)(7)\left(2\frac{1}{4}\right)$ 186

56. $\left(3\frac{3}{5}\right)\left(4\frac{1}{3}\right)(3)\left(2\frac{7}{9}\right)$ 130

57. $\left(\frac{8}{11}\right)\left(3\frac{2}{3}\right)\left(4\frac{1}{2}\right)\left(1\frac{1}{5}\right)$ $14\frac{2}{5}$

58. $\left(\frac{5}{16}\right)\left(4\frac{5}{7}\right)\left(2\frac{4}{5}\right)\left(5\frac{4}{9}\right)$ $22\frac{11}{24}$

Divide. Write as a mixed number if possible.

59. $31\frac{1}{3} \div 1\frac{1}{9}$ $28\frac{1}{5}$

60. $21\frac{3}{7} \div 8\frac{1}{3}$ $2\frac{4}{7}$

61. $10\frac{2}{3} \div 2\frac{2}{7}$ $4\frac{2}{3}$

62. $22\frac{2}{3} \div 6\frac{6}{7}$ $3\frac{11}{36}$

63. $33\frac{1}{3} \div 11\frac{1}{9}$ 3

64. $16\frac{2}{3} \div 2\frac{7}{9}$ 6

65. $20\frac{5}{6} \div 3\frac{4}{7}$ $5\frac{5}{6}$

66. $18\frac{2}{5} \div 17\frac{1}{4}$ $1\frac{1}{15}$

67. $15\frac{3}{7} \div 14$ $1\frac{5}{49}$

68. $13 \div 7\frac{3}{7}$ $1\frac{3}{4}$

$$\frac{2}{5} < \frac{4}{5} \text{ means } ``\frac{2}{5} \text{ is less than } \frac{4}{5} "$$

$$\frac{4}{5} > \frac{1}{5} \text{ means } ``\frac{4}{5} \text{ is greater than } \frac{1}{5} "$$

If fractions to be compared do not have a common denominator, then one or more must be renamed so that all have a common denominator. The preferred common denominator is the least common multiple (LCM) of all the denominators.

To list $\frac{5}{8}, \frac{7}{16}, \frac{1}{2}$, and $\frac{9}{16}$ from the smallest to largest, we write each with a common denominator and then compare the numerators. We note that the LCM of all the denominators is 16. Therefore, we build each fraction so that it has a denominator of 16:

$$\frac{5}{8} = \frac{10}{16} \qquad \frac{7}{16} = \frac{7}{16} \qquad \frac{1}{2} = \frac{8}{16} \qquad \frac{9}{16} = \frac{9}{16} \qquad \text{Each fraction now has a denominator of 16.}$$

We arrange those fractions whose denominator is 16 in order from the smallest to largest:

$$\frac{7}{16} < \frac{8}{16} < \frac{9}{16} < \frac{10}{16} \qquad \text{They are now listed in order from the smallest to largest with a common denominator of 16.}$$

We replace each fraction by the original, so

$$\frac{7}{16} < \frac{1}{2} < \frac{9}{16} < \frac{5}{8} \qquad \text{They are now listed in order from the smallest to largest}$$

▶ **To list fractions from smallest to largest**

1. Build the fractions so that they have a common denominator. Use the LCM of the denominators.
2. List the fractions (with common denominators) with numerators from smallest to largest.
3. Reduce.

Examples F–I   **Warm Ups F–I**

Directions: Tell which fraction is larger.

Strategy: Write the fractions with a common denominator. The fraction with the larger numerator is the larger.

F. $\frac{6}{11}$ or $\frac{1}{2}$ F. $\frac{8}{13}$ or $\frac{3}{5}$

Solution: The LCM of 11 and 2 is 22. Build each fraction so it has 22 for a denominator.

$$\frac{6}{11} = \frac{12}{22} \qquad \text{and} \qquad \frac{1}{2} = \frac{11}{22}$$

$\frac{6}{11}$ is larger $12 > 11$. That is, $\frac{6}{11} > \frac{1}{2}$.

Answer to warm up: **F.** $\frac{8}{13}$

Directions: List the group of fractions from smallest to largest.

Strategy: Build each of the fractions to a common denominator. List the fractions from smallest to largest by the value of the numerator. Reduce to lowest terms.

G. $\dfrac{2}{3}$, $\dfrac{3}{8}$, and $\dfrac{3}{4}$

G. $\dfrac{5}{6}$, $\dfrac{7}{8}$, and $\dfrac{4}{5}$

Solution:

$\dfrac{2}{3} = \dfrac{16}{24}$ $\dfrac{3}{8} = \dfrac{9}{24}$ The LCM of 3, 8, and 4 is 24. Build the fractions to the denominator 24.

$\dfrac{3}{4} = \dfrac{18}{24}$

$\dfrac{9}{24}, \dfrac{16}{24}, \dfrac{18}{24}$ List the fractions in the order of the numerators: $9 < 16 < 18$

The list is $\dfrac{3}{8}$, $\dfrac{2}{3}$, and $\dfrac{3}{4}$.   Reduce.

H. $3\dfrac{1}{2}$, $3\dfrac{5}{6}$, and $3\dfrac{5}{8}$

H. $4\dfrac{3}{5}$, $4\dfrac{4}{9}$, and $4\dfrac{2}{3}$

Solution: Since the whole number part is the same in each mixed number, they can be listed in the order of the fractions.

$3\dfrac{1}{2} = 3\dfrac{12}{24}$ $3\dfrac{5}{6} = 3\dfrac{20}{24}$ The LCM of 2, 6, and 8 is 24. Write with common denominators.

$3\dfrac{5}{8} = 3\dfrac{15}{24}$

$3\dfrac{12}{24}, 3\dfrac{15}{24}, 3\dfrac{20}{24}$ Write the numbers in the order of the numerators, smallest to largest.

The list is $3\dfrac{1}{2}$, $3\dfrac{5}{8}$, and $3\dfrac{5}{6}$.   Reduce.

I. 🌐 The Acme Hardware Store sells bolts with diameters of $\dfrac{5}{16}$, $\dfrac{3}{8}$, $\dfrac{1}{2}$, $\dfrac{5}{8}$, $\dfrac{1}{4}$, and $\dfrac{7}{16}$ inch. List the diameters from smallest to largest.

I. The Acme Hardware Store also sells ''rebar'' with diameters of $\dfrac{3}{4}$, $\dfrac{7}{8}$, $\dfrac{7}{16}$, $\dfrac{15}{32}$, $\dfrac{15}{64}$, and $\dfrac{7}{12}$ inch. List the diameters from smallest to largest.

Solution:

$\dfrac{5}{16} = \dfrac{5}{16}$ $\dfrac{3}{8} = \dfrac{6}{16}$ $\dfrac{1}{2} = \dfrac{8}{16}$

$\dfrac{5}{8} = \dfrac{10}{16}$ $\dfrac{1}{4} = \dfrac{4}{16}$ $\dfrac{7}{16} = \dfrac{7}{16}$ Write each diameter using the common denominator, 16.

---

22. $\dfrac{1}{2}, \dfrac{3}{5}, \dfrac{7}{10}$

$\dfrac{1}{2}, \dfrac{3}{5}, \dfrac{7}{10}$

23. $\dfrac{1}{2}, \dfrac{3}{8}, \dfrac{1}{3}$

$\dfrac{1}{3}, \dfrac{3}{8}, \dfrac{1}{2}$

24. $\dfrac{2}{3}, \dfrac{8}{15}, \dfrac{3}{5}$

$\dfrac{8}{15}, \dfrac{3}{5}, \dfrac{2}{3}$

Are the following statements true or false?

25. $\dfrac{1}{4} < \dfrac{3}{4}$ True   **26.** $\dfrac{5}{9} > \dfrac{7}{9}$ False   **27.** $\dfrac{11}{16} > \dfrac{7}{8}$ False   **28.** $\dfrac{9}{16} < \dfrac{5}{8}$ True

B

Write four fractions equivalent to each of the given fractions by multiplying by $\dfrac{2}{2}, \dfrac{3}{3}, \dfrac{4}{4},$ and $\dfrac{5}{5}$.

29. $\dfrac{4}{10}$ $\dfrac{8}{20}, \dfrac{12}{30}, \dfrac{16}{40}, \dfrac{20}{50}$ **30.** $\dfrac{3}{9}$ $\dfrac{6}{18}, \dfrac{9}{27}, \dfrac{12}{36}, \dfrac{15}{45}$ **31.** $\dfrac{7}{3}$ $\dfrac{14}{6}, \dfrac{21}{9}, \dfrac{28}{12}, \dfrac{35}{15}$ **32.** $\dfrac{6}{5}$ $\dfrac{12}{10}, \dfrac{18}{15}, \dfrac{24}{20}, \dfrac{30}{25}$

Find the missing numerator.

33. $\dfrac{3}{4} = \dfrac{?}{36}$ 27   **34.** $\dfrac{2}{3} = \dfrac{?}{24}$ 16   **35.** $\dfrac{1}{5} = \dfrac{?}{75}$ 15

36. $\dfrac{5}{9} = \dfrac{?}{45}$ 25   **37.** $\dfrac{?}{72} = \dfrac{5}{6}$ 60   **38.** $\dfrac{?}{36} = \dfrac{11}{12}$ 33

Which fraction is larger?

39. $\dfrac{5}{4}, \dfrac{13}{10}$ $\dfrac{13}{10}$ **40.** $\dfrac{5}{3}, \dfrac{3}{2}$ $\dfrac{5}{3}$ **41.** $2\dfrac{3}{8}, 2\dfrac{5}{16}$ $2\dfrac{3}{8}$

42. $5\dfrac{4}{9}, 5\dfrac{3}{7}$ $5\dfrac{4}{9}$ **43.** $\dfrac{5}{11}, \dfrac{3}{9}$ $\dfrac{5}{11}$ **44.** $\dfrac{5}{6}, \dfrac{3}{4}$ $\dfrac{5}{6}$

List these fractions from the smallest to largest.

45. $\dfrac{4}{5}, \dfrac{2}{3}, \dfrac{3}{4}$ $\dfrac{2}{3}, \dfrac{3}{4}, \dfrac{4}{5}$ **46.** $\dfrac{5}{8}, \dfrac{7}{10}, \dfrac{3}{4}$ $\dfrac{5}{8}, \dfrac{7}{10}, \dfrac{3}{4}$ **47.** $\dfrac{13}{15}, \dfrac{4}{5}, \dfrac{5}{6}, \dfrac{9}{10}$ $\dfrac{4}{5}, \dfrac{5}{6}, \dfrac{13}{15}, \dfrac{9}{10}$

NAME _____ _____ CLASS _____ DATE _____

48. $\dfrac{7}{9}, \dfrac{2}{3}, \dfrac{3}{4}, \dfrac{5}{6}$ $\dfrac{2}{3}, \dfrac{3}{4}, \dfrac{7}{9}, \dfrac{5}{6}$

49. $2\dfrac{3}{4}, 2\dfrac{7}{8}, 2\dfrac{5}{6}$ $2\dfrac{3}{4}, 2\dfrac{5}{6}, 2\dfrac{7}{8}$

50. $1\dfrac{3}{8}, 1\dfrac{5}{16}, 1\dfrac{1}{4}$ $1\dfrac{1}{4}, 1\dfrac{5}{16}, 1\dfrac{3}{8}$

Are the following statements true or false?

51. $\dfrac{3}{10} > \dfrac{7}{15}$ False

52. $\dfrac{5}{8} > \dfrac{13}{12}$ False

53. $\dfrac{5}{9} < \dfrac{2}{7}$ False

54. $\dfrac{6}{7} > \dfrac{7}{8}$ False

C

Find the missing numerator.

55. $\dfrac{?}{12} = \dfrac{2}{3}$ 8

56. $\dfrac{?}{66} = \dfrac{3}{11}$ 18

57. $\dfrac{23}{6} = \dfrac{?}{12}$ 46

58. $\dfrac{9}{5} = \dfrac{?}{100}$ 180

59. $\dfrac{?}{300} = \dfrac{7}{15}$ 140

60. $\dfrac{6}{9} = \dfrac{?}{108}$ 72

61. $\dfrac{?}{126} = \dfrac{19}{42}$ 57

62. $\dfrac{?}{147} = \dfrac{16}{7}$ 336

63. $\dfrac{15}{18} = \dfrac{?}{144}$ 120

64. $\dfrac{11}{16} = \dfrac{?}{144}$ 99

65. Find the LCM of the denominators of $\dfrac{1}{2}, \dfrac{2}{3}, \dfrac{1}{6}$, and $\dfrac{5}{8}$. Build the four fractions so that each has the LCM as the denominator.
LCM = 24; $\dfrac{12}{24}, \dfrac{16}{24}, \dfrac{4}{24}, \dfrac{15}{24}$

66. Find the LCM of the denominators of $\dfrac{1}{4}, \dfrac{4}{13}$, and $\dfrac{5}{26}$. Build the fractions so that each has the LCM as the denominator.
LCM = 52; $\dfrac{13}{52}, \dfrac{16}{52}, \dfrac{10}{52}$

List these fractions from smallest to largest.

67. $\dfrac{11}{24}, \dfrac{17}{36}, \dfrac{35}{72}$
$\dfrac{11}{24}, \dfrac{17}{36}, \dfrac{35}{72}$

68. $\dfrac{3}{5}, \dfrac{8}{25}, \dfrac{31}{50}, \dfrac{59}{100}$
$\dfrac{8}{25}, \dfrac{59}{100}, \dfrac{3}{5}, \dfrac{31}{50}$

69. $\dfrac{13}{28}, \dfrac{17}{35}, \dfrac{6}{14}$
$\dfrac{6}{14}, \dfrac{13}{28}, \dfrac{17}{35}$

70. $\dfrac{11}{15}, \dfrac{17}{20}, \dfrac{9}{12}$
$\dfrac{11}{15}, \dfrac{9}{12}, \dfrac{17}{20}$

71. $\dfrac{7}{18}, \dfrac{2}{5}, \dfrac{11}{30}, \dfrac{17}{45}$

$\dfrac{11}{30}, \dfrac{17}{45}, \dfrac{7}{18}, \dfrac{2}{5}$

72. $\dfrac{47}{80}, \dfrac{9}{16}, \dfrac{13}{20}, \dfrac{5}{8}$

$\dfrac{9}{16}, \dfrac{47}{80}, \dfrac{5}{8}, \dfrac{13}{20}$

73. $\dfrac{29}{30}, \dfrac{14}{15}, \dfrac{19}{20}, \dfrac{11}{12}$

$\dfrac{11}{12}, \dfrac{14}{15}, \dfrac{19}{20}, \dfrac{29}{30}$

74. $\dfrac{7}{8}, \dfrac{1}{2}, \dfrac{2}{3}, \dfrac{5}{6}$

$\dfrac{1}{2}, \dfrac{2}{3}, \dfrac{5}{6}, \dfrac{7}{8}$

Are the following statements true or false?

75. $\dfrac{5}{8} < \dfrac{47}{80}$ False

76. $\dfrac{8}{25} < \dfrac{59}{100}$ True

77. $\dfrac{15}{20} < \dfrac{55}{75}$ False

78. $\dfrac{19}{40} > \dfrac{31}{60}$ False

79. $\dfrac{11}{30} < \dfrac{7}{18}$ True

80. $\dfrac{11}{27} > \dfrac{29}{36}$ False

Applications

81. Janie answers $\dfrac{4}{5}$ of the problems correctly on her Chapter I test. If there are 40 problems on the Chapter III test, how many must she get correct to answer the same fractional amount?   32 problems

82. Five of every eight packages of gum sold at the Maxi-Mart are bubble gum. At that rate, how many packages of bubble gum are sold if a total of 136 packages of gum are sold?   85 packages

83. The night nurse at Malcolm X Community Hospital finds bottles containing codeine tablets out of the usual order. The bottles contain tablets having the following strengths of codeine: $\dfrac{1}{8}, \dfrac{3}{32},$ $\dfrac{5}{16}, \dfrac{3}{8}, \dfrac{9}{16}, \dfrac{1}{2},$ and $\dfrac{1}{4}$ grain, respectively. Arrange the bottles in order of the strength of codeine from the smallest to largest.

$\dfrac{3}{32}, \dfrac{1}{8}, \dfrac{1}{4}, \dfrac{5}{16}, \dfrac{3}{8}, \dfrac{1}{2}, \dfrac{9}{16}$

84. Joe, an apprentice, is given the task of sorting a bin of bolts according to their diameters. The bolts have the following diameters: $\dfrac{11}{16}, \dfrac{7}{8}, 1\dfrac{1}{16}, \dfrac{3}{4},$ $1\dfrac{1}{8},$ and $1\dfrac{3}{32}$ inches. How should he list the diameters from the smallest to largest?

$\dfrac{11}{16}, \dfrac{3}{4}, \dfrac{7}{8}, 1\dfrac{1}{16}, 1\dfrac{3}{32}, 1\dfrac{1}{8}$

85. Four pickup trucks are advertised in the local car ads. The load capacities listed are $\dfrac{3}{4}$ ton, $\dfrac{5}{8}$ ton, $\dfrac{7}{16}$ ton, and $\dfrac{1}{2}$ ton. Which capacity is the smallest and which is the largest?

largest: $\dfrac{3}{4}$ ton; smallest: $\dfrac{7}{16}$ ton

86. A container of a chemical is weighed by three people. Mary records the weight as $3\dfrac{1}{8}$ lb. George reads the weight as $3\dfrac{3}{16}$ lb. Chang reads the weight as $3\dfrac{1}{4}$ lb. Whose measurement is heaviest?

Chang's

NAME _____ CLASS _____ DATE _____

87. Three rulers are marked in inches. On the first ruler the spaces are divided into tenths, on the second they are divided into sixteenths, and on the third they are divided into eighths. All are used to measure a line on a scale drawing. The nearest mark on the first ruler is $5\frac{7}{10}$, the nearest mark on the second is $5\frac{11}{16}$, and the nearest mark on the third is $5\frac{6}{8}$. Which is the largest (longest) measurement? $5\frac{6}{8}$ inches

88. Four National Forest plots are analyzed for the amount of old growth trees. The first plot has $\frac{34}{55}$ old growth, plot two has $\frac{47}{70}$ old growth, plot three has $\frac{53}{77}$ old growth, and the fourth plot has $\frac{15}{22}$ old growth. List the plots, by name, from the least amount of old growth to the most old growth.   Plots 1, 2, 4, 3

89. Three fourths of a serving of Tostie-Os is fiber. How many ounces of fiber are there in 120 ounces of Tostie-Os?   90 ounces

90. During one week on her diet, Samantha ate five servings of chicken, each containing $\frac{3}{16}$ ounce of fat. During the same period her brother ate four servings of beef, each containing $\frac{6}{25}$ ounce of fat. Who ate the greatest amount of fat from these entrees?   Her brother

State Your Understanding

91. State the difference between reducing and building fractions.

92. Why is it important to build fractions to the same denominator to find out which is larger?

Challenge

93. List $\frac{12}{25}, \frac{14}{29}, \frac{29}{60}, \frac{35}{71}, \frac{39}{81}$, and $\frac{43}{98}$ from smallest to largest.

$\frac{43}{98}, \frac{12}{25}, \frac{39}{81}, \frac{14}{29}, \frac{29}{60}, \frac{35}{71}$

94. Build $\frac{5}{7}$ so that it has denominators of 70, 91, 161, 784, and 4067.

$\frac{50}{70}, \frac{65}{91}, \frac{115}{161}, \frac{560}{784}, \frac{2905}{4067}$

95. Fernando and Filipe are hired to sell tickets for the holiday raffle. Fernando sells $\frac{14}{17}$ of his quota of 765 tickets. Filipe sells $\frac{19}{23}$ of his quota of 759 tickets. Who sells the most of his quota? Who sells the most tickets?   Filipe; Fernando

Group Activity

96. We saw that $\frac{2}{5}$ was less than $\frac{4}{5}$ by looking at a rectangle representing each fraction. Show the sum, $\frac{2}{5} + \frac{4}{5}$, visually using a rectangle divided into five parts. Similarly, show $\frac{2}{7} + \frac{3}{7}$.

Maintain Your Skills (Sections 1.2, 1.3, 1.8, 2.3, 2.4, 2.6, 3.1, 3.2)

97. Find the sum of 3796, 43, 296, 4099, and 5310.
13,544

98. Is 611 a prime or a composite number?
Composite

99. List all the factors of 996.
1, 2, 3, 4, 6, 12, 83, 166, 249, 332, 498, 996

100. Round 65,458,999 to the nearest ten thousand.
65,460,000

101. Find the LCM of 25, 35, 45, and 63.   1575

102. Reduce $\frac{812}{928}$ to lowest terms. $\frac{7}{8}$

103. Change $27\frac{5}{8}$ to an improper fraction. $\frac{221}{8}$

104. Change $\frac{217}{12}$ to a mixed number. $18\frac{1}{12}$

105. The Forest Service rents a two-engine plane at $625 per hour and a single-engine plane at $365 per hour to drop fire retardant. During a forest fire, the two-engine plane was used for four hours and the single-engine plane was used for two hours. What was the cost of using the two planes?
$3230

106. Ms. Wallington is taking one capsule containing 250 mg of a drug every eight hours. Beginning next Wednesday her doctor's instructions are to increase the dosage to 500 mg every six hours. How many 250-mg capsules should the pharmacist give her for the following week (seven days)?
56 capsules

3.6   ADDING FRACTIONS

Objectives

  1   Add like fractions.

  2   Add unlike fractions.

Application

Sheila Fankowski is assembling a composting bin for her lawn and garden debris. She needs a bolt that will reach through a $\frac{1}{32}$-inch thick washer, a $\frac{3}{16}$-inch thick plastic bushing, a $\frac{3}{4}$-inch piece of steel tubing, a second $\frac{1}{32}$-inch thick washer, and a $\frac{1}{4}$-inch thick nut. How long a bolt does she need?

Vocabulary

Like fractions are fractions with common denominators. **Unlike fractions** are fractions with different denominators.

How and Why 1

What is the sum of $\frac{1}{5} + \frac{2}{5}$? The denominators tell the number of parts in the unit. The numerator tells us how many of these parts are shaded. By adding the numerators we find the total number of shaded parts. The common denominator keeps track of the size of the parts. (See Fig. 3.10.)

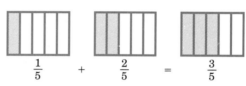

$$\frac{1}{5} \qquad + \qquad \frac{2}{5} \qquad = \qquad \frac{3}{5}$$

Figure 3.10

▶ **To add like fractions**

1. Add the numerators.
2. Write the sum over the common denominator.

Examples A–D   **Warm Ups A–D**

Directions: Add and reduce.

Strategy: Add the numerators and retain the common denominator. Reduce to lowest terms.

A. $\dfrac{3}{7} + \dfrac{2}{7}$ A. $\dfrac{4}{9} + \dfrac{3}{9}$

Solution:

$$\frac{3}{7} + \frac{2}{7} = \frac{5}{7} \qquad \text{Add.}$$

Answer to warm up: **A.** $\dfrac{7}{9}$

B. $\dfrac{1}{3} + \dfrac{2}{3} + \dfrac{1}{3}$

Solution:

$$\dfrac{1}{3} + \dfrac{2}{3} + \dfrac{1}{3} = \dfrac{4}{3} \qquad \text{Add.}$$

B. $\dfrac{1}{6} + \dfrac{5}{6} + \dfrac{5}{6}$

C. $\dfrac{2}{6} + \dfrac{1}{6} + \dfrac{1}{6}$

Solution:

$$\dfrac{2}{6} + \dfrac{1}{6} + \dfrac{1}{6} = \dfrac{4}{6} = \dfrac{2}{3} \qquad \text{Add and reduce.}$$

C. $\dfrac{3}{10} + \dfrac{2}{10} + \dfrac{1}{10}$

D. The stock of the Wesin Corporation rose $\dfrac{1}{8}$ point on Monday, $\dfrac{3}{8}$ point on Tuesday, $\dfrac{1}{8}$ point on Wednesday, $\dfrac{5}{8}$ point on Thursday, and $\dfrac{5}{8}$ point on Friday. What was the total rise of the stock for the week?

Solution: To find the total gain, add the gains for each day.

$$\dfrac{1}{8} + \dfrac{3}{8} + \dfrac{1}{8} + \dfrac{5}{8} + \dfrac{5}{8} = \dfrac{15}{8} \qquad \text{Add the gains.}$$

$$= 1\dfrac{7}{8} \qquad \text{Write as a mixed number.}$$

The stock rose $1\dfrac{7}{8}$ points during the week.

D. The previous week the Wesin Corporation stock rose $\dfrac{1}{8}$ point on Monday, $\dfrac{7}{8}$ point on Tuesday, $\dfrac{1}{8}$ point on Wednesday, $\dfrac{3}{8}$ point on Thursday, and $\dfrac{1}{8}$ point on Friday. What was the total rise of the stock for the week?

How and Why   2   The sum $\dfrac{1}{2} + \dfrac{1}{5}$ cannot be worked in this form. A look at Figure 3.11 shows that the parts are not the same size.

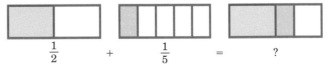

$$\dfrac{1}{2} \qquad + \qquad \dfrac{1}{5} \qquad = \qquad ?$$

Figure 3.11

To add, rename $\dfrac{1}{2}$ and $\dfrac{1}{5}$ as like fractions. The LCM (least common multiple) of the two denominators serves as the least common denominator. The LCM of 2 and 5 is 10. We can now write

$$\dfrac{1}{2} = \left(\dfrac{1}{2}\right)\left(\dfrac{5}{5}\right) = \dfrac{5}{10} \qquad \text{and} \qquad \dfrac{1}{5} = \left(\dfrac{1}{5}\right)\left(\dfrac{2}{2}\right) = \dfrac{2}{10}$$

Answers to warm ups: **B.** $\dfrac{11}{6}$ or $1\dfrac{5}{6}$ **C.** $\dfrac{3}{5}$ **D.** $\dfrac{13}{8}$ or $1\dfrac{5}{8}$

and the problem can now be seen in Figure 3.12:

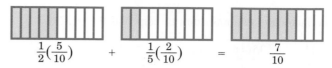

$$\frac{1}{2}\left(\frac{5}{10}\right) \quad + \quad \frac{1}{5}\left(\frac{2}{10}\right) \quad = \quad \frac{7}{10}$$

Figure 3.12

▶ **To add unlike fractions**

1. Build the fractions so that they have a common denominator.
2. Add and reduce.

Examples E–J   **Warm Ups E–J**

Directions: Add and reduce.

Strategy: Build each of the fractions to a common denominator.

E. $\dfrac{3}{8} + \dfrac{1}{4}$ **E.** $\dfrac{2}{3} + \dfrac{1}{6}$

Solution:

$$\frac{3}{8} + \frac{1}{4} = \frac{3}{8} + \frac{2}{8} \qquad \text{The LCM of 8 and 4 is 8.}$$

$$= \frac{5}{8} \qquad \text{Add.}$$

F. $\dfrac{5}{12} + \dfrac{2}{9}$ **F.** $\dfrac{5}{8} + \dfrac{1}{6}$

Solution:

$$\frac{5}{12} + \frac{2}{9} = \frac{15}{36} + \frac{8}{36} \qquad \text{The LCM of 12 and 9 is 36.}$$
$$\frac{5}{12} \cdot \frac{3}{3} = \frac{15}{36} \qquad \frac{2}{9} \cdot \frac{4}{4} = \frac{8}{36}$$

$$= \frac{23}{36} \qquad \text{Add.}$$

G. $\dfrac{1}{6} + \dfrac{7}{10}$ **G.** $\dfrac{2}{3} + \dfrac{1}{12}$

Solution:

$$\frac{1}{6} + \frac{7}{10} = \frac{5}{30} + \frac{21}{30} \qquad \text{The LCM of 6 and 10 is 30.}$$

$$= \frac{26}{30} \qquad \text{Add.}$$

$$= \frac{13}{15} \qquad \text{Reduce.}$$

Answers to warm ups: **E.** $\dfrac{5}{6}$ **F.** $\dfrac{19}{24}$ **G.** $\dfrac{3}{4}$

H. $\dfrac{11}{96} + \dfrac{35}{72}$

H. $\dfrac{13}{45} + \dfrac{28}{75}$

Solution: Prime factor the denominators to help find their LCM.

$$\dfrac{11}{96} + \dfrac{35}{72} = \dfrac{11(3)}{288} + \dfrac{35(4)}{288} \qquad 96 = 2^5 \cdot 3, \; 72 = 2^3 \cdot 3^2$$

$$\qquad\qquad\qquad\qquad\qquad LCM = 2^5 \cdot 3^2 = 288$$

$$= \dfrac{33}{288} + \dfrac{140}{288}$$

$$= \dfrac{173}{288} \qquad\qquad \text{Add.}$$

I. 🖩 $\dfrac{15}{84} + \dfrac{37}{60}$

I. $\dfrac{13}{28} + \dfrac{14}{35}$

Solution:

ENTER	15	$a^{b/c}$	84	+
DISPLAY	15.	15⌐. 15⌐84. 5⌐28.		
ENTER	37	$a^{b/c}$	60	=
DISPLAY	37.	37⌐. 37⌐60. 167⌐210.		

So $\dfrac{15}{84} + \dfrac{37}{60} = \dfrac{167}{210}$.

J. 🌐 Sheila Fankowski is assembling a composting bin for her lawn and garden debris. She needs a bolt that will reach through a $\dfrac{1}{32}$-inch thick washer, a $\dfrac{3}{16}$-inch thick plastic bushing, a $\dfrac{3}{4}$-inch piece of steel tubing, a second $\dfrac{1}{32}$-inch thick washer, and a $\dfrac{1}{4}$-inch thick nut. How long a bolt does she need?

J. A nail must reach through three thicknesses of wood and penetrate the fourth thickness $\dfrac{1}{4}$ inch. If the first piece of wood is $\dfrac{5}{16}$ inch, the second is $\dfrac{3}{8}$ inch, and the third is $\dfrac{9}{16}$ inch, how long must the nail be?

Solution: Add the thicknesses of each part together to find the length needed.

$\dfrac{1}{32} + \dfrac{3}{16} + \dfrac{3}{4} + \dfrac{1}{32} + \dfrac{1}{4}$ \qquad The LCM of 32, 16, and 4 is 32.

$\dfrac{1}{32} + \dfrac{6}{32} + \dfrac{24}{32} + \dfrac{1}{32} + \dfrac{8}{32}$ \qquad Build each fraction to the denominator, 32

$= \dfrac{40}{32}$ \qquad\qquad Add.

$\dfrac{5}{4} = 1\dfrac{1}{4}$ \qquad\qquad Reduce and write as a mixed number.

The bolt must be $1\dfrac{1}{4}$ inches long.

Answers to warm ups: **H.** $\dfrac{149}{225}$ **I.** $\dfrac{121}{140}$ **J.** $1\dfrac{1}{2}$ inches

NAME _____ CLASS _____ DATE _____

EXERCISES 3.6

A

Add and reduce.

1. $\dfrac{4}{11} + \dfrac{5}{11}$ $\dfrac{9}{11}$

2. $\dfrac{5}{12} + \dfrac{2}{12}$ $\dfrac{7}{12}$

3. $\dfrac{1}{9} + \dfrac{4}{9} + \dfrac{1}{9}$ $\dfrac{2}{3}$

4. $\dfrac{3}{8} + \dfrac{1}{8} + \dfrac{2}{8}$ $\dfrac{3}{4}$

5. $\dfrac{3}{4} + \dfrac{5}{4}$ 2

6. $\dfrac{5}{7} + \dfrac{9}{7}$ 2

7. $\dfrac{3}{10} + \dfrac{4}{10} + \dfrac{1}{10}$ $\dfrac{4}{5}$

8. $\dfrac{5}{12} + \dfrac{4}{12} + \dfrac{1}{12}$ $\dfrac{5}{6}$

9. $\dfrac{3}{13} + \dfrac{6}{13} + \dfrac{1}{13}$ $\dfrac{10}{13}$

10. $\dfrac{5}{11} + \dfrac{2}{11} + \dfrac{1}{11}$ $\dfrac{8}{11}$

11. $\dfrac{4}{12} + \dfrac{3}{12} + \dfrac{8}{12}$ $1\dfrac{1}{4}$

12. $\dfrac{7}{16} + \dfrac{8}{16} + \dfrac{5}{16}$ $1\dfrac{1}{4}$

13. $\dfrac{1}{6} + \dfrac{3}{8}$ $\dfrac{13}{24}$

14. $\dfrac{2}{3} + \dfrac{1}{6}$ $\dfrac{5}{6}$

15. $\dfrac{1}{8} + \dfrac{7}{24}$ $\dfrac{5}{12}$

16. $\dfrac{7}{15} + \dfrac{1}{3}$ $\dfrac{4}{5}$

17. $\dfrac{5}{16} + \dfrac{5}{8}$ $\dfrac{15}{16}$

18. $\dfrac{4}{9} + \dfrac{5}{18}$ $\dfrac{13}{18}$

19. $\dfrac{1}{3} + \dfrac{1}{5} + \dfrac{1}{10}$ $\dfrac{19}{30}$

20. $\dfrac{1}{4} + \dfrac{2}{5} + \dfrac{3}{20}$ $\dfrac{4}{5}$

21. $\dfrac{2}{5} + \dfrac{3}{10}$ $\dfrac{7}{10}$

22. $\dfrac{4}{15} + \dfrac{3}{5}$ $\dfrac{13}{15}$

B

23. $\dfrac{3}{16} + \dfrac{3}{16} + \dfrac{2}{16}$ $\dfrac{1}{2}$

24. $\dfrac{7}{32} + \dfrac{8}{32} + \dfrac{5}{32}$ $\dfrac{5}{8}$

25. $\dfrac{5}{48} + \dfrac{7}{48} + \dfrac{3}{48}$ $\dfrac{5}{16}$

26. $\dfrac{3}{16} + \dfrac{2}{16} + \dfrac{5}{16}$ $\dfrac{5}{8}$

27. $\dfrac{8}{30} + \dfrac{9}{30} + \dfrac{1}{30}$ $\dfrac{3}{5}$

28. $\dfrac{13}{50} + \dfrac{7}{50} + \dfrac{2}{50}$ $\dfrac{11}{25}$

29. $\dfrac{5}{24} + \dfrac{7}{24} + \dfrac{9}{24}$ $\dfrac{7}{8}$

30. $\dfrac{3}{20} + \dfrac{9}{20} + \dfrac{3}{20}$ $\dfrac{3}{4}$

31. $\dfrac{3}{35} + \dfrac{8}{21}$ $\dfrac{7}{15}$

32. $\dfrac{9}{14} + \dfrac{5}{21}$ $\dfrac{37}{42}$

33. $\dfrac{3}{10} + \dfrac{9}{20} + \dfrac{11}{30}$ $1\dfrac{7}{60}$

34. $\dfrac{7}{8} + \dfrac{7}{12} + \dfrac{1}{6}$ $1\dfrac{5}{8}$

71. Chef Ramon prepares a punch for the stockholders' meeting of the Northern Corporation. The punch calls for $\frac{1}{4}$ gallon lemon juice, $\frac{3}{4}$ gallon raspberry juice, $\frac{2}{4}$ gallon cranberry juice, $\frac{1}{4}$ gallon lime juice, $\frac{5}{4}$ gallon 7-Up, and $\frac{3}{4}$ gallon vodka. How many gallons of punch does the recipe make? $3\frac{3}{4}$ gallons

72. A physical therapist prescribes that Belinda swim $\frac{5}{16}$ mile on Monday and increase the distance by $\frac{1}{16}$ mile each day from Tuesday through Friday. How much total swimming was prescribed for the five days? $2\frac{3}{16}$ miles

73. In order to make a certain project, Charles needs $\frac{1}{10}$ inch of foam, $\frac{3}{10}$ inch of metal, $\frac{4}{10}$ inch of wood, and $\frac{7}{10}$ inch of fabric. What will be the total thickness of this project when these materials are piled up? $1\frac{1}{2}$ inches

74. Jonnie Lee Simms is assembling a rocking horse for his granddaughter. He needs a bolt to reach through a $\frac{7}{8}$-inch piece of steel tubing, a $\frac{1}{16}$-inch bushing, a $\frac{1}{2}$-inch piece of tubing, a $\frac{1}{8}$-inch thick washer, and a $\frac{1}{4}$-inch thick nut. How long a bolt does he need? $1\frac{13}{16}$ inches

75. On the American Stock Exchange, Joan's stock rose $\frac{1}{8}$ point the first hour and an additional $\frac{3}{16}$ point during the remainder of the day. What was the total rise for the day? $\frac{5}{16}$ point

76. What is the total distance (perimeter) around this triangle? $1\frac{11}{12}$ yd

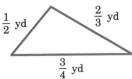

$\frac{1}{2}$ yd $\frac{2}{3}$ yd

$\frac{3}{4}$ yd

NAME _____ CLASS _____ DATE _____

77. Find the length of this pin: $\frac{3}{4}$ in.

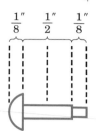

$\frac{1''}{8}$ $\frac{1''}{2}$ $\frac{1''}{8}$

78. An elephant-ear bamboo grew $\frac{1}{2}$ inch on Tuesday, $\frac{3}{8}$ inch on Wednesday, and $\frac{1}{4}$ inch on Thursday. How much did it grow in the three days?

$1\frac{1}{8}$ inches

79. The Chico family spends $\frac{2}{15}$ of their income on rent, $\frac{1}{4}$ on food, $\frac{1}{20}$ on clothes, $\frac{1}{10}$ on transportation, and $\frac{5}{24}$ on taxes. What fraction of their income is spent on these costs?

$\frac{89}{120}$ of income

80. Find the length of the rod in the figure. Assume that the grooves and teeth are uniform in length.

$\frac{7''}{8}$ $\frac{3''}{16}$ $\frac{1''}{8}$ $\frac{3''}{4}$

$3\frac{3}{8}$ inches

81. An electronics mogul leaves $\frac{2}{9}$, $\frac{1}{5}$, and $\frac{4}{15}$ shares of her estate to her three children. What share of the estate will the children receive? $\frac{31}{45}$ share

State Your Understanding

82. Explain why $\frac{1}{2} + \frac{2}{5}$ is not equal to $\frac{3}{7}$.

83. Why is it important to write fractions with a common denominator before adding?

▶ **To subtract fractions**

1. Build each fraction to a common denominator.
2. Subtract the numerators and write the difference over the common denominator.
3. Reduce, if possible.

Examples A–F

Warm Ups A–F

Directions: Subtract and reduce.

Strategy: Build each fraction to a common denominator.

A. $\dfrac{11}{20} - \dfrac{5}{20}$

A. $\dfrac{15}{16} - \dfrac{11}{16}$

Solution:

$$\dfrac{11}{20} - \dfrac{5}{20} = \dfrac{6}{20} \qquad \text{Subtract the numerators.}$$
$$= \dfrac{3}{10} \qquad \text{Reduce.}$$

B. $\dfrac{7}{8} - \dfrac{2}{3}$

B. $\dfrac{11}{12} - \dfrac{4}{5}$

Solution:

$$\dfrac{7}{8} - \dfrac{2}{3} = \dfrac{21}{24} - \dfrac{16}{24} \qquad \text{The LCM of 8 and 3 is 24.}$$
$$= \dfrac{5}{24} \qquad \text{Subtract the numerators.}$$

C. $\dfrac{7}{15} - \dfrac{1}{4}$

C. $\dfrac{15}{32} - \dfrac{1}{3}$

Solution:

$$\dfrac{7}{15} - \dfrac{1}{4} = \dfrac{28}{60} - \dfrac{15}{60} \qquad \text{The LCM of 15 and 4 is 60.}$$
$$= \dfrac{13}{60} \qquad \text{Subtract the numerators.}$$

Answers to warm ups: **A.** $\dfrac{1}{4}$ **B.** $\dfrac{7}{60}$ **C.** $\dfrac{13}{96}$

D. $\dfrac{25}{48} - \dfrac{13}{80}$

D. $\dfrac{71}{72} - \dfrac{31}{90}$

Solution:

$$\dfrac{25}{48} - \dfrac{13}{80} = \dfrac{125}{240} - \dfrac{39}{240} \qquad \text{The LCM of 48 and 80 is 240.}$$

$$= \dfrac{86}{240} \qquad \text{Subtract the numerators.}$$

$$= \dfrac{43}{120} \qquad \text{Reduce.}$$

E. $\dfrac{39}{50} - \dfrac{8}{15}$

E. $\dfrac{43}{48} - \dfrac{23}{32}$

Solution:

ENTER	39	$a^{b/c}$	50		$-$	
DISPLAY	39.	39⌐.	39⌐50.	39⌐50.		
ENTER	8	$a^{b/c}$	15		$=$	
DISPLAY	8.	8⌐.	8⌐15.	37⌐150.		

So $\dfrac{39}{50} - \dfrac{8}{15} = \dfrac{37}{150}$.

F. Lumber mill operators must plan for the shrinkage of "green" (wet) boards when they cut logs. If the shrinkage for a $\dfrac{5}{8}$-inch thick board is expected to be $\dfrac{1}{16}$ inch, what will be the thickness of the dried board?

Solution: To find the thickness of the dried board, subtract the shrinkage from the thickness of the green board.

$$\dfrac{5}{8} - \dfrac{1}{16} = \dfrac{10}{16} - \dfrac{1}{16} \qquad \text{Build } \dfrac{5}{8} \text{ to have a denominator of 16.}$$

$$= \dfrac{9}{16}$$

The dried board will be $\dfrac{9}{16}$ inch thick.

F. Mike must plane $\dfrac{3}{32}$ inch from the thickness of a board. If the board is now $\dfrac{3}{8}$ inch thick, how thick will it be after he has planed it?

Answers to warm ups: **D.** $\dfrac{77}{120}$ **E.** $\dfrac{17}{96}$ **F.** $\dfrac{9}{32}$ inch

CAUTION

Do not write $\dfrac{18}{20}$. If we "borrow" 1 from 8, we must add 1 $\left(\dfrac{20}{20}\right)$ to $\dfrac{8}{20}$.

The example can now be completed.

$$8\dfrac{2}{5} = 8\dfrac{8}{20} = 7\dfrac{28}{20} \qquad \text{Rename by ''borrowing'' 1.}$$

$$3\dfrac{3}{4} = 3\dfrac{15}{20} = 3\dfrac{15}{20}$$

$$= 4\dfrac{13}{20} \qquad \text{Subtract.}$$

▶ **To subtract two mixed numbers**

1. Build the fractions to a common denominator.
2. Subtract the fractions. If the fractions cannot be subtracted, rename the first mixed number by "borrowing" 1 from the whole-number part and adding it to the fraction part, and then subtract the fractions.
3. Subtract the whole numbers.
4. Reduce, if possible.

Examples A–H | **Warm Ups A–H**

Directions: Subtract. Write as a mixed number.

Strategy: Subtract the fractions and subtract the whole numbers. If necessary borrow. Reduce.

A. $47\dfrac{5}{8} - 36\dfrac{3}{7}$

A. $48\dfrac{5}{9} - 22\dfrac{2}{5}$

Solution: Write the mixed numbers in columns to group the whole numbers and to group the fractions.

$$47\dfrac{5}{8} = 47\dfrac{35}{56} \qquad \text{Build the fractions to the common denominator, 56.}$$

$$36\dfrac{3}{7} = 36\dfrac{24}{56}$$

$$= 11\dfrac{11}{56} \qquad \text{Subtract.}$$

B. $13\dfrac{2}{3} - 8$

B. $21\dfrac{5}{8} - 17$

Solution:

$$13\dfrac{2}{3} - 8 = 5\dfrac{2}{3} \qquad \text{Subtract the whole numbers.}$$

Answers to warm ups: **A.** $26\dfrac{7}{45}$ **B.** $4\dfrac{5}{8}$

C. $19\dfrac{11}{30} - 12\dfrac{1}{5}$

C. $32\dfrac{17}{40} - 27\dfrac{1}{8}$

Solution:

$$19\dfrac{11}{30} = 19\dfrac{11}{30}$$

Write in columns and build $\dfrac{1}{5}$ to a denominator of 30.

$$12\dfrac{1}{5} = 12\dfrac{6}{30}$$

$$= 7\dfrac{5}{30} = 7\dfrac{1}{6}$$

Subtract and reduce.

D. $15\dfrac{5}{12} - 7\dfrac{7}{12}$

D. $18\dfrac{11}{15} - 8\dfrac{12}{15}$

Solution: Since $\dfrac{7}{12}$ cannot be subtracted from $\dfrac{5}{12}$, we will need to borrow.

$$15\dfrac{5}{12} = 14 + 1\dfrac{5}{12} = 14\dfrac{17}{12}$$

Borrow 1 from 15 and then change the mixed number to an improper fraction.

$$7\dfrac{7}{12} \qquad\quad = 7\dfrac{7}{12}$$

$$= 7\dfrac{10}{12}$$

Subtract.

$$= 7\dfrac{5}{6}$$

Reduce.

E. $43\dfrac{7}{12} - 21\dfrac{11}{15}$

E. $47\dfrac{3}{8} - 32\dfrac{14}{15}$

Solution:

$$43\dfrac{7}{12} = 43\dfrac{35}{60} = 42 + 1\dfrac{35}{60} = 42\dfrac{95}{60}$$

The LCM of 12 and 15 is 60.

$$21\dfrac{11}{15} = 21\dfrac{44}{60} \qquad\qquad = 21\dfrac{44}{60}$$

Borrow 1 from 43 and then change the mixed number to an improper fraction.

$$= 21\dfrac{51}{60}$$

Subtract.

$$= 21\dfrac{17}{20}$$

Reduce.

F. $11 - 2\dfrac{5}{9}$

F. $33 - 11\dfrac{5}{7}$

Solution: The whole number, 11, must be written as a mixed number so we can subtract the fraction. We may think of the mixed number as $11\dfrac{0}{9}$ in order to get a common denominator for the improper fraction. Or think: $11 = 10 + 1 = 10 + \dfrac{9}{9} = 10\dfrac{9}{9}$.

Answers to warm ups: **C.** $5\dfrac{3}{10}$ **D.** $9\dfrac{14}{15}$ **E.** $14\dfrac{53}{120}$

23. $76\dfrac{7}{15}$

$50\dfrac{1}{12}$

$26\dfrac{23}{60}$

24. $9\dfrac{9}{16}$

$3\dfrac{5}{12}$

$6\dfrac{7}{48}$

25. $37\dfrac{2}{3}$

$15\dfrac{11}{12}$

$21\dfrac{3}{4}$

26. $28\dfrac{1}{3}$

$15\dfrac{7}{9}$

$12\dfrac{5}{9}$

27. $30\dfrac{7}{16}$

$22\dfrac{5}{6}$

$7\dfrac{29}{48}$

28. $33\dfrac{17}{30}$

$25\dfrac{7}{9}$

$7\dfrac{71}{90}$

29. 45

$16\dfrac{2}{3}$

$28\dfrac{1}{3}$

30. 76

$26\dfrac{2}{3}$

$49\dfrac{1}{3}$

31. $5\dfrac{31}{32}$

$3\dfrac{}{16}$

$5\dfrac{25}{32}$

32. $8\dfrac{11}{20}$

$9\dfrac{}{10}$

$7\dfrac{13}{20}$

33. $7\dfrac{13}{18}$

$5\dfrac{}{12}$

$7\dfrac{11}{36}$

34. $9\dfrac{1}{6}$

$5\dfrac{}{8}$

$8\dfrac{13}{24}$

35. $43\dfrac{5}{6}$

21

$22\dfrac{5}{6}$

36. $48\dfrac{6}{11}$

17

$31\dfrac{6}{11}$

37. $64\dfrac{13}{15}$

$28\dfrac{29}{40}$

$36\dfrac{17}{120}$

38. $70\dfrac{11}{18}$

$58\dfrac{41}{45}$

$11\dfrac{7}{10}$

39. $75\dfrac{7}{12} - 47\dfrac{13}{18}$ $27\dfrac{31}{36}$ **40.** $82\dfrac{4}{15} - 56\dfrac{7}{12}$ $25\dfrac{41}{60}$

C

41. $34\dfrac{2}{39}$

$7\dfrac{21}{26}$

$26\dfrac{19}{78}$

42. $18\dfrac{5}{24}$

$11\dfrac{3}{40}$

$7\dfrac{2}{15}$

43. $25\dfrac{7}{12}$

$14\dfrac{11}{15}$

$10\dfrac{17}{20}$

44. $37\dfrac{2}{9}$

$18\dfrac{7}{12}$

$18\dfrac{23}{36}$

45. $125\dfrac{31}{36}$

$30\dfrac{17}{24}$

$95\dfrac{11}{72}$

46. $47\dfrac{8}{15}$

$29\dfrac{7}{20}$

$18\dfrac{11}{60}$

47. $143\dfrac{19}{24}$

$58\dfrac{7}{16}$

$85\dfrac{17}{48}$

48. $178\dfrac{11}{15}$

$97\dfrac{5}{9}$

$81\dfrac{8}{45}$

NAME _____   CLASS _____   DATE _____

49. $17\dfrac{1}{2}$

$9\dfrac{5}{18}$

$8\dfrac{2}{9}$

50. $22\dfrac{1}{8}$

$19\dfrac{3}{5}$

$2\dfrac{21}{40}$

51. $28 - 4\dfrac{8}{9}$ $23\dfrac{1}{9}$

52. $17 - 3\dfrac{7}{15}$ $13\dfrac{8}{15}$

53. $6\dfrac{1}{3} - 5\dfrac{5}{6}$ $\dfrac{1}{2}$

54. $3\dfrac{11}{15} - 2\dfrac{9}{10}$ $\dfrac{5}{6}$

55. 16

$14\dfrac{17}{20}$

$1\dfrac{3}{20}$

56. 41

$29\dfrac{17}{36}$

$11\dfrac{19}{36}$

57. $47\dfrac{24}{35} - 19$ $28\dfrac{24}{35}$

58. $78\dfrac{43}{58} - 39$ $39\dfrac{43}{58}$

59. $140\dfrac{44}{45}$

$82\dfrac{27}{60}$

$58\dfrac{19}{36}$

60. $103\dfrac{29}{30}$

$84\dfrac{75}{75}$

$18\dfrac{29}{30}$

Applications

61. Han Kwong trims bone and fat from a $6\dfrac{3}{4}$-pound roast. The meat left weighs $5\dfrac{1}{4}$ pounds. How many pounds does she trim off? $1\dfrac{1}{2}$ pounds

62. Patti has a piece of lumber that measures $10\dfrac{7}{12}$ ft, and it is to be used in a spot that calls for a length of $8\dfrac{5}{12}$ ft. How much of the board must be cut off? $2\dfrac{1}{6}$ ft

63. Dick harvests $30\dfrac{3}{4}$ tons of wheat. He sells $12\dfrac{3}{10}$ tons to the Cartwright Flour Mill. How many tons of wheat does he have left? $18\dfrac{9}{20}$ tons

64. A $14\dfrac{3}{4}$-inch casting shrinks $\dfrac{3}{16}$ inch on cooling. Find the size when the casting is cold. $14\dfrac{9}{16}$ inches

GETTING READY FOR ALGEBRA

Objective   Solve equations of the form $x + \dfrac{a}{b} = \dfrac{c}{d}$ where a, b, c, and d are whole numbers.

Application   On Tuesday $2\dfrac{3}{8}$ inches of rain fell on Kansas City. This brought the total for the last five consecutive days to $14\dfrac{1}{2}$ inches. What was the rainfall for the first four days?

How and Why   We have solved equations in which whole numbers were either added to or subtracted from a variable. Now we solve equations where fractions or mixed numbers are either added to or subtracted from the variable. We use the same procedure as with whole numbers.

Examples A–C	Warm Ups A–C

Directions: Solve.

Strategy: Add or subtract the same number from each side of the equation to isolate the variable.

A. $x - \dfrac{4}{5} = 3\dfrac{1}{2}$ A. $x - \dfrac{5}{8} = 3\dfrac{7}{8}$

Solution:

$$x - \frac{4}{5} = 3\frac{1}{2}$$

$$x - \frac{4}{5} + \frac{4}{5} = 3\frac{1}{2} + \frac{4}{5} \qquad \text{Eliminate the subtraction by adding}$$
$$\frac{4}{5} \text{ to each side of the equation.}$$

$$x = 3\frac{1}{2} + \frac{4}{5}$$

$$x = 3\frac{5}{10} + \frac{8}{10} \qquad \text{Build each fraction to the denominator, 10.}$$

$$x = 3\frac{13}{10} \qquad \text{Change the improper fraction to a mixed number and add.}$$

$$x = 4\frac{3}{10}$$

CHECK:

$$4\frac{3}{10} - \frac{4}{5} = 3\frac{1}{2} \qquad \text{Substitute } 4\frac{3}{10} \text{ for } x \text{ in the original equation.}$$

$$3\frac{1}{2} = 3\frac{1}{2}$$

The solution is $x = 4\dfrac{3}{10}$.

Answer to warm up: **A.** $x = 4\dfrac{1}{2}$

53. Find the average of $5\frac{1}{3}$, $6\frac{2}{5}$, and $9\frac{13}{15}$. $7\frac{1}{5}$

54. Find the average of $\frac{1}{2}$, $1\frac{1}{6}$, $\frac{7}{9}$, and $5\frac{1}{3}$. $1\frac{17}{18}$

Applications

55. Wayne catches six salmon. The salmon measure $23\frac{1}{4}$ inches, $31\frac{5}{8}$ inches, $42\frac{3}{4}$ inches, $28\frac{5}{8}$ inches, $35\frac{3}{4}$ inches, and 40 inches in length. What is the average length of the salmon? $33\frac{2}{3}$ in.

56. Nurse Louise weighs five new babies at General Hospital. They weigh $6\frac{1}{2}$ lb, $7\frac{3}{4}$ lb, $9\frac{3}{8}$ lb, $7\frac{1}{2}$ lb, and $8\frac{7}{8}$ lb. What is the average weight of the babies?   8 lb

57. A class of 15 students took a ten-problem quiz. Their results were as follows:

Number of Students	Fraction of Problems Correct
1	$\frac{10}{10}$ (all correct)
2	$\frac{9}{10}$
3	$\frac{8}{10}$
5	$\frac{7}{10}$
1	$\frac{6}{10}$
2	$\frac{5}{10}$
1	$\frac{2}{10}$

What was the class average? $\frac{7}{10}$ correct

58. On the second quiz, the class in Exercise 57 scored as follows:

Number of Students	Fraction of Problems Correct
2	$\frac{10}{10}$ (all correct)
1	$\frac{9}{10}$
2	$\frac{8}{10}$
2	$\frac{7}{10}$
4	$\frac{5}{10}$
3	$\frac{3}{10}$
1	$\frac{2}{10}$

What was the class average? $\frac{6}{10}$ correct

NAME _____   CLASS _____   DATE _____ _____

59. Coho Inc. packs a variety carton of canned seafood. Each carton contains three $3\frac{1}{2}$-oz cans of smoked sturgeon, five $6\frac{3}{4}$-oz cans of tuna, four $5\frac{1}{2}$-oz cans of salmon, and four $10\frac{1}{2}$-oz cans of sardines. How many ounces of seafood are in the carton? If the carton sells for \$52, to the nearest cent, what is the average cost per ounce? $108\frac{1}{4}$ oz; 48¢

60. In a walk for charity seven people walk $2\frac{7}{8}$ miles, six people walk $3\frac{4}{5}$ miles, nine people walk $4\frac{1}{4}$ miles, and five people walk $5\frac{3}{4}$ miles. What are the total miles walked? If the charity raises \$2355, to the nearest dollar, what is the average amount raised per mile? $109\frac{37}{40}$ miles; \$21

61. Tom Peterson's Appliances buys 48 television sets for \$14,976. They sell one third of the sets for \$450 each, one fourth for \$462, and five twelfths for \$482. What is the profit from the sale of the sets?   \$7408

62. A 1575-acre farm is subdivided and sold. Three fifths of the farm sells for \$245 an acre, one third of the farm sells for \$375 an acre, and the rest sells for \$610 an acre. What is the total sale price for the farm?   \$492,450

State Your Understanding

63. Is the following exercise worked correctly? If not, why not?

$$6\frac{12}{25} - 3\frac{1}{5} + 2\left(1\frac{1}{2}\right)^2$$

$$\frac{162}{25} - \frac{16}{5} + 2\left(\frac{3}{2}\right)^2$$

$$\frac{162}{25} - \frac{16}{5} + (3)^2$$

$$\frac{162}{25} - \frac{16}{5} + 9$$

$$\frac{162}{25} - \frac{80}{25} + \frac{225}{25}$$

$$\frac{82}{25} + \frac{225}{25}$$

$$\frac{310}{25} = \frac{62}{5} = 12\frac{2}{5}$$

64. Must the average of a group of numbers be larger than the smallest number and smaller than the largest number? Why?

D. 19.53   D. 17.06

Solution:

Nineteen	First, write the word name for the whole number.
Nineteen and	Second, write ''and'' for the decimal point.
Nineteen and fifty-three	Third, write the word name for the whole number to the right of the decimal point, 53.
Nineteen and fifty-three hundredths	Fourth, write the place value of the digit 3.

Directions: Write the place-value name.

Strategy: Write the digit symbols for the corresponding words. Replace the word ''and'' with a decimal point.

E.   fifteen ten-thousandths   E.   twenty-nine thousandths

Solution:

15	First, write the number for fifteen. The place value ''ten-thousandths'' indicates four decimal places, so write two zeros *before* the numeral 15 and then a decimal point. This puts the numeral 5 in the ten-thousandths place. Since the value is between zero and one, we write ''0'' in the ones place.
.0015	
0.0015	

F.   four hundred five and four hundred five thousandths   F.   seven hundred three and three hundred seven thousandths

Solution:

405	The whole-number part is 405.
405.	Write a decimal point for ''and.''
405.405	''Thousandths'' indicates three decimal places.

G.   four hundred five and four hundred five ten-thousandths   G.   seven hundred three and three hundred seven ten-thousandths

Solution:

405	The whole-number part is 405.
405.	Write a decimal point for ''and''
405.0405	''Ten-thousandths'' indicates four decimal places.

Answers to warm ups: **D.** seventeen and six hundredths   **E.** 0.029   **F.** 703.307   **G.** 703.0307

H. Both three hundred-thousandths and three hundred thousandths

Solution:

0.00003	''Hundred-thousandths'' indicates the fifth place to the right of the decimal point. The hyphen in the name is part of the word name. So, three hundred-thousandths has five decimal places.
0.300	There are three decimal places since the place value is ''thousandths.'' Note that 0.300 = 0.3

H. Both thirty hundredths and three hundredths

I. Each year approximately 35.8 million Americans have a Christmas tree to discard. Each year a large number of these still end up in landfills when they could be recycled. Write the word name for the number of trees that are discarded.

Solution:

Thirty-five and eight tenths million trees

I. One corporation states that it can recycle 2.4 billion tin cans per year. Write this number of cans in word form.

How and Why 3   The expanded form shows the place value of each digit:

Place-Value Name	Expanded Form Indicated Sum of Values
0.346	$\dfrac{3}{10} + \dfrac{4}{100} + \dfrac{6}{1000}$
32.9	$30 + 2 + \dfrac{9}{10}$
8.6421	$8 + \dfrac{6}{10} + \dfrac{4}{100} + \dfrac{2}{1000} + \dfrac{1}{10,000}$

The number 0.346 can be written: 3 tenths + 4 hundredths + 6 thousandths.

▶ **To change from place-value name to expanded form**

Write the indicated sum of the values of each of the digits.

▶ **To change from expanded form to place-value name**

Find the sum and write as a decimal.

Use the graph to answer Exercises 39 to 42. The graph shows the precipitation for four weeks in a southern city.

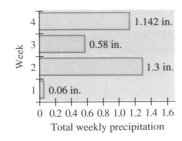

39. Write the word name for the number of inches of precipitation during the second week.
one and three tenths

40. Write the word name for the number of inches of precipitation during the fourth week.
one and one hundred forty-two thousandths

41. Write the word name for the number of inches of precipitation during the first week.   six hundredths

42. Write the word name for the number of inches of precipitation during the third week.
fifty-eight hundredths

Write the place-value name.

43. five thousandths   0.005

44. seventeen thousandths   0.017

45. twenty-five ten-thousandths   0.0025

46. fifty-two ten-thousandths   0.0052

Write the number in expanded form.

47. 0.532
$\frac{5}{10} + \frac{3}{100} + \frac{2}{1000}$

48. 0.793
$\frac{7}{10} + \frac{9}{100} + \frac{3}{1000}$

49. 0.004
$\frac{0}{10} + \frac{0}{100} + \frac{4}{1000}$

50. 0.009
$\frac{0}{10} + \frac{0}{100} + \frac{9}{1000}$

Write the number in place-value form.

51. $\frac{6}{1000}$ 0.006

52. $\frac{5}{1000}$ 0.005

53. $20 + 5 + \frac{8}{10} + \frac{0}{100} + \frac{1}{1000}$
25.801

54. $50 + 8 + \frac{0}{10} + \frac{0}{100} + \frac{9}{1000}$
58.009

C

Write the word name.

55. 2.03041
two and three thousand forty-one hundred-thousandths

56. 6.54321
six and fifty-four thousand three hundred twenty-one hundred-thousandths

57. 404.00011
four hundred four and eleven hundred-thousandths

58. 40,400.011
forty thousand four hundred and eleven thousandths

Write the place-value name.

59. two hundred thirty-three thousandths   0.233

60. two hundred and thirty-three thousandths   200.033

61. forty hundred-thousandths   0.00040

62. four hundred thousandths   0.400

Write the number in expanded form.

63. 92.432 $90 + 2 + \frac{4}{10} + \frac{3}{100} + \frac{2}{1000}$

64. 239.034 $200 + 30 + 9 + \frac{0}{10} + \frac{3}{100} + \frac{4}{1000}$

NAME _____ CLASS _____ DATE _____

65. 524.0046 $500 + 20 + 4 + \dfrac{0}{10} + \dfrac{0}{100} + \dfrac{4}{1000} + \dfrac{6}{10,000}$ **66.** 201.0004 $200 + 0 + 1 + \dfrac{0}{10} + \dfrac{0}{100} + \dfrac{0}{1000} + \dfrac{4}{10,000}$

Applications

67. Dan Ngo buys a deep fryer that has a marked price of $64.79. What word name does he write on the check?   Sixty-four and seventy-nine hundredths

68. Fari Alhadet buys a truckload of organic fertilizer for her yard. The price of the load is $106.75. What word name does she write on the check?   One hundred six and seventy-five hundredths

69. A newspaper reported that NASA's one-year budget a few years ago was $23.3 billion. What is the place value of the digit 2?   ten billion

70. A financial magazine estimates that NASA's budget next year will be $17.4 billion. What is the place value of the digit 7?   one billion

71. A retail warehouse club reports earnings of $112.7 million. What digit is in the millions place?   2

72. In Exercise 71, what digit is in the hundred thousands place?   7

State Your Understanding

73. Explain why you believe that magazines and newspapers use both numerals *and* words in writing numbers like those in Exercises 69 to 71.

74. Explain, in words, the meaning of the values of 4 in the numeral 43.34. Include some comment on how and why the values of the digit 4 are alike and how and why they are different.

Challenge

75. What is the place value of the digit 8 in 3,082,000,000,000,000?   ten trillion

76. What is the place value of the digit 8 in 0.0000000082?   billionths

Group Activity

77. Have each group member find an example of the use of numerals where the place value is not significant or is ignored when writing or reading. One example might be a phone number. Discuss your findings with the group. Do you agree with the examples offered by the other members?

Maintain Your Skills (Sections 3.2, 3.3, 3.5, 3.6, 3.9)

Build the fractions as indicated.

78. $\dfrac{11}{12} = \dfrac{?}{36}$ 33

79. $\dfrac{7}{8} = \dfrac{?}{48}$ 42

Reduce the fractions.

80. $\dfrac{75}{80}$ $\dfrac{15}{16}$

81. $\dfrac{75}{120}$ $\dfrac{5}{8}$

Write the reciprocal.

82. $\dfrac{22}{25}$ $\dfrac{25}{22}$

83. $4\dfrac{7}{8}$ $\dfrac{8}{39}$

True or false?

84. $\dfrac{2}{3} < \dfrac{7}{9}$ True

85. $1\dfrac{1}{5} > 1\dfrac{2}{7}$ False

86. Trina buys $\dfrac{1}{2}$ lb of chocolates, $\dfrac{1}{4}$ lb of peanut brittle, and $\dfrac{1}{2}$ lb of gumdrops. How many pounds of candy does she buy? $1\dfrac{1}{4}$ pounds

87. Saul needs eight and one-half ounces of tomato paste for a recipe. He already has three and seven-eighths ounces left over from an earlier meal. How many more ounces of tomato paste does he need? $4\dfrac{5}{8}$ ounces

| **4.2** | **CHANGING DECIMALS TO FRACTIONS; LISTING IN ORDER** |

Objectives

1. Change a decimal to a fraction.

2. List two or more decimals in order from smallest to largest.

Application

🌐 The chance (probability) that a coin will land heads up when flipped once is 0.5. Write this decimal as a reduced fraction.

How and Why   1

Consider 0.625.

READ: six hundred twenty-five thousandths

WRITE: $\dfrac{625}{1000}$

So, $0.625 = \dfrac{625}{1000} = \dfrac{5}{8}$.

▶ **To change a decimal to a fraction**

1. Read the decimal word name.
2. Write the fraction that has the same name.
3. Reduce if possible.

Notice that because of place value, the number of decimal places in a decimal tells us the number of zeros in the denominator of the fraction. This fact can be used as another way to write the fraction or to check that the fraction is correct:

$$2.78 \quad = 2\dfrac{78}{100} = 2\dfrac{39}{50} \quad \text{or} \quad \dfrac{278}{100} = 2\dfrac{39}{50}$$

Two decimal places   Two zeros

Examples A–D   **Warm Ups A–D**

Directions: Change the decimal to a fraction or mixed number.

Strategy: Say the word name to yourself and write the fraction that is equivalent. Reduce.

A.   0.85   **A.**   0.12

Solution:

$0.85 = \dfrac{85}{100} = \dfrac{17}{20}$ Read "eighty-five hundredths," then write the fraction and reduce.

Answer to warm up: **A.** $\dfrac{3}{25}$

B. 12.3

B. 13.7

Solution:

$$12.3 = 12\frac{3}{10}$$ Read "twelve and three tenths," then write the mixed number.

In the decimal 12.3, the place value of the last place is "tenths." We can also write

$$12.3 = \frac{123}{10} = 12\frac{3}{10}$$

C. 5.075 and 0.0075

C. 3.125 and 0.625

Solution:

$$5.075 = 5\frac{75}{1000} = 5\frac{3}{40}$$

$$0.0075 = \frac{75}{10,000} = \frac{3}{400} \qquad \frac{75}{10,000} = \frac{3 \cdot 25}{400 \cdot 25} = \frac{3}{400}$$

D. 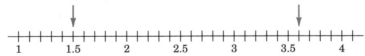 The chance (probability) that a coin will land heads up when flipped once is 0.5. Write this decimal as a reduced fraction.

D. The chance that a pair of dice will land with a sum of five or six is 0.25. Write this as a reduced fraction.

Solution:

$$0.5 = \frac{5}{10} = \frac{1}{2}$$ Write the fraction for "five tenths," and reduce.

The chance of getting heads is $\frac{1}{2}$, or one in every two flips.

How and Why   **2**   Fractions can be listed in order, when they have a common denominator, by ordering the numerators. This idea can be extended to decimals when they have the same number of decimal places. For instance, $0.26 = \frac{26}{100}$ and $0.37 = \frac{37}{100}$ have a common denominator when written in fraction form. So 0.26 is less than 0.37; or $0.26 < 0.37$.

We can see that $1.5 < 3.6$ because 1.5 is to the left of 3.6 on the number line.

The decimals 0.3 and 0.15 have a common denominator when a zero is placed after the 3. Thus

$$0.3 = \frac{3}{10} = \frac{3}{10} \cdot \frac{10}{10} = \frac{30}{100} = 0.30$$

---

so that

$$0.3 = \frac{30}{100} \quad \text{and} \quad 0.15 = \frac{15}{100}$$

Then, since $\frac{15}{100} < \frac{30}{100}$, we conclude that $0.15 < 0.3$.

To list three or more decimals in order from smallest to largest we proceed in a similar manner, see Examples H–J.

▶ **To list decimals in order**

1. Make sure that all numbers have the same number of decimal places to the right of the decimal point by placing zeros to the right of the last digit when necessary.
2. Write the numbers in order from the smallest to largest, ignoring the decimal point.
3. Remove the extra zeros.

Examples E–J

Warm Ups E–J

Directions: Is the statement true or false?

Strategy: Write each numeral with the same number of decimal places. Compare the values without regard to the decimal point.

E. $0.45 > 0.41$

Solution:

| $0.45 > 0.41$ | True | The decimal points can be ignored since both numbers have two decimal places. Then, since $45 > 41$, the statement is true. |

E. $2.09 > 2.001$

F. $0.92 < 0.919$

Solution:

| $0.92 < 0.919$ | False | Write 0.92 as 0.920. Since $920 < 919$ is false, the statement is false. |

F. $0.5 < 0.499$

G. $1.003 > 1.01$ and $53.0001 > 53.009$

Solution:

| $1.003 > 1.01$ | False | Write 1.01 as 1.010. Since $1003 > 1010$ is false, the statement is false. |
| $53.0001 < 53.009$ | True | Since $530{,}001 < 530{,}090$ is true. |

G. $33.7 > 33.6989$ and $0.0001 < 0.000004$

Answers to warm ups: **E.** True   **F.** False   **G.** True; false

$56.65 \approx 56. It is common for retail stores to round up for any amounts smaller than one cent. Thus, $1.333 \approx 1.34. There is also a rule for rounding numbers in science, which is sometimes referred to as the "even/odd" rule. You might need to learn and use a different round-off rule depending on what kind of work you are doing.

Examples A–F	Warm Ups A–F

Directions: Round as indicated.

Strategy: Draw an arrow under the place value indicated. Examine the digit to the right of the arrow to determine whether to round up or down.

A.   0.3582 to the nearest hundredth

Solution:

$0.3582 \approx 0.36$ Draw an arrow under the digit 5 in the hundredths
    ↑   place. The digit to the right is 8, so we round up.

A.   0.3548 to the nearest hundredth

B.   3582.9 to the nearest thousand

Solution:

$3582.9 \approx 4000$ Draw an arrow under the digit 3 in the thousands
    ↑   place. The digit to the right is 5 so we round up by
             adding $3 + 1$. Three zeros must be written after the
             digit 4 to keep it in the thousands place.

In Example B, we see that $4000 > 3582.9$

B.   3489.5 to the nearest thousand

CAUTION

Do not round by working from right to left. In Example C the "99" is ignored. Only the digit 4 to the right of the arrow is used for rounding.

C.   16.3499 to the nearest tenth

Solution:

$16.3499 \approx 16.3$ Draw an arrow under the digit 3 in the tenths
    ↑   place. The digit to the right is 4, so we round
             down.

C.   16.7506 to the nearest tenth

D.   249.7 to the nearest unit

Solution:

$249.7 \approx 250$ Draw an arrow under the digit 9 in the units place.
    ↑   The digit to the right is 7, so we round up by adding
             $249 + 1$.

D.   370.2 to the nearest unit

Answers to warm ups: **A.** 0.35   **B.** 3000   **C.** 16.8   **D.** 370

E. 37.2828 and 3.9964 to the nearest unit, the nearest tenth, the nearest hundredth, and the nearest thousandth.

Solution:

	Unit	Tenth	Hundredth	Thousandth
37.2828 ≈	37 ≈	37.3 ≈	37.28 ≈	37.283
3.9964 ≈	4 ≈	4.0 ≈	4.00 ≈	3.996

E. 12.8947 to the nearest unit, the nearest tenth, the nearest hundredth, and the nearest thousandth.

CAUTION

In Example E the zeros in 4.0 and 4.00 are required to display the accuracy of the rounded approximation.

F. Juan is reading the instructions about listing deductions on his income-tax return. The instructions are to round each deduction to the nearest dollar. If he is going to deduct $832.57 for mortgage interest he paid, what will he enter on his return?

Solution:

832.57 ≈ 833   Draw an arrow under the digit 2 in the units place.
↑   The next digit is 5 so round up by adding 2 + 1.

Juan will enter $833 on his return.

F. If Juan can deduct $204.48 for charitable contributions, what will he enter on his return?

B. $1.05 + 0.723 + 72.6 + 8$

Solution:

1.050	Write each numeral with three decimal places. The whole
0.723	number 8 can be written 8. or 8.0 or 8.00 or 8.000 because
72.600	the decimal point follows the units place.
8.000	
82.373	

B. $7.09 + 0.385 + 37.7 + 12$

C.   ⊞ $6.3975 + 0.0116 + 3.410 + 18.624$

Solution:

ENTER	$\boxed{6.3975}$ $\boxed{+}$ $\boxed{.0116}$ $\boxed{+}$
DISPLAY	6.3975 6.3975 0.0116 6.4091
ENTER	$\boxed{3.41}$ $\boxed{+}$ $\boxed{18.624}$ $\boxed{=}$
DISPLAY	3.41 9.8191 18.624 28.4431

The sum is 28.4431. Extra zeros do not need to be entered on the calculator. The place values will be added correctly by the calculator.

C. $8.4068 + 0.0229 + 4.56 + 34.843$

D.   🌐 What is the total cost of an automobile tire if the retail price is $57.95, the federal excise tax is $2.05, the state sales tax is $3.48, and local sales tax is $1.16?

Solution:

Retail price	$57.95	To find the total cost, add the retail
Excise tax	2.05	price and the taxes. Since prices are in
State sales tax	3.48	dollars and cents, every decimal already
Local sales tax	1.16	has the same number of decimal places.
Total	$64.64	

D.   What is the total cost of a pair of emerald earrings if the retail price is $83.95, the federal tax is $3.06, the state sales tax is $2.78, and the city sales tax is $0.67?

Answers to warm ups: **B.** 57.175   **C.** 47.8327   **D.** $90.46

NAME _____ CLASS _____ DATE _____

EXERCISES 4.4

A

Add.

1. 0.4
0.2
0.6

2. 0.8
0.1
0.9

3. 0.6
1.2
1.8

4. 2.5
1.3
3.8

5. 1.4 + 2.1 + 4.2   7.7

6. 3.2 + 1.1 + 2.4   6.7

7. 23.3 + 4.4   27.7

8. 17.7 + 2.2   19.9

9. 0.113
0.121
0.443
0.677

10. 0.233
0.311
0.132
0.676

11. 3.41
2.14
1.32
6.87

12. 4.31
3.21
2.22
9.74

13. 5 + 9.3   14.3

14. 7 + 8.8   15.8

15. 4.72 + 9   13.72

16. 3.94 + 12   15.94

B

17. 8.3
5.541
13.841

18. 7.6
6.44
14.04

19. 8.28
0.28
12.3
2.54
23.4

20. 9.06
0.82
11.5
4.35
25.73

21. 0.438 + 0.834 + 1.483   2.755

22. 1.254 + 1.425 + 0.524   3.203

23. 0.0017 + 1.007 + 7 + 1.071   9.0797

24. 1.0304 + 1.4003 + 1.34 + 0.403   4.1737

25. 37.008 + 38.007 + 3.87 + 3.708   82.593

26. 82.005 + 8.25 + 2.085 + 28.55   120.89

27. 0.00043 + 0.0034 + 0.304 + 3.04   3.34783

28. 1.00603 + 6.0301 + 3.16 + 10.3006   20.49673

$$\begin{array}{r} {}^{12} \\ 7\,\cancel{2}\,11 \\ 5.8\,\cancel{3}\,\cancel{1} \\ 0.2\,8\,7 \\ \hline 5.5\,4\,4 \end{array}$$

Since we cannot subtract 8 hundredths from 2 hundredths, we regroup again. We borrow 1 tenth from the 8 in the tenths place to add to the 2 in the hundredths place. (1 tenth = 10 hundredths)

CHECK:

$$\begin{array}{r} 0.287 \\ \underline{5.544} \\ 5.831 \end{array}$$ Check by addition.

The difference is 5.544.

CAUTION

Be sure to align the decimal points so that the place values will be lined up.

B. $6 - 2.94$

B. $9.382 - 5.736$

Solution:

$$\begin{array}{r} 6.00 \\ \underline{2.94} \end{array}$$ We write the 6 as 6.00 so that both numerals will have the same number of decimal places.

$$\begin{array}{r} {}^{5\ 10} \\ \cancel{6}.\cancel{0}\,\cancel{0} \\ 2.9\,4 \end{array}$$ We need to borrow to subtract in the hundredths place. Since there is a 0 in the tenths place, we start by borrowing 1 from the ones place. (1 one = 10 tenths)

$$\begin{array}{r} {}^{9} \\ {}^{5\ \cancel{10}\ 10} \\ \cancel{6}.\cancel{0}\,\cancel{0} \\ 2.9\,4 \\ \hline 3.0\,6 \end{array}$$ Now borrow 1 tenth to add to the hundredths place (1 tenth = 10 hundredths) and then subtract.

CHECK:

$$\begin{array}{r} 2.94 \\ \underline{3.06} \\ 6.00 \end{array}$$ Check by addition.

The difference is 3.06.

C. $6.271 - 3.845$

C. $13 - 7.88$

Solution:

$$\begin{array}{r} {}^{5\ 12\ 6\ 11} \\ \cancel{6}.\cancel{2}\,\cancel{7}\,\cancel{1} \\ 3.8\,4\,5 \\ \hline 2.4\,2\,6 \end{array}$$ Each numeral has three decimal places, so when we write one under the other, the place values line up. The check is left for the student.

The difference is 2.426.

D. 127.9635 − 96.938

Solution:

ENTER	127.9635	−	96.938	=
DISPLAY	127.9635	127.9635	96.938	31.0255

The difference is 31.0255.

D. 340.7225 − 278.897

E. Marta purchases a small radio for $13.89. She gives the clerk a $20 bill to pay for the radio. How much change does she get?

Solution:

```
20.00       We subtract to find the amount of change.
13.89
─────
 6.11
```

Marta should get $6.11 in change.

Clerks sometimes make change by counting backwards, that is, by adding to $13.89 the amount necessary to equal $20.

$13.89 + a penny = $13.90
$13.90 + a dime   = $14.00
$14.00 + 1 dollar = $15.00
$15.00 + 5 dollars = $20.00

So the change is 0.01 + 0.10 + 1.00 + 5.00 = $6.11.

E. Micky buys a video for $18.69. She gives the clerk a $20 bill to pay for the cassette. How much change should she get?

23. The price of an energy-efficient hot-water heater decreased by $46.98 over the past two years. What was the price two years ago if the heater now sells for $359.99? $406.97

24. In one state the use of household biodegradable cleaners increased by 2444.67 pounds per month because of state laws banning phosphates. How many pounds of these cleaners were used before the new laws if the average use now is 5780.5 pounds?   3335.83 lb

4.6   MULTIPLYING DECIMALS

Objective   Multiply decimals.

Application   If exactly eight strips of metal, each 3.875 inches wide, are to be cut from a piece of sheet metal, what is the smallest (in width) piece of sheet metal that can be used?

How and Why   The "multiplication table" for decimals is the same as for whole numbers. In fact, decimals are multiplied the same way as whole numbers, with one exception. The exception is in locating the decimal point. To locate the decimal point in (0.3)(0.8), change the decimals to fractions:

Decimals	Fractions	Product of Fractions	Product of Decimals
0.3×0.8	$\dfrac{3}{10} \times \dfrac{8}{10}$	$\dfrac{24}{100}$	0.24
11.2×0.07	$\dfrac{112}{10} \times \dfrac{7}{100}$	$\dfrac{784}{1000}$	0.784
7.2×0.13	$\dfrac{72}{10} \times \dfrac{13}{100}$	$\dfrac{936}{1000}$	0.936

The shortcut is to multiply the numbers and insert the decimal point. If necessary, insert zeros so that there are enough decimal places. The product 0.2×0.3 has two decimal places, since tenths multiplied by tenths yields hundredths.

$$0.2 \times 0.3 = 0.06 \qquad \left(\text{Note that } \frac{2}{10} \times \frac{3}{10} = \frac{6}{100} \right)$$

▶ **To multiply two decimals**

1. Multiply the numbers as if they were whole numbers.
2. Locate the decimal point by counting the number of decimal places (to the right of the decimal point) in both factors. The total of these two counts is the number of decimal places the product must have.
3. If necessary, zeros are inserted at the *left of the numeral* so there are enough decimal places (see Example F).

Examples A–H   **Warm Ups A–H**

Directions: Multiply.

Strategy: First multiply the numbers, ignoring the decimal point. Place the decimal point in the product by counting the number of decimal places in the two factors. Insert zeros if necessary to preserve the number of required places.

A. 0.7×6

Solution:

$0.7 \times 6 = 4.2$ Multiply 7×6 to get 42. The total count of decimal
places is one (1), so there is one decimal place
in the product.

We can verify the product by writing (or better, thinking)

$\dfrac{7}{10} \times 6 = \dfrac{42}{10} = 4.2.$

B. 7×0.6

Solution:

$7 \times 0.6 = 4.2$ Again, there is one decimal place.

C. 0.7×0.6

Solution:

$0.7 \times 0.6 = 0.42$ This time there are two decimal places, since
each factor contains one decimal place.

We can verify the product by thinking $\dfrac{7}{10} \times \dfrac{6}{10} = \dfrac{42}{100} = 0.42.$

D. $11(0.33)$

Solution:

$$\begin{array}{r} 0.33 \\ \underline{11} \\ 33 \\ \underline{33} \\ 3.63 \end{array}$$

Since 0.33 has two decimal places and 11 has none, the product
has two decimal places.

E. $2.31(3.4)$

Solution:

$$\begin{array}{r} 2.31 \\ \underline{3.4} \\ 924 \\ \underline{693} \\ 7.854 \end{array}$$

There are three decimal places in the factors (two in 2.31
and one in 3.4), so the product has three decimal places.

A. 0.8×7

B. 8×0.7

C. 0.8×0.7

D. $14(0.27)$

E. $6.2(5.78)$

Answers to warm ups: **A.** 5.6   **B.** 5.6   **C.** 0.56   **D.** 3.78   **E.** 35.836

NAME

EXEF

A

Multiply

1. 0.3
   $\underline{8}$
   2.4

5. 0.9
   $\underline{2}$
   1.8

9. 0.5
   $\underline{0.7}$
   0.35

13. 0.21
    $\underline{4}$
    0.84

17. 0.05
    $\underline{0.3}$
    0.015

B

Multiply.

19. 7.3ᶦ
    $\underline{0.00\,}$
    0.0147

23. 34.6
    $\underline{6.5}$
    224.9

27. 8.2
    $\underline{0.68}$
    5.576

31. 0.059

CAUTION

Insert zeros when necessary to preserve the correct number of decimal places.

F. 0.21(0.14)

Solution:

0.2 1	There are four decimal places in the factors. Since the
0.1 4	product must also have four decimal places we insert a 0
8 4	before the 2.
2 1	
0.0 2 9 4	

F. 0.09(0.35)

G. 🖩 62.75(136.492)

Solution:

ENTER	62.75	×	136.492	=
DISPLAY	62.75	62.75	136.492	8564.873

The product is 8564.873.

G. 3.456(82.74)

H. 🌐 If exactly eight strips of metal, each 3.875 inches wide, are to be cut from a piece of sheet metal, what is the smallest (in width) piece of sheet metal that can be used?

Solution:

3.875	To find the width of the piece of sheet metal, we multiply.
8	We can drop the extra zeros.
31.000	

The piece must be at least 31 inches wide.

H. If 12 strips, each 6.45 centimeters wide, are to be cut from a piece of sheet metal, what is the narrowest piece of sheet metal that can be used?

Answers to warm ups: **F.** 0.0315　**G.** 285.94944　**H.** 77.4 inches wide

© 1995 Saundeɪ

J. 0.00000501

J. 0.0000907

Solution:

ENTER	.0000907	×	
DISPLAY	0.0000907	9.07 −05	

The calculator displays scientific notation by showing the number between 1 and 10, then the power of 10. The base of 10 is not displayed.

So $0.0000907 = 9.07 \times 10^{-5}$.

Scientific and graphing calculators have settings to display numbers in scientific notation. If the steps above do not give you the same display, consult your calculator manual.

NAME _____ CLASS _____ _____ DATE _____

EXERCISES 4.7

A

Multiply or divide as indicated.

1. $42.5 \div 10$ 4.25   **2.** $4.67 \div 10$ 0.467   **3.** $1.83(100)$ 183   **4.** $6.275(100)$ 627.5

5. $0.8214(1000)$ 821.4   **6.** $682.34(10)$ 6823.4   **7.** $276 \div 100$ 2.76   **8.** $2195 \div 100$ 21.95

9. $2143.61 \div 1000$ **10.** $217.16 \div 1000$
    2.14361   0.21716

Write the numbers in scientific notation.

11. 1000 1×10^3 **12.** 100,000 1×10^5 **13.** 0.0001 1×10^{-4} **14.** 0.00001 1×10^{-5}

Change the numbers to place-value form.

15. 1×10^4 10,000   **16.** 1×10^7 10,000,000   **17.** 1×10^{-2} 0.01   **18.** 1×10^{-7} 0.0000001

Multiply or divide as indicated.

19. $36.95 \div 10,000$ 0.003695   **20.** $756 \div 10,000$ 0.0756   **21.** $26(100,000)$ 2,600,000

22. $314.5(10,000)$ 3,145,000   **23.** $122.31 \div 1000$ 0.12231   **24.** $41.62 \div 1000$ 0.04162

Write the numbers in scientific notation.

25. 700 7×10^2 **26.** 950 9.5×10^2 **27.** 0.078 7.8×10^{-2}

28. 0.002 2×10^{-3} **29.** 15,000 1.5×10^4 **30.** 24,000 2.4×10^4

Change the numbers to place-value form.

31. 6×10^4 60,000   **32.** 9×10^5 900,000   **33.** 1.22×10^{-1} 0.122

34. 5.7×10^{-2} 0.057   **35.** 2.34×10^3 2340   **36.** 4.57×10^2 457

Multiply or divide as indicated.

37. $0.00214(10,000)$ 21.4   **38.** $0.000214(100)$ 0.0214   **39.** $0.832 \div 100$ 0.00832

40. $0.068 \div 10,000$ 0.0000068   **41.** 0.08216×100 8.216   **42.** $0.2317 \div 10$ 0.02317

Write the number in scientific notation.

43. 70,000 7×10^4

44. 7,500,000 7.5×10^6

45. 0.00816 8.16×10^{-3}

46. 0.00000000044 4.4×10^{-10}

47. 627,000 6.27×10^5

48. 0.0000461 4.61×10^{-5}

Change the numbers to place-value form.

49. 6×10^9 6,000,000,000

50. 3×10^{15} 3,000,000,000,000,000

51. 4.44×10^{-5} 0.0000444

52. 2.3×10^{-7} 0.00000023

53. 7.851×10^5 785,100

54. 3.492×10^{-3} 0.003492

Applications

55. Ken's Shoe Store buys 100 pairs of shoes that cost $22.29 per pair. What is the total cost of the shoes? $2229

56. If Mae's Shoe Store buys 100 pairs of shoes and the total cost is $4897.50, what is the cost of each pair of shoes? $48.975

57. Ms. James buys 100 acres of land at a cost of $985 per acre. What is the total cost of her land? $98,500

58. If 1000 bricks weigh 5900 pounds, how much does each brick weigh? 5.9 pounds

59. Mr. Tuck loads 1000 boxes of paper on his trailer. If each box weighs 12.5 pounds, what is the total weight of the boxes that he loads? 12,500 pounds

60. The total land area of Earth is approximately 52,000,000 square miles. What is the total area written in scientific notation? 5.2×10^7 square miles

61. The local computer store offers a small computer with 1152K (1,152,000) bytes of memory. Write the number of bytes in scientific notation. 1.152×10^6 bytes

62. The length of a red light ray is 0.000000072 cm. Write this length in scientific notation. 7.2×10^{-8} cm

63. The time it takes light to travel one kilometer is approximately 0.0000033 second. Write this time in scientific notation. 3.3×10^{-6} second

64. The speed of light is approximately 1.116×10^7 miles per minute. Write this speed in place-value form. 11,160,000 miles per minute

65. Earth is approximately 1.5×10^8 kilometers from the sun. Write this distance in place-value form. 150,000,000 kilometers

66. The shortest wavelength of visible light is approximately 4×10^{-5} centimeter. Write this length in place-value form. 0.00004 centimeter

NAME _____   _____   CLASS _____   DATE _____

67. A family in the Northeast used 3.276×10^8 BTUs of energy during 1989. A family in the Midwest used 3.312×10^8 BTUs in the same year. A family in the South used 3.933×10^8 and a family in the West used 1.935×10^8 BTUs. Write the total energy usage for the four families in place-value form.   1,245,600,000 BTUs

68. In 1990 the per capita consumption of fish was 15.5 pounds. In the same year the per capita consumption of poultry was 63.6 pounds and of red meat was 112.3 pounds. Write the total amount in each category consumed by 100,000 people in scientific notation.   fish: 1.55×10^6 lb; poultry: 6.36×10^6 lb; red meat: 1.123×10^7 lb

69. The population of Cabot Cove was approximately 10,000 in 1991. During this time, the community consumed a total of 276,000 gallons of milk. What was the per capita consumption of milk in Cabot Cove in 1991?   27.6 gallons

70. In 1980, $24,744,000,000 was spent on air pollution abatement. Ten years later, $26,326,000,000 was spent. In scientific notation, how much more money was spent in 1990 than in 1980? What is the average amount of increase per year during this period? 1.582×10^9; 1.582×10^8

State Your Understanding

71. Find a pair of numbers whose product is larger than ten trillion. Explain how scientific notation makes it possible to multiply these factors on a calculator. Why is it not possible without scientific notation?

Challenge

72. Simplify: $\dfrac{(3.25 \times 10^{-3})(2.4 \times 10^3)}{(4.8 \times 10^{-4})(2.5 \times 10^{-3})}$ 6.5×10^6

73. Simplify: $\dfrac{(3.25 \times 10^{-7})(2.4 \times 10^6)}{(4.8 \times 10^4)(2.5 \times 10^{-3})}$ 6.5×10^{-3}

Group Activity

74. Find the 1990 population for the ten largest cities and the five smallest cities in your state. Round these numbers to the nearest thousand. Find the total number of pounds of fruit, at the rate of 92.3 pounds per person, and the total number of pounds of vegetables, at the rate of 111.2 pounds per person, consumed in each of the fifteen cities.

The bar written above the sequence of digits, 428571, indicates that these digits are repeated endlessly. Whenever a fraction is changed to a decimal, we have one of two possibilities:

1. The quotient is exact, as in $\dfrac{2}{5} = 0.4$. This decimal is a "terminating decimal."

2. The quotient is a nonterminating, repeating decimal, as in

$$\frac{2}{3} = 0.6666666\ldots = 0.\overline{6}$$

In practical applications we stop the division process one place value beyond the accuracy required by the situation and then round. Therefore

$$2.34 \div 7 \approx 0.33 \qquad \text{to the nearest hundredth}$$

$$2.34 \div 7 \approx 0.3343 \qquad \text{to the nearest ten-thousandth}$$

If the divisor contains a decimal point, we change the problem:

$$0.7\overline{)2.338} = 0.7\overline{)2.338} = 7\overline{)23.38} \qquad \text{because} \qquad \frac{2.338}{0.7} \cdot \frac{10}{10} = \frac{23.38}{7}$$

$$0.014\overline{)78} = 0.014\overline{)7.800} = 14\overline{)7800} \qquad \text{because} \qquad \frac{7.8}{0.014} \cdot \frac{1000}{1000} = \frac{7800}{14}$$

$$0.23\overline{)7.2} = 0.23\overline{)7.20} = 23\overline{)720} \qquad \text{because} \qquad \frac{7.2}{0.23} \cdot \frac{100}{100} = \frac{720}{23}$$

▶ **To divide two numbers**

1. If the divisor is not a whole number, move both decimal points to the right the same number of decimal places until the divisor is a whole number. In other words, multiply both the divisor and the dividend by the same power of ten so the divisor is a whole number.
2. Place the decimal point in the quotient above the decimal point in the dividend.
3. Divide as if both numbers were whole numbers.
4. Round to the given place value. (If no round-off place is given, divide until the remainder is zero or round as appropriate in the problem. For instance, in problems with money, round to the nearest cent.)

Planning for a nursing career, Georgeanna Jeffers is a fulltime student at Maple Woods Community College in Kansas City, MO. Georgeanna was a winner of the Barker/Rogers/Van Dyke problem-posing contest. Her math teacher was Martha Haehl.

Examples A–G   **Warm Ups A–G**

Directions: Divide. Round as indicated.

Strategy: If the divisor has a decimal point, move both decimal points to the right. Move the decimals the same number of places until the divisor is a whole number. The decimal point in the quotient is found by writing it directly above the decimal (as moved) in the dividend.

A. $13\overline{)13.026}$ **A.** $15\overline{)45.105}$

Solution:

$$13\overline{)13.026}$$ quotient 1.002

$$
\begin{array}{r}
1.002 \\
13\overline{)13.026} \\
\underline{13} \\
0\,0 \\
\underline{0\,0} \\
02 \\
\underline{00} \\
26 \\
\underline{26} \\
0
\end{array}
$$

The numerals in the answer are lined up in columns that have the same place value. Check by multiplying 13×1.002.

$$
\begin{array}{r}
1.002 \\
\underline{13} \\
3\,006 \\
\underline{10\,02} \\
13.026
\end{array}
$$

The quotient is 1.002.

CAUTION

Write the decimal point for the quotient directly above the decimal point in the dividend.

B. $1.88 \div 8$ **B.** $2.16 \div 16$

Solution:

$$
\begin{array}{r}
0.23 \\
8\overline{)1.88} \\
\underline{1\,6} \\
28 \\
\underline{24} \\
4
\end{array}
$$

Here the remainder is not zero, so the division is not complete. We write a zero on the right (1.880) without changing the value of the dividend and continue dividing.

$$
\begin{array}{r}
0.235 \\
8\overline{)1.880} \\
\underline{1\,6} \\
28 \\
\underline{24} \\
40 \\
\underline{40} \\
0
\end{array}
$$

Both the quotient (0.235) and the rewritten dividend (1.880) have three decimal places. Check by multiplying 8×0.235.

$$
\begin{array}{r}
0.235 \\
\underline{8} \\
1.880
\end{array}
$$

The quotient is 0.235.

Answers to warm ups: **A.** 3.007   **B.** 0.135

C. $486.5 \div 23$; round to the nearest hundredth.

Solution:

```
        21.152
   23)486.500
       46
       ‾‾
       26
       23
       ‾‾
        3 5
        2 3
        ‾‾‾
        1 20
        1 15
        ‾‾‾‾
          50
          46
          ‾‾
           4
```

It is necessary to place two zeros on the right in order to round to the hundredths place.

The quotient is approximately 21.15.

C. $241.3 \div 21$; round to the nearest hundredth.

D. $1.32 \div 0.7$; round to the nearest hundredth.

Solution:

```
  0.7)1.32
```

First, move both decimal places one place to the right so the divisor is the whole number, 7. The same result is obtained by multiplying both divisor and dividend by 10.

```
      1.8
   7)13.2
      7
      ‾
      6 2
      5 6
      ‾‾‾
        6
```

$$\frac{1.32}{0.7} \times \frac{10}{10} = \frac{13.2}{7}$$

```
     1.885
  7)13.200
     7
     ‾
     6 2
     5 6
     ‾‾‾
       60
       56
       ‾‾
       40
       35
       ‾‾
        5
```

The number of zeros you place on the right depends on either the directions for rounding or your own choice of the number of places. Here we find the approximate quotient rounded to the nearest hundredth.

The quotient is approximately 1.89.

D. $2.48 \div 0.7$; round to the nearest hundredth.

E. $0.47891 \div 0.072$; round to the nearest thousandth.

Solution:

```
  0.072)0.47891
```

E. $0.75593 \div 0.043$; round to the nearest thousandth.

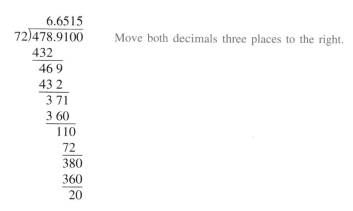

```
      6.6515
72)478.9100      Move both decimals three places to the right.
    432
    46 9
    43 2
      3 71
      3 60
        110
         72
        380
        360
         20
```

The quotient is approximately 6.652.

F.  78.1936 ÷ 8.705; round to the nearest thousandth.

Solution:

ENTER	78.1936	÷	8.705	=

DISPLAY   78.1936   78.1936   8.705   8.9826077

The quotient is 8.983, to the nearest thousandth.

F. 103.843 ÷ 4.088; round to the nearest thousandth.

G. What is the cost per ounce of a 12-ounce can of root beer that costs 45¢? This is called the "unit price" and is used for comparing prices. Many stores are required to show this price for the food they sell.

Solution:

```
      3.75
12)45.00         To find the unit price (cost per ounce), we divide the cost
   36            by the number of ounces.
    9 0
    8 4
     60
     60
```

The root beer costs 3.75¢ per ounce.

G. What is the unit price of potato chips if a 7-ounce bag costs $1.26?

Answers to warm ups: **E.** 17.580   **F.** 25.402   **G.** 18¢ per ounce

CHECK:

$18.2 = \dfrac{231.14}{12.7}$ Substitute 231.14 for a in the original equation and simplify.

$18.2 = 18.2$

The solution is $a = 231.14$.

C. $22.3y = 62.44$

Solution:

$\dfrac{22.3y}{22.3} = \dfrac{62.44}{22.3}$ Divide both sides by 22.3 to eliminate the multiplication and simplify.

$y = 2.8$

CHECK:

$22.3(2.8) = 62.44$ Substitute 2.8 for y in the original equation and simplify.

$62.44 = 62.44$

The solution is $y = 2.8$.

C. $0.075a = 1.065$

D. $\dfrac{c}{0.234} = 1.2$

Solution:

$(0.234)\dfrac{c}{0.234} = (0.234)(1.2)$ Multiply both sides by 0.234 and simplify.

$c = 0.2808$

CHECK:

$\dfrac{0.2808}{0.234} = 1.2$ Substitute 0.2808 for c in the original equation and simplify.

$1.2 = 1.2$

The solution is $c = 0.2808$.

D. $\dfrac{x}{0.508} = 3.5$

E.   The total number of calories, T, is given by the formula $T = sC$ where s represents the number of servings and C represents the number of calories per serving. Find the number of calories per serving in 7.5 servings if the total number of calories is 948.

E. Use the formula in Example E to find the number of calories per serving if there is a total of 4039 calories in 35 servings.

Solution: First substitute the known values into the formula:

$T = sC$

$948 = 7.5C$ Substitute $T = 948$ and $s = 7.5$.

$\dfrac{948}{7.5} = \dfrac{7.5C}{7.5}$ Divide both sides by 7.5 to eliminate the multiplication.

$126.4 = C$

Since $7.5(126.4) = 948$, the number of calories per serving is 126.4.

NAME _____ CLASS _____ DATE _____

EXERCISES

Solve.

1. $2.3x = 13.8$ $\quad x = 6$

2. $1.7x = 0.408$ $\quad x = 0.24$

3. $0.07y = 14.28$ $\quad y = 204$

4. $0.03w = 0.378$ $\quad w = 12.6$

5. $0.123 = 2.05t$ $\quad 0.06 = t$

6. $367.72 = 11.6x$ $\quad 31.7 = x$

7. $1.1m = 0.044$ $\quad m = 0.04$

8. $0.004p = 8$ $\quad p = 2000$

9. $0.016q = 7$ $\quad q = 437.5$

10. $6 = 0.004w$ $\quad 1500 = w$

11. $8 = 0.016h$ $\quad 500 = h$

12. $\dfrac{x}{2.6} = 9.4$ $\quad x = 24.44$

13. $\dfrac{y}{8.1} = 0.33$ $\quad y = 2.673$

14. $0.03 = \dfrac{b}{0.23}$ $\quad 0.0069 = b$

15. $0.215 = \dfrac{c}{0.48}$ $\quad 0.1032 = c$

16. $\dfrac{w}{0.04} = 2.66$ $\quad w = 0.1064$

17. $0.0425 = \dfrac{x}{23}$ $\quad 0.9775 = x$

18. $0.09 = \dfrac{t}{7.14}$ $\quad 0.6426 = t$

19. $\dfrac{w}{0.06} = 0.235$ $\quad w = 0.0141$

20. $\dfrac{y}{12.3} = 1.07$ $\quad y = 13.161$

21. $\dfrac{z}{14.5} = 2.08$ $\quad z = 30.16$

22. $\dfrac{c}{9.07} = 1.003$ $\quad c = 9.09721$

E. 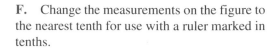 $\dfrac{49}{69}$; round to the nearest thousandth.

E. $\dfrac{33}{71}$; round to the nearest thousandth.

Solution:

ENTER	49	÷	69	=
DISPLAY	49.	49.	69.	0.7101449

So $\dfrac{49}{69} \approx 0.710$ to the nearest thousandth.

F. 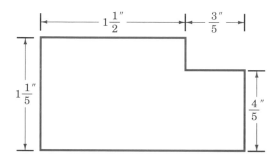 Jan needs to make a pattern of the shape shown below. Her ruler is marked in tenths. Change all the measurements to tenths so she can make an accurate pattern.

F. Change the measurements on the figure to the nearest tenth for use with a ruler marked in tenths.

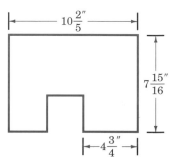

Solution: So that Jan can use her ruler for more accurate measure, each fraction is changed to a decimal rounded to the nearest tenth.

$1\dfrac{1}{2} = 1\dfrac{5}{10} = 1.5$

$\dfrac{3}{5} = \dfrac{6}{10} = 0.6$

$1\dfrac{1}{5} = 1\dfrac{2}{10} = 1.2$

$\dfrac{4}{5} = \dfrac{8}{10} = 0.8$

Each fraction and mixed number can be changed by either building each to a denominator of ten as shown or by dividing the numerator by the denominator. The measurements on the drawing can be labeled:

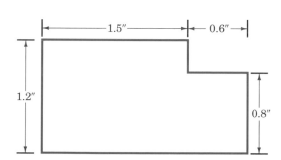

NAME _____ CLASS _____ DATE _____

EXERCISES 4.9

A

Change to a decimal.

1. $\dfrac{1}{8}$ 0.125   **2.** $\dfrac{1}{4}$ 0.25   **3.** $\dfrac{3}{8}$ 0.375

4. $\dfrac{5}{8}$ 0.625   **5.** $\dfrac{11}{16}$ 0.6875   **6.** $\dfrac{13}{16}$ 0.8125

7. $\dfrac{1}{32}$ 0.03125   **8.** $\dfrac{1}{16}$ 0.0625   **9.** $\dfrac{7}{16}$ 0.4375

Change to a decimal. Round as indicated.

	TENTH	HUNDREDTH
10. $\dfrac{3}{7}$	0.4	0.43
12. $\dfrac{2}{9}$	0.2	0.22
14. $\dfrac{1}{11}$	0.1	0.09

	TENTH	HUNDREDTH
11. $\dfrac{1}{9}$	0.1	0.11
13. $\dfrac{4}{7}$	0.6	0.57
15. $\dfrac{5}{11}$	0.5	0.45

B

Change to a decimal.

16. $\dfrac{11}{20}$ 0.55   **17.** $\dfrac{13}{20}$ 0.65   **18.** $\dfrac{3}{125}$ 0.024   **19.** $\dfrac{99}{125}$ 0.792

Change to a decimal. Round as indicated.

	TENTH	HUNDREDTH
20. $\dfrac{5}{6}$	0.8	0.83
22. $\dfrac{4}{11}$	0.4	0.36

	TENTH	HUNDREDTH
21. $\dfrac{7}{9}$	0.8	0.78
23. $\dfrac{2}{13}$	0.2	0.15

D. ▦ $2.55 \div 17 + (2.3)(4.5) + 1.37$

D. $1.82 \div 1.3 + (0.3)(14.4) + 3.79$

Solution: All but the least expensive calculators have algebraic logic. The operations can be entered in the same order as the exercise.

ENTER	2.55	÷	17	+	2.3	×	4.5	+	1.37	=
DISPLAY	2.55	2.55	17.	0.15	2.3	2.3	4.5	10.5	1.37	11.87

The result is 11.87.

How and Why 2 — The method for finding the average of a group of decimals is the same as that for whole numbers and fractions.

Examples E–F

Warm Ups E–F

Directions: Find the average.

Strategy: Use the same procedure as for whole numbers and fractions.

E. 0.1, 0.27, 0.48, and 0.03

E. 0.7, 5.2, 1.18, 0.5, and 2.4

Solution:

$$0.1 + 0.27 + 0.48 + 0.03 = 0.88 \qquad \text{First, add the numbers.}$$

$$0.88 \div 4 = 0.22 \qquad \text{Second, divide by 4, the number of numbers.}$$

The average is 0.22.

F. 🌐 Wanda has a morning and an evening rural paper route. She must drive her car to make the deliveries. During one week she made these "fill-ups":

Monday	12.8 gallons
Tuesday	16.3 gallons
Wednesday	13.2 gallons
Thursday	15.6 gallons
Friday	18.3 gallons
Saturday	17.5 gallons
Sunday	8.8 gallons

What is her average daily purchase, rounded to the nearest tenth of a gallon?

F. During another week, Wanda made these "fill-ups":

Monday	13.7 gallons
Tuesday	12.6 gallons
Wednesday	13.9 gallons
Thursday	14.4 gallons
Friday	27.7 gallons
Saturday	12.8 gallons
Sunday	0 gallons

What was her average daily purchase (not counting Sunday, since there was a typesetters' strike that day)?

Solution:

$$12.8 + 16.3 + 13.2 + 15.6 + 18.3 + 17.5 + 8.8 = 102.5 \qquad \text{Find the sum and divide by 7.}$$

$$102.5 \div 7 \approx 14.64$$

Wanda's average daily purchase is approximately 14.6 gallons.

Answers to warm ups: **D.** 9.51   **E.** 1.996   **F.** 15.85 gallons

NAME _____ CLASS _____ DATE _____

EXERCISES 4.10

A

Perform the indicated operations.

1. $0.6 + 0.2 - 0.3$ 0.5   **2.** $0.9 - 0.4 + 0.3$ 0.8   **3.** $0.21 \div 7 + 0.02$ 0.05

4. $0.32 \div 4 + 0.03$ 0.11   **5.** $1.8 - 2(0.8)$ 0.2   **6.** $2.4 - 3(0.3)$ 1.5

7. $2(1.2) + 0.1(30)$ 5.4   **8.** $3(2.1) + 0.2(20)$ 10.3   **9.** $0.08 + (0.2)^2$ 0.12

10. $0.41 + (0.3)^2$ 0.5

Find the average.

11. $1.2, 3.4$ 2.3   **12.** $4.5, 6.3$ 5.4   **13.** $2.2, 2.3, 2.4$ 2.3

14. $4.1, 4.3, 4.5$ 4.3   **15.** $2.7, 2.3, 4$ 3   **16.** $7.2, 4.8, 6$ 6

B

Perform the indicated operations.

17. $5.03 - 2.19 + 0.75 - 1.17$ 2.42   **18.** $0.08 + 2.37 - 1.6 + 0.98$ 1.83

19. $4.97 \div (0.07)(3.1)$ 220.1   **20.** $(52.5) \div (0.05)(0.2)$ 210

21. $(25.6)(0.08) \div 0.02$ 102.4   **22.** $(6.5)(2.14) \div (0.13)$ 107

23. $(6.3)^2 - 12.02$ 27.67   **24.** $(0.5)^2(2.1 \div 1.05)$ 0.5

25. $(4.6)(0.3)^3 \div 2.07$ 0.06   **26.** $(1.4)^3 - (0.2)^2$ 2.704

19. Multiply: 0.00216(10,000)   21.6 [4.7-1]

20. Write the place-value name for

$$20 + 5 + \frac{7}{10} + \frac{0}{100} + \frac{9}{1000}$$ 25.709 [4.1-3]

21. Write in scientific notation: 32,750
3.275×10^4 [4.7-2]

22. Write as an approximate decimal to the nearest thousandth: $7\frac{3}{11}$ 7.273 [4.9]

23. Divide: 0.08 ÷ 100   0.0008 [4.7-1]

24. Multiply: (7.6)(0.0018)   0.01368 [4.6]

25. For each of the four Sundays of February, the offering at the Chapel on the Hill was $68.25, $76.55, $82.76, and $71.33. What was the average Sunday offering? $74.72 [4.10-2]

26. Add: 1.07 + 0.659 + 12.36 + 8.9   22.989 [4.4]

27. Divide: $25\overline{)1.375}$ 0.055 [4.8]

28. During a canned vegetable sale Ted buys 14 cans of various vegetables. If the sale price is 4 cans for $1.79, how much does Ted pay for the canned vegetables? $6.27 [4.10-1]

Ratio and Proportion

Personal satisfaction is the reward for a long-distance runner determined to reach her goal. Setting a goal is the critical first step, for the runner and for the student of mathematics. (Lori Adamski Peek/ Tony Stone Images)

25. 800 miles to (per) 16 hours $\dfrac{50 \text{ miles}}{1 \text{ hour}}$

26. 700 feet to (per) 35 seconds $\dfrac{20 \text{ feet}}{1 \text{ second}}$

27. $42 to 14 pairs of socks $\dfrac{\$3}{1 \text{ pair}}$

28. 36 lb to $15 $\dfrac{12 \text{ lb}}{\$5}$

29. 220 miles to 4 hours $\dfrac{55 \text{ miles}}{1 \text{ hour}}$

30. 375 pies to 50 sales $\dfrac{15 \text{ pies}}{2 \text{ sales}}$

C

Write as a ratio or a rate.

31. 24 cups of sugar for 16 cakes $\dfrac{3 \text{ cups}}{2 \text{ cakes}}$

32. 750 people for 3000 tickets $\dfrac{1 \text{ person}}{4 \text{ tickets}}$

33. $7.50 to $8.50 $\dfrac{15}{17}$

34. $10.25 to $15.25 $\dfrac{41}{61}$

35. 8775 households to 6 cable companies
$\dfrac{2925 \text{ households}}{2 \text{ cable companies}}$

36. 234, the number of teeth in a large gear, to 36, the number of teeth in a small gear $\dfrac{13}{2}$

Write as a unit rate.

37. 825 miles to 22 gallons of gasoline $\dfrac{37.5 \text{ miles}}{1 \text{ gallon}}$

38. 729 miles to 27 gallons of gasoline $\dfrac{27 \text{ miles}}{1 \text{ gallon}}$

39. 1056 feet to 12 seconds $\dfrac{88 \text{ feet}}{1 \text{ second}}$

40. 12,096 pounds to 48 square inches $\dfrac{252 \text{ pounds}}{1 \text{ square inch}}$

41. 340 miles to 8 hours $\dfrac{42.5 \text{ miles}}{1 \text{ hour}}$

42. 228 gallons to 15 minutes $\dfrac{15.2 \text{ gallons}}{1 \text{ minute}}$

NAME _____ CLASS _____ DATE _____

Applications

43. The parking lot in the lower level of the Knew Office Building has 28 spaces for compact cars and 40 spaces for larger cars. (See the drawing below.)

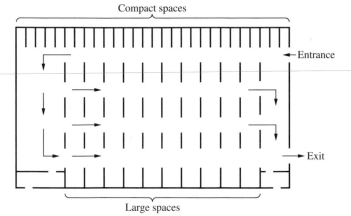

Compact spaces

←Entrance

→ Exit

Large spaces

a. What is the rate of the number of compact spaces to larger spaces?

b. What is the rate of compact spaces to the total number of spaces?

a. $\frac{7}{10}$ b. $\frac{7}{17}$

44. The Reliable Auto Repair Service building has ten stalls for repairing automobiles and five stalls for repairing small trucks.

a. What is the rate of the number of stalls for small trucks to the number of stalls for automobiles?

b. What is the rate of the number of stalls for small trucks to the total number of stalls?

a. $\frac{1}{2}$ b. $\frac{1}{3}$

45. One section of the country has 3500 TV sets per 1000 houses. A second section has 500 sets per 150 houses. Are the unit rates equal?   No

46. In City A there are 5000 automobiles per 3000 households. In City B there are 8000 automobiles per 4800 households. Are the unit rates the same?   Yes

47. What is the population density of Dryton if 22,450 people live there and the area is 230 square miles? Reduce to a one-square-mile comparison, rounded to the nearest tenth. $\frac{97.6 \text{ people}}{1 \text{ square mile}}$

48. What is the population density of Struvaria if there are 950,000 people and the area is 18,000 square miles? Reduce to a one-square-mile comparison, rounded to the nearest tenth. $\frac{52.8 \text{ people}}{1 \text{ square mile}}$

49. What was the population density of your city in 1990? Your county? Your state?   Answers will vary.

50. A store buys a sofa for a cost of $175 and sells it for $300. What is the ratio of the cost to the selling price? $\frac{7}{12}$

51. A store buys a bicycle for $350 and advertises it to sell for $600. What is the ratio of the cost to the selling price? $\dfrac{7}{12}$

Sale price $600

52. In Exercise 51, what is the ratio of the markup (the difference between the cost and the selling price) to the cost? $\dfrac{5}{7}$

53. In Exercise 51, what is the ratio of the markup to the selling price? $\dfrac{5}{12}$

54. A potted plant is regularly priced at $9.99, but during a sale its price is $6.66. What is the ratio of the sale price to the regular price? $\dfrac{2}{3}$

Regular price $9.99
Sale price $6.66

55. In Exercise 54, what is the ratio of the discount (difference between the sale price and the regular price) to the regular price? $\dfrac{1}{3}$

56. In accounting, the current ratio is defined as

$$\text{Current ratio} = \frac{\text{current assets}}{\text{current liabilities}}$$

What is the current ratio for a business if the current assets are $3,840,000 and the current liabilities are $2,560,000? $\dfrac{3}{2}$

NAME _____ CLASS _____ DATE _____

57. Using the formula in Exercise 56, what is the Current Ratio for a business if the current assets are $7,750,000 and the current liabilities are $5,500,000? $\frac{31}{22}$

58. In a recent study on multiple sclerosis, a new drug was given to 15 patients while 15 other patients were given a placebo. Only 6 out of the first 15 had attacks, while 12 of the second 15 had attacks. Write a ratio of attacks to patients with the new drug and then a ratio of attacks to patients without the new drug. Finally write a ratio for attacks to total patients. $\frac{2}{5}; \frac{4}{5}; \frac{3}{5}$

59. In the United States, four people use an average of 250 gallons of water per day. One hundred gallons are used to flush the toilet, 80 gallons in baths/showers, 35 gallons doing the laundry, 15 gallons washing dishes, 12 gallons for cooking/drinking, and 8 gallons in the bathroom sink. Write the following ratios:

a. Laundry use to toilet use
b. Bathing/showering use to dishwashing use
c. Cooking/drinking use to dishwashing use
d. Rate of laundry use per person

a. $\frac{7}{20}$ b. $\frac{16}{3}$ c. $\frac{4}{5}$ d. $\frac{8.75}{1}$ gallons per person

60. Drinking water is considered to be polluted when a pollution index of 0.05 mg of lead per liter is reached. At that rate how many mg of lead are needed to pollute 25 liters of drinking water?

1.25 mg

61. Data indicate that 3 out of every 20 rivers in the United States showed an increase in water pollution from 1974 to 1983. Determine how many rivers are in your state. At the same rate, determine how many of that number had an increased pollution level during the same period. Answers will vary.

State Your Understanding

62. Explain the difference between a ratio and a rate.

63. Explain the difference between a rate and a unit rate.

Challenge

Are the two ratios equal?

64. $\dfrac{3(7-5)}{2(8-7)}; \dfrac{8(7+2)}{6(8-4)}$ Yes

65. $\dfrac{41-5(8-3)}{32+(2\cdot5-6)}; \dfrac{8\cdot5}{90}$ Yes

66. $\dfrac{0.8(0.15+0.25)}{1.2(2-0.5)+1}; \dfrac{0.5[2(0.8)-4(0.2)]}{0.7(5)}$ Yes

67. Write the ratio of 0.25 to 0.7 as a fraction reduced to lowest terms. $\dfrac{5}{14}$

68. Write the ratio of 0.88 to 1.2 as a fraction reduced to lowest terms. $\dfrac{11}{15}$

69. Each gram of fat contains 9 calories. Chicken sandwiches at various fast-food places contain the following total calories and grams of fat:

		Calories	Grams of Fat
a.	RB's Light Roast Chicken Sandwich	276	7
b.	KB's Broiler Chicken Sandwich	267	8
c.	Hard B's Chicken Filet	370	13
d.	LJS's Baked Chicken	130	4
e.	The Major's Chicken Sandwich	482	27
f.	Mickey's Chicken	415	19
g.	Tampico's Soft Chicken Taco	213	10
h.	Winston's Grilled Chicken Sandwich	290	7

Determine the ratio of fat calories to total calories.

a. $\dfrac{21}{92}$ **b.** $\dfrac{24}{89}$ **c.** $\dfrac{117}{370}$ **d.** $\dfrac{18}{65}$ **e.** $\dfrac{243}{482}$ **f.** $\dfrac{171}{415}$ **g.** $\dfrac{30}{71}$ **h.** $\dfrac{63}{290}$

NAME _____ CLASS _____ DATE _____

Group Activity

70. Each group is to select one of the following surveys to conduct in class or outside of class.

   a. Survey of people's current ages.

   b. Survey of people who normally eat breakfast, lunch, and dinner.

   c. Survey of beverages that people drink in one day.

Each group is to make a chart for the survey chosen. Decide which ratios to use for each group. Combine each group result to get a classroom result. Make a chart of these results. Determine the same ratios as those determined in the group. Compare the class ratios with the group ratios. Which are greater? Which are the same?

Maintain Your Skills (Sections 4.1, 4.2, 4.3, 4.6, 4.8)

71. Write the word name for 4800.005.

   Four thousand, eight hundred and five thousandths

72. Change 0.125 to a fraction. $\frac{1}{8}$

73. True or false? $0.08 > 0.789$ False

74. List these decimals from the smallest to the largest: 6.03, 6.003, 6.087, 6.006, 6.023

   6.003, 6.006, 6.023, 6.03, 6.087

75. Round 0.89923 to the nearest hundredth.   0.90

76. Round 5.49987 to the nearest unit.   5

77. Multiply: (11.895)(0.56)   6.6612

78. Multiply: (11.089)(0.056)   0.620984

79. Jill goes to the gasoline station and has her automobile's tank filled. It takes 8.9 gallons to fill the tank and the gasoline costs $1.299 per gallon. Does she need to give the attendant one or two $10 bills to pay for the gasoline? (Round the cost to the nearest cent.) In any event, how much change will she receive?   2 tens; $8.44

80. A hospital patient is scheduled to be given 1250 cubic centimeters of an IV solution during the next eight hours. How many cubic centimeters per minute is this, rounded to the nearest tenth?

   2.6 cubic centimeters per minute

5.2   SOLVING PROPORTIONS

Objectives

1 Determine whether a proportion is true or false.

2 Solve a proportion.

Application

🌐 If $\frac{1}{5}$ of the people purchased products with no plastic wrapping $\frac{1}{5}$ of the time, 144 tons of plastic would be eliminated from our landfills each year. At the same rate, how many tons would be eliminated if $\frac{1}{5}$ of the people purchased products with no plastic wrapping $\frac{3}{4}$ of the time?

Vocabulary

A **proportion** is a statement that two ratios are equal. **Cross multiplication** in a proportion means multiplying the numerator of each ratio times the denominator of the other. **Cross products** are the products obtained from cross multiplication.

In proportions we use a letter to hold the place of a missing number. The letter that is used is called an unknown or a **variable.** Finding the missing number that will make the proportion true is called **solving the proportion.**

How and Why 1

The statement $\frac{3}{4} = \frac{6}{8}$ is a proportion. Moreover, it is a true proportion since $\frac{6}{8}$ reduces to $\frac{3}{4}$. Other proportions may be true or false. The test to tell whether a proportion is true or false is called "cross multiplication." To perform this test, multiply each numerator times the denominator on the other side of the equal sign. If the cross products are equal, the proportion is true. If the cross products are not equal, the proportion is false. To test whether $\frac{3}{4} = \frac{6}{8}$ is true or false, we write

$$\frac{3\searrow}{4\nearrow} = \frac{\nearrow 6}{\searrow 8} \qquad \text{Multiply in the direction of the arrows.}$$

$$3(8) = 4(6)$$

$$24 = 24 \qquad \text{The cross products are equal so the proportion is true.}$$

The cross-product process will always determine the validity of a proportion since if

$$\frac{a}{b} = \frac{c}{d} \qquad \text{then} \qquad \frac{a}{b} \cdot \frac{d}{d} = \frac{c}{d} \cdot \frac{b}{b} \qquad \begin{array}{l}\text{Build each fraction to} \\ \text{a common denominator.}\end{array}$$

so

$$\frac{ad}{bd} = \frac{bc}{bd} \qquad \begin{array}{l}\text{These two fractions are} \\ \text{equal since the original} \\ \text{fractions were equal.}\end{array}$$

Since the two fractions are equal and the denominators are the same, the numerators must be equal. Therefore, if $\frac{a}{b} = \frac{c}{d}$, then $ad = bc$.

▶ **To tell whether a proportion is true or false**

1. If the proportion contains rates, check that the units are the same.
2. Cross multiply.
3. If the cross products are equal, the proportion is true.

Examples A–C   **Warm Ups A–C**

Directions: Determine whether a proportion is true or false.

Strategy: Check the cross products. If they are equal, the proportion is true.

A. $\dfrac{6}{5} = \dfrac{72}{60}$ **A.** $\dfrac{7}{8} = \dfrac{42}{48}$

Solution:

$\dfrac{6}{5} = \dfrac{72}{60}$ Find the cross products.

$6(60) = 360$

$5(72) = 360$ The cross products are equal.

The proportion is true.

B. $\dfrac{4.1}{7.1} = \dfrac{4}{7}$ **B.** $\dfrac{5.6}{6.3} = \dfrac{5}{6}$

Solution:

$\dfrac{4.1}{7.1} = \dfrac{4}{7}$ Find the cross products.

$(4.1)(7) = 28.7$

$(7.1)(4) = 28.4$ The cross products are *not* equal.

The proportion is false.

C. $\dfrac{1 \text{ dollar}}{3 \text{ quarters}} = \dfrac{8 \text{ dimes}}{12 \text{ nickels}}$ **C.** $\dfrac{1 \text{ dollar}}{2 \text{ quarters}} = \dfrac{16 \text{ nickels}}{4 \text{ dimes}}$

Solution: The rates do not have the same units. We change everything to cents and drop the common unit.

$\dfrac{1 \text{ dollar}}{3 \text{ quarters}} = \dfrac{8 \text{ dimes}}{12 \text{ nickels}}$

$\dfrac{100 \text{ cents}}{75 \text{ cents}} = \dfrac{80 \text{ cents}}{60 \text{ cents}}$

$\dfrac{100}{75} = \dfrac{80}{60}$

$(100)(60) = 6000$ Check the cross products.

$(75)(80) = 6000$ They are equal.

The proportion is true.

How and Why Proportions are used to solve many problems in science, technology, and business. There are four numbers in a proportion. If three numbers are given, we can find the missing number.

What number is to 5 as 15 is to 25? To answer this, we use x to hold the place of the missing number.

$$\frac{x}{5} = \frac{15}{25}$$

Since the cross products are equal, we have

$$25(x) = 5(15)$$
$$25(x) = 75$$

Any multiplication problem has two related division problems. The product divided by either factor gives the other factor. So

$$x = 75 \div 25 \qquad \text{or} \qquad x = 3$$

The missing number is 3.

▶ **To solve a proportion**

1. Cross multiply.
2. Do the related division problem to find the missing number.

Examples D–I   Warm Ups D–I

Directions: Solve the proportion.

Strategy: Cross multiply and do the related division problem to find the missing number.

D. $\dfrac{4}{9} = \dfrac{8}{x}$ **D.** $\dfrac{5}{9} = \dfrac{10}{x}$

Solution:

$\dfrac{4}{9} = \dfrac{8}{x}$

$4(x) = 9 \cdot 8$ Cross multiply.

$4(x) = 72$ Simplify the right side.

$x = 72 \div 4$ Do related division.

$x = 18$

CHECK: Substitute 18 for x in the original proportion. To check, cross multiply.

$\dfrac{4}{9} = \dfrac{8}{18}$

$4 \cdot 18 = 9 \cdot 8$

$72 = 72$ The proportion is true.

The missing number is 18.

E. $\dfrac{5}{3} = \dfrac{y}{8}$

E. $\dfrac{7}{5} = \dfrac{a}{4}$

Solution:

$$\dfrac{5}{3} = \dfrac{y}{8}$$

$5 \cdot 8 = 3(y)$

$40 = 3(y)$ Multiply.

$40 \div 3 = y$

$13\dfrac{1}{3} = y$ The check is left for the student.

F. $\dfrac{0.6}{x} = \dfrac{0.16}{0.96}$

F. $\dfrac{0.8}{x} = \dfrac{0.12}{0.72}$

Solution:

$$\dfrac{0.6}{x} = \dfrac{0.16}{0.96}$$

$(0.6)(0.96) = (0.16)x$

$0.576 = (0.16)x$ Simplify the left side.

$0.576 \div 0.16 = x$

$3.6 = x$ The check is left for the student.

G. $\dfrac{\dfrac{3}{4}}{1\dfrac{2}{3}} = \dfrac{\dfrac{1}{2}}{x}$

G. $\dfrac{\dfrac{5}{6}}{\dfrac{3}{4}} = \dfrac{\dfrac{2}{3}}{x}$

Solution:

$$\dfrac{\dfrac{3}{4}}{1\dfrac{2}{3}} = \dfrac{\dfrac{1}{2}}{x}$$

$\dfrac{3}{4}x = \left(1\dfrac{2}{3}\right)\left(\dfrac{1}{2}\right)$

$\dfrac{3}{4}x = \left(\dfrac{5}{3}\right)\left(\dfrac{1}{2}\right)$ Change the mixed number to an improper fraction.

$\dfrac{3}{4}x = \dfrac{5}{6}$ Simplify.

$x = \dfrac{5}{6} \div \dfrac{3}{4}$ The related division problem.

$x = \left(\dfrac{5}{\cancel{6}}\right)\left(\dfrac{\cancel{4}^{\,2}}{3}\right)$ Invert the divisor and multiply. Reduce.

Answers to warm ups: **E.** $b = \dfrac{28}{5}$ or $5\dfrac{3}{5}$ **F.** $x = 4.8$

$$x = \frac{10}{9} = 1\frac{1}{9}$$ The check is left for the student.

H. 🖩 $\dfrac{3}{x} = \dfrac{9.6}{11.52}$

H. $\dfrac{4}{x} = \dfrac{1.28}{3.28}$

Solution:

$3(11.52) = (9.6)x$

$3(11.52) \div 9.6 = x$ Related division problem.

ENTER	3	×	11.52	÷	9.6	=

DISPLAY   3.   3.   11.52 34.56 9.6   3.6

Therefore $x = 3.6$.

I. 🌐 If $\dfrac{1}{5}$ of the people purchased products with no plastic wrapping $\dfrac{1}{5}$ of the time, 144 tons of plastic would be eliminated from our landfills each year. At the same rate, how many tons would be eliminated if $\dfrac{1}{5}$ of the people purchased products with no plastic wrapping $\dfrac{3}{4}$ of the time?

Solution: The ratio of the fractions and the ratio of the tons eliminated should be the same. This will form our proportion.

$$\frac{\frac{1}{5}}{\frac{3}{4}} = \frac{144 \text{ tons}}{x \text{ tons}}$$

$\dfrac{1}{5}x = \dfrac{3}{4}(144)$ Cross multiply.

$\dfrac{1}{5}x = 108$ Simplify.

$x = 108 \div \dfrac{1}{5}$

$x = 540$

So 540 tons of plastic would be eliminated from our landfills.

I. If $\dfrac{1}{5}$ of the people bought products with no plastic wrapping $\dfrac{11}{20}$ of the time, how much plastic would be eliminated from our landfills each year? (Assume the same rate as in Example I.)

Answers to warm ups: **G.** $x = \dfrac{3}{5}$ **H.** $x = 10.25$ **I.** 396 tons eliminated

NAME _____ CLASS _____ DATE _____

EXERCISES 5.2

A

Determine whether the proportion is true or false.

1. $\dfrac{4}{2} = \dfrac{8}{4}$ True

2. $\dfrac{2}{3} = \dfrac{4}{6}$ True

3. $\dfrac{6}{9} = \dfrac{2}{3}$ True

4. $\dfrac{6}{8} = \dfrac{3}{4}$ True

5. $\dfrac{11}{12} = \dfrac{3}{4}$ False

6. $\dfrac{3}{7} = \dfrac{4}{14}$ False

Solve.

7. $\dfrac{7}{9} = \dfrac{a}{18}$ 14

8. $\dfrac{13}{3} = \dfrac{52}{c}$ 12

9. $\dfrac{b}{10} = \dfrac{2}{5}$ 4

10. $\dfrac{16}{v} = \dfrac{2}{5}$ 40

11. $\dfrac{14}{5} = \dfrac{28}{x}$ 10

12. $\dfrac{6}{a} = \dfrac{8}{12}$ 9

13. $\dfrac{c}{5} = \dfrac{20}{25}$ 4

14. $\dfrac{9}{x} = \dfrac{36}{12}$ 3

15. $\dfrac{10}{12} = \dfrac{15}{x}$ 18

16. $\dfrac{x}{7} = \dfrac{21}{49}$ 3

17. $\dfrac{6}{8} = \dfrac{12}{x}$ 16

18. $\dfrac{x}{42} = \dfrac{5}{7}$ 30

19. $\dfrac{9}{3} = \dfrac{n}{2}$ 6

20. $\dfrac{8}{4} = \dfrac{b}{3}$ 6

B

Determine whether the proportion is true or false.

21. $\dfrac{18}{12} = \dfrac{15}{10}$ True

22. $\dfrac{16}{10} = \dfrac{24}{15}$ True

23. $\dfrac{35}{30} = \dfrac{22}{20}$ False

24. $\dfrac{24}{36} = \dfrac{32}{38}$ False

25. $\dfrac{27}{30} = \dfrac{45}{60}$ False

26. $\dfrac{45}{36} = \dfrac{25}{20}$ True

Solve.

27. $\dfrac{7}{2} = \dfrac{x}{3}$ $\dfrac{21}{2}$ or 10.5

28. $\dfrac{5}{4} = \dfrac{x}{3}$ $\dfrac{15}{4}$ or 3.75

29. $\dfrac{x}{2} = \dfrac{11}{5}$ $\dfrac{22}{5}$ or 4.4

30. $\dfrac{12}{16} = \dfrac{x}{3}$ $\dfrac{9}{4}$ or 2.25

31. $\dfrac{16}{x} = \dfrac{24}{16}$ $\dfrac{32}{3}$

32. $\dfrac{9}{x} = \dfrac{11}{15}$ $\dfrac{135}{11}$

33. $\dfrac{15}{6} = \dfrac{w}{21}$ $\dfrac{105}{2}$ or 52.5

34. $\dfrac{12}{15} = \dfrac{w}{16}$ $\dfrac{64}{5}$ or 12.8

35. $\dfrac{28}{50} = \dfrac{7}{x}$ $\dfrac{25}{2}$ or 12.5

36. $\dfrac{0.3}{x} = \dfrac{0.4}{8}$ 6

37. $\dfrac{0.1}{0.2} = \dfrac{x}{1.2}$ 0.6

38. $\dfrac{0.5}{x} = \dfrac{0.2}{0.6}$ 1.5

39. $\dfrac{0.3}{0.4} = \dfrac{12}{x}$ 16

40. $\dfrac{0.2}{0.3} = \dfrac{8}{x}$ 12

C

Determine whether the proportion is true or false.

41. $\dfrac{18.48}{18.18} = \dfrac{27.72}{27.27}$ True

42. $\dfrac{0.005}{0.015} = \dfrac{0.018}{0.054}$ True

43. $\dfrac{2\frac{3}{4}}{12} = \dfrac{11}{48}$ True

44. $\dfrac{21}{5\frac{3}{4}} = \dfrac{12}{3\frac{2}{7}}$ True

45. $\dfrac{\frac{3}{5}}{\frac{1}{4}} = \dfrac{8}{5}$ False

46. $\dfrac{\frac{2}{3}}{1\frac{1}{3}} = \dfrac{\frac{8}{9}}{1\frac{7}{9}}$ True

Solve.

47. $\dfrac{w}{90} = \dfrac{45}{18}$ 225

48. $\dfrac{7.4}{37} = \dfrac{15}{m}$ 75

49. $\dfrac{x}{0.014} = \dfrac{50}{70}$ 0.01

NAME _____ CLASS _____ DATE _____

50. $\dfrac{2}{5} = \dfrac{a}{3.5}$ 1.4

51. $\dfrac{0.9}{0.05} = \dfrac{4.5}{b}$ 0.25

52. $\dfrac{2.7}{1.2} = \dfrac{w}{3.4}$ 7.65

53. $\dfrac{7}{42} = \dfrac{\frac{1}{2}}{w}$ 3

54. $\dfrac{b}{30} = \dfrac{2}{\frac{3}{4}}$ 80

55. $\dfrac{\frac{1}{8}}{9} = \dfrac{3}{y}$ 216

56. $\dfrac{x}{40} = \dfrac{\frac{3}{4}}{5}$ 6

57. $\dfrac{3\frac{1}{2}}{10\frac{1}{2}} = \dfrac{8}{y}$ 24

58. $\dfrac{2\frac{1}{2}}{3\frac{1}{3}} = \dfrac{4\frac{1}{4}}{w}$ $5\frac{2}{3}$

Solve. Round to the nearest tenth.

59. $\dfrac{\frac{1}{4}}{0.5} = \dfrac{b}{0.9}$ 0.5

60. $\dfrac{\frac{1}{4}}{c} = \dfrac{1.5}{8}$ 1.3

61. $\dfrac{9}{35} = \dfrac{12}{x}$ 46.7

62. $\dfrac{7}{50} = \dfrac{c}{18}$ 2.5

Solve. Round to the nearest hundredth.

63. $\dfrac{9}{16} = \dfrac{x}{14}$ 7.88

64. $\dfrac{5}{z} = \dfrac{15}{16}$ 5.33

65. $\dfrac{1.5}{4.5} = \dfrac{b}{0.85}$ 0.28

66. $\dfrac{4.5}{0.28} = \dfrac{8}{b}$ 0.50

67. $\dfrac{285}{128} = \dfrac{c}{8}$ 17.81

68. $\dfrac{84}{a} = \dfrac{225}{52}$ 19.41

69. $\dfrac{4.76}{r} = \dfrac{28}{8.2}$ 1.39

70. $\dfrac{0.88}{x} = \dfrac{0.36}{1.75}$ 4.28

Applications

71. Data show that it takes the use of 18,000,000 gasoline-powered lawn mowers to produce the same amount of air pollution as 3,000,000 new cars. Determine the number of gasoline-powered lawn mowers that will produce the same amount of air pollution as 50,000 new cars.   300,000 lawn mowers

72. Older shower heads use eight gallons of water per minute. Newer showers use three gallons per minute. Time your next shower and determine how many gallons of water you use if you have an old shower head. Determine the number of gallons of water you use if you have the new shower head. Answers will vary.

73. For every 10 people in the United States, it is believed that 7 suffer from some form of migraine headache.

  a. Determine how many migraine sufferers would be in a group of 350 people.   245 people
  b. If three times as many women as men suffer from migraines, find the number of men that suffer from migraines if in a certain group it is known that 306 women are affected with migraines.   102 men
  c. It is believed that headaches in 8 out of every 40 migraine sufferers are related to diet. At this rate, determine the number of migraine headaches that could be related to diet in a group of 350 migraine sufferers.
  70 headaches

State Your Understanding

74. If $\dfrac{a}{b} = \dfrac{c}{d}$ is true, is it correct to say that $\dfrac{d}{c} = \dfrac{b}{a}$ is also true? Why?

75. If $\dfrac{a}{b} = \dfrac{c}{d}$ is true, is it correct to say that $\dfrac{a}{c} = \dfrac{b}{d}$ is also true? Why?

Challenge

Solve.

76. $\dfrac{8+4}{5+10} = \dfrac{8}{x}$ 10

77. $\dfrac{25-10}{7 \cdot 5 - 8} = \dfrac{x}{3 \cdot 3}$ 5

78. $\dfrac{5 \cdot 9 - 2 \cdot 5}{8 \cdot 6 - 3 \cdot 2} = \dfrac{8 \cdot 5}{x}$ 48

NAME _____ CLASS _____ DATE _____

Group Activity

79. Five ounces of decaffeinated coffee contains approximately 3 mg of caffeine while five ounces of regular coffee contains an average of 120 mg of caffeine. Five ounces of tea brewed for one minute contains an average of 21 mg of caffeine. Twelve ounces of regular cola contains an average of 54 mg of caffeine. Six ounces of hot cocoa contains an average of 11 mg of caffeine. Twelve ounces of iced tea contains an average of 72 mg of caffeine. Determine the total amount of caffeine each member of your group consumed yesterday. Make a chart to illustrate this information. Combine this information with the other groups in your class to make a class amount. Make a class chart to illustrate this information. Determine the average amount of caffeine consumed by each member of the group and then by each member of the class. Compare these averages by making ratios. Discuss the similarities or differences.

Maintain Your Skills (Sections 4.6, 4.8, 4.10)

Multiply.

80. $(0.875)(29)$
25.375

81. $(3.0087)(0.28)$
0.842436

82. $(12.75)(8.09)$
103.1475

83. $(400.8)(5.07)$
2032.056

Divide.

84. $0.35\overline{)0.70035}$ 2.001

85. $0.72\overline{)3.6}$ 5

86. Divide 8.2 by 66 and round to the nearest hundredth.   0.12

87. Divide 66 by 8.2 and round to the nearest thousandth.   8.049

88. If the cost of gasoline is $1.249 per gallon, how much should Jean pay the attendant if it takes 12.8 gallons to fill her automobile's tank? (Don't forget to round your answer to the nearest cent.) $15.99

89. A barrel of liquid weighs 429.5 pounds. If the barrel weighs 22.5 pounds and the liquid weighs approximately 7.4 pounds per gallon, how many gallons does the barrel contain?   55 gallons

5.3 APPLICATIONS OF PROPORTIONS

Objective   Solve word problems using proportions.

Application   It is claimed that if 250 people each recycle one can a day for a year, the equivalent of approximately 2500 gallons of gasoline can be saved each year. At the same rate, if 200,000 people recycle one can a day for a year, how many gallons of gasoline can be saved in one year?

How and Why   If the rate of comparison of two quantities is constant, the rate can be used to find the missing part of a second rate. For instance, if two pounds of grapes cost $0.98, what will 12 pounds cost?

	Case I	Case II
Pounds of Grapes	2	12
Cost in Dollars	0.98	

In the chart the cost in Case II is missing. Call the missing value y.

	Case I	Case II
Pounds of Grapes	2	12
Cost in Dollars	0.98	y

Write the proportion using the rates as shown in the chart.

$$\frac{2 \text{ lb of grapes}}{\$0.98} = \frac{12 \text{ lb of grapes}}{\$y}$$

Cross multiplying gives us

$$(2 \text{ lb of grapes})(\$y) = (12 \text{ lb of grapes})(\$0.98)$$
$$\$y = (12 \text{ lb})(\$0.98) \div (2 \text{ lb})$$
$$\$y = \$11.76 \div 2$$
$$\$y = \$5.88$$

Notice that if we drop the units, since they are the same on both sides, we arrive at the equation

$$y = 5.88$$

We will solve these problems without using the common units. However, we must remember to insert the correct unit when giving the answer.

▶ **To solve word problems involving proportions**

1. Write the two rates and form the proportion. (A chart with two columns and two rows will help organize the data. The proportion will be shown in the boxes.)
2. Solve the proportion.

Examples A–C   **Warm Ups A–C**

Directions: Solve the word problem involving proportions.

Strategy: Make a chart. Fill in each space with the appropriate information and solve the proportion.

A.   On a road map of Oregon, $\frac{1}{4}$ inch represents 50 miles. How many miles are represented by $1\frac{3}{4}$ inches?

A.   On a road map of Jackson County, $\frac{1}{4}$ inch represents 25 miles. How many miles are represented by $2\frac{1}{4}$ inches?

Solution: Make a chart, label the columns Case I and Case II. The first row is inches, the second is miles. Enter the appropriate measure in each box. The letter N represents the number of miles represented by $1\frac{3}{4}$ inches.

	Case I	Case II
Inches	$\frac{1}{4}$	$1\frac{3}{4}$
Miles	50	N

$\dfrac{\frac{1}{4}}{50} = \dfrac{1\frac{3}{4}}{N}$ The proportion is shown in the boxes. We do not write the units in the proportion.

$\frac{1}{4}(N) = \left(1\frac{3}{4}\right)(50)$ Cross multiply.

$\frac{1}{4}(N) = \left(\frac{7}{\cancel{4}_2}\right)\left(\frac{\cancel{50}^{25}}{1}\right)$ Change the mixed numbers to improper fractions and simplify.

$\frac{1}{4}(N) = \frac{175}{2}$

$N = \frac{175}{2} \div \frac{1}{4}$ The related division problem.

$N = \frac{175}{\cancel{2}_1} \cdot \frac{\cancel{4}^2}{1}$ Simplify.

$N = 350$

Therefore $1\frac{3}{4}$ inches on the map represents 350 miles.

B. The city fire code requires a school to have at least 50 square feet of floor space in a classroom for each three students that are in the class. What is the minimum number of square feet needed for 30 students?

Solution: Make a chart, label the columns Case I and Case II. The first row is labeled students while the second row is square feet. Enter the appropriate measures in each box. Let S represent the number of square feet needed for 30 students.

	Case I	Case II
Students	3	30
Square Feet	50	S

$\dfrac{3}{50} = \dfrac{30}{S}$ The proportion is shown in the boxes.

$3S = (50)(30)$ Cross multiply.

$3S = 1500$ Multiply on the right.

$S = 1500 \div 3$ The related division problem.

$S = 500$ Simplify.

The room must have at least 500 square feet for 30 students.

C. 🌐 It is claimed that if 250 people each recycle one can a day for a year, the equivalent of approximately 2500 gallons of gasoline can be saved each year. At the same rate, if 200,000 people recycle one can a day for a year, how many gallons of gasoline can be saved in one year?

Solution: Make a chart. Label the columns. The first row is people, the second is energy saved.

	Case I	Case II
People	250	200,000
Energy Saved	2500 gal	x

$\dfrac{250}{2500} = \dfrac{200,000}{x}$ Write the proportion.

$250(x) = (2500)(200,000)$ Cross multiply.

$250x = 500,000,000$ Simplify the right side.

$x = 500,000,000 \div 250$ The related division problem.

$x = 2,000,000$

If 200,000 people recycle one can per day for a year, approximately the equivalent of 2,000,000 gallons of gasoline can be saved.

B. In another city the fire code requires a school to have at least 86 square feet for each 5 students. What is the minimum area needed for 30 students?

C. If 350,000 people recycle one can a day for a year, how many gallons of gasoline can be saved in one year?

Answers to warm ups: **B.** 516 square feet   **C.** 3,500,000 gallons

NAME _____ CLASS _____ DATE _____

EXERCISES 5.3

A

A photograph that measures 6 inches wide and 4 inches high is to be enlarged so that the width will be 15 inches. What will be the height of the enlargement?

15 in.

6 in. x in.

4 in.

	Case I	Case II
Width	(a)	(c)
Height	(b)	(d)

1. What goes in box (a)?   6

2. What goes in box (b)?   4

3. What goes in box (c)?   15

4. What goes in box (d)? x

5. What is the proportion for the problem? $\frac{6}{4} = \frac{15}{x}$

6. What is the height of the enlargement?
10 inches

If a fir tree is 30 feet tall and casts a shadow of 18 feet, how tall is a tree that casts a shadow of 48 feet?

	First Tree	Second Tree
Height	(1)	(3)
Shadow	(2)	(4)

7. What goes in box (1)?   30

8. What goes in box (2)?   18

9. What goes in box (3)? x

10. What goes in box (4)?   48

11. What is the proportion for the problem? $\dfrac{30}{18} = \dfrac{x}{48}$ **12.** How tall is the second tree? 80 feet

Jean and Jim are building a fence around their yard. From past experience they know that they are able to build 48 feet in 8 hours. If they work at the same rate, how many hours will it take them to complete the job if the perimeter of the yard is 288 feet?

	Case I	Case II
Time	(5)	(7)
Length of Fence	(6)	(8)

13. What goes in box (5)? 8

14. What goes in box (6)? 48

15. What goes in box (7)? x

16. What goes in box (8)? 288

17. What is the proportion for the problem?
$\dfrac{8}{48} = \dfrac{x}{288}$

18. How many hours will it take to build the fence?
48 hours

B

The Midvale Junior High School expects a fall enrollment of 910 students. The district assigns teachers at the rate of 3 teachers for every 65 students. The district currently has 38 teachers assigned to the school. How many additional teachers does the district need to assign to the school?

	Case I	Case II
Teachers	3	(e)
Students	65	(f)

19. What goes in box (e)? x

20. What goes in box (f)? 910

21. What is the proportion for the problem?
$\dfrac{3}{65} = \dfrac{x}{910}$

22. How many teachers will be needed at the school next year? 42 teachers

23. How many additional teachers will need to be assigned? 4 teachers

A home owner in Central City pays $1125 property taxes on a house that is valued at $75,000. A neighbor's house is valued at $180,000. How much property tax will the neighbor pay?

	Case I	Case II
Taxes	$1125	(g)
Value	$75,000	(h)

NAME _____   CLASS _____   DATE _____

24. What goes in box (g)? x

25. What goes in box (h)? $180,000

26. What is the original ratio? $\dfrac{1125}{75,000}$

27. What is the proportion? $\dfrac{1125}{75,000} = \dfrac{x}{180,000}$

28. How much property tax will the neighbor pay?
$2700

The Logan Valley Community College basketball team won 12 of its first 15 games. At this rate how many games will they win if they play a 30-game schedule?

	Case I	Case II
Games Won	12	x
Games Played	15	30

29. What goes in each of the four boxes?

30. What is the proportion for the problem? $\dfrac{12}{15} = \dfrac{x}{30}$

31. How many games should they win with a 30-game schedule? 24 games

32. Merle is knitting a sweater. The knitting is six rows to the inch. How many rows must she knit to complete $11\dfrac{1}{2}$ inches of the sweater? 69 rows

33. Floyd has 65 yards of fabric to make shirts. Every 2 shirts takes 5 yards of fabric. How many shirts can he make from this fabric? 26 shirts

34. For every 2 hours a week that Helen is in class, she plans to spend 5 hours a week doing her homework. If she is in class 18 hours each week, how many hours will she plan to study each week? 45 hours

35. John must do 25 hours of work to pay for the tuition for 3 college credits at the local university. If John is going to take 15 credits in the fall, how many hours will he need to work to pay for his tuition? 125 hours

36. If John (see Exercise 35) works 40 hours per week, how many weeks will he need to work to pay for his tuition? (Any part of a week counts as a full week.) 4 weeks

37. Larry sells men's clothing at the University Men's Shop. If he sells $100 worth of clothing, he makes $15. How much does he make if he sells $340 worth of clothes? $51

38. Hazel sells automobiles at the Quality Used Car Company. If she sells an automobile for $1200 she is paid $60. If she sells an automobile for $2900, how much is she paid? $145

39. If 30 lb of fertilizer covers 1500 square feet of lawn, how much fertilizer is needed to cover 2500 square feet?   50 lb

40. If gasoline sells for $1.229 per gallon, how many gallons can be purchased for $24.58?   20 gallons

41. If 44 ounces of soap powder costs $4.84, what does 20 ounces cost? $2.20

42. It takes four secretaries from the pool one day to type 72 pages of a technical manuscript. At this rate how many pages could nine secretaries type in one day?   162 pages

43. In Jean's Vegetable Market, onions are priced at two pounds for $0.63. If Mike buys six pounds, what is his cost? $1.89

44. Twenty-five pounds of tomatoes cost $23.70 at the local market. At this rate, what is the cost of ten pounds? $9.48

45. A new car travels 369 miles in 8.2 hours. At the same rate, how long does it take to go 900 miles?   20 hours

46. A brine solution is made by dissolving 1.5 pounds of salt in one gallon of water. At this rate, how many gallons of water are needed when 9 pounds of salt are used?   6 gallons

47. Celia earns a salary of $900 per month from which she saves $45 each month. Her salary is increased to $980 per month. How much must she save each month to save at the same rate? $49

48. Ginger and George have a room in their house that needs to be carpeted. It is determined that a total of 33 yards of carpet are needed for the job. Hickson's Carpet Emporium will install the 33 yards of carpet for $526.35. If Ginger and George decide to have a second room of their house carpeted and the room will need 22 yards of carpet, at the same rate how much will it cost to have the second room carpeted? $350.90

NAME _____ CLASS _____ DATE _____

C

49. The counter on a tape recorder registers 576 after the recorder has been running for 18 minutes. What does the counter register after 28 minutes?
896

50. During the first 309 miles on their vacation trip the Scaberys use 15 gallons of gasoline. At this rate, how many gallons are needed to finish the remaining 515 miles?   25 gallons

51. The Utah Construction Company has a job that takes four people 16 hours to do. How many of these jobs can the four people do in 112 hours?
7 jobs

52. A map of the United States has a scale in which $\frac{3}{4}$ inch represents 75 miles. How many miles is it between San Diego and Seattle if on the map it is 12 inches?   1200 miles

53. If Wayne receives $810 for $\frac{3}{4}$ ton of strawberries, how much does he receive for $1\frac{7}{8}$ tons? $2025

54. If Nora receives $600 for 0.5 ton of raspberries, how much does she receive for 3.5 tons? $4200

55. Billy Merker is a waiter at the Grand Ballroom Restaurant. He serves a group in which the total bill is $120 and receives a tip of $18. At the same rate, how much would he receive from a group in which the total bill was $90? $13.50

56. Jill Johnson can detail 3 cars in eight hours. At this rate how long would it take her to detail 12 cars?   32 hours

57. Seventy-five gallons of paint covers 30,000 square feet of surface. If Joe has 32 gallons of paint on hand, how many square feet of surface can he paint?   12,800 square feet

58. Eight double rolls of wallpaper cover 320 square feet of wall. How many square feet of wall do 20 double rolls cover?   800 square feet

59. A 16-ounce can of pears costs $0.98 and a 29-ounce can costs $1.69. Is the price per ounce the same in both cases? If not, then what should be the price of the 29-ounce can to equalize the price per ounce?   No; $1.78

60. A doctor requires that Ida, the nurse, give 8 milligrams of a certain drug to a patient. The drug is in a solution that contains 20 milligrams in one cubic centimeter. How many cubic centimeters should Ida use for the injection?

0.4 cubic centimeter

61. If a 24-foot beam of structural steel contracts 0.0036 inch for each drop of five degrees in temperature, then at the same rate, how much does a 50-foot beam of structural steel contract for a drop of five degrees in temperature?   0.0075 inch

62. If a package of gum drops weighing 1.5 ounces costs 45¢, at the same rate what is the cost of one pound (16 ounces) of the gum drops? $4.80

63. The ratio of boys to girls taking math is 5 to 4. How many boys are in a math class of 81 students? (*Hint:* Fill in the rest of the table.)

45 boys

	Case I	Case II
Number of Boys		
Number of Students	9	81

64. Betty prepares a mixture of nuts that has cashews and peanuts in a ratio of 3 to 7. How many pounds of each will she need to make 40 pounds of the mixture?

12 pounds of cashews, 28 pounds of peanuts

65. The Local Health-Food Store is making a cereal mix that has nuts to cereal in a ratio of 2 to 7. If they want to make 126 ounces of the mix, how many ounces of nuts will they need?

28 ounces

66. Debra is making green paint by using 3 quarts of blue paint for every 4 quarts of yellow paint. How much blue paint will she need to make 98 quarts of green paint?   42 quarts

67. A concrete mix takes 3 bags of cement for every 2 bags of sand and every 3 bags of gravel. How many bags of cement are necessary if 80 bags of the concrete mix are needed?   30 bags

68. Mario makes meatballs for his famous spaghetti sauce by using 10 pounds of ground round to 3 pounds of additives. How many pounds of ground round should he buy for 91 pounds of meatballs?

70 pounds

NAME _____   CLASS _____ DATE _____

69. Martha makes her own glue by mixing seven parts flour to three parts water. How much flour will she need to make five quarts of glue?   3.5 quarts

70. The estate of the late Ms. June Redgrave is to be divided among her three nephews in the ratio of 4 to 3 to 3. How much of the $84,930 estate will each nephew receive? $33,972; $25,479; $25,479

71. A brass alloy is four parts copper and three parts zinc. How many kilograms of copper are needed to make 200 kilograms of the alloy (to the nearest tenth of a kg)?   114.3 kg

72. A yard (cubic yard) of concrete will make a 4-inch-thick slab that is 81 ft². How many yards of concrete (to the nearest tenth of a yard) are needed to pour a 4-inch-thick garage floor of 440 ft²?   5.4 yards

73. Jean paid a total of $848 to the bank when she borrowed $800 for one year. The bank still charges the same rate when she wants to borrow money again. What is the total amount she will pay to the bank if she borrows $950 and keeps it for one year? $1007

74. If George pays back $1008 when he borrows $900 for one year, how much will he pay back if he borrows $750 and keeps it for one year? $840

75. The Corner Grocery Store bought $6875 worth of goods and sold them for $7700. At the same rate, what would goods cost that were sold for $5600? $5000

76. The Slightly Used Auto Company bought an automobile for $7500 and sold it for $9000. If the company bought another automobile for $8200, at the same rate, for what price would the company expect to sell it? $9840

77. When $1 is worth ¥108 (Japanese yen) and a fan costs ¥14,580, what is the cost in dollars? $135

78. When $1 (U.S. dollars) is worth $1.25 (Canadian dollars) and an automobile costs $13,750 Canadian, what is the cost in U.S. dollars? $11,000

79. When $1 is worth 210 drachma (Greek currency) and a used refrigerator costs $247, what is the cost in drachmas?   51,870 drachmas

80. When $1 is worth £0.65 (British pound) and a computer costs $2300, what is the cost in pounds?   £1495

81. When $1 is worth 1455 lire (Italian currency), a pair of shoes costs 69,840 lire. What is the cost in dollars? $48

82. Auto batteries are sometimes priced proportionally to the number of years they are expected to last. If a $35.85 battery is expected to last 36 months, what is the comparable price of a 60-month battery? $59.75

83. In 1960 only 6.7 of every 100 pounds of waste was recovered. In 1970, this rose to 7.1 pounds. By 1980, the amount was 9.7 pounds. In 1988 the amount was up to 13.1 pounds. Determine the amount of waste recovered from 56,000,000 pounds of waste in each of these years.
1960 — 3,752,000 lb; 1970 — 3,976,000 lb; 1980 — 5,432,000 lb; 1988 — 7,336,000 lb

84. The amount of ozone contained in 1 cubic meter of air may not exceed 235 mg or the air is considered to be polluted. What is the greatest amount of ozone that can be contained in 12 cubic meters of air and not be considered polluted?
2820 mg

State Your Understanding

85. Explain the difference between a ratio and a proportion.

86. Explain the difference between a rate and a proportion.

Challenge

87. In 1982 approximately 25 California condors were alive. This was due to hunting, habitat loss, and poisoning. The United States Fish and Wildlife Service instituted a program that has resulted in 73 condors alive in 1992. If this increase continues proportionally, predict how many condors will be alive in 2017.   193 condors

88. The tachometer of a sports car shows the engine speed is 2800 revolutions per minute. The transmission ratio (engine speed to drive shaft speed) for the car is 2.5 to 1. Find the drive shaft speed.   1120 rpm

89. Two families rented a beach house for 21 days at a cost of $2060. The Parisi family stayed for 11 days and the Nguyen family stayed for 10 days. How much does it cost each family? Round the rents to the nearest dollar.　Parisi: $1079; Nguyen: $981

Group Activity

90. List all of the recycling done by you and your classmates. Determine how many people engage in each of these activities. Determine ratios for each kind of recycling. Find the population of your city or county. Using your class ratios, determine how many people in your area are recycling each type of material. Make a chart to illustrate your findings. Contact your local recycling center to see how your ratios compare to their estimates. Explain the differences or similarities.

Maintain Your Skills (Sections 4.2, 4.3, 4.6, 4.8, 4.9, 4.10)

Change each decimal to a fraction.

91. 0.865　$\dfrac{173}{200}$

92. 0.01175　$\dfrac{47}{4000}$

Change each fraction to a decimal to the nearest thousandth.

93. $\dfrac{123}{225}$　0.547

94. $\dfrac{29}{350}$　0.083

Perform the indicated operations.

95. $0.7(0.25) + (0.82)(8) - (0.5)(0.6)$
6.435

96. $(0.088)(0.0004) \div 0.016 + (0.8)(0.6)$
0.4822

97. Divide 42 by 0.66 and round to the nearest hundredth.　63.64

98. Divide 81 by 36 and round to the nearest tenth.
2.3

99. What is the cost of 17.2 gallons of gasoline that cost $1.229 per gallon? Round your answer to the nearest cent.　$21.14

100. What is the cost per quart of a package of drink mix if a 4.6-oz package costs $5.76 and makes eight quarts of drink?　$0.72 per quart or 72¢ per quart

NAME _____ CLASS _____ DATE _____

| CHAPTER 5 | **Concept Review** |

Check your understanding of the language of basic mathematics. Tell whether each of the following statements is True (always true) or False (not always true). For those statements that you judge to be false, revise them to make them true.

1. A ratio is a comparison of two fractions. False: A ratio is a comparison of two numbers or measures written as a fraction. [5.1-1]

2. A proportion is a comparison of two ratios. True [5.2-1]

3. The cross products of a proportion are always equal. False: The cross products of a proportion are equal if the proportion is true. [5.2-1]

4. Five people is an example of a measurement. True [5.1-1]

5. To determine whether a proportion is true or false, the ratios must have the same units. True [5.2-1]

6. To solve a proportion one needs to find the replacement for the missing number that will make the proportion true. True [5.2-2]

Use the following information to answer questions 7–10 as being True or False.

If a fir tree that is 18 ft tall casts a shadow of 17 ft, how tall is a tree that casts a shadow of 25 ft?

7. The following chart can be used to solve the given problem.

	First Tree	Second Tree
Height	17	18
Shadow	x	25

False: The table should look like the following:

	First Tree	Second Tree
Height	18	x
Shadow	17	25

[5.3]

8. The following chart can be used to solve the given problem.

	First Tree	Second Tree
Shadow	17	25
Height	18	x

True [5.3]

9. The proportion $\dfrac{18}{17} = \dfrac{x}{25}$ can be used to solve the given problem.   True [5.3]

10. The height of the second tree will be less than the length of its shadow.   False: The height of the second tree will be greater than the length of its shadow. [5.3]

NAME _____ CLASS _____ DATE _____

CHAPTER 5 Test

1. Write a ratio to compare 12 pounds to 15 pounds.
$\frac{4}{5}$ [5.1-1]

2. On a test Ken answered 24 of 30 questions correctly. At the same rate, how many would he answer correctly if there were 100 questions on a test? 80 correct [5.3]

3. Solve the proportion: $\dfrac{2.4}{8} = \dfrac{0.36}{w}$.
$w = 1.2$ [5.2-2]

4. Is the following proportion true or false?
$$\frac{16}{34} = \frac{24}{51}$$ True [5.2-1]

5. Is the following proportion true or false?
$$\frac{9 \text{ inches}}{2 \text{ feet}} = \frac{6 \text{ inches}}{16 \text{ inches}}$$ True [5.2-1]

6. Solve the proportion: $\dfrac{13}{36} = \dfrac{y}{18}$.
$y = 6.5$ [5.2-2]

7. If Mary is paid $49.14 for 7 hours of work, how much should she expect to earn for 12 hours of work? $84.24 [5.3]

8. Write a ratio to compare six hours to three days and reduce. (Compare in hours.) $\frac{1}{12}$ [5.1-1]

9. There is a canned food sale at the supermarket. A case of 24 cans of peas is priced at $19.68. What is the price of 10 cans of peas? $8.20 [5.3]

10. If 40 pounds of beef contains 7 pounds of bones, how many pounds of bones may be expected in 100 pounds of beef? 17.5 lb [5.3]

11. Solve the proportion: $\dfrac{0.3}{0.9} = \dfrac{0.8}{x}$.
$x = 2.4$ [5.2-2]

12. A charter fishing boat has been catching an average of 3 salmon for every 4 people they take fishing. At that rate, how many fish will they catch if over a period of time they take a total of 32 people fishing? 24 fish [5.3]

13. On a trip to see her parents, Jennie used 12.5 gallons of gasoline. The trip odometer on her automobile registered 295 miles for the round trip. She is now planning a trip to see a friend that lives a distance of 236 miles from her home. How much gasoline should Jennie expect to need to make the round trip?   20 gal [5.3]

14. Solve the proportion: $\dfrac{a}{6} = \dfrac{3.21}{3.6}$.

$a = 5.35$ [5.2-2]

CHAPTER 6

Percent

Dedicated practice with the tools of the trade achieves masterful results for this woodcarver. In business and science, the tools of the trade are mathematical skills: Practice leads to mastery, mastery to achievement.
(Tony Stone Images)

GOOD ADVICE FOR STUDYING

Low-Stress Tests

It's natural to be anxious before an exam. In fact, a *little* anxiety is actually good: It keeps you alert and on your toes. Obviously, too much stress over tests is not good. Here are some proven tips for taking low-stress tests.

1. Before going to the exam, find a place on campus where you can physically and mentally relax. Don't come into the classroom in a rush.

2. Arrive in time to arrange all the tools you will need for the test: sharpened pencils, eraser, plenty of scratch paper, and a water bottle. Try to avoid talking with classmates about the test. Instead, concentrate on deep-breathing and relaxation.

3. Before starting the test, on a separate piece of paper, write all the things you may forget while you are busy taking the test: formulas, rules, definitions, and reminders to yourself. Doing so relieves the load on your short-term memory.

4. Read all the test problems and mark the easiest ones. *Don't skip reading the directions.* Note point values so that you don't spend too much time on problems that count only a little, at the expense of problems that count a lot.

5. Do the easiest problems first; do the rest in order of difficulty for you.

6. Estimate a reasonable answer for a problem before you make calculations. When you finish the problem, check to see that your answer agrees with your estimate.

7. If you get stuck on a problem, mark it so you will remember to come back to it later. Then go on to another problem.

8. When you have finished trying all the problems, go back to the problems you didn't finish and do what you can. Show all steps, because you may get partial credit even if you cannot complete the problem.

9. When you are finished, if time permits, go back over the test to see that all the problems are as complete as possible and that you have indicated your final answer. Use all the time allotted, unless you are sure that there is nothing more you can do.

10. Turn in your test and be confident that you did the best job you could. Congratulate yourself on a low-stress test!

If you find yourself feeling anxious during the test, it may help you to have a "calming card," a 3×5 card on which you list all the ways you have found to relax and stay focused. It may include any or all of the following: (a) a personal coping statement such as "I have studied hard and prepared well for this test; I will do fine"; (b) a brief description of your peaceful scene; and (c) a reminder to stop, breathe, and relax your tense muscles.

By now, you should be closer to taking control over math instead of allowing math to control you. You are avoiding learned helplessness (believing that other people or influences control your life). Questioning "Why try?" and lack of motivation are indicators of this type of attitude. Perfectionism, procrastination, fear of failure, and blaming others are also ineffective attitudes that block your power of control. Take responsibility, and believe that you have the power within to control your life situation.

6.1 THE MEANING OF PERCENT

Objective

Write a percent to express a comparison of two numbers.

Application

After a strong nonsmoking campaign in one state, 276 restaurants out of 300 banned smoking areas. What percent of the restaurants are nonsmoking?

Vocabulary

When ratios are used to compare numbers, the denominator is called the **base unit.** In comparing 80 to 100 $\left(\text{as the ratio } \dfrac{80}{100}\right)$, 100 is the base unit. The **percent comparison,** or just the **percent,** is a ratio with a base unit of 100. The percent $\dfrac{80}{100} = (80)\left(\dfrac{1}{100}\right)$ is usually written 80%. The symbol % is read "percent," and $\% = \dfrac{1}{100} = 0.01$.

How and Why

The word "percent" means "by the hundred." It is from the Roman word *percentum.* In Rome, taxes were collected by the hundred. For example, if you had 100 cattle, the tax collector might take 14 of them to pay your taxes. Hence, 14 per one hundred, or 14 percent, would be the tax rate.

Look at Figure 6.1 to see an illustration of the concept of "by the hundred." The base unit is 100, and 24 of the 100 parts are shaded. The ratio of shaded parts to total parts is $\dfrac{24}{100} = 24\left(\dfrac{1}{100}\right) = 24\%$. We say that 24% of the unit is shaded.

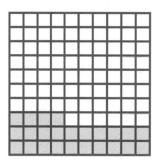

Figure 6.1

Figure 6.1 also illustrates that if the numerator is smaller than the denominator, then not all of the base unit will be shaded, and hence the comparison will be less than 100%. If the numerator equals the denominator, the entire unit will be shaded and the comparison will be 100%. If the numerator is larger than the denominator, more than one entire unit will be shaded, and the comparison will be more than 100%.

The ratio of two numbers can be used to find the percent when the base unit is not 100. Compare 7 to 20. The ratio is $\dfrac{7}{20}$. Now find the equivalent ratio with a denominator of 100.

$$\frac{7}{20} = \frac{35}{100} = 35 \cdot \frac{1}{100} = 35\%$$

If the equivalent ratio with a denominator of 100 cannot be found easily, solve as a proportion. See Example F.

▶ **To find the percent comparison of two numbers**

1. Write the ratio of the first number to the base number.
2. Find the equivalent ratio with denominator 100.
3. $\dfrac{\text{numerator}}{100} = \text{numerator} \cdot \dfrac{1}{100} = \text{numerator } \%$

The following chart shows some common fractions and their decimal equivalents. Some of the decimals are repeating decimals. Remember that a repeating decimal is shown by the bar over the digits that repeat. These fractions occur often in applications of percents. They should be memorized so that you can recall the patterns when they appear.

$\dfrac{1}{2} = 0.5$

$\dfrac{1}{3} = 0.33\overline{3}$ $\dfrac{2}{3} = 0.66\overline{6}$

$\dfrac{1}{4} = 0.25$ $\dfrac{3}{4} = 0.75$

$\dfrac{1}{5} = 0.2$ $\dfrac{2}{5} = 0.4$ $\dfrac{3}{5} = 0.6$ $\dfrac{4}{5} = 0.8$

$\dfrac{1}{6} = 0.166\overline{6}$ $\dfrac{5}{6} = 0.833\overline{3}$

$\dfrac{1}{8} = 0.125$ $\dfrac{3}{8} = 0.375$ $\dfrac{5}{8} = 0.625$ $\dfrac{7}{8} = 0.875$

For example, $2.66\overline{6} = 2\dfrac{2}{3}$, $8.166\overline{6} = 8\dfrac{1}{6}$, and $17.125 = 17\dfrac{1}{8}$.

Examples A–H	Warm Ups A–H

Directions: Write the percent of each region that is shaded.

Strategy: (1) Count the number of parts in each unit. (2) Count the number of parts that are shaded. (3) Write the ratio of these as a fraction and build the fraction to a denominator of 100. (4) Write the percent using the numerator in step 3.

A.

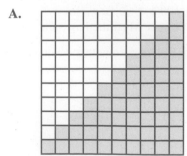

A.

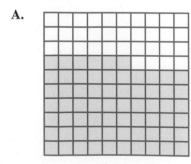

Solution:

55 out of 100 parts or   There are 100 small squares in the base
                               unit.

$\dfrac{55}{100} = 55 \cdot \dfrac{1}{100} = 55\%$ There are 55 shaded squares.

B.

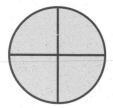

B.

Solution:

4 out of 4   Four out of the four parts are shaded.

$\dfrac{4}{4} = \dfrac{100}{100}$

$= 100 \cdot \dfrac{1}{100}$

$= 100\%$

C.

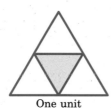

One unit   One unit

C.

One unit   One unit

Solution:

$\dfrac{5}{4} = \dfrac{125}{100} = 125\%$ Each triangle is divided into four parts. All four
                                              parts in one unit and one part in the second
                                              unit are shaded. The number of shaded parts
                                              must be compared to four. So more than 100%
                                              is shaded.

Directions: Write the percent for the comparison.

Strategy: Write the comparison in fraction form. Build the fraction to hundredths and write the percent using the numerator.

D. At a football game, 30 women are among the first 100 people to enter. What percent are women?

D. At the last basketball game of the season, of the first 100 tickets sold, 61 were student tickets. What percent were student tickets?

Answers to warm ups: **A.** 66%   **B.** 100%   **C.** 175%

Solution:

$$\frac{30}{100} = 30 \cdot \frac{1}{100} = 30\%$$ The comparison of women to people is 30 to 100. Write the fraction and change to percent.

E. The ratio of 42 to 25.

Solution:

$$\frac{42}{25} = \frac{168}{100} = 168 \cdot \frac{1}{100}$$ Write the ratio, then build this fraction to one with a denominator of 100.

$$= 168\%$$

E. The ratio of 80 to 50.

F. The ratio of 12 to 18.

Solution:

$$\frac{12}{18} = \frac{R}{100}$$ Since we cannot build the fraction to one with a denominator of 100, we write a proportion to find the percent.

$$12(100) = 18(R)$$ Cross multiply.

$$1200 \div 18 = R$$

$$66\frac{2}{3} = R \text{ or } 66.\overline{66} = R$$ We can write the remainder in fraction form or as a repeating decimal.

So, $$\frac{12}{18} = \frac{66\frac{2}{3}}{100}$$ Replace R in the original proportion with $66\frac{2}{3}$.

$$= 66\frac{2}{3} \cdot \frac{1}{100}$$

$$= 66\frac{2}{3}\%$$ Change to a percent.

F. The ratio of 10 to 12.

G. 🖩 The ratio of 35 to 280.

Solution:

$$\frac{35}{280} = \frac{R}{100}$$

$$280 \cdot R = 35 \cdot 100$$ Since percents can be found from proportions, a calculator can be used the same way as in Chapter 5.

$$R = (35 \cdot 100) \div 280$$

G. The ratio of 45 to 240.

Answers to warm ups: **D.** 61%   **E.** 160%   **F.** $83\frac{1}{3}\%$

ENTER   [35] [×] [100] [÷] [280] [=]

DISPLAY   35.   35.   100.   3500. 280. 12.5

The comparison is 12.5.%.

With a [%] key you can save two steps.

Solution:

ENTER   [35] [÷] [280] [%]

DISPLAY   35.   35.   280.   12.5   We read the percent from the
                                                  display. Some calculators
                                                  require pressing the

So, 35 is 12.5% of 280.   [=] key also.

H. ⊙ After a strong nonsmoking campaign in one state, 276 restaurants out of 300 banned smoking areas. What percent of the restaurants are nonsmoking?

Solution:

$$\frac{276}{300} = \frac{92}{100}$$ Write the ratio comparison and reduce.

$$= 92 \cdot \frac{1}{100} = 92\%$$ Change to percent.

Nonsmoking restaurants make up 92% of the total.

H. Of 200 fish caught in Olive Lake, 34 were tagged. What percent of the fish were tagged?

Answers to warm ups: **G.** 18.75%   **H.** 17%

NAME _____ CLASS _____ DATE _____

EXERCISES 6.1

A

What percent of each of the following regions is shaded?

1. 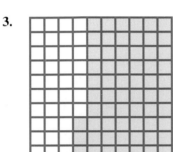 15%

2. 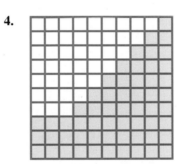 56%

3. 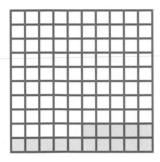 63%

4. 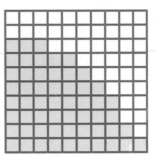 58%

Write an exact percent for these comparisons; use fractions when necessary.

5. 17 out of 100   17%

6. 78 per 100   78%

7. 6 to 100   6%

8. 13 to 100   13%

9. 7 per 50   14%

10. 10 per 50   20%

11. 10 out of 25   40%

12. 11 out of 25   44%

13. 12 to 25   48%

14. 20 to 25   80%

15. 9 per 20   45%

16. 12 per 20   60%

B

17. 16 to 10   160%

18. 300 to 120   250%

19. 160 out of 160   100%

20. 62 to 62   100%

21. 124 to 100   124%

22. 215 to 100   215%

23. 30 to 10   300%

24. 24 to 16   150%

25. 30 to 25   120%

26. 70 to 200   35%

27. 65 to 50   130%

28. 120 to 80   150%

© 1995 Saunders College Publishing.

29. 9 per 15   60%

30. 53 per 500 $10\frac{3}{5}\%$

31. 93 to 80 $116\frac{1}{4}\%$

32. 75 to 80 $93\frac{3}{4}\%$

C

33. 106 to 1000 $10\frac{3}{5}\%$

34. 118 to 1000 $11\frac{4}{5}\%$

35. 7 parts per 16 parts $43\frac{3}{4}\%$

36. 11 parts per 16 parts $68\frac{3}{4}\%$

37. 95 to 114 $83\frac{1}{3}\%$

38. 28 to 42 $66\frac{2}{3}\%$

39. 49 to 56 $87\frac{1}{2}\%$

40. 11 to 12 $91\frac{2}{3}\%$

41. 29 to 60 $48\frac{1}{3}\%$

42. 11 to 15 $73\frac{1}{3}\%$

43. 62 to 93 $66\frac{2}{3}\%$

44. 78 to 117 $66\frac{2}{3}\%$

45. 133 to 152 $87\frac{1}{2}\%$

46. 119 to 136 $87\frac{1}{2}\%$

47. 105 to 25   420%

48. 130 to 25   520%

49. 105 to 15   700%

50. 245 to 35   700%

Applications

51. Carol spends $65 on a new outfit. If she has $100, what percent of her money does she spend on the outfit?   65%

52. The fact that 12% of all people are blonde indicates that ___?___ out of 100 people are blonde.   12

53. In a recent election, out of every 100 eligible voters, 62 cast their ballots. What percent of the eligible voters exercised the right to vote?   62%

54. Of the people who use Shiny toothpaste, 37 out of 100 report that they have fewer cavities. Out of every 100 people who report, what percent do not report fewer cavities?   63%

NAME _____   CLASS _____   DATE _____

55. If the telephone tax rate is 8 cents per dollar, what percent is this?   8%

56. For every $100 spent on gasoline, the state receives $6 tax. What percent of the price of gasoline is the state tax?   6%

57. A bank pays $3.25 interest per year for every $100 in savings. What is the annual interest rate? $3\frac{1}{4}$%

58. A graphing calculator originally priced at $100 is on sale for $93. What is the percent of discount? (Discount is the difference between the original price and the sale price.)   7%

59. James has $500 in his savings account. Of that amount, $25 is interest that was paid to him. What percent of the total amount is the interest?   5%

60. Mickie bought a TV and makes monthly payments to pay for it. Last year she paid a total of $600. Of the total that she paid, $90 was interest. What percent of the total was the interest?   15%

61. Last year Mr. and Mrs. Average were informed that the property tax rate on their house was $3 per $100 of the house's assessed value. What percent is the tax rate?   3%

62. Salespeople are often paid by commission, which is expressed as a percent. If Pat is told that she will receive $8 for every $100 worth of merchandise she sells, what is her rate of commission?   8%

State Your Understanding

63. Explain the difference in meaning of the symbols 12% and 112%. In your explanation, use diagrams to illustrate the meanings. Contrast the similarities and differences in the diagrams.

Challenge

64. Write the ratio of 101 to 500 as a fraction and as a percent. $\frac{101}{500}$; $20\frac{1}{5}$% or 20.2%

65. Write the ratio of 503 to 800 as a fraction and as a percent. $\frac{503}{800}$; $62\frac{7}{8}$% or 62.875%

Group Activity

66. Have the members of your group use the resource center to find out some background about the percent symbol (%). Divide the task so that one member looks in a large dictionary, some look in different encyclopedias, and others look in other mathematics books. Together, make a short report to the rest of the class on your findings.

Maintain Your Skills (Sections 4.7, 4.9, 4.10)

Change to a decimal.

67. $\dfrac{15}{32}$ 0.46875

68. $\dfrac{35}{64}$ 0.546875

Change to a decimal rounded to the hundredths place.

69. $\dfrac{17}{18}$ 0.94

70. $\dfrac{31}{24}$ 1.29

Find the average.

71. 16.2, 13.9, 15.6, 20.8, 17.5   16.8

72. 216.7, 345.77, 256.03, 198.54   254.26

Divide.

73. $456.003 \div 10^4$ 0.0456003

74. $55{,}000 \div 10^7$ 0.0055

75. Bill goes to the store with $10. He uses his calculator to keep track of the money he is spending. He decides that he could make the following purchases. Is he correct?   Yes

Article	Cost
2 loaves of bread	$0.89 each
5 cans of soup	$0.38 each
1 box of crackers	$0.97
2 lb hamburger	$1.19 per lb
6 cans of root beer	6 cans for $2.49

76. Ms. Henderson earns $5.62 per hour and works the following hours during one month. How much are her monthly earnings? $734.35

Week	Hours
1	$28\frac{1}{2}$
2	$32\frac{1}{4}$
3	33
4	$30\frac{1}{6}$
5	$6\frac{3}{4}$

	6.2	**CHANGING DECIMALS TO PERCENTS**

Objective Write a given decimal as a percent.

Application 🌐 The tax rate on a building lot is given as 0.03. What is the tax rate expressed as a percent?

How and Why In multiplication, where one factor is $\dfrac{1}{100}$, the indicated multiplication can be read as a percent. That is, $75\left(\dfrac{1}{100}\right) = 75\%$, $0.8\left(\dfrac{1}{100}\right) = 0.8\%$, and $\dfrac{3}{4}\left(\dfrac{1}{100}\right) = \dfrac{3}{4}\%$.

To write a number as a percent, multiply by $100 \cdot \dfrac{1}{100}$, a name for one. This is shown in the following table.

Number	Multiply by 1 $100\left(\dfrac{1}{100}\right) = 1$	Multiply by 100	Percent
0.45	$0.45\,(100)\left(\dfrac{1}{100}\right)$	$45.\left(\dfrac{1}{100}\right)$	45%
0.2	$0.2\,(100)\left(\dfrac{1}{100}\right)$	$20.\left(\dfrac{1}{100}\right)$	20%
5	$5\,(100)\left(\dfrac{1}{100}\right)$	$500.\left(\dfrac{1}{100}\right)$	500%

In each case the decimal point is moved two places to the right and the percent symbol (%) is inserted.

▶ **To change a decimal to a percent**

1. Move the decimal point two places to the right. (Write zeros on the right if necessary.)
2. Write the percent symbol (%) on the right.

Examples A–G   **Warm Ups A–G**

Directions: Change the decimal to percent.

Strategy: Move the decimal point two places to the right and write the percent sign on the right.

A. 0.35   **A.** 0.79

Solution:

$0.35 = 35\%$ Move the decimal point two places to the right. Write the percent symbol on the right.

Answer to warm up: **A.** 79%

B. 0.04

Solution:

$0.04 = 004\% = 4\%$ Since the zeros are to the left of 4 we can drop them.

C. 0.217

Solution:

$0.217 = 21.7\%$

D. 0.003

Solution:

$0.003 = 000.3\% = 0.3\%$ This is three tenths of one percent.

E. 9

Solution:

$9 = 9.00 = 900\%$ Insert two zeros on the right so we can move two decimal places. Nine hundred percent is 9 times 100%.

F. $0.25\overline{3}$

Solution:

$0.25\overline{3} = 25.\overline{3}\% = 25\dfrac{1}{3}\%$ The repeating decimal is $0.33\overline{3} = \dfrac{1}{3}$.

G. 🌐 The tax rate on a building lot is given as 0.03. What is the tax rate expressed as a percent?

Solution:

$0.03 = 003\% = 3\%$ Move the decimal point two places to the right and insert the percent symbol.

B. 0.08

C. 0.237

D. 0.002

E. 4

F. $0.22\overline{6}$

G. The tax code lists the tax rate on a zone 3 lot at 0.025. What is the tax rate expressed as a percent?

Answers to warm ups: **B.** 8%   **C.** 23.7%   **D.** 0.2%   **E.** 400%   **F.** $22\dfrac{2}{3}\%$ **G.** 2.5%

NAME _____   CLASS _____   DATE _____

EXERCISES 6.2

A

Write each decimal as a percent.

1. 0.36   36%   **2.** 0.24   24%   **3.** 4.76   476%   **4.** 8.33   833%

5. 0.08   8%   **6.** 0.06   6%   **7.** 1.6   160%   **8.** 2.4   240%

9. 12   1200%   **10.** 11   1100%   **11.** 0.009   0.9%   **12.** 0.003   0.3%

13. 0.531   53.1%   **14.** 0.555   55.5%   **15.** 0.29   29%   **16.** 0.74   74%

17. 1   100%   **18.** 2   200%

B

19. 0.214   21.4%   **20.** 0.083   8.3%   **21.** 7   700%   **22.** 27   2700%

23. 13.21   1321%   **24.** 1.27   127%   **25.** 0.005   0.5%   **26.** 0.745   74.5%

27. 0.7   70%   **28.** 0.4   40%   **29.** 3.2   320%   **30.** 1.85   185%

31. 0.0317   3.17%   **32.** 0.265   26.5%   **33.** 2.84   284%   **34.** 1.23   123%

35. 0.008   0.8%   **36.** 0.007   0.7%

C

37. 5.75   575%   **38.** 7.36   736%   **39.** 0.5625   56.25%   **40.** 4.23   423%

41. $0.741\overline{66}$ $74\frac{1}{6}\%$ **42.** $0.66\overline{6}$ $66\frac{2}{3}\%$ **43.** 0.2051   20.51%   **44.** 0.3618   36.18%

45. 0.1025   10.25% or $10\frac{1}{4}\%$ **46.** 0.205   20.5% or $20\frac{1}{2}\%$ **47.** 0.052   5.2% or $5\frac{1}{5}\%$ **48.** $0.033\overline{3}$ $3\frac{1}{3}\%$

49. 0.0009   0.09%   **50.** 0.0001   0.01%   **51.** 10   1000%   **52.** 12   1200%

53. 1.234   123.4%   **54.** 2.145   214.5%

© 1995 Saunders College Publishing.

Applications

55. If the tax rate on a person's income is 0.22, what is the rate expressed as a percent?   22%

56. The completion rate in a certain math class is 0.85. What is this rate as a percent?   85%

57. A class has completed 0.62 of its class work. Express this as a percent.   62%

58. The sales tax in a certain state is 0.055. Express this as a percent. 5.5% or $5\frac{1}{2}\%$

59. If 0.375 of the contestants in a race withdraw, what is the percent of withdrawals?   37.5%

60. During the blizzard of 1977, the price of a snow blower increased by 1.87. Express this as a percent.   187%

61. Mary Ellen measured the July rainfall. She found it was 0.235 of the year's total. Express this as a percent.   23.5%

62. Social Security paid by employees is found by multiplying the gross wages by 0.062. The Medicare payment is found by multiplying the gross wages by 0.0145. Express the sum of these amounts as a percent.   7.65%

63. Cholesterol levels in Americans have dropped from 0.26 in 1981 to 0.2 in 1993. Express the difference as a percent.   6%

64. Of all the rice eaten in America, 0.9 is grown in the United States. Express this as a percent.   90%

State Your Understanding

65. Write two sentences that illustrate the use of a decimal. Write the same two sentences replacing the decimal with a percent. Which form do you prefer? Why?

Challenge

66. Write 0.024 and $0.02\overline{4}$ as percents. 2.4%; $2\frac{4}{9}\%$

67. Write 0.425 and $0.42\overline{5}$ as percents. 42.5%; $42\frac{5}{9}\%$

Group Activity

68. Baseball batting averages are written as decimals. A batter with an average of 238 has hit an average of 238 times out of 1000 times at bat (0.238). Find the batting averages of the top five players in the American and National Leagues for the last five years. Express these numbers as percents.

NAME _____ CLASS _____ DATE _____

Maintain Your Skills (Sections 4.3, 4.10)

69. Round to the nearest thousandth: 3.87245   3.872

70. Round to the nearest thousand: 3872.45   4000

Perform the indicated operations.

71. $(0.37)(0.4) + 2.5 - (0.04)(0.02)$ 2.6472

72. $(0.75) - (0.5)(0.3) + (1.8)(0.2)$ 0.96

73. $(0.18)(3.6) \div 18 - (1.2)(0.01)$ 0.024

74. $0.5^2 - 0.2^3$ 0.242

75. $[2.3^2 + 7.3(0.1)](0.3)^2 - 0.041$ 0.5008

76. $23 - 3.7^3(0.1)$ 17.9347

77. Marilyn needs to buy four textbooks for this semester. She goes to the bookstore to find out how much they cost:

Algebra	$27.45
Chemistry	$31.50
Psychology	$26.85
American history	$34.35

What is the total cost of the books that she needs? What is the average cost of the books?

$120.15; $30.04

78. Bill is making a table top. The two ends of the piece of wood he is using need to be trimmed and sanded. The piece of wood is 52.25 inches long. If he requires a length of 48.5 inches, the saw removes $\dfrac{1}{8}$ inch during each cut, and he wants to allow $\dfrac{1}{16}$ inch for finishing sanding on each end, how much should he cut from each end?

1.6875 inches

Patty Cortez and Chris Lindal work together in the math lab at Seattle Central Community College in Seattle, Washington.

6.3 CHANGING PERCENTS TO DECIMALS

Objective Write a given percent as a decimal.

Application 🌐 When ordering fresh vegetables, a grocer orders 7.4% more than is needed to allow for spoilage. What decimal is entered into the computer to calculate the amount of extra vegetables to be added to the order?

How and Why The percent symbol indicates multiplication by $\dfrac{1}{100}$, so

$$17\% = 17 \cdot \frac{1}{100} = \frac{17}{100} = 17 \div 100$$

To divide a number by 100, move the decimal point two places to the left.

$$17\% = 17 \div 100 = 0.17$$

▶ **To change a percent to a decimal**

1. Move the decimal point two places to the left. (Write zeros on the left if necessary.)
2. Drop the percent symbol (%).

Examples A–H

Warm Ups A–H

Directions: Change the percent to a decimal.

Strategy: Move the decimal point two places to the left and drop the percent symbol.

A. 14.5%

A. 94.7%

Solution:

14.5% = 0.145   Move the decimal point two places left. Drop the percent symbol.

B. 35%

B. 67%

Solution:

35% = 0.35

C. 295%

C. 165%

Solution:

295% = 2.95   A value over 100% becomes a mixed number or a whole number.

Answers to warm ups: **A.** 0.947   **B.** 0.67   **C.** 1.65

D. $83\dfrac{1}{2}\%$

D. $12\dfrac{3}{5}\%$

Solution:

$83\dfrac{1}{2}\% = 83.5\%$ Change the fraction to a decimal.

     $= 0.835$ Move the decimal point left and drop the percent symbol.

E. $4\dfrac{5}{6}\%$; round to the nearest thousandth.

E. $83\dfrac{1}{6}\%$; round to the nearest thousandth.

Solution:

$4\dfrac{5}{6}\% = 4.8\overline{3}\%$ By division, $\dfrac{5}{6} = 0.8\overline{3}$.

     $= 0.048\overline{3}$ Move the decimal point left and drop the percent symbol.

     ≈ 0.048

F. 0.8%

F. 0.24%

Solution:

$0.8\% = 00.8\%$ We need two zeros to the left of the decimal point so we can move two left.

     $= 0.008$

G. $\dfrac{3}{5}\%$

G. $\dfrac{3}{4}\%$

Solution:

$\dfrac{3}{5}\% = 0.6\%$ Change the fraction to a decimal.

     $= 0.006$ $\dfrac{3}{5} = 0.6$. Move the decimal two places left and drop the percent symbol.

H. 🌐 When ordering fresh vegetables, a grocer orders 7.4% more than is needed to allow for spoilage. What decimal is entered into the computer to calculate the amount of extra vegetables to be added to the order?

H. When ordering cement, a contractor orders 2.5% more than is needed to allow for waste. What decimal will she enter into the computer to calculate the extra amount to be added to the order?

Solution:

$7.4\% = 07.4\% = 0.074$ Write a zero before the 7 so that there will be two places to allow the move left.

Answers to warm ups: **D.** 0.126   **E.** 0.832   **F.** 0.0024   **G.** 0.0075   **H.** 0.025

NAME _____ CLASS _____ DATE _____

EXERCISES 6.3

A

Write each of the following as a decimal.

1. 16%   0.16   **2.** 59%   0.59   **3.** 82%   0.82   **4.** 36%   0.36

5. 73%   0.73   **6.** 57%   0.57   **7.** 2.15%   0.0215   **8.** 3.75%   0.0375

9. 312%   3.12   **10.** 563%   5.63   **11.** 110.6%   1.106   **12.** 53.7%   0.537

13. 0.04%   0.0004   **14.** 0.08%   0.0008   **15.** 2.79%   0.0279   **16.** 1.79%   0.0179

17. 17.9%   0.179   **18.** 179%   1.79

B

19. 314.7%   3.147   **20.** 261.3%   2.613   **21.** 0.12%   0.0012   **22.** 0.52%   0.0052

23. $\frac{1}{2}$%   0.005   **24.** $\frac{1}{4}$%   0.0025   **25.** 0.25%   0.0025   **26.** 0.75%   0.0075

27. 1%   0.01   **28.** 100%   1   **29.** 200%   2   **30.** 0.082%   0.00082

31. 0.058%   0.00058   **32.** 0.002%   0.00002   **33.** 125%   1.25   **34.** 234%   2.34

35. $\frac{5}{8}$%   0.00625   **36.** $\frac{4}{5}$%   0.008

C

37. $29\frac{3}{4}$%   0.2975   **38.** $22\frac{2}{5}$%   0.224   **39.** $475\frac{1}{2}$%   4.755   **40.** $325\frac{1}{5}$%   3.252

41. $\frac{7}{8}$%   0.00875   **42.** $\frac{1}{8}$%   0.00125   **43.** $1\frac{1}{4}$%   0.0125   **44.** $2\frac{7}{8}$%   0.02875

45. $\frac{7}{5}$%   0.014   **46.** $\frac{11}{8}$%   0.01375   **47.** 72.61%   0.7261   **48.** 81.94%   0.8194

Change to a decimal rounded to the nearest thousandth.

49. $\dfrac{1}{6}\%$ 0.002

50. $\dfrac{2}{3}\%$ 0.007

51. $35\dfrac{5}{6}\%$ 0.358

52. $48\dfrac{1}{3}\%$ 0.483

53. $\dfrac{11}{6}\%$ 0.018

54. $\dfrac{5}{3}\%$ 0.017

Applications

55. Employees just settled their new contract and got a 4.7% raise. Express this as a decimal.   0.047

56. When bidding for a job, an estimator adds 10% to cover unexpected expenses. What decimal part is this?   0.1

57. Interest rates are expressed as percents. The Last Federal Bank charges 7% interest on auto loans. What decimal will they use to compute the interest?
0.07

58. What decimal is used to compute the interest on a mortgage that has an interest rate of 5.75%?
0.0575

59. Unemployment is down 0.2%. Express this as a decimal.   0.002

60. The cost of living rose 0.7% during June. Express this as a decimal.   0.007

61. In industrialized countries 60% of river pollution is due to agricultural runoff. Change this to a decimal.
0.6

62. Recycling aluminum consumes 95% less energy than smelting new stocks of metal. Change this to a decimal.   0.95

63. In 1993, Americans had 4% less blood cholesterol than in 1981. Change this to a decimal.   0.04

64. Find today's interest rates for home mortgages for 15 and 30 years. Express these as decimals.
Answers will vary.

State Your Understanding

65. Every percent can be written as a decimal. Write two sentences that illustrate the use of percent. Rewrite each sentence replacing the percent with the equivalent decimal. Which form best communicates the intent of your original sentences?

Challenge

66. Change $1\dfrac{2}{7}\%$ to a decimal rounded to the nearest tenth and the nearest thousandth.   0.0; 0.013

67. Change $56\dfrac{5}{12}\%$ to a decimal rounded to the nearest tenth and the nearest thousandth.
0.6; 0.564

NAME _____ CLASS _____ DATE _____

Group Activity

68. Determine the major causes of the greenhouse effect. Find out which substances cause the greenhouse effect and the percent contributed by each. Write these percents in decimal form. Discuss ways to reduce the greenhouse effect in class and write group reports on your findings.

Maintain Your Skills (Sections 4.2, 4.5, 4.9, 4.10)

Change to a decimal.

69. $\dfrac{7}{8}$ 0.875

70. $\dfrac{9}{64}$ 0.140625

71. $\dfrac{19}{16}$ 1.1875

72. $\dfrac{24}{75}$ 0.32

73. $\dfrac{27}{15}$ 1.8

74. $\dfrac{117}{65}$ 1.8

Change to a fraction.

75. 0.715 $\dfrac{143}{200}$

76. 0.1025 $\dfrac{41}{400}$

77. In one week George earns $245. His deductions (income tax, Social Security, and so on) total $38.45. What is his "take-home" pay? $206.55

78. The cost of gasoline is reduced from $0.419 per liter to $0.379 per liter. How much money is saved on an automobile trip that requires 230 liters? $9.20

6.4 CHANGING FRACTIONS TO PERCENTS

Objective Change a fraction or mixed number to a percent.

Application A motor that needs repair is only turning $\dfrac{3}{16}$ the number of revolutions per minute that is normal. What percent of the normal rate is this?

How and Why We already know how to change fractions to decimals and decimals to percent. We combine the two ideas to change fractions to a percent.

▶ **To change a fraction or mixed number to a percent**

1. Change to a decimal with two decimal places. The decimal is rounded or carried out as directed.
2. Change the decimal to percent.

Unless directed to round, the division is completed or else the quotient is written as a repeating decimal.

Examples A–I

Warm Ups A–I

Directions: Change the fraction or mixed number to a percent.

Strategy: Change the number to a decimal and then to a percent.

A. $\dfrac{4}{5}$

A. $\dfrac{3}{5}$

Solution:

$\dfrac{4}{5} = 0.8 = 80\%$ Divide 4 by 5 to change the fraction to a decimal. Move the decimal point two places right and write the percent symbol on the right.

B. $\dfrac{7}{16}$

B. $\dfrac{1}{8}$

Solution:

$\dfrac{7}{16} = 0.4375 = 43.75\%$

Answers to warm ups: **A.** 60% **B.** 12.5%

Group Activity

66. Keep a record of everything you eat for one entire day. Use exact amounts as much as possible. With a calorie and fat counter, compute the percent of fat in each item. Then find the percent of fat you consumed that day. The latest recommendations suggest that the fat content not exceed 30% per day. How did you do? Which foods have the highest and which the lowest fat content? Was this a typical day for you? Continue this exercise for one week and compare your daily percent of fat with others in your group. Compute a weekly average individually and as a group.

Maintain Your Skills (Sections 4.6, 4.8)

Multiply.

67. $(8.003)(0.87)$ 6.96261

68. $(19)(0.0115)$ 0.2185

69. $(0.02)(0.2)(2.02)$ 0.00808

70. $(1.45)(4.05)(1.4)$ 8.2215

Divide.

71. $0.38\overline{)5.738}$ 15.1

72. $6.22\overline{)0.202772}$ 0.0326

73. Divide 48 by 6.2 and round to the nearest hundredth.   7.74

74. Divide 62 by 480 and round to the nearest thousandth.   0.129

75. If Abel works 37 hours and earns a total of $197.95, what is his hourly rate? $5.35

76. If Spencer loses 11.6 lb in two weeks, what is his rate of weight loss per day (that is, what is the average loss per day) to the nearest hundredth of a pound?   0.83 lb

6.5 CHANGING PERCENTS TO FRACTIONS

Objective   Change percents to fractions or mixed numbers.

Application   A biological study shows that spraying for gypsy moths to save a forest is 92% successful. What fraction (ratio) of the moths yet remain?

How and Why   The expression 6.5% is equal to $6.5 \times \dfrac{1}{100}$. This gives a very efficient method for changing a percent to a fraction. Change 6.5 to a fraction and multiply. See Example C.

▶ **To change a percent to a fraction or a mixed number**

1. Replace the percent symbol (%) with the fraction $\left(\dfrac{1}{100}\right)$.
2. Rewrite the other factor (if necessary) as a fraction.
3. Multiply.

Examples A–F   **Warm Ups A–F**

Directions: Change the percent to a fraction.

Strategy: Change the percent symbol to the fraction $\dfrac{1}{100}$ and multiply.

A. 35%   **A.** 45%

Solution:

$35\% = 35 \cdot \dfrac{1}{100}$ Replace the percent symbol (%) with $\dfrac{1}{100}$.

$= \dfrac{35}{100} = \dfrac{7}{20}$ Multiply and reduce.

CAUTION

You need to multiply by $\dfrac{1}{100}$, not just write it down.

B. 312%   **B.** 145%

Solution:

$312\% = 312 \cdot \dfrac{1}{100}$ Substitute, multiply, change to a mixed number, and reduce.

$= \dfrac{312}{100} = 3\dfrac{3}{25}$

C. 6.5%   **C.** 8.2%

Answers to warm ups: **A.** $\dfrac{9}{20}$ **B.** $\dfrac{29}{20}$ or $1\dfrac{9}{20}$

66. Write a ratio to compare $39,000,000 to 75,000,000 people. $\dfrac{\$13}{25 \text{ people}}$

67. Reduce Exercise 66 to a one-person comparison. $\dfrac{\$0.52}{1 \text{ person}}$

68. Write a ratio to compare 14,765,000 gallons of water to 100,000 people. $\dfrac{2953 \text{ gallons}}{20 \text{ people}}$

69. Reduce Exercise 68 to a one-person comparison. $\dfrac{147.65 \text{ gallons}}{1 \text{ person}}$

70. The taxes on a home valued at $89,000 are $2225. At the same rate, what are the taxes on a house valued at $75,000? $1875

71. Five measurements of the diameter of a wire are taken with a micrometer screw gauge. The five estimated measurements are 2.31 mm, 2.32 mm, 2.30 mm, 2.34 mm, and 2.30 mm. What is the average estimate? (Note that although 2.3 = 2.30, writing 2.30 mm shows greater precision than writing 2.3 mm.)   2.314 mm

6.6 FRACTIONS, DECIMALS, PERCENTS: A REVIEW

Objectives

1. Write a percent as a decimal and as a fraction.
2. Write a fraction as a percent and as a decimal.
3. Write a decimal as a percent and as a fraction.

Application   The average American uses about 200 pounds of plastic a year. Approximately 60% of this is used for packaging and about 4% of it is recycled. Write the percent used for packaging as a decimal and as a fraction.

How and Why 1 2 3   Decimals, fractions, and percents can each be expressed in terms of the others:

$$50\% = 50 \cdot \frac{1}{100} = \frac{50}{100} = \frac{1}{2} \quad \text{and} \quad 50\% = 0.50$$

$$\frac{3}{4} = 3 \div 4 = 0.75 \quad \text{and} \quad \frac{3}{4} = 0.75 = 75\%$$

$$0.65 = 65\% \quad \text{and} \quad 0.65 = \frac{65}{100} = \frac{13}{20}$$

Examples A–B   **Warm Ups A–B**

Directions: Fill in the table with the related fraction, decimal, or percent.

Strategy: Use the procedures of the previous sections.

A.

Fraction	Decimal	Percent
		30%
$\frac{7}{8}$		
	0.62	

A.

Fraction	Decimal	Percent
$\frac{2}{3}$		
		27%
	0.72	
$\frac{73}{100}$		
		160%
	1.3	

Solution:

Fraction	Decimal	Percent
$\frac{3}{10}$	0.30	30%
$\frac{7}{8}$	0.875	87.5% or $87\frac{1}{2}\%$
$\frac{31}{50}$	0.62	62%

$30\% = 0.30 = \frac{30}{100} = \frac{3}{10}$

$\frac{7}{8} = 0.875 = 87.5\% = 87\frac{1}{2}\%$

$0.62 = 62\% = \frac{62}{100} = \frac{31}{50}$

Answer to warm up: **A.**

Fraction	Decimal	Percent
$\frac{2}{3}$	$0.66\overline{6}$	$66\frac{2}{3}\%$
$\frac{27}{100}$	0.27	27%
$\frac{18}{25}$	0.72	72%

Fraction	Decimal	Percent
$\frac{73}{100}$	0.73	73%
$1\frac{3}{5}$	1.6	160%
$1\frac{3}{10}$	1.3	130%

B. 🌐 The average American uses about 200 pounds of plastic a year. Approximately 60% of this is used for packaging and about 4% of it is recycled. Write the percent used for packaging as a decimal and as a fraction.

Solution:

$$60\% = 0.60 = \frac{60}{100} = \frac{3}{5}$$

Move the decimal point two places to the left and drop the percent symbol. Then change to a fraction.

B. In Example B, write the percent that is recycled as a decimal and as a fraction.

Answer to warm up: **B.** 0.04; $\frac{1}{25}$

NAME _____ CLASS _____ DATE _____

EXERCISES 6.6

Fill in the empty spaces with the related percent, decimal, or fraction.

	Fraction	Decimal	Percent
*	$\dfrac{1}{10}$	0.1	
*	$\dfrac{3}{10}$	0.3	30%
*	$\dfrac{3}{4}$	0.75	
*	$\dfrac{9}{10}$	0.9	
	$1\dfrac{9}{20}$	1.45	145%
*	$\dfrac{3}{8}$	0.375	
	$\dfrac{1}{1000}$	0.001	
*	$\dfrac{1}{1}$ or 1	1	
	$2\dfrac{1}{4}$	2.25	
*	$\dfrac{4}{5}$	0.8	
	$\dfrac{11}{200}$	0.055	$5\dfrac{1}{2}\%$
*	$\dfrac{7}{8}$	0.875	
	$\dfrac{1}{200}$	0.005	$\dfrac{1}{2}\%$
*	$\dfrac{3}{5}$	0.6	
*	$\dfrac{5}{8}$	0.625	$62\dfrac{1}{2}\%$
	$\dfrac{1}{2}$	0.50	50%
	$\dfrac{43}{50}$	0.86	
	$\dfrac{5}{6}$	0.8333	

*If you are going to be working with problems that will involve percent in your job or in your personal finances (loans, savings, insurance, and so on), it is advisable to know (memorize) these special relationships.

	Fraction	Decimal	Percent
	$\dfrac{2}{25}$	0.08	8%
	$\dfrac{2}{3}$	$0.66\overline{6}$	$66\dfrac{2}{3}\%$
*	$\dfrac{1}{4}$	0.25	25%
*	$\dfrac{1}{5}$	0.20	20%
*	$\dfrac{2}{5}$	0.4	40%
*	$\dfrac{1}{3}$	$0.33\overline{3}$	$33\dfrac{1}{3}\%$
*	$\dfrac{1}{8}$	0.125	12.5% or $12\dfrac{1}{2}\%$
*	$\dfrac{7}{10}$	0.7	70%

Applications

1. Louis goes to buy new tires for his truck. He finds them on sale for $\dfrac{1}{4}$ off. What percent is this?   25%

2. George buys a new VCR at a 50%-off sale. What fraction is this? $\dfrac{1}{2}$

3. Michael went on a diet. He now weighs $66\dfrac{2}{3}\%$ of his original weight. What fraction is this? $\dfrac{2}{3}$

4. Melinda is researching the best place to buy a computer. Family Computers offers $\dfrac{1}{8}$ off, Computer will give a 12% discount, and Machines ETC will allow a 0.13 discount. Where does she get the best deal?   Machines ETC

5. Teresa is negotiating a business deal. The client has offered a 5% increase in price, while her boss has authorized up to 0.0526 more. A competitor has offered a deal that is $\dfrac{1}{18}$ more. Who has offered the least?   Client

6. A local department store is having its red tag sale. All merchandise will now be 20% off. What fraction is this? $\dfrac{1}{5}$

NAME _____ CLASS _____ DATE _____

7. Randy is trading in his swimming pool for a larger model. Prices are the same for Model PS+ and Model PT. PS+ has 11% more water while PT has $\frac{1}{9}$ more water. Which should he choose to get the most value for his money?   PT

8. During the month of August the grocery store has a special on sweet corn: $\frac{3}{8}$ or 35% more corn for 1 cent. Which is the better deal? $\frac{3}{8}$

State Your Understanding

9. Write a short paragraph with examples that illustrate when to use fractions, when to use decimals, and when to use percents to show comparisons.

Challenge

10. Fill in the table.

Fraction	Decimal	Percent
$\frac{14}{3}$	$4.6\overline{6}$	$466\frac{2}{3}\%$
$\frac{19}{16}$	1.1875	118.75%
$\frac{101}{1600}$	0.063125	6.3125%

Group Activity

11. Have each member of your group make up a table like the one in Example A. Exchange your table with the other group members and fill in the blanks. Check your answers with the rest of the group.

Maintain Your Skills (Sections 5.2, 5.3)

Solve the following proportions.

12. $\frac{25}{30} = \frac{x}{45}$ $x = 37.5$

13. $\frac{45}{81} = \frac{16}{y}$ $y = 28.8$

14. $\frac{x}{72} = \frac{38}{9}$ $x = 304$

15. $\frac{x}{9.5} = \frac{125}{250}$ $x = 4.75$

16. $\dfrac{\frac{1}{2}}{100} = \dfrac{A}{40}$ $A = 0.2$

17. $\dfrac{50}{100} = \dfrac{70}{B}$ $B = 140$

18. $\dfrac{R}{100} = \dfrac{8}{27}$; round R to the nearest tenth. $R = 29.6$

19. $\dfrac{17}{100} = \dfrac{A}{22.3}$; round A to the nearest tenth. $A = 3.8$

20. Sean drives 413 miles and uses 11.8 gallons of gasoline. At that rate, how many gallons will he need to drive 1032.5 miles?   29.5 gallons

21. The Bacons' house is worth $78,000 and is insured so that the Bacons will be paid four fifths of the value for any damage. One third of the house is totally destroyed by fire. How much insurance should they collect? $20,800

6.7 SOLVING PERCENT PROBLEMS

Objectives

1. Solve percent problems using the formula.

2. Solve percent problems using a proportion.

Application

Applications of these objectives come from a variety of fields. These applications are so important that they all appear in Section 6.8.

Vocabulary

To **solve** a percent problem means to do one of the following:

1. Find A, given R and B.
2. Find B, given R and A.
3. Find R, given A and B.

In the statement "$R\%$ of B is A,"

R is the **rate** of percent.

B is the **base** unit and follows the word "of."

A is the **amount** that is compared to B.

How and Why 1

We show two methods for solving percent problems. We will refer to these as

The formula $RB = A$ or $R(B) = A$ See Examples A–E

The proportion method   See Examples F–H

In each method we must identify the rate of percent (R), the base (B), and the amount (A). To help determine these, keep in mind that

R is associated with the percent symbol ($\%$).

B follows the words "of" or "percent of."

A, sometimes called the *percentage,* is the amount compared to B.

The method you choose to solve percent problems should depend on

1. The method your instructor recommends.
2. Your major field of study.
3. How you use percent in your day-to-day activities.

In the formula $RB = A$, the percent symbol is part of R.

What percent of B is A? The word "of" in this context and in other places in mathematics indicates multiplication. The word "is" describes the relationship "is equal to" or "=." Thus we may write:

$$R \text{ of } B \text{ is } A$$
$$\downarrow \qquad \downarrow$$
$$R \cdot B = A$$

For example, what percent of 65 is 22.1?

$R(B) = A$	Substitute $B = 65$ (65 follows the word "of") and $A = 22.1$. The rate, R, is unknown.
$R(65) = 22.1$	
$R = 22.1 \div 65$	Divide.
$R = 0.34 = 34\%$	Change the decimal to a percent.

So, 22.1 is 34% of 65.

The triangle below is a useful device to remind you where to place R, A, and B. The triangle will also remind you when to multiply and when to divide.

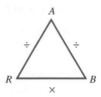

When the unknown value is covered, the positions of the uncovered (known) values help us remember how to see what operations to use:

When A is covered, we see $R \times B$, reading from left to right.

When B is covered, we see $A \div R$, reading from top to bottom.

When R is covered, we see $A \div B$, reading from top to bottom.

For example, what percent of 65 is 22.1? Since R is unknown, $B = 65$ (follows "of"), and $A = 22.1$, cover R in the triangle.

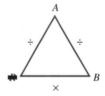

Reading from the top, we see A is divided by B. Therefore,

$$R = A \div B$$
$$R = 22.1 \div 65 = 0.34 \qquad \text{Divide to find } R, \text{ then change}$$
$$= 34\% \qquad \text{to a percent.}$$

So 22.1 is 34% of 65.

Examples A–E	**Warm Ups A–E**

Directions: Solve the percent problem using the formula.

Strategy: Write the percent equation $R(B) = A$. Substitute the known values and find the unknown value.

A.   45% of what number is 9?

Solution:

45% of B is 9

$0.45B = 9$

$B = 9 \div 0.45$

$B = 20$

So 45% of 20 is 9.

The % symbol follows 45 so $R = 45\%$. The base B (following the word "of") is unknown.

A.   75% of what number is 9?

B.   7 is what percent of 35?

B.   7 is what percent of 42?

Solution:

What percent of 35 is 7?   Reword to use the formula $RB = A$.

R of 35 is 7   The rate of percent R is unknown.

$R(35) = 7$ $B = 35$ and $A = 7$.

$R = 7 \div 35$ Divide.

$R = 0.2 = 20\%$ Change the decimal to a percent.

So 7 is 20% of 35.

C.   What is $33\frac{1}{3}\%$ of 105?

C.   What is $66\frac{2}{3}\%$ of 111?

Solution:

$33\frac{1}{3}\%$ of 105 is what?   Reword to use the formula $RB = A$.

$\dfrac{100}{3} \cdot \dfrac{1}{100} \cdot 105 = A$ $R = 33\frac{1}{3}\% = \dfrac{100}{3} \cdot \dfrac{1}{100}$ and $B = 105$.

$35 = A$ Reduce and multiply.

So 35 is $33\frac{1}{3}\%$ of 105.

D.   45% of what number is 27.9?

D.   45% of what number is 32.4?

Solution:

$R = 45\%$ and $A = 27.9$ The percent symbol follows R. The base B, following "of," is unknown.

In the percent triangle, cover B and read "$A \div R$."

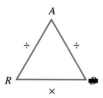

$B = A \div R$

$B = 27.9 \div 0.45$ $A = 27.9$ and $R = 45\% = 0.45$.

$B = 62$ Divide.

So 45% of 62 is 27.9.

Answers to warm ups: **B.** $16\frac{2}{3}\%$ **C.** 74   **D.** 72

E.   9.15 is what percent of 75?

E.   9.2 is what percent of 80?

Solution:

$B = 75$ and $A = 9.15$ $B = 75$ since it follows "of," R is unknown, and $A = 9.15$.

Cover R and read "$A \div B$."

$R = A \div B$
$R = 9.15 \div 75$
$R = 0.122$ Divide.
$R = 12.2\%$ Change the decimal to a percent.

So 12.2% of 75 is 9.15.

How and Why 2   Since R is a comparison of A to B, and we have seen earlier that this comparison can be written as a ratio, we can write the percent ratio equal to the ratio of A and B. In the proportion, the percent symbol is not part of R.

$$\frac{R}{100} = \frac{A}{B}$$ In this proportion, R is the number before "%."

When any one of the values of R, A, and B is unknown it can be found by solving the proportion.

For example, what percent of 65 is 22.1?

$$\frac{R}{100} = \frac{A}{B}$$ In the proportion $R\% = \dfrac{R}{100}$.

$$\frac{R}{100} = \frac{22.1}{65}$$

$65(R) = 100(22.1)$ Cross multiply.

$65(R) = 2210$

$R = 2210 \div 65$

$R = 34$

So 22.1 is 34% of 65.

Examples F–H   **Warm Ups F–H**

Directions: Solve the percent problem using a proportion.

Strategy: Write the proportion, $\dfrac{R}{100} = \dfrac{A}{B}$, fill in the known values, and solve.

F.   25% of 60 is what?

F.   65% of 60 is what?

Answer to warm up: **E.** 11.5%

Solution:

$$\frac{R}{100} = \frac{A}{B}$$ Proportion for solving percent exercises.

$$\frac{25}{100} = \frac{A}{60}$$ $R\% = 25\% = \frac{25}{100}$, $B = 60$, and A is unknown.

$$25(60) = 100(A)$$ Cross multiply.

$$1500 = 100(A)$$

$$1500 \div 100 = A$$

$$15 = A$$

So 25% of 60 is 15.

G.   135% of ___?___ is 54.

G.   140% of ___?___ is 105.

Solution:

$$\frac{R}{100} = \frac{A}{B}$$ Proportion for solving percent exercises.

$$\frac{135}{100} = \frac{54}{B}$$ $R = 135$, B is unknown, and $A = 54$.

$$135(B) = 100(54)$$ Cross multiply.

$$135(B) = 5400$$

$$B = 5400 \div 135$$

$$B = 40$$

So 135% of 40 is 54.

H.   50 is what percent of 180? Round to the nearest tenth of 1 percent.

H.   78 is what percent of 162 to the nearest tenth of 1 percent?

Solution:

$$\frac{R}{100} = \frac{A}{B}$$

$$\frac{R}{100} = \frac{50}{180}$$ R is unknown, $A = 50$, and $B = 180$.

$$180(R) = 100(50)$$ Cross multiply.

$$180(R) = 5000$$

$$R = 5000 \div 180$$

$$R \approx 27.77$$ Carry out division to two decimal places.

$$R \approx 27.8$$ Round to the nearest tenth.

So 50 is 27.8% of 180 to the nearest tenth of 1 percent.

Answers to warm ups: **F.** 39   **G.** 75   **H.** 48.1%

NAME _____ CLASS _____ DATE _____

EXERCISES 6.7

A

Solve.

1. 9 is 50% of ___?___. 18

2. 9 is 90% of ___?___. 10

3. What is 75% of 80? 60

4. What is 45% of 70? 31.5

5. 3 is ___?___% of 1. 300%

6. 8 is ___?___% of 4. 200%

7. ___?___% of 60 is 30. 50%

8. ___?___% of 65 is 13. 20%

9. 70% of ___?___ is 28. 40

10. 80% of ___?___ is 28. 35

11. 80% of 45 is ___?___. 36

12. ___?___ is 80% of 25. 20

13. 64 is ___?___% of 80. 80%

14. ___?___% of 56 is 14. 25%

15. 19% of ___?___ is 19. 100

16. 16 is ___?___% of 16. 100%

17. $\frac{1}{2}$% of 200 is __?__.   1

18. $\frac{1}{4}$% of 800 is __?__.   2

B

19. 140% of __?__ is 35.   25

20. 175% of __?__ is 52.5.   30

21. 9.5% of 60 is __?__.   5.7

22. 8.5% of 80 is __?__.   6.8

23. 0.4 is __?__% of 20.   2%

24. 78 is 52% of __?__.   150

25. 45 is 36% of __?__.   125

26. 1 is __?__% of 1000.   0.1%

27. 48% of 40 is __?__.   19.2

28. 72% of 80 is __?__.   57.6

29. 76% of __?__ is 152.   200

30. 27% of __?__ is 162.   600

31. 135% of __?__ is 48.6.   36

32. 165% of __?__ is 112.2.   68

33. 76 is __?__% of 125.   60.8%

34. 84 is __?__% of 160.   52.5%

NAME _____ CLASS _____ DATE _____

35. 15.6% of 80 is ___?___.   12.48

36. 24.3% of 90 is ___?___.   21.87

C

37. 3.2% of 0.7 is ___?___.   0.0224

38. ___?___ is $\frac{1}{2}$% of 0.5.   0.0025

39. $11\frac{1}{9}$% of 1845 is ___?___.   205

40. $16\frac{2}{3}$% of 3522 is ___?___.   587

41. $83\frac{1}{3}$% of ___?___ is 1040.   1248

42. $57\frac{1}{7}$% of ___?___ is 1008.   1764

43. 28% of ___?___ is 36 (to the nearest tenth).   128.6

44. ___?___ is 31.6% of 57.8 (to the nearest tenth).   18.3

45. What percent of 75 is 8 (to the nearest tenth of one percent)?   10.7%

46. What percent of 92 is 56 (to the nearest tenth of one percent)?   60.9%

47. 47 is ___?___% of 30 (to the nearest tenth of one percent).   156.7%

48. 82.5 is ___?___% of 37.6 (to the nearest whole-number percent).   219%

49. 1.25% of 1250 is ___?___.   15.625

50. 219 is 12% of ___?___.   1825

51. $5\frac{1}{3}\%$ of $6\frac{1}{2}$ is ___?___ (as a fraction). $\frac{26}{75}$

52. ___?___ is 53% of $15\frac{2}{3}$ (as a mixed number). $8\frac{91}{300}$

53. ___?___% of 82 is 105.5 (to the nearest tenth of one percent).   128.7%

54. $5\frac{1}{2}\%$ of ___?___ is 34.5 (to the nearest hundredth).   627.27

State Your Understanding

55. Explain the inaccuracies in this statement: "Strawbak Industries charges 70¢ for a part that costs them 30¢ to make. They're making 40% profit."

Challenge

56. $\frac{1}{2}\%$ of $33\frac{1}{3}$ is what fraction? $\frac{1}{6}$

57. $\frac{2}{5}\%$ of $66\frac{2}{3}$ is what fraction? $\frac{4}{15}$

Maintain Your Skills (Sections 5.2, 5.3)

Solve the proportions.

58. $\frac{14}{24} = \frac{x}{30}$ $x = 17.5$

59. $\frac{4.8}{2.5} = \frac{96}{y}$ $y = 50$

60. $\frac{a}{\frac{5}{8}} = \frac{1\frac{1}{2}}{3\frac{3}{4}}$ $a = 0.25$ or $\frac{1}{4}$

61. $\frac{1\frac{1}{2}}{t} = \frac{5\frac{5}{8}}{1\frac{2}{3}}$ $t = \frac{4}{9}$

62. $\frac{1.3}{0.07} = \frac{w}{3.01}$ $w = 55.9$

63. $\frac{1.3}{0.07} = \frac{5.59}{t}$ $t = 0.301$

Exercises 64–67: On a certain map, $1\frac{1}{2}$ inches represent 60 miles.

64. How many miles are represented by $2\frac{7}{8}$ inches?   115 miles

65. How many miles are represented by $3\frac{3}{16}$ inches? $127\frac{1}{2}$ miles

66. How many inches are needed to represent 820 miles? $20\frac{1}{2}$ inches

67. How many inches are needed to represent 22 miles?   0.55 inches

6.8 APPLICATIONS OF PERCENTS

Objectives

1 Solve percent word problems.

2 Solve business-related percent problems.

Application

🌐 In a statistical study of 285 people surveyed, 114 said they preferred eating whole wheat bread. What percent of the people surveyed preferred eating whole wheat bread?

How and Why 1 When a word problem is translated to the simpler word form, "What percent of what is what?" the unknown value can be found using one of the methods of the previous section. For example, "What percent of the loan is the interest?" (See Example A.)

Both methods of Section 6.7 are used in the examples.

When a value, B, is increased by an amount, A, the rate of percent, R, is called the *percent of increase*. When a value, B, is decreased by an amount, A, the rate of percent, R, is called the *percent of decrease*.

Examples A–H

Warm Ups A–H

Directions: Solve the percent word problem.

Strategy: Write the problem in the form, "What percent of what is what?" Fill in the known values and find the unknown value.

A. Rod buys a motorcycle with a 15% one-year loan. The interest payment is $75. How much is his loan?

A. Jamie buys a motorcycle with a 14% one-year loan. If the interest payment is $112, how much is the loan?

Solution:

15% of what is $75?   The $75 interest is 15% of the loan, so
$0.15(B) = 75$ $R = 15\% = 0.15$ and $A = \$75$. Substitute
$\quad B = 75 \div 0.15$ these values in the formula $R(B) = A$ and
$\quad B = 500$ solve.

Rod's loan is for $500.

B. This year the population of Century County is 130% of its population ten years ago. The population ten years ago was 117,000. What is its population this year?

B. The cost of a Kosmos is now 140% of what it was five years ago. If the cost of the automobile five years ago was $7850, what is the cost now?

Solution:

130% of 117,000 is what? $R = 130\%$ and $B = 117{,}000$.

$$\frac{130}{100} = \frac{A}{117{,}000}$$ Substitute these values into the

$$15{,}210{,}000 = 100A$$ proportion $\dfrac{R}{100} = \dfrac{A}{B}$, cross

$$15{,}210{,}000 \div 100 = A$$ multiply, and solve.

$$152{,}100 = A$$

The population this year is 152,100.

Answers to warm ups: **A.** $800   **B.** $10,990

C.   A pickup has depreciated to 65% of its original cost. If the value of the pickup is $8060, what did it cost originally?

C.   A tractor has depreciated to 52% of its original cost. If the value of the tractor is now $8216, what did it cost originally?

Solution:

65% of what is 8060? $R = 65\%$ and $A = 8060$.

Cover B and read "$A \div R$."

$B = A \div R$

$B = 8060 \div 0.65$ Change 65% to a decimal, 0.65.

$B = 12{,}400$ Divide.

The original cost was $12,400.

D.   The Davidson Bakery has 500 loaves of day-old bread they want to sell. If the price was originally 92¢ a loaf and they sell it for 64¢ a loaf, what percent discount, based on the original price, should the bakery advertise?

D.   The bakery also has 200 packages of day-old buns to sell. If the price was originally $1.08 per package and they sell them for 81¢ per package, what percent discount, based on the original price, will they advertise?

Solution:

$92 - 64 = 28$ First determine the discount amount.

What % of 92 is 28? $A = 28$ and $B = 92$ because we are seeking the percent of the discount based on the original price.

$R(92) = 28$

$R = 28 \div 92$

$R \approx 0.304$ Round to the nearest thousandth.

$R \approx 30.4\%$ Change the decimal to percent.

The discount is about 30.4%, so the bakery will probably advertise "over 30% off."

E.   A student newspaper polls a group of students. Two of them say they walk to school, seven others say they ride the bus, ten drive in car pools, and three drive their own cars. What percent of the group ride the bus?

E.   A list of the grades in a math class revealed that 7 students received A's, 15 received B's, 23 received C's, and 5 received D's. What percent of the students received a grade of B?

Solution:

What % of 22 is 7?   There are 22 students in the group so $B = 22$ and seven ride the bus so $A = 7$.

$\dfrac{R}{100} = \dfrac{7}{22}$

$22(R) = 700$ Cross multiply.

$R = 700 \div 22$

$R \approx 31.8$ Round to the nearest tenth.

$\approx 31.8\%$

Approximately 32% of the group ride the bus.

F. 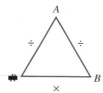 In a statistical study of 285 people surveyed, 114 said they preferred eating whole wheat bread. What percent of the people surveyed preferred eating whole wheat bread?

F. In a similar study of 372 people, 93 said they jog for exercise. What percent of those surveyed jog?

Solution:

What % of 285 is 114? $B = 285$ and $A = 114$.

Cover R and read "$A \div B$."

$R = A \div B$

$R = 114 \div 285$

$R = 0.4$ Divide.

$R - 40\%$ $0.4 = 0.40 = 40\%$

Therefore 40% of the people surveyed preferred eating whole wheat bread.

Directions: Find the percent of increase or decrease.

Strategy: Use one of the two methods to solve for R.

G. The percent of increase from 360 to 432.

G. The percent of increase from 360 to 450.

Solution:

$432 - 360 = 72$ The difference, 72, is the *amount* of increase from 360 to 432. The percent of increase is the amount, 72, based on 360.

$R(360) = 72$ What percent of 360 is 72?

$R = 72 \div 360$

$R = 0.2 = 20\%$

There is a 20% increase from 360 to 432.

H. The percent of decrease from 556 to 361.4.

H. The percent of decrease from 450 to 360.

Solution:

$556 - 361.4 = 194.6$ The difference, 194.6, is the *amount* of decrease from 556 to 361.4. The percent of decrease is the amount, 194.6, based on 556.

$R(556) = 194.6$ What percent of 566 is 194.6?

$R = 194.6 \div 556$

$R = 0.35 = 35\%$

There is a 35% decrease from 556 to 361.4.

Answers to warm ups: **F.** 25%   **G.** 25%   **H.** 20%

How and Why   2   Businesses use percent in a variety of ways. Among these are percent of markup, percent of discount, percent of profit, interest rates, taxes, salary increases, and commissions. These words and phrases are explained in the next set of examples.

Examples I–N	Warm Ups I–N

Directions: Solve the business-related word problem.

Strategy: Write the problem in the simpler word form, "What percent of what is what?" Fill in the known values and find the unknown value.

I. The cost of an electric iron is $18.50. The markup is 30% of the cost. What is the selling price of the iron?

I. The cost of a coffee maker is $28.50. The markup is 40% of the cost. What is the selling price of the coffee maker?

Solution:

SIMPLER WORD FORM

Markup is 30% of cost.

$M = 30\%(\$18.50)$

$M = 0.30(\$18.50)$

$M = \$5.55$

Markup is the amount added to the cost, by the store, of an article so the store can pay its expenses and make a profit. Let M represent the markup. Use the formula $R(B) = A$ where $R = 0.30$ and $B = \$18.50$.

The markup is $5.55.

S.P. = cost + markup

= $18.50 + $5.55

= $24.05

To find the selling price, add the cost and the markup. Let S.P. represent the price.

The selling price of the iron is $24.05.

J. The regular price of a portable radio is $29.98. What is the sale price of the radio if it is discounted 30%? Round to the nearest cent.

J. The price of a CD player is $179.95. What is the sale price of the player if the percent of discount is 18%? Round to the nearest cent.

Solution:

SIMPLER WORD FORM

Amount of discount is 30% of S.P.

Amount of discount = 0.30($29.98)

= $8.994

Sale price = $29.98 − $8.994

= $20.986 ≈ $20.99

The *amount of discount* is the amount subtracted from the regular price. The *percent of discount* is 30%. Use the formula $R(B) = A$.

Subtract discount from price. Round to the nearest cent.

The sale price is $20.99.

Answers to warm ups: **I.** $39.90   **J.** $147.56

K.   A toaster-oven is priced to sell for $29.95. The markup is 40% of the selling price. What is the cost of the oven?

Solution:

SIMPLER WORD FORM

M is 40% of the selling price

$$\frac{40}{100} = \frac{M}{29.95}$$

$$40(29.95) = 100(M)$$

$$1198 \div 100 = M$$

Let M represent the markup.

Use the proportion $\dfrac{R}{100} = \dfrac{A}{B}$.

$R = 40\% = \dfrac{40}{100}$ and $B = 29.95$.

Markup can be based on the cost to the store (as in Example I) or on the selling price, as here.

The markup is $11.98.

Cost = S.P. − markup

= 29.95 − 11.98

= 17.97

The (store) cost of the toaster-oven is $17.97.

K.   A camera is priced to sell for $189.95. If the markup is 40% of the selling price, what is the cost of the camera?

L.   A phone company buys a new car that costs $15,000. During the first year it will depreciate $12\frac{1}{2}\%$ of its original value. What will its value be at the end of the year?

Solution:

SIMPLER WORD FORM

Depreciation is $12\frac{1}{2}\%$ of price

Depreciation $= 12\frac{1}{2}\%(\$15{,}000)$

$= 0.125(\$15{,}000)$

$= \$1875$

Depreciation is the name given to the decrease in value caused by age or use. Use the formula.

The depreciation is $1875.

Value = $15,000 − $1875 = $13,125

The value of the car at the end of the first year is $13,125.

L.   The phone company buys a new truck at the same time for $28,530. If the depreciation rate for the truck is $11\frac{1}{9}\%$, what will its value be at the end of the year?

M. Jean's rate of pay is $6.48 per hour. She gets time and one-half for each hour over 40 hours worked in one week. What are her earnings if in one week she works for 46.5 hours?

M. What are Jean's earnings for a week in which she works 49.75 hours at the same pay rate as in Example M?

Solution:

SIMPLER WORD FORM
Overtime is 150% of regular pay
Overtime = 150%($6.48)

Time and one-half means that she will earn 1.5 times or 150% of her regular hourly wage.

Cover *A* and read "*R* × *B*."

Overtime = $R(B)$ = 150%($6.48)

Overtime = 1.5($6.48)

   = $9.72

Earnings = 40($6.48) + 6.5($9.72)

   = $259.20 + $63.18

   = $322.38

Add the overtime wages to the pay for the first 40 hours.

Jean earns $322.38 for the week.

N. Mr. Jordan sells men's clothing. He receives a salary of $180 per week plus a commission of 7.5% of his total sales. One week he sells $1530 worth of clothing. What are his total earnings for the week?

N. What are Mr. Jordan's total earnings for a week in which his sales total $975, if his salary and commission are the same as in Example N?

Solution:

SIMPLER WORD FORM
Commission is 7.5% of sales

Commission = 7.5%($1530)

   = 0.075($1530)

   = $114.75

Commission is the money salespeople earn based on the goods they sell.

Total earnings = salary + commission

   = $180 + $114.75

   = $294.75

Mr. Jordan's total earnings for the week are $294.75.

NAME _____ CLASS _____ DATE _____

EXERCISES 6.8

Applications

1. If there is a 4% sales tax on a television set costing $119.95, how much is the tax? $4.80

2. Dan buys a used motorcycle for $955. He makes a down payment of 18%. How much cash does he pay as down payment? $171.90

3. Last year Joan had 14% of her salary withheld for taxes. If the total amount withheld was $2193.10, what is Joan's yearly salary? $15,665

4. The manager of a fruit stand loses $16\frac{2}{3}\%$ of his bananas to spoilage and sells the rest. He discards three boxes of bananas in two weeks. How many boxes does he have in stock at the beginning of the two weeks?   18 boxes

5. A state sales tax is 7%. Rich pays $480 for a new TV, not including the sales tax. How much sales tax does Rich pay? $33.60

6. Ilga buys a new van for $15,980. She pays 12% down. How much does she still owe? $14,062.40

7. Janet pays $225 as a down payment on her new appliances. The appliances cost $2500. What percent does she pay as down payment? How much does she still owe?   9%; $2275

8. To pass a test to qualify for a job interview, Carol must score at least 70%. If there are 40 questions on the test, how many must Carol get correct to score 70%?   28 questions

9. Kathy's house is valued at $65,000 and rents for $4875 per year. What percent of the value of the house is the annual income from rent? Round to the nearest tenth of a percent.   7.5%

10. Eddy and his family go to a restaurant for dinner. The dinner check is $19.75. He leaves the waiter a tip of $3. What percent of the check is the tip? Round to the nearest whole-number percent.   15%

11. Floyd earns a monthly salary of $805. He spends $130 a month at the supermarket. What percent of his salary is spent at the supermarket? Round to the nearest whole-number percent.   16%

Exercises 12–16 refer to the same family.

12. Marline and Julio Martin spend 35% of their combined net income on their house payment. What is their house payment if they net $2500 per month? $875

13. The Martin family spends $180 on property taxes per month. What percent of their income is this?   7.2%

14. Julio donates $71.25 to a local charity one month. This is 5% of his monthly net income. What is his monthly net income? $1425

15. What percent of their combined net income is Marline's net income?   43%

16. Julio Martin gets a 4.5% raise in his net income. How much is this? Round to the nearest cent. $64.13

17. Adams High School's basketball team finishes the season with a record of 15 wins and 9 losses. What percent of the games played were won? $62\frac{1}{2}$%

18. A state charges a gasoline tax of 9% of the cost. The federal tax is 4¢ per gallon. If gasoline costs $1.30 per gallon before taxes, what is the total price per gallon including taxes? $1.457

19. The police department sets up a vehicle inspection station at the high school parking lot. Of the 128 cars inspected on a particular day, 6.25% are found to have faulty brakes. How many vehicles do not have faulty brakes?   120 cars

20. The town of Verboort has a population of 15,560, which is 45% male. Of the men, 32% are 40 years or older. How many men are there in Verboort who are younger than 40?   4761 men

21. If the population of Sparse County decreased from 2305 to 2289, what is the percent of decrease? Round to the nearest tenth.   0.7%

NAME _____ CLASS _____ DATE _____

22. After an 8% increase in population, the city of Croburg has 1998 inhabitants. What was the former population?   1850 people

23. James suffers a 5% cut in his hourly wages. If after the pay cut he receives $4.75 per hour, what were his wages before the cut? $5 per hour

24. The population of Port City increased 15% since the last census. If the former population was 124,000, what is the present population?   142,600

25. For customers who use a bank's credit card, there is a $1\frac{3}{4}$% finance charge on monthly accounts that have a balance of $400 or less. Merle's finance charge for August is $4.69. How much is the balance of her account for that month? $268

26. In preparing a mixture of concrete, Lily uses 300 pounds of gravel, 100 pounds of cement, and 200 pounds of sand. What percent of the mixture is gravel?   50%

27. St. Josef's Hospital has 8 three-bed wards, 20 four-bed wards, 100 two-bed wards, and 10 private rooms. What percent of the capacity of St. Josef's Hospital is in private rooms? Round to the nearest tenth of a percent.   3.2%

28. Airica receives a weekly salary of $85 plus 9% of the price of everything she sells. Last week she earned $226.30. What was her sales total for that week? $1570

29. An article that costs a store owner $8.43 is to be marked up $2.81. What is the percent of markup based on the cost? $33\frac{1}{3}$%

30. In Exercise 29, what is the percent of the markup based on the selling price?   25%

31. A screwdriver that costs a hardware merchant $8.40 is to be marked up 30% of the cost. What is the selling price? $10.92

32. In Exercise 31, what percent of the selling price is the markup? Round to the nearest percent.   23%

33. People pay 7.51% of their salary to Social Security. What will Jon pay to Social Security on a monthly salary of $1576? Round to the nearest cent. $118.36

34. Jill gives 0.5% of her weekly salary to United Way. Last week she gave $9.25. What was her salary last week? $1850

35. Marica makes $1900 per month. She contributes 12% toward retirement and $1\frac{1}{4}$% to the Salvation Army. How much does she give to each per month?
$228 retirement; $23.75 Salvation Army

36. Last year the Chief Executive Officer of the Sweet Tooth Candy Company received a bonus of $12,824. The CEO receives 4% of the profits as bonus. What were the company's profits last year?
$320,600

37. Mary's base rate of pay is $7.82 per hour. She receives 150% of the base rate for all hours over 40 that she works in one week. What were her total earnings if she worked 47 hours last week?
$394.91

38. Jamie's base rate of pay is $6.72 per hour. He receives 150% of the base rate for all hours over 40 that he works in one week. What were his total earnings if he worked 42 hours last week?
$288.96

39. A new automobile depreciates 14% during the first year. If its original cost was $10,950, what is its depreciated value at the end of the first year? (*Hint:* The depreciated value is the original value minus the depreciation.) $9417

40. A new machine acquired by the Hot-Blast Foundry costs $11,728. At the end of the first year it has depreciated to a value of $10,262. What is the rate of depreciation for the first year?   12.5%

41. Four people decide to become business partners. The first partner buys 25% of a business, the second partner buys 20%, the third partner buys 32%, and the fourth partner buys 23%. The profits are to be divided among the four according to their share of the ownership. The company profits for last month were $18,256. How much does each partner receive? $4564; $3651.20; $5841.92; $4198.88

NAME _____   CLASS _____   DATE _____

42. Three people resolve to become business associates. The first associate pays 36% for a share of a franchise, the second associate pays 29%, and the third associate pays for the remaining 35% of the franchise. The profits are to be divided among the three according to each associate's share of the ownership. The profits for last month were $5274. How much does each associate receive?

$1898.64; $1529.46; $1845.90

43. During one week Tami Williams sells a total of $12,875 worth of hardware to the stores in her territory. She receives a 3% commission on sales of $2000 or less, 4% on the portion of her sales from $2001 to $8000, and 5% on all sales over $8000. What is her total commission for the week?

$543.75

44. One week earlier, Ms. Williams (in Exercise 43) sold $14,280 worth of appliances at the same commission rate. How much commission did she earn? $614

45. The base price of an automobile is $8400. The optional equipment on the car increases the price to $11,200. What percent of the base price is the cost of the optional equipment? $33\frac{1}{3}\%$

46. In Exercise 45, what percent of the total price is the optional equipment?   25%

47. The tax rate in a rural township is $3.20 per $100 of assessed value. What is the tax rate in percent form?   3.2%

48. Using the tax rate in Exercise 47, what are the taxes on a house with an assessed value of $68,950? $2206.40

49. The taxes levied on a piece of property are $2238.30, and the property has an assessed value of $82,900. What is the percent tax rate in the district where the property is located?   2.7%

50. A toaster sells for $28.96. If the markup is $33\frac{1}{3}\%$ of the cost, what is the most the store can afford to pay for the toaster? $21.72

51. A labor union renegotiated their contract with the Bobcat manufacturing company. The average wage under the new contract will increase 4.25%. The average wage under the old contract was $8.52 per hour. What will be the average wage under the new contract? $8.88

3. How many cars used the highway on Tuesday?
4. How many cars used the highway on the weekend?

3. How many people rode the bus on Friday?
4. How many people rode the bus during the week?

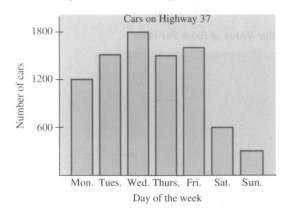

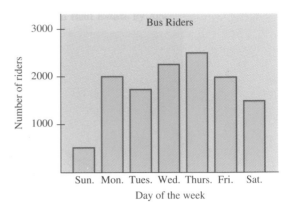

Solution:

1. Wednesday   The tallest bar shows the largest number of cars.
2. Sunday   The shortest bar shows the least number of cars.
3. 1500   Read the vertical scale at the top of the bar for Tuesday. The value is estimated since the top of the bar is not on a scale line.
4. 900   Add the number of cars for Saturday and Sunday.

B. The total sales from hot dogs, soda, T-shirts, and buttons during an air show are in the pictograph.

1. What item has the largest dollar sales?
2. What were the total sales from hot dogs and buttons?
3. How many more dollars were realized from the sale of T-shirts than from buttons?

B. The number of birds spotted during a recent expedition of the Huntsville Bird Society is shown in the pictograph.

1. Which species was spotted most often?
2. How many woodpeckers and wrens were spotted?
3. How many more canaries were spotted than crows?

Item	Sales at Air Show $\,$= \$1000 $\,$= \$500	
Hot dogs	$ $ $	
Soda	$ $ $	
T-shirts	$ $ $ $ $	
Buttons	$	

Species	Birds Spotted = 50 = 25	
Crows	🐦	
Woodpeckers	🐦 🐦 🐦	
Wrens	🐦 🐦 🐦 🐦	
Canaries	🐦 🐦	

Solution:

1. T-shirts

There are more bills representing dollar sales in the T-shirt row than any other row. The three bills represent $3000 in sales for hot dogs. The half bill represents $500 in sales for buttons. Add these.

2. Hot dogs: $3000
   Buttons: $ 500
   Total: $3500
3. T-shirts: $5000
   Buttons: $ 500

   The sale from T-shirts was $4500 more than from buttons.

Subtract the sales of buttons from the sales of T-shirts.

Answers to warm ups: **A.** 1. Thursday 2. Sunday 3. 2000 4. 12,500 **B.** 1. Wrens 2. 350 3. 50

C. The sources of City Community College's revenue are shown in the circle graph.

1. What percent of the revenue is from the federal government?
2. What percent of the revenue is from tuition and property taxes?
3. What percent of the revenue is from the federal and state governments?

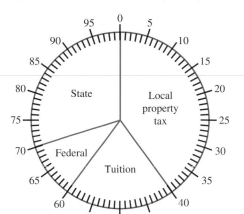

C. The percent of sales from food, sundries, drugs, and hardware at the Mini-Mart are shown in the circle graph.

1. What is the area of highest sales?
2. What percent of the total sales are from sundries and drugs?
3. What percent of the total sales are from food and hardware?

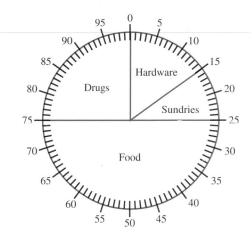

Solution:

1. 10%   Read directly from the graph.
2. 60%   Add the percents from tuition and property taxes.
3. 40%   Add the percents from state and federal sources.

How and Why 2   Let us construct a bar graph to show the variation in used car sales at Oldies but Goldies used car lot. The data are shown in the following table:

Month	Jan.	Feb.	Mar.	Apr.	May	Jun.
Cars Sold	30	15	25	20	15	35

To draw and label the bar graph for these data, we show the number of cars sold on the vertical scale and the months on the horizontal scale. This is a logical display as we will most likely be asked to find the highest and lowest months of car sales and a vertical display of numbers is easier to read than a horizontal display of numbers. This is the typical way bar graphs are displayed. Be sure to write the names on the vertical and horizontal scales as soon as you have chosen how the data will be displayed. Now title the graph so that the reader will recognize the data it contains.

The next step is to construct the two scales of the graph. Since each monthly total is divisible by five, we choose multiples of five for the vertical scale. We could have chosen one for the vertical scale, but the bars would be very long and the graph would take up a lot of space. If we had chosen a larger scale, say ten, then the graph might be too compact and we would need to find fractional values on the scale. It is easier to draw the graph if we use a scale that divides each unit of data. The months are displayed on the horizontal scale. Be sure to draw the bars with uniform width, for each of them represents a month of

---

sales. A vertical display of between 5 and 12 units is typical. The vertical display should start with zero.

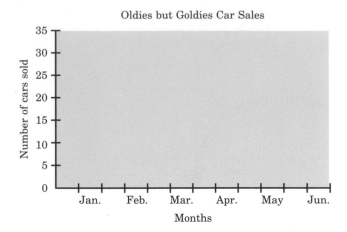

We stop the vertical scale at 35, since that is the maximum number of cars to be displayed. The next step is to draw the bars. Start by finding the number of cars for January. Since 30 cars were sold in January, we draw the bar for January until the height of 30 is reached. This is the top of the bar. Now draw the solid bar for January.

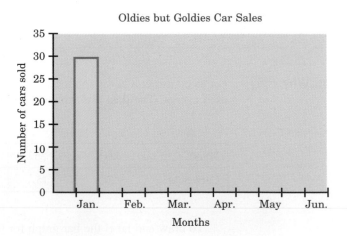

Complete the graph by drawing the bars for the other months.

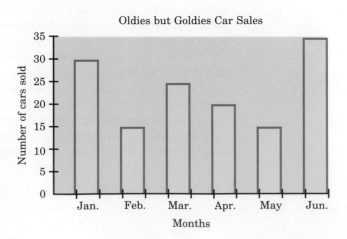

A line graph is similar to a bar graph in that it has vertical and horizontal scales. The data are represented by points rather than bars and the points are connected by line segments. We use a line graph to display the following data:

Property Taxes	
Year	**Tax Rate (per $1000)**
1970	12.00
1975	15.00
1980	14.00
1985	16.00
1990	20.00

We will let the vertical scale represent the tax rate and each unit represent $2. This requires using a half space for the $15.00 rate, since using $1 would make the graph too tall. The horizontal scale represents the years.

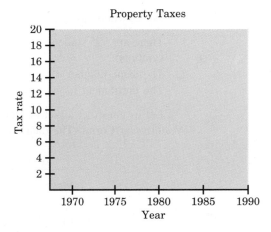

To find the points that represent the data, find the points that are at the intersection of the horizontal line through the tax rate and the vertical line through the corresponding year. Once all the points have been located, connect them with line segments.

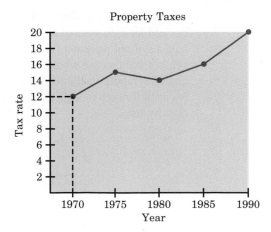

From the graph we can conclude the following:

1. Only during one five-year period (1975–1980) did the tax rate decline.
2. The largest increase in the tax rate took place from 1985 to 1990.
3. The tax rate has increased $8 per thousand from 1970 to 1990.

The third type of graph we consider is a pictograph. A pictograph is similar to a bar graph where symbols replace the bar to represent the data. Consider the following graph:

Class	Mathematics Students at City College ♟ = 50 students ♟ = 25 students
Prealgebra	♟ ♟
Algebra	♟ ♟ ♟ ♟
Geometry	♟ ♟
Calculus	♟ ♟
Statistics	♟

We can draw the following conclusions from the graph:

1. There are 525 students enrolled in mathematics courses at City College (value of all symbols).
2. The same number of students take prealgebra and calculus.
3. The enrollment in geometry is 25 more than the enrollment in statistics.

Let us construct a pictorial graph to show the number of cars sold, by model, at the Western Car Corral. The data are shown in the following table:

Make	**Car Sales at Western Car Corral**
Ford	50
Chrysler	35
Honda	60
Toyota	25
Pontiac	20

First select a symbol and the number of cars it represents. Here we use a picture of a car and let each symbol represent ten cars. By letting each symbol represent ten cars and half a symbol represent five cars, we can save space. We could have chosen five cars per symbol, but then we would need to display 12 symbols to represent the number of Hondas, and 12 symbols would make the graph quite large. Next, determine the number of symbols we need for each model. The number of symbols can be found by dividing each number of cars by ten:

Make	**Number**	**Number of Symbols**
Ford	50	5
Chrysler	35	$3\frac{1}{2}$
Honda	60	6
Toyota	25	$2\frac{1}{2}$
Pontiac	20	2

Now draw the graph using the symbols (pictures) to represent the data:

Model	Car Sales at Western Car Corral
	🚗 = 10 cars 🚙 = 5 cars
Ford	🚗 🚗 🚗 🚗 🚗
Chrysler	🚗 🚗 🚗 🚙
Honda	🚗 🚗 🚗 🚗 🚗 🚗
Toyota	🚗 🚗 🚙
Pontiac	🚗 🚗

The circle graph is used to show how a whole unit is divided into parts, or in this case percents. Consider the following graph:

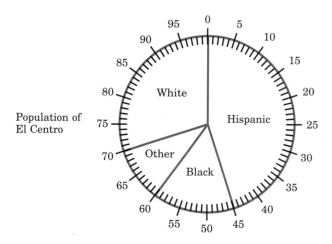

Population of El Centro

From the graph we can conclude:

1. The largest ethnic group in El Centro is Hispanic.
2. The white population is twice the black population.
3. Blacks and Hispanics make up 60% of the population.

If the population of El Centro is 125,000, we can also compute the approximate number of each group. For instance, the number of blacks is found by

$$RB = A$$
$$15\%(125,000) = A$$
$$0.15(125,000) = A$$
$$18,750 = A$$

So, there are approximately 18,750 blacks in El Centro.

Construct a circle graph to show the percent of age groups in Central City. The data are listed in the following chart:

Age Groups	0–21	22–50	Over 50
Population	14,560	29,120	14,560

The first step is to find the size of the whole unit or total population. The sum of the population by age groups is 58,240. The second step is to determine the percent of the population in each age group. Since the total population is 58,240, the percents are

$$0\text{--}21: \quad \frac{14560}{58240} = 0.25 = 25\% \qquad 50+: \quad \frac{14560}{58240} = 0.25 = 25\%$$

$$22\text{--}50: \quad \frac{29120}{58240} = 0.5 = 50\%$$

From the percents we see that we must divide the circle in half (each half is 50%), and then divide one of the halves. Draw the graph, label the segments, and give the graph a title.

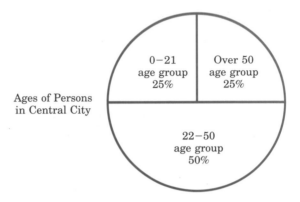

Ages of Persons in Central City

Many circle graphs are divided into sectors using a degree as the unit of measurement. We do not discuss degrees in this text but instead divide the circumference of the circle using increments of 1%. A more accurate graph can be drawn when you have learned about degree measurement.

| **Example D** | **Warm Up D** |

Directions: Construct a bar graph.

Strategy: List the related values in pairs and draw two scales to show the pairs of values.

D. The number of babies born during the first six months at Tuality Hospital: January, 15; February, 9; March, 7; April, 18; May, 10; June, 6.

D. The number of plants sold at the Pick-a-Posey Nursery: geraniums, 45; fuchsias, 60; marigolds, 150; impatiens, 90; daisies, 120.

Solution:

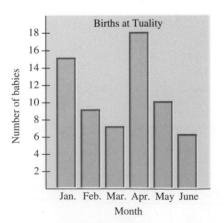

Choose a scale of 1 unit = 2 babies for the vertical scale.

Divide the horizontal scale so that it will accommodate six months with a common unit between them.

Construct the graph, label the scales, and give the graph a title.

Answer to warm up: **D.**

NAME _____ CLASS _____ DATE _____

EXERCISES 6.9

A

The following graph shows the variation in the number of phone calls during normal business hours:

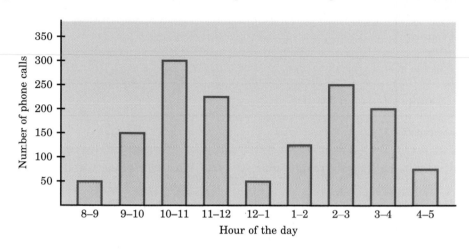

1. At what hour of the day is the number of phone calls greatest?   10–11

2. At what hour of the day is the number of phone calls least?   8–9 and 12–1

3. What is the number of phone calls made between 2 and 3?   250

4. What is the number of phone calls made between 8 and 12?   725

5. What is the total number of phone calls made during the times listed?   1425

The following graph displays the way the Andrews spend their monthly income:

6. What percent of their income is spent on food?
25%

7. What percent of their income is spent on rent?
30%

8. Do the Andrews spend more money per month on automobile expenses or clothes?   automobile expenses

9. What percent of the Andrews' income is spent on clothes and miscellaneous items?   25%

10. What percent of the Andrews' income is spent on food and rent?   55%

The following graph shows the number of cars in the shop for repair during a given year:

Type of car	1988 Repair Intake Record
	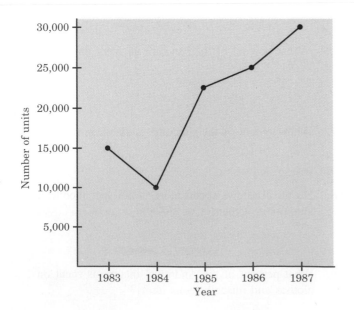 = 20 cars
Compact	🚗 🚗 🚗 · 🚗
Full size	🚗 🚗 🚗 🚗 🚗 🚗 🚗 🚗
Van	🚗 🚗
Subcompact	🚗 🚗 🚗 🚗 🚗 🚗

11. How many vans were in the shop for repair during the year?   40 vans

12. What type of car had the most cars in for repair?   full size

13. How many compacts and subcompacts were in for repair during the year?   200

14. How many cars were in for repair during the year?   400

15. Were more subcompacts or compacts in for service during the year?   subcompacts

B

The following graph shows the number of production units at What-Co during the period 1983–1987:

16. What was the greatest production year?   1987

17. What was the year of least production?   1984

18. What was the increase in production between 1984 and 1985?   12,500 units

19. What was the decrease in production between 1983 and 1984?   5000 units

20. What was the percent increase in production from 1983 to 1987?   100%

NAME _____ CLASS _____ DATE _____

The following circle graph shows how dollars are spent in a particular industry:

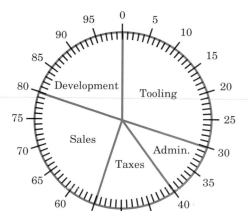

The following graph shows the amounts paid for raw materials:

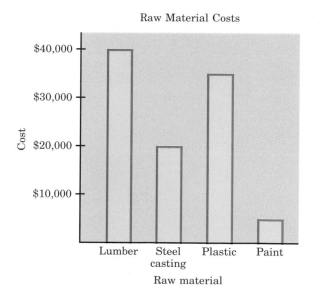

21. What department has the greatest expenditure of funds?   tooling department

22. Which is more costly, development or taxes? development

23. If the total expenditures of the industry are $2,500,000, how much is spent on development? $500,000

24. Using the total expenditures in Exercise 23, how much is spent on tooling? $750,000

25. What is the total paid for paint and lumber? $45,000

26. How much less is paid for steel castings than for plastics? $15,000

27. What is the total amount paid for raw materials? $100,000

28. What percent of the total cost of raw materials is paid for lumber?   40%

29. What two raw materials account for 45% of the total cost?   lumber and paint

C

In Exercises 30–42 be sure to name the graph and label the parts. Draw bar graphs to display the following data.

30. Distribution of grades in an algebra class: A, 8; B, 6; C, 15; D, 8; F, 4.

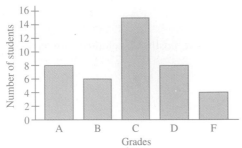

31. Dinner choices at the LaPlante restaurant in one week: Steak, 45; Salmon, 80; Chicken, 60; Lamb, 10; Others, 25.

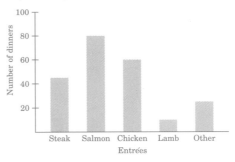

32. The distribution of monthly income: Rent, $350; Automobile, $300; Taxes, $250; Clothes, $100; Food, $250; Miscellaneous, $100.

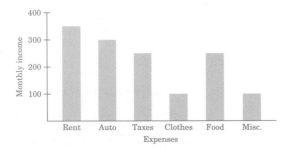

33. The type of television sets sold in one week at an appliance store: Black and White, 15; Color, 25; Color with Stereo, 5; Miniature, 10.

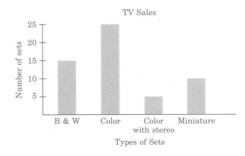

34. Career preference as expressed by a senior class: Business, 120; Law, 20; Medicine, 40; Science, 100; Public Service, 80; Armed Service, 40.

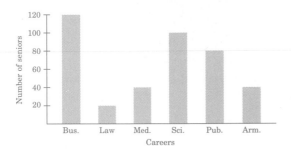

Draw circle graphs to display the following data.

35. The distribution of male and female workers in the Acme Corporation: Males, 75%; Females, 25%.

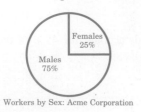

36. The type of fish caught during the Far West Angling Tournament: Salmon, 44; Trout, 22; Sturgeon, 11; Sea Bass, 11.

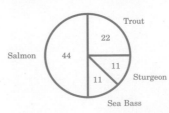

NAME _____ CLASS _____ DATE _____

Draw line graphs to display the following data.

37. Daily sales at the local men's store: Monday, $1500; Tuesday, $2500; Wednesday, $1500; Thursday, $3500; Friday, $4000; Saturday, $6000; Sunday, $4500.

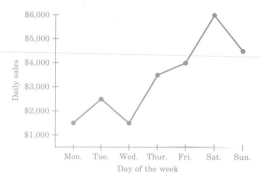

38. The gallons of water used each quarter of the year by a certain city:

        Jan.–Mar. 20,000,000 gallons
        Apr.–June 30,000,000 gallons
        July–Aug. 45,000,000 gallons
        Sept.–Dec. 25,000,000 gallons

39. Income from various sources for a given year: Wages, $32,000; Interest, $2000; Dividends, $4000; Sale of Property, $16,000.

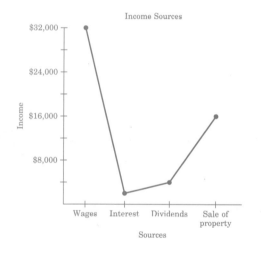

Draw pictorial graphs to display the following data.

40. The cost of an average three-bedroom house in Oregon:

Year	Cost
1960	$45,000
1965	$55,000
1970	$60,000
1975	$70,000
1980	$75,000
1985	$70,000

41. The population of Wilsonville over 20 years of age: 1965, 15,000; 1970, 17,500; 1975, 22,500; 1980, 30,000; 1985, 32,500.

42. The oil production from a local well over a five-year period:

Year	Barrels Produced
1980	500
1981	1500
1982	3000
1983	2250
1984	1250

	= 500	= 250
1980		
1981		
1982		
1983		
1984		

State Your Understanding

43. Explain the advantages of each type of graph and chart. Which do you prefer?

Challenge

44. The figures for United States casualties in four declared wars of the 20th century are: World War I, 321,000; World War II, 1,076,000; Korean War, 158,000; Vietnam War, 211,000. Draw three graphs to illustrate the information. Make a bar graph, a line graph, and a circle graph. Which of your graphs do you think does the best job?

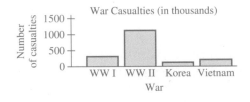

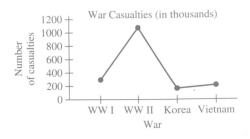

Group Activity

45. Have each group member select a country and find the most recent population statistics for that country. Put the numbers together and have each member draw a different kind of graph of the populations.

Maintain Your Skills (Sections 4.7, 4.10, 5.2)

Find the unknown value.

46. $\dfrac{30}{36} = \dfrac{x}{42}$ $x = 35$

47. $\dfrac{72}{80} = \dfrac{y}{220}$ $y = 198$

48. $\dfrac{12}{x} = \dfrac{102}{17}$ $x = 2$

49. $\dfrac{52}{a} = \dfrac{286}{44}$ $a = 8$

50. $\dfrac{8.4}{3.5} = \dfrac{12}{b}$ $b = 5$

51. $\dfrac{4}{x} = \dfrac{8}{21}$ $x = 10.5$

52. $\dfrac{3.4}{5} = \dfrac{8.5}{x}$ $x = 12.5$

53. Find the average of 18.3, 13.58, 21.6, 1.02, and 3.5.   11.6

54. Multiply: 8614.371×10^2.   861,437.1

55. Divide: $2.384 \div 10^3$.   0.002384

6.10 READING AND INTERPRETING TABLES

Objective Read and interpret information given in a table.

Application 🌐 The following table displays nutritional information about four breakfast cereals:

Nutritional Value per 1-oz Serving

Ingredient	Oat Bran	Rice Puffs	Raisin Bran	Wheat Flakes
Calories	90	110	120	110
Protein	6 g	2 g	3 g	3 g
Carbohydrate	17 g	25 g	31 g	23 g
Fat	0 g	0 g	1 g	1 g
Sodium	5 mg	290 mg	230 mg	270 mg
Potassium	180 mg	35 mg	260 mg	4 mg

1. Which cereal has the most calories per serving?
2. How many grams (g) of carbohydrates are there in five ounces of Rice Puffs?
3. How many more milligrams (mg) of sodium are there in a one-ounce serving of Wheat Flakes as compared to Raisin Bran?
4. How many ounces of Oat Bran can one eat before consuming the same amount of sodium as in one ounce of Rice Puffs?

Vocabulary A **table** is a method of displaying data in an array using a horizontal and vertical arrangement to distinguish the type of data. A **row** of a table is a horizontal line of a table and reads left or right across the page. A **column** of a table is a vertical line of a table and reads up or down the page. For example, in the table

Column

134	**56**	89	102
14	**116**	7	98
65	**45**	**12**	**67**
23	**32**	7	213

Row

the number "45" is in row 3 and column 2.

How and Why Data are often displayed in the form of a table. We see tables in the print media, in advertisements, and in business presentations. Reading a table involves finding the correct column and row that describes the needed information and then reading the data at the intersection of that column and that row; for example,

Student Course Enrollment

Class	Mathematics	English	Science	Humanities
Freshman	950	1500	500	1200
Sophomore	600	700	650	1000
Junior	450	200	950	1550
Senior	400	250	700	950

To find the number of sophomores who take English, find the column headed English and the row headed Sophomore and read the number at the intersection. The number of sophomores taking English is 700.

We can use the table for predicting by scaling the values in the table upward or downward. If the number of seniors doubles next year, we can assume the number of seniors taking humanities will also double. So the number of seniors taking humanities next year will be 1900, since $2 \cdot 950 = 1900$.

We can also find the percent of the enrollments listed by subject area. For instance, to find the percent of those enrolled in mathematics that are freshmen, we divide the freshman enrollment in mathematics by the total mathematics enrollment:

$$\frac{950}{950 + 600 + 450 + 400} = \frac{950}{2400} \approx 0.39583 \approx 39.6\%$$

So about 39.6% of the mathematics enrollment are freshmen.

Other ways to interpret data from a table are shown in the examples.

Examples A–C

Warm Ups A–C

Directions: Answer the questions associated with the table.

Strategy: Examine the rows and columns of the table to determine the values that are related.

A. This table shows the decline in the number of railroad workers in four western states.

1. Which state had the most railroad workers in 1980?
2. Which state had the least number of railroad workers in 1988?
3. Which state suffered the greatest loss in the number of railroad workers?
4. What was the percent of decrease in the number of railroad workers in Wyoming from 1980 to 1988?

A. Use the table in Example A to answer.

1. What was the total number of railroad workers in 1980 in the four states?
2. How many more railroad workers did Idaho have than Oregon in 1988?
3. What was the total number of railroad workers in Wyoming and Utah in 1988?
4. The railroad workers in Idaho represent what percent of the total railroad workers in 1988? Round to the nearest percent.

Railroad Workers

State	1980	1988
Oregon	2991	1338
Idaho	3368	1748
Wyoming	3416	1486
Utah	3046	1717

Solution:

1. Wyoming

Read down the column headed "1980" to locate the largest number of workers, 3416. Now read across the row to find the state, Wyoming.

2. Oregon

Read down the column headed "1988" to find the least number of workers, 1338. Then read across the row to find the state, Oregon.

3. Oregon: $2991 - 1338 = 1653$
   Idaho: $3368 - 1748 = 1620$
   Wyoming: $3416 - 1486 = 1930$
   Utah: $3046 - 1717 = 1329$

   Wyoming suffered the greatest loss.

Find the difference in the number of workers for each state.

The difference 1930 is the greatest of the four numbers.

4. $\dfrac{1930}{3416} \approx 0.564988$

Divide the loss in workers by the number in 1980.

≈ 0.565

Round to three decimal places to find the percent to the nearest tenth.

$= 56.5\%$

Change to percent.

B.   This table shows the value of homes sold in the Portland metropolitan area for a given month in 1993.

1. In which location was the highest-priced home sold?
2. What was the price difference between the average cost of a house and the lowest cost of a house in Lake Oswego?
3. The lowest-priced house is what percent of the highest-priced house in West Portland? Round to the nearest percent.
4. What percent of the average-priced house in Beaverton is the average-priced house in S.E. Portland? Round to the nearest percent.

B.   Use the table in Example B to answer.

1. Which area has the highest average sale price?
2. What is the difference between the highest- and lowest-priced house in Beaverton?
3. What is the percent of increase from the average-priced house in N.E. Portland to the highest-priced house in N.E. Portland? Round to the nearest percent.
4. What is the percent of increase from the cost of the lowest-priced house to the highest-priced house in West Portland? Round to the nearest percent.

Value of Houses Sold

Location	Price		
	Lowest	*Highest*	*Average*
North Portland	$16,000	$ 58,500	$ 34,833
N.E. Portland	$18,000	$120,000	$ 47,091
S.E. Portland	$18,000	$114,000	$ 51,490
Lake Oswego	$40,000	$339,000	$121,080
West Portland	$29,500	$399,000	$112,994
Beaverton	$20,950	$165,000	$ 78,737

Answer to warm up: **A.** 1. 12,821 2. 410 3. 3203 4. 28%

Solution:

1. West Portland   Read down the "highest" cost column and find the largest price, $399,000.

2.
$$\begin{array}{r} \$121,080 \\ - \ 40,000 \\ \hline \$ \ 81,080 \end{array}$$
Subtract the lowest cost from the average cost for Lake Oswego to find the price difference.

The price difference is $81,080.

3. $\dfrac{\$29,500}{\$399,000} \approx 0.073934$ Divide the lowest price by the highest price.

     $= 7.3934\%$ Change to percent.

     $\approx 7\%$ Round to the nearest percent.

The lowest-priced house is 7% of the highest-priced house.

4. $\dfrac{\$51,490}{\$78,737} \approx 0.65394$ Divide the average cost in S.E. Portland by the average cost in Beaverton.

     $= 65.394\%$ Change to percent.

     $\approx 65\%$ Round to the nearest percent.

The average-priced S.E. house is 65% of the average-priced Beaverton house.

C.   The following table displays nutritional information about four breakfast cereals:

Nutritional Value per 1-oz Serving

Ingredient	Oat Bran	Rice Puffs	Raisin Bran	Wheat Flakes
Calories	90	110	120	110
Protein	6 g	2 g	3 g	3 g
Carbohydrate	17 g	25 g	31 g	23 g
Fat	0 g	0 g	1 g	1 g
Sodium	5 mg	290 mg	230 mg	270 mg
Potassium	180 mg	35 mg	260 mg	4 mg

1. Which cereal has the most calories per serving?
2. How many grams (g) of carbohydrates are there in five ounces of Rice Puffs?
3. How many more milligrams (mg) of sodium are there in a one-ounce serving of Wheat Flakes as compared to Raisin Bran?
4. How many ounces of Oat Bran can one eat before consuming the same amount of sodium as in one ounce of Rice Puffs?

C.   Use the table in Example C to answer.

1. Which cereal has the most sodium per one-ounce serving?
2. How many milligrams (mg) of potassium are there in six ounces of Wheat Flakes?
3. Mary's doctor has counseled her to eat 18 grams (g) of protein for breakfast. How many servings of Raisin Bran will she need to eat to meet the recommendation?
4. How many ounces of Wheat Flakes can one eat before consuming the same amount of potassium as in one ounce of Rice Puffs?

Solution:

1. Raisin Bran

    Find the largest value in the calorie row, 120, then read the cereal heading at the top of that column, Raisin Bran.

2. $5(25 \text{ g}) = 125 \text{ g}$

    Multiply the grams of carbohydrates in Rice Puffs by 5.

3. $(270 - 230) \text{ mg} = 40 \text{ mg}$

    Subtract the milligrams of sodium in Raisin Bran from that of Wheat Flakes.

4. $\dfrac{290 \text{ mg}}{5 \text{ mg}} = 58$

    Divide the number of milligrams of sodium in Rice Puffs by the number in Oat Bran.

Answer to warm up: **C.** 1. Rice Puffs 2. 24 mg 3. 6 servings 4. 8.75 ounces

NAME _____   CLASS _____   DATE _____

EXERCISES   6.10

Applications

Use the table for Exercises 1 to 12.

Telephone Network Monthly Access Charges

City	1-Party Line	2-Party Line	4-Party Line
Portland	$18.00	$15.69	$13.84
Seattle	$18.31	$16.00	$14.15
Tampa	$17.33	$15.02	$13.17
Dallas	$19.34	$17.03	$15.18
Boston	$18.61	$16.30	$14.45

1. What is the cost of a one-party line in Seattle?
   $18.31

2. What is the cost of a four-party line in Boston?
   $14.45

3. Which city has the highest two-party rate?   Dallas

4. Which city has the lowest one-party rate?   Tampa

5. What are the monthly savings of a two-party line over a one-party line in Portland? $2.31

6. How much more does it cost a person in Dallas to have a four-party line than it does a person in Tampa? $2.01

7. How much more does it cost to have a one-party line than a two-party line in Tampa? $2.31

8. How much can be saved on a yearly basis by using a two-party line instead of a one-party line in Seattle? $27.72

9. How much will be saved yearly when José moves from Dallas to Tampa and keeps a two-party line?
   $24.12

10. What is the percent of increase in the cost from a four-party line to a one-party line in Boston? (To the nearest percent.)   29%

11. What is the percent of increase in the cost of a one-party line in Dallas as compared to Portland? (To the nearest percent.)   7%

12. How much monthly income is realized by the phone company in Seattle from 3500 four-party lines? $49,525

15. If a tire costs the dealer $48.52 and the markup is 30% of the cost, what is the selling price of the tire? · $63.08 [6.8-2]

16. Given the following graph showing auto sales distribution for a local dealer,

Car Sales ACME Motors

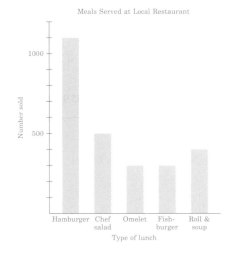

a. What make of auto had the greatest sales?

b. What was the total number of Pontiacs and Chevrolets sold?

c. How many more Buicks were sold than Oldsmobiles?

a. Chevrolet   b. 700   c. 100 [6.9]

17. Given the following table,

Employees by Division
Exacto Electronics

Division	Day Shift	Swing Shift
A	350	175
B	400	125
C	125	25

a. Which division has the greatest number of employees?

b. How many more employees are in the day shift in Division A as compared to Division C?

c. What percent of Exacto's employees are in Division B?

a. Division A and Division B have the same number.

b. 225   c. 43.75% [6.10]

18. Construct a bar graph to display the type of lunch that was purchased at the local fast-food bar over one week: Hamburger, 1100; Chef Salad, 500; Omelet, 300; Fishburger, 300; Roll and Soup, 400. [6.9]

Meals Served at Local Restaurant

CHAPTER 7

Measurement

Regular physical exercise keeps the body fit; regular mathematical exercise keeps the mind fit. Like this mountain biker, you can arrange a pleasant setting for your ''exercising.''
(Mike Hewitt/ Tony Stone Images)

Table 7.1   U.S. Monetary System

					Metric Prefixes
		1 mil	=	0.001 dollar	milli
10 mils	=	1 cent	=	0.01 dollar	centi
10 cents	=	1 dime	=	0.1 dollar	deci
10 dimes	=	1 dollar	=	1 dollar	base unit
10 dollars	=	1 $10 bill	=	10 dollars	deka
10 $10 bills	=	1 $100 bill	=	100 dollars	hecto
10 $100 bills	=	1 $1000 bill	=	1000 dollars	kilo

For most purposes, the units of meter, gram, and liter, along with their multiples, are sufficient.

A line 6 centimeters long requires six 1-centimeter measurements to show the length.

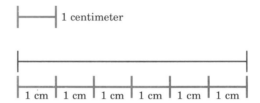

We can say that the line segment is $6 \cdot (1 \text{ cm})$ long, or 6 cm. Three liters of water represent three 1-liter measurements:

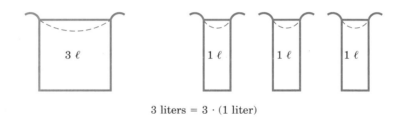

3 liters = 3 · (1 liter)

These examples show a useful way of thinking about metric measurements:

$$1.5 \text{ meters} = 1.5(1 \text{ meter})$$
$$15 \text{ kilometers} = 15(1 \text{ kilometer})$$
$$0.45 \text{ kilogram} = 0.45(1 \text{ kilogram})$$

▶ **To multiply a measurement times a number**

1. Multiply the two numbers.
2. Write the unit of measure.

If a container holds 6 quarts of water, how many quarts does it contain when it is $\frac{1}{3}$ full?

$$\frac{1}{3} \text{ of 6 quarts} = \frac{1}{3} \cdot 6 \text{ quarts} = 2 \text{ quarts}$$

▶ **To divide a measurement by a number**

1. Divide the two numbers.
2. Write the unit of measure.

If a beam that measures 36 meters in length is divided into 5 equal lengths, what is the measure of each?

$$(36 \text{ meters}) \div 5 = (36 \div 5) \text{ meters} = 7.2 \text{ meters}$$

Examples A–E   **Warm Ups A–E**

Directions: Multiply or divide.

Strategy: Multiply or divide the numbers and write the unit of measure.

A. Multiply 16 pints by 5.   **A.** Multiply 34 ounces by 6.

Solution:

$$(16 \text{ pints})(5) = (16 \cdot 5) \text{ pints} \qquad \text{Group the numbers.}$$
$$= 80 \text{ pints} \qquad \text{Simplify.}$$

B. Divide 63 liters into 5 equal amounts.   **B.** Divide 93 meters into 6 equal lengths.

Solution:

$$(63 \text{ liters}) \div 5 = \frac{63}{5} \text{ liters} \qquad \text{Divide the numbers.}$$
$$= 12.6 \text{ liters} \qquad \text{Simplify.}$$

C. What is the total weight of four packages of cheese if each weighs 0.86 kilogram?

Solution: To find the weight of four packages, multiply the weight of one by four.

$$4(0.86 \text{ kg}) = 4(0.86)\text{kg} \qquad \text{Multiply the weight of 1 package by 4.}$$
$$= 3.44 \text{ kg}$$

The weight of four packages of cheese is 3.44 kg.

C. A package of microwave popcorn weighs 101 grams. What is the weight of nine packages?

D. If 486 pounds of peanut brittle are divided equally among 54 sacks, how much goes into each sack?

Solution: To find how much goes into one sack, divide the total amount by the number of sacks.

$$486 \text{ lb} \div 54 = \frac{486}{54} \text{ lb} \qquad \text{Divide the weight by the number of sacks.}$$
$$= 9 \text{ lb}$$

Each sack will contain 9 pounds.

D. If 288 quarts of soup are divided equally among 48 families, how many quarts will each receive?

Answers to warm ups: **A.** 204 ounces   **B.** 15.5 meters   **C.** 909 grams   **D.** 6 quarts

Group Activity

67. With your group discuss ways to add measures that have different units. For instance, how can you add 1 hour + 25 minutes + 12 seconds or 4 yards + 2 feet + 6 inches?

Maintain Your Skills (Sections 5.3, 6.2, 6.3, 6.4, 6.5)

Change to a percent.

68. $\dfrac{9}{32}$ 28.125%

69. $\dfrac{17}{125}$ 13.6%

70. 0.82   82%

71. 3.775   377.5%

Change to a fraction.

72. 72% $\dfrac{18}{25}$

73. 37.8% $\dfrac{189}{500}$

Change to a decimal.

74. 72%   0.72

75. 37.8%   0.378

76. A map of Canada is scaled so that 2.5 cm represents approximately 64 kilometers. How many kilometers is it between Vancouver, British Columbia, and Regina, Saskatchewan, if the distance on the map is 70 cm?   1792 kilometers

77. Mrs. Hagen owns an apartment complex. She figures that for each three apartments that are occupied she will pay a monthly water bill of $19.00. At present, 47 apartments are occupied. How much should she plan to spend for water this month, to the nearest cent? $297.67

7.2 CONVERTING UNITS IN THE SAME SYSTEM

Objective   Convert the units within a system of a given measurement.

Application   🌐 Sidley Electronics wants to change Jean's hourly wage of $8.40 to an equal piece-work wage. If Jean averages 2.5 circuit boards per hour, what would be the equal wage per board?

How and Why   Since 12 inches = 1 foot, these two are equivalent measurements. Consider the division (12 inches) ÷ (1 foot). The division asks "how many" units of measure 1 foot it will take to make 12 inches. Since they measure the same length, the answer is 1.

$$\frac{12 \text{ inches}}{1 \text{ foot}} = \frac{1 \text{ foot}}{12 \text{ inches}} = 1$$

This idea, along with the multiplication property of one, is used to convert from one measure to another. The units of measure are treated like factors and are divided out (reduced) before multiplying.

To convert 48 inches to feet, we do the following.

$$48 \text{ inches} = (48 \text{ inches}) \cdot 1 \qquad \text{Multiply by 1.}$$

$$48 \text{ inches} = \frac{48 \text{ inches}}{1} \cdot \frac{1 \text{ foot}}{12 \text{ inches}} \qquad \text{Substitute } \frac{1 \text{ foot}}{12 \text{ inches}} \text{ for 1, so the unit inches will divide out.}$$

$$= \frac{48}{12} \text{ feet} \qquad \text{Simplify.}$$

$$= 4 \text{ feet}$$

In some cases it may be necessary to multiply by several different names for one. Convert 2300 milligrams (mg) to grams (g).

$$2300 \text{ mg} = (2300 \text{ mg}) \cdot 1 \cdot 1 \cdot 1$$

$$2300 \text{ mg} = \frac{2300 \text{ mg}}{1} \cdot \frac{1 \text{ cg}}{10 \text{ mg}} \cdot \frac{1 \text{ dg}}{10 \text{ cg}} \cdot \frac{1 \text{ g}}{10 \text{ dg}}$$

$$= \frac{2300}{1000} \text{ g}$$

$$= 2.3 \text{ g}$$

▶ **To convert the units of a measurement**

1. Multiply by fractions formed by equivalent measures (names for 1) so that the unwanted unit(s) reduces and the desired unit(s) remains.
2. Simplify.

An alternate method for conversion within the metric system utilizes the fact that it uses the base-ten place-value system. The following metric conversion chart, based on the prefixes and the base unit, will help.

To convert to a new metric measure, move the decimal point the same number of places and in the same direction as you would to go from the original prefix to the new one on the preceding chart. This is the same process that was used when dividing or multiplying by powers of ten. For instance,

23 hg = ? dg

			base			
k	h	da	unit	d	c	m
2	3	.0		0	0	

23 hg = 23,000 dg

The "d" prefix is three places to the right of the "h" prefix, so move the decimal point three places to the right.

Also,

56 mℓ = ? kℓ
56 mℓ = 0.000056 kℓ

The "k" prefix is six places to the left of the "m" prefix, so move the decimal point six places to the left.

Examples A–H

Warm Ups A–H

Directions: Convert the units of measurement.

Strategy: Multiply the given unit of measure by fractions formed by equivalent measures. Use a conversion chart if necessary.

A. 4 gallons to pints

A. 4 hours to seconds

Solution:

4 gallons = (4 gallons) · 1 · 1   Multiply by 1 twice.

$$= \frac{4 \text{ gallons}}{1} \cdot \frac{4 \text{ quarts}}{1 \text{ gallon}} \cdot \frac{2 \text{ pints}}{1 \text{ quart}}$$

Multiply by quarts/gallon to get quarts and then by pints/quart to get pints.

= 4 · 4 · 2 pints

= 32 pints

So 4 gallons is equivalent to 32 pints.

B. 91.36 kg to cg

B. 3.79 m to mm

Solution: It is necessary to multiply by 1 five times to change kg to cg.

$$91.36 \text{ kg} = \frac{91.36 \text{ kg}}{1} \cdot \frac{1}{1} \cdot \frac{1}{1} \cdot \frac{1}{1} \cdot \frac{1}{1} \cdot \frac{1}{1}$$

$$= \frac{91.36 \text{ kg}}{1} \cdot \frac{10 \text{ hg}}{1 \text{ kg}} \cdot \frac{10 \text{ dag}}{1 \text{ hg}} \cdot \frac{10 \text{ g}}{1 \text{ dag}} \cdot \frac{10 \text{ dg}}{1 \text{ g}} \cdot \frac{10 \text{ cg}}{1 \text{ dg}}$$

$$= 9,136,000 \text{ cg}$$

or

91.36 kg = 9,136,000 cg   Using the alternate method, move the decimal point five places to the right as cg is five places to the right of kg.

So 91.36 kg is equivalent to 9,136,000 cg.

C. 50 dm to cm

C. 80 g to mg

Solution: Use the alternate method of moving the decimal point.

50 dm = 500 cm   Move the decimal point one place to the right, since cm is one place to the right of dm.

So 50 dm is equivalent to 500 cm.

D. 4 m to km

D. 6 mℓ to ℓ

Solution: Use the alternate method of moving the decimal point.

4 m = 0.004 km   Move the decimal point three places to the left since km is three places to the left of m.

So 4 m is equivalent to 0.004 km.

E. 3 ft² to in.²

E. 6 yd² to ft²

Solution: Recall that the exponent 2 means to use it as a factor twice, so

$$\text{ft}^2 = (\text{ft})(\text{ft}) \text{ and in.}^2 = (\text{in.})(\text{in.})$$

$$3 \text{ ft}^2 = 3(1 \text{ ft})(1 \text{ ft}) \cdot \frac{12 \text{ in.}}{1 \text{ ft}} \cdot \frac{12 \text{ in.}}{1 \text{ ft}} \qquad \text{Multiply by in./ft twice.}$$

$$= 3(12)(12)(\text{in.})(\text{in.})$$

$$= 432 \text{ in.}^2$$

So 3 ft² is equivalent to 432 in.²

Answers to warm ups: **B.** 3790 mm   **C.** 80,000 mg   **D.** 0.006 ℓ   **E.** 54 ft²

Applications

61. If a secretary can type 90 words per minute $\left(\dfrac{90 \text{ words}}{1 \text{ minute}}\right)$, how many words can he type in 1 second? $1\frac{1}{2}$ words per second

62. Shirley is going on a diet that will cause her to lose 4 ounces every day. At this rate, how many pounds will she lose in 6 weeks? $10\frac{1}{2}$ pounds

63. A physician orders 0.01 g of Elixir Chlor-Trimeton. The available dose has a label that reads 2 mg per cc (cubic centimeter). How many cubic centimeters are needed to fill the doctor's order?   5 cc

64. Nurse Paul sees that the doctor has ordered 0.9 g of Tetracyn for his patient. If the available capsules contain 150 mg of Tetracyn, how many capsules will he give the patient?   6 capsules

65. Larry's family eats an average of three boxes of Wheat Bran Flakes per week. If each box contains 536 grams of cereal, how many kilograms of the cereal will Larry's family eat in one year?

83.616 kg

66. The Iowa State Game Department uses an average of 800 pounds of fish food per week at the Charles River Fish Hatchery. How many tons of fish food are used in one year at the hatchery?   20.8 tons

67. During a fund raiser to save the black rhino, Greg's Sports Shop agrees to donate 1¢ for every yard Rita jogs during one week. Rita jogs 2 miles every day that week. How much does Greg's Sport Shop donate to save the black rhino? $246.40

68. During a fund raiser to preserve land to save the African elephant, the Jungle Society agrees to donate 10¢ a milligram for the largest bass caught during the club's annual Bass Contest. If the largest bass caught weighs 1.45 kilograms, how much does the Jungle Society donate to save the African elephant?

$145,000

NAME _____ CLASS _____ DATE _____

69. During a bicycle vacation the Trong family travels at an average of 22 feet per second. At this rate, how many miles will they average in a 7-hour day of cycling? How many days will it take the Trong family to get 350 miles from their home in Des Moines, Iowa?   105 miles; $3\frac{1}{3}$ days

70. The Koko Company makes a chocolate bar that weighs 4.3 grams. What is the weight, in kilograms, of a box of 144 bars? If the box weighs 250 grams and it costs $5 per kilogram to ship the candy to Waco, Texas, what is the cost of shipping 10 boxes of the candy to Waco?   0.6192 kg; $43.46

71. The Fashion Plate Company makes a hair gel that weighs 64 pounds per cubic foot. The company sells the gel in bottles that contain 2 cubic inches of the gel. How many ounces, to the nearest tenth, of gel is sold in one bottle? If the gel is priced at $1.25 per ounce, what is the price of one bottle? [*Hint:* 1 cubic foot = $1 \text{ ft}^3 = (1 \text{ ft})(1 \text{ ft})(1 \text{ ft})$ and 1 cubic inch = $1 \text{ in.}^3 = (1 \text{ in.})(1 \text{ in.})(1 \text{ in.})$]
1.2 ounces; $1.50

72. A mosquito repellent weighs 100 kilograms per cubic meter. The AntiPest Company sells the repellent in bottles containing 300 cubic centimeters. How many grams of repellent are sold in one bottle? If the repellent is priced at 15 cents per gram, what is the price of one bottle?
30 g; $4.50

73. The Lobos Company plans to change the way they pay employees from an hourly rate to a piecework wage. The current pay rate is $9.80 per hour and the average employee produces 2.8 articles in one hour. What will be the new pay rate per piece?
$3.50 per piece

74. An intravenous (IV) solution contains 20 cc of medicine and 250 cc of solution for a total of 270 cc. Each cc of the IV solution contains 10 drops. Dr. Stem orders the IV to run 3 hours for her patient. How many drops per minute should Nurse Gomez give the patient?   15 drops/minute

State Your Understanding

75. Explain how to convert 12,000 seconds to hours.

76. Describe how the basic principle of fractions is used to convert units.

Challenge

77. Convert $\dfrac{16,000 \text{ lb}}{\text{yd}^3}$ to $\dfrac{\text{oz}}{\text{in.}^3}$. (Round to the nearest tenth of an ounce.)   5.5 oz/in.³

78. If a chain made of precious metal is priced at $7.20 per inch, what is the cost of 4 yd 2 ft 4 in. of the chain? $1238.40

23. $\dfrac{55 \text{ lb}}{1 \text{ ft}} = \dfrac{? \text{ g}}{1 \text{ m}}$ $\dfrac{81{,}848.6 \text{ g}}{1 \text{ m}}$

24. $\dfrac{40 \text{ miles}}{1 \text{ hr}} = \dfrac{? \text{ meters}}{1 \text{ second}}$ $\dfrac{17.9 \text{ m}}{1 \text{ sec}}$

25. $\dfrac{75 \text{ km}}{1 \text{ hr}} = \dfrac{? \text{ mi}}{1 \text{ hr}}$ $\dfrac{46.6 \text{ mi}}{1 \text{ hr}}$

26. $\dfrac{9.6 \text{ g}}{1 \text{ cm}} = \dfrac{? \text{ oz}}{1 \text{ in.}}$ $\dfrac{0.9 \text{ oz}}{1 \text{ in.}}$

27. $\dfrac{8.3 \text{ lb}}{\text{ft}^2} = \dfrac{? \text{ g}}{\text{cm}^2}$ $\dfrac{4.1 \text{ g}}{\text{cm}^2}$

28. $\dfrac{38 \text{ ft}}{\text{sec}} = \dfrac{? \text{ m}}{\text{sec}}$ $\dfrac{11.6 \text{ m}}{\text{sec}}$

29. $\dfrac{525 \text{ g}}{\ell} = \dfrac{? \text{ lb}}{\text{qt}}$ $\dfrac{1.1 \text{ lb}}{\text{qt}}$

30. $\dfrac{\$1.52}{\text{lb}} = \dfrac{\$ \, ?}{\text{kg}}$ $\dfrac{\$3.35}{\text{kg}}$

Applications

31. A box of Wheat Bran cereal weighs 18.9 ounces. To the nearest tenth, how many grams does it weigh?

535.8 g

32. A farmer's harvest of strawberries averages 10 tons per acre. To the nearest tenth, express the harvest in kilograms per acre.   9071.8 kg

33. The Heatherton Corporation reimburses its employees 30¢ per mile when they use their private car on company business. The company is opening a plant in Canada. What reimbursement per kilometer should the company pay, to the nearest cent per kilometer?   19 cents/km

34. The Williams Company advertises that a water pump will deliver water at 35 gallons per minute. Nyen needs to put an ad in a Canadian paper. How many liters per minute should he put in the ad, to the nearest liter per minute?   132 liters/min

35. A newborn baby elephant at the Oxnard Zoo weighs 295 pounds. Express the weight in kilograms.   133.8 kg

36. The Japanese fishing fleet has a weekly catch of 110,000 kilograms of whiting. Express the catch in tons.   121 tons

NAME _____ CLASS _____ DATE _____

37. The Georgia Pacific Corporation grows trees for poles. A typical pole measures 95 feet in length. Express the length in meters.   29.0 m

38. The average length of a salmon returning to the Oakridge Hatchery is 37 inches. Express the length in centimeters.   94.0 cm

39. The Coffee Company packages 3 kilograms of coffee that sells in Canada for $18.95. The company also packages 6 pounds of coffee that sells for $17.95 in the United States. Assuming both dollar amounts are in American currency, which is the better buy?

The Canadian pack

40. Laura drives 67 miles to work each day. Her cousin Mabel, who lives in a foreign country, drives 115 kilometers to work each day. Who has the shorter drive?   Laura

41. The average rainfall in Freeport, Florida, is 26.83 inches. Express the average to the nearest tenth of a centimeter.   68.1 cm

42. The Toyo Tire Company recommends that its premium tire be inflated to 1.5 kilograms per square centimeter. In preparation to sell the tire in America, Mishi must convert the pressure to pounds per square inch. What measure, to the nearest pound per square inch, must she use?
21 lb/in.^{2}

State Your Understanding

43. Write your opinion about which measurement system, English or metric, is easier to use and why.

44. Explain how to convert $\dfrac{3 \text{ g}}{\text{cm}^2}$ to $\dfrac{\text{oz}}{\text{in}^2}$.

45. Explain why you might get different answers when converting 25 meters to feet using different conversion units from the charts in this section.

B.   A rectangle with $\ell = 12$ m and $w = 8$ m.

B.   A rectangle with $\ell = 24$ ft and $w = 17$ ft.

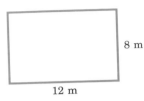

8 m

12 m

Solution:

$A = \ell w$ Formula for the area of a rectangle.

$A = (12\text{ m})(8\text{ m})$ Substitute $\ell = 12$ m and $w = 8$ m.

$\quad = 96\text{ m}^2$ Multiply.

The area of the rectangle is 96 square meters (or 96 m²).

C.   A triangle with base 14.2 cm and height 7 cm.

C.   A triangle with base 35.4 ft and height 9.6 ft.

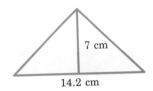

7 cm

14.2 cm

Solution:

$A = \dfrac{1}{2}bh$ Formula for the area of a triangle.

$\quad = \dfrac{1}{2}(14.2\text{ cm})(7\text{ cm})$ Substitute $b = 14.2$ cm and $h = 7$ cm.

$\quad = 49.7\text{ cm}^2$ Multiply.

The area of the triangle is 49.7 square centimeters (or 49.7 cm²).

D.   A parallelogram with base 1 foot and height 4 inches.

D.   A parallelogram with base 6 yards and height 5 feet.

Solution:

$A = bh$

$\quad = (1\text{ ft})(4\text{ in.})$

$\quad = (12\text{ in.})(4\text{ in.})$ or $(1\text{ ft})\left(\dfrac{1}{3}\text{ ft}\right)$

$\quad = 48\text{ in.}^2$ or $\dfrac{1}{3}\text{ ft}^2$

We can multiply the measures only if the units are the same. So either change feet to inches or inches to feet.

The area is shown both ways.

The area of the parallelogram is 48 in.² or $\dfrac{1}{3}$ ft².

Answers to warm ups: **B.** 408 ft²   **C.** 169.92 ft²   **D.** 90 ft² or 10 yd²

E. A trapezoid with $b_1 = 17$ feet, $b_2 = 13$ feet, and $h = 7$ feet.

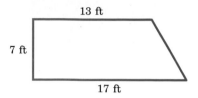
13 ft

7 ft

17 ft

E. A trapezoid with bases of 51 m and 36 m and a height of 12 m.

Solution:

$$A = \frac{1}{2}(b_1 + b_2)h \qquad \text{Formula for the area of a trapezoid.}$$

$$= \frac{1}{2}(17 \text{ ft} + 13 \text{ ft})(7 \text{ ft}) \qquad \text{Substitute and simplify.}$$

$$= \frac{1}{2}(30 \text{ ft})(7 \text{ ft})$$

$$= 105 \text{ ft}^2$$

The area of the trapezoid is 105 ft^2.

F. A circle with $r = 8$ cm.

8 cm

F. A circle with diameter 18 feet. Let $\pi \approx 3.14$.

Solution:

$$A = \pi r^2 \qquad \text{Formula for the area of a circle.}$$

$$\approx (3.14)(8 \text{ cm})^2 \qquad \text{Substitute } \pi \approx 3.14 \text{ and } r = 8 \text{ cm.}$$

$$\approx (3.14)(64 \text{ cm}^2)$$

$$\approx 200.96 \text{ cm}^2$$

The area of the circle is 200.96 cm^2.

G. 🌐 A gallon of deck paint will cover 400 ft^2. George has a rectangular deck that he wants to paint. The length is 26 feet and the width is 15 feet. Will one gallon be enough to paint this deck?

Solution:

$$A = \ell w \qquad \text{First find the area of the deck.}$$

$$A = (26 \text{ ft})(15 \text{ ft})$$

$$A = 390 \text{ ft}^2 \qquad \begin{array}{l} \text{The area of the deck is less than the area a} \\ \text{gallon will cover } (390 < 400). \end{array}$$

One gallon will be enough to paint the deck.

G. Marta finds 45 square yards of plush carpet on sale for $15 per square yard. Marta's living room is circular with a radius of 11 ft. Is there enough carpet to cover her living room?

Answers to warm ups: **E.** 522 m² **F.** 254.34 ft² **G.** Yes

NAME _____ CLASS _____ DATE _____

EXERCISES 7.5

A

Find the area of the following. Let $\pi \approx 3.14$.

1.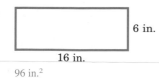

6 in.

16 in.

96 in.²

2.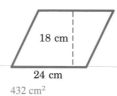

18 cm

24 cm

432 cm²

3.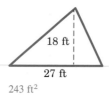

18 ft

27 ft

243 ft²

4.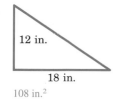

12 in.

18 in.

108 in.²

5.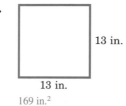

13 in.

13 in.

169 in.²

6.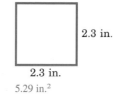

2.3 in.

2.3 in.

5.29 in.²

7.

4 km

2 km

5 km

9 km²

8.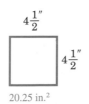

4 yd

2 yd

2 yd

6 yd²

9.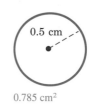

0.5 cm

0.785 cm²

10.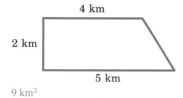

6 ft

28.26 ft²

11.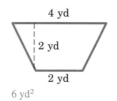

$4\frac{1}{2}''$

$4\frac{1}{2}''$

20.25 in.²

12.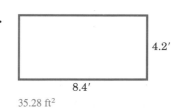

4.2'

8.4'

35.28 ft²

13.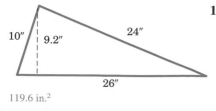

10″   9.2″   24″

26″

119.6 in.²

14.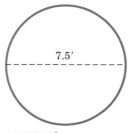

7.5'

44.15625 ft²

B

15.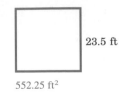

23.5 ft

552.25 ft²

16.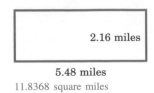

2.16 miles

5.48 miles

11.8368 square miles

17.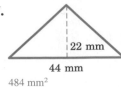

22 mm

44 mm

484 mm²

18.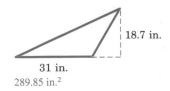

18.7 in.

31 in.

289.85 in.²

19.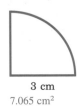

3 cm

7.065 cm²

20.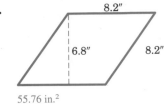

8.2″

6.8″

8.2″

55.76 in.²

21.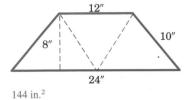

12″

8″   10″

24″

144 in.²

22.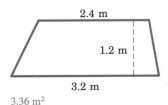

2.4 m

1.2 m

3.2 m

3.36 m²

23. Answer in square yards.

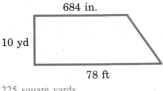

684 in.

10 yd

78 ft

225 square yards

24. Answer in square inches.

$1\frac{1}{6}$ ft

153.86 in.²

C

25. Find the area of a rectangle with a length of 16 inches and a width of 12 inches.   192 in.²

26. Find the area of a circle with a diameter of 16 centimeters.   200.96 cm²

27. Find the area of a parallelogram that has a base of 18.9 meters and a height of 17.3 meters.   326.97 m²

28. Find the area of a trapezoid with bases of 2 ft 4 in. and 3 ft 2 in. and a height of 9 in.   297 in.²

NAME _____ CLASS _____ DATE _____

29. One roll of wallpaper will cover 32 square feet. How many rolls are needed for a windowless wall that measures 15 feet by 8 feet? (You cannot buy part of a roll.)   4 rolls

30. How many square yards of vinyl floor covering are needed for a kitchen floor that measures 10 feet by 12 feet? $13\frac{1}{3}$ square yards

Applications

31. The side of Jane's house that has no windows measures 35 ft by 22 ft. If one gallon of stain will cover 250 ft², will 2 gallons of stain be enough to stain this side?   No

32. If the south side of Jane's house measures 85 ft by 22 ft and has two windows, each 4 ft by 6 ft, will 4 gallons of the stain be enough for this side? (See Exercise 31.)   No

33. How many square inches of glass are in a circular mirror of diameter 36 inches?   1017.36 in.²

34. How many square yards of carpet will Peggy need to carpet a rectangular floor that measures 21 ft by 30 ft?   70 square yards

35. If one ounce of weed killer treats one square meter of lawn, how many ounces of weed killer will Debbie need to treat a rectangular lawn that measures 30 m by 8 m?   240 ounces

36. Lily intends to make a swimming pool cover for her circular pool that is 25 feet in diameter. She will make the cover circular with an extra 2 feet around the outside of the pool for overhang. How much fabric will she need for the cover? The canvas she will use costs $5.65 per square yard. What will be the total cost?   660.185 ft²; $414.45

37. One acre is equivalent to 43,560 square feet. How many square feet are in a parcel of land that measures 18 acres? The owner of this acreage wants to divide it into smaller parcels measuring 30 feet by 100 feet. How many complete parcels can be made available for sale? How many square feet of land remain?   784.080 ft²; 261 parcels; 1080 ft²

38. How many square feet of sheathing are needed for the gable end of a house that has a rise of 9 ft and a span of 36 ft?

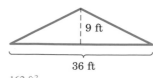

9 ft

36 ft

162 ft²

State Your Understanding

39. What is the meaning of the word "area"?

Challenge

40. Troy is going to cover his kitchen floor. Along the outside he will put black squares that are 6 inches on each side. The next (inside) row will be white squares that are 6 inches on each side. The remaining inside rows will alternate between black and white squares that are 1 foot on each side. How many squares of each kind will he need for the kitchen floor that measures 9 feet by 10 feet?

72 six-inch black squares; 64 six-inch white squares; 36 one-foot black squares; 20 one-foot white squares

Group Activity

41. Determine the coverage of 1 gallon of white semi-gloss paint. How much of this paint is needed to paint your classroom, excluding chalkboards, windows, and doors? What would it cost? Repeat this for your bathroom and kitchen at home. Compare the results in class.

Maintain Your Skills (Sections 6.7, 6.8)

42. On a test Mildred answered 18 questions correctly and missed 7. What percent did she answer correctly?   72%

43. Bill answered 37 questions correctly and missed 3. What percent did he miss?   7.5%

44. The local high school basketball team won 21 games and lost 7. What percent did it win?   75%

45. In the eight baseball games that Lew Slugger played last week he hit safely 12 times, struck out 8 times, and flied out 12 times. What percent of the time did Lew hit safely?   37.5%

46. In Exercise 45, what percent of the time did Lew strike out?   25%

47. Inflation last year was 4.5%. If John earned $7000 last year, what should he earn this year, to the nearest ten dollars, to keep up with inflation? $7320

48. Approximately 6% of the keys on Myra's harpsichord do not function. If there are 51 keys on the keyboard, how many are in working order?   48 keys

49. Bonita discovers that 13% of the 455 forms she has to check have been filled out incorrectly. To the nearest ten, how many of the forms are filled out correctly?   400 forms

50. On a particular math test you can pass if you get only 45% of the problems correct. There are 50 questions on the test. How many can you miss and still pass?   27 problems

51. One family saves 5% of their monthly income and uses 85% for rent, food, heat, and other monthly expenses. They have $52.10 left for entertainment. What is the dollar amount of their monthly expenses? $442.85

7.6 A SECOND LOOK AT AREAS

Objective   Find the area of geometric figures that are a combination of two or more geometric figures.

Application   An oval piece of sheet metal is to be made from a rectangular piece as shown. How much of the metal will be wasted? (Let $\pi \approx 3.14$.)

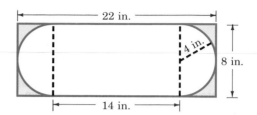

The shaded portion is the waste.

How and Why   Some figures can be divided into two or more common shapes. The sum of the areas of each of these common figures is the area of the entire region.

Consider the following shapes:

The figure on the left can be divided into a rectangle with a triangle attached, as shown on the right. We can find the area of the rectangle and the area of the triangle. The sum of these areas is the area of the entire region.

Consider the following shapes:

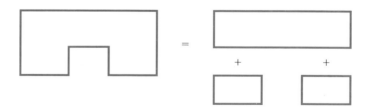

The figure on the left can be divided into three rectangles, as shown on the right. We can find the area of each rectangle. The sum of these areas is the area of the entire region.

In some figures it is helpful to attach a region to the original figure so that it can be divided into the common figures. For example,

The figure on the left is a semicircle and a rectangle minus a triangle, as shown on the right. We can find the area of the semicircle, the rectangle, and the triangle. Then we find the sum of the areas of the semicircle and the rectangle, and subtract the area of the triangle to find the area of the entire region.

Applications

27. The following diagram shows the Smiths' yard with respect to their house. How much grass seed is needed to sow the lawn if one pound of seed will sow 1000 ft²?

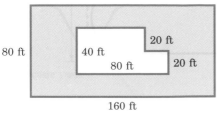

10 lb

28. The floor of a shop (floor plan shown below) is to be poured concrete. If concrete costs $3.35 a square yard, what will the floor cost?

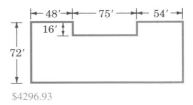

$4296.93

29. How many squares of aluminum siding are needed for the shed shown below? Assume that there are no windows and that the door will be made of the siding. A different material will be used for the roof. (100 ft² = 1 square of siding)

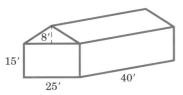

21.5 squares of aluminum

30. Kassandra and Alfredo's house was originally a rectangle that measured 50 feet by 20 feet. Soon after they bought it, they added a kitchen and eating area on one of the short sides. This addition is a square that is 25 feet on a side. The front of the house remained straight. A few years later they added an enclosed porch along the entire front of the house. The porch is 7 feet wide. What is the floor area of the house now?   2150 ft²

31. The Brighton Parent-Student-Teacher Group is constructing a new playground. A circular area with a diameter of 9 feet is needed for the jungle gym. A rectangular area measuring 10 feet by 25 feet is needed for the swings. Around each of these areas is a 2-foot blacktop strip. What is the smallest area needed for the playground? Round to the nearest tenth.   538.7 ft²

32. Find the area of a football field that measures 120 yards by 160 feet. Now assume there is a 10-foot-wide track around the entire playing field. Compute the entire area of the field and track. Find each of the areas in both square feet and square yards.
57,600 ft² or 6400 yd²; 68,400 ft² or 7600 yd²

State Your Understanding

33. Describe a situation in your own experience in which knowing the area of a region was useful.

NAME _____   CLASS _____ DATE _____

Challenge

34. A cylindrical can has a diameter of 10 inches and a height of 8 inches. It is painted red on top and bottom and green on the sides. What is the area of the can that is painted red? Green?

157 in.²; 251.2 in.²

Group Activity

35. Select any building on campus and determine the amount of paint that is required to paint the entire outside of the building. Allow for windows and doors.

Maintain Your Skills (Sections 6.7, 6.8)

36. If a saline solution is 20% salt and 80% water, how much salt is in 40 pounds of the mixture?   8 pounds

37. If a saline solution is 40% salt and 60% water, how much solution can be made using 36 pounds of salt?   90 pounds

38. An attorney collects a debt of $500 for a client. The attorney charges $75 for her services. What rate of commission does she charge?   15%

39. One month the price of eggs was 95¢ per dozen. The following month the price was 76¢. What was the percent of decrease in the price?   20%

40. The pilot of a transcontinental airplane is instructed to increase the speed of his airplane from 480 miles per hour to 510 miles per hour. What is the percent of increase?   6.25%

41. If the cost of gasoline is $1.20 per gallon and the tax on a gallon of gasoline is 12¢, what percent of the cost of gasoline is the tax?   10%

42. The price of hamburger rose 12% last month. This was 15¢ more than it had been. What was the price before? $1.25

43. Wayne and Susan caught one salmon 10% of the times they went fishing. On 2% of the trips they caught two salmon. On the other 88% of their fishing trips they caught nothing. On their 50 trips together, how many salmon did they catch?

7 salmon

11. Find the volume. Round to the nearest tenth.

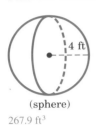

(sphere)

267.9 ft³

12. Find the volume of a sphere with a diameter of 30 meters.   14,130 m³

13. Find the volume:

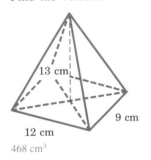

13 cm

12 cm

9 cm

468 cm³

14. Find the volume of a pyramid whose base is a square with a side 150 feet and whose height is 30 feet.   225,000 ft³

15. Find the volume of two identical fuzzy dice tied to the mirror of a '57 Chevy if one edge measures 6 inches.   432 in.³

16. Find the volume of a can if the radius is 7 centimeters and the height is 18 centimeters.   2769.48 cm³

C

17. Find the volume in cubic inches of a cylinder that has a radius of 9 inches and a height of 2 feet.   6104.16 in.³

18. Find the volume of a cylinder that has a 13″ diameter and is 4′ tall. Round to the nearest cubic inch.   6368 in.³

19. Find the volume of a pyramid that has a height of 37 ft and the triangular base shown below:

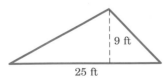

9 ft

25 ft

1387.5 ft³

20. Find the volume in cubic meters of a pyramid with a height of 37 meters and a square base that is 2500 centimeters on each side. Round to the nearest tenth.   7708.3 m³

NAME _____   CLASS _____   DATE _____

21. Find the volume in cubic millimeters. Round to the nearest tenth.

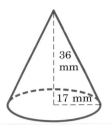

36 mm

17 mm

10,889.5 mm³

22. Find the volume in cubic inches of a sphere with a diameter of $2\frac{1}{3}$ ft. Round to the nearest cubic inch.

11,488 in.³

Applications

23. A water tank is a cylinder that is 22 inches in diameter and $3\frac{1}{2}$ feet high. If there are 231 in.³ in a gallon, how many gallons of water will the tank hold?   69.08 gallons

24. An excavation is being made for a basement. The hole is 24 ft wide, 35 ft long, and 9 ft deep. If the bed of a truck holds 14 yd³, how many truckloads of dirt will need to be hauled away?   20 truckloads

25. A farming corporation is building three new cylindrical silos. They will have diameters of 50 feet, 20 feet, and 15 feet. Each is 60 feet tall. Find the total volume available in these silos. Round to the nearest tenth.   147,187.5 ft³

26. A sphere is being cast out of wire mesh to represent the world at a state fair. What is the volume of this sphere if the diameter is 22 meters? Round to the nearest hundredth?   5572.45 m³

State Your Understanding

27. What is the difference between ''inches,'' ''square inches,'' and ''cubic inches''? How do you remember the difference between the measures of perimeter, area, and volume?

Challenge

28. A swimming pool that is 30 feet long and 10 feet wide is filled to a depth of 60 inches. How many cubic feet of water are in the pool? If one cubic foot of water is approximately 7.5 gallons, how many gallons of water are in the pool?
1500 ft³; 11,250 gallons

GOOD ADVICE FOR STUDYING

The Long and the Short of It

To become proficient at mathematics takes two important steps. First, you must develop strategies to begin working on a problem; second, you must learn the processes that enable you to do the problem. It's a combination of first thinking and then doing. After you have rehearsed enough problems, the thinking part becomes automatic, and the doing part becomes faster. It's like learning to drive a car. In the beginning, you think about every move you make; there are many things to remember. After learning to drive, you don't think about the driving process any longer — you just drive.

When you learn something, you store it in either short-term or long-term memory. Short-term memory is for information you need temporarily. For instance, you might remember a phone number just long enough to dial it. Information about driving a car is stored in long-term memory. You would NOT want to relearn this skill every time you needed to drive! The mathematics you have learned is also not something you want to forget — you want the information in long-term memory. The concepts you learned at the beginning of this book have been rehearsed often. Concepts in the last chapter have been practiced the least. Most recently learned concepts are the soonest forgotten; if you want to retain this information, you need to rehearse or review it, especially if you have more math classes to take.

If you have a break until your next math course, you should use the term to look over recently learned material so that you can start the next course well prepared. You should try not to take a term off completely from math so all of the information stays fresh in your mind. It is helpful to keep your textbook, if you can, as a reference in the next course. It will help you because you have spent many hours working from it, you know where everything is, and you are familiar with the author's style.

You may also want to determine your own learning style. Doing so can dramatically improve the effectiveness of your math study skills. To assess what type of learner you are and what patterns of learning are best suited to your type, you may take the Myers-Briggs Type Indicator (MBTI).[1] This instrument indicates learning style on four different scales.

Two of the scales show where you prefer to focus your attention: externally, to people on the outside; or internally, to your own thoughts and reflections. You can apply this information to your study habits. If your focus is external, your preference will be to work through ideas by talking. So a study group will be helpful. If your focus is inward, you will prefer to study and work alone, asking questions later if you don't understand a concept.

Just remember that your preferences cause basic differences in learning styles, and that no one style is better or worse than another. Knowing your own style can give you added confidence and the ability to adapt study skills to your learning style.

The bottom line for studying and succeeding in mathematics is the bottom line for any challenging activity: The rewards are many, and they are waiting for you. You are not powerless over math anxiety. You *can* overcome it. And once you do, you make way for learning the vital mathematics you'll use again and again, every day.

[1] Inquire at your campus counseling department to find a local source that can administer the MBTI.

8.1 OPPOSITES AND ABSOLUTE VALUE

Objectives

[1] Find the opposite of a signed number.

[2] Find the absolute value of a signed number.

Application

 If 10% of Americans purchased products with no plastic packaging just 10% of the time, approximately 144,000 pounds of plastic would be eliminated (taken out of or decreased) from our landfills.

1. Write this decrease as a signed number.
2. Write the opposite of eliminating (decreasing) 225,000 pounds of plastic from our landfills as a signed number.

Vocabulary

Positive numbers are the numbers of arithmetic and are greater than zero. **Negative numbers** are numbers less than zero. Zero is neither positive nor negative. Positive numbers, zero, and negative numbers are called **signed numbers.**

The **opposite** or **additive inverse** of a signed number is the number on the number line that is the same distance from zero but on the opposite side. Zero is its own opposite. The opposite of 5 is written -5. This can be read "the opposite of 5" or "negative 5," since they both name the same number.

The **absolute value** of a signed number is the number of units between the number and zero. The expression $|7|$ is read "the absolute value of 7."

How and Why [1]

Exercises such as

$$3 - 4 \qquad 8 - 22 \qquad 16 - 17 \qquad \text{and} \qquad 1 - 561$$

do not have answers in the numbers of arithmetic. The answer to each is a signed number. Signed numbers (which include both numbers to the right of zero and to the left of zero) are used to represent quantities with opposite characteristics. For instance,

right and left
up and down
above zero and below zero
gain and loss

A few signed numbers are shown on the following number line:

$$\begin{array}{ccccccccccccc} + & + & + & + & + & + & + & + & + & + & + & + \\ -4 & -3.6 & -3 & -2.4 & -2 & & -1 & & 0 & \frac{1}{2} & 1 & 1.4 & 2 & & 3 \end{array}$$

The negative numbers are to the left of zero. The negative numbers have a dash, or negative sign, in front of them. The numbers to the right of zero are called positive (and may be written with a plus sign). Zero is neither positive nor negative.

7	Seven or positive seven
-3	Negative three
-0.12	Negative twelve hundredths
0	Zero is neither positive nor negative
$+\dfrac{1}{2}$	One half or positive one half

51. $|7 - 2.3|$ 4.7   **52.** $|0|$ 0   **53.** $|8 + 7|$ 15   **54.** $|20 - 16|$ 4

55. $|-244|$ 244   **56.** $|-482|$ 482   **57.** $|0.0071|$ 0.0071   **58.** $|-0.0099|$ 0.0099

Find the value of the following:

59. Opposite of $\left|-\dfrac{4}{9}\right|$ $-\dfrac{4}{9}$ **60.** Opposite of $\left|\dfrac{5}{8}\right|$ $-\dfrac{5}{8}$

61. Opposite of $|46|$ -46 **62.** Opposite of $|-41|$ -41

Applications

63. At the New York Stock Exchange, positive and negative numbers are used to record changes in stock prices on the board. What is the opposite of a gain of five eighths $\left(+\dfrac{5}{8}\right)$? $-\dfrac{5}{8}$

64. At the American Stock Exchange a stock is shown to have taken a loss of three-eighths point $\left(-\dfrac{3}{8}\right)$. What is the opposite of this loss? $\dfrac{3}{8}$

65. On a thermometer temperatures above zero are listed as positive and those below zero as negative. What is the opposite of a reading of 12°C? $-12°C$

66. On a thermometer such as the one in Exercise 65, what is the opposite of a reading of 23°C? $-23°C$

67. The modern calendar counts the years after the birth of Christ as positive numbers (A.D. 1993 or $+1993$). Years before Christ are listed using negative numbers (2045 B.C. or -2045). What is the opposite of 1875 B.C. or -1875?   1875 A.D.

68. The empty-weight center of gravity of an airplane is determined. A generator is installed at a moment of -278. At what moment could a weight be placed so that the center of gravity remains the same? (Moment is the product of a quantity such as weight and its distance from a fixed point. In this application the moments must be opposites to keep the same center of gravity.)   278

69. A cyclist travels up a mountain 1685 feet then turns around and travels down the mountain 1246 feet. Represent each trip as a signed number. $+1685$ feet, -1246 feet

70. How far is the cyclist from her starting point? (See Exercise 69.) Write the distance as a signed number. $+439$ feet

71. An energy audit indicates that the Gates family could reduce their average electric bill by $28.76 per month by doing some minor repairs, insulating their attic and crawl space, and caulking around the windows and other cracks in the siding.
  a. Express this savings as a signed number.
  b. Express the opposite of the savings as a signed number.
  a. $-\$28.76$ b. $\$28.76$

72. If 80 miles north is represented by $+80$, how would you represent 80 miles south? -80

NAME _____ CLASS _____ DATE _____

73. The Buffalo Bills are playing a football game against the Seattle Seahawks. On the first play the Seahawks lose 8 yards. Represent this as a signed number. What is the opposite of a loss of 8 yards? Represent this as a signed number.   −8 yd, 8 yd

74. The Dallas Cowboys and the New York Giants are having an exhibition game in London, England. The Cowboy offensive team runs a gain of 6 yards, a loss of 8 yards, a gain of 21 yards, and a loss of 15 yards. Represent these yardages as signed numbers.   6 yd, −8 yd, 21 yd, −15 yd

75. The Golden family is on a vacation in the southwestern United States. Consider north and east as positive directions and south and west as negative directions. On one day they drive north 97 miles then east 152 miles. The next day they drive west 72 miles then 18 miles south. Represent each of these distances as signed numbers.
97 mi, 152 mi, −72 mi, −18 mi

State Your Understanding

76. Is zero the only number that is its own opposite? Justify your answer.

77. Is there a set of numbers for which the absolute value of each number is the number itself? If yes, identify that set and tell why this is true.

78. Is there a set of numbers for which the absolute value of each number is the opposite of the number itself? If yes, identify that set and tell why this is true.

Challenge

79. If n is a positive number, what kind of number is $-n$?   Negative

80. If n is a negative number, what kind of number is $-n$?   Positive

81. For what numbers is $|n| = n$ true?
For all numbers greater than or equal to zero.

82. For what numbers is $|-n| = n$ always true?
For all numbers greater than or equal to zero.

83. For what numbers is $|n| = -n$ always true?
For all numbers less than or equal to zero.

A. $37 + (-12)$

Solution: Since the signs are unlike, subtract their absolute values.

$$|37| - |-12| = 37 - 12$$
$$= 25$$

Because the positive number has the larger absolute value, the sum is positive.

$$37 + (-12) = 25$$

A. $48 + (-29)$

B. $-52 + 28$

Solution:

$$|-52| - |28| = 52 - 28$$
$$= 24$$
$$-52 + 28 = -24 \qquad \text{The sum is negative since } -52 \text{ has the larger absolute value.}$$

B. $-51 + 34$

C. $41 + (-63)$

Solution:

$$|-63| - |41| = 63 - 41$$
$$= 22$$
$$41 + (-63) = -22 \qquad \text{The sum is negative since } -63 \text{ has the larger absolute value.}$$

C. $29 + (-75)$

D. $-0.33 + (-1.7)$

Solution: The signs are the same, so add their absolute values.

$$|-0.33| + |-1.7| = 0.33 + 1.7$$
$$= 2.03$$
$$-0.33 + (-1.7) = -2.03 \qquad \text{The numbers are negative, therefore the sum is negative.}$$

D. $-1.3 + (-2.5)$

E. $\dfrac{4}{5} + \left(-\dfrac{3}{2}\right)$

Solution:

$$\left|-\frac{3}{2}\right| - \left|\frac{4}{5}\right| = \frac{15}{10} - \frac{8}{10}$$
$$= \frac{7}{10}$$
$$\frac{4}{5} + \left(-\frac{3}{2}\right) = -\frac{7}{10} \qquad \text{Since the negative number has the larger absolute value, the sum is negative.}$$

E. $\dfrac{7}{8} + \left(-\dfrac{5}{6}\right)$

Answers to warm ups: **A.** 19   **B.** -17 **C.** -46 **D.** -3.8 **E.** $\dfrac{1}{24}$

F. $-13 + 53 + (-27) + (-21)$

Solution: Where there are more than two numbers to add, it may be easier to add the numbers with the same sign first.

$$
\begin{array}{r}
-13 \\
-27 \\
-21 \\
\hline
-61
\end{array}
$$

Add the negative numbers. Add their sum to 53. Since the signs are different, find the difference in their absolute values.

$$
\begin{aligned}
-61 + 53 &= |-61| - |53| \\
&= 8
\end{aligned}
$$

$-13 + 53 + (-27) + (-21) = -8$ The sum is negative since -61 has the larger absolute value.

F. $-35 + 76 + (-101) + 37$

G. $-0.1 + 0.5 + (-3.4) + 0.8$

Solution: Add the negative numbers and add the positive numbers.

$$
\begin{array}{rr}
-0.1 & 0.5 \\
-3.4 & 0.8 \\
\hline
-3.5 & 1.3
\end{array}
$$

The signs are different so subtract their absolute values.

$$
\begin{aligned}
-3.5 + 1.3 &= |-3.5| - |1.3| \\
&= 2.2
\end{aligned}
$$

$-0.1 + 0.5 + (-3.4) + 0.8 = -2.2$ Since -3.5 has the larger absolute value, the sum is negative.

G. $0.32 + (-0.54) + (-0.73) + 1.2$

H. $-\dfrac{3}{4} + \dfrac{7}{8} + \left(-\dfrac{1}{2}\right) + \left(-\dfrac{7}{8}\right)$

Solution: First, add the negative numbers.

$$
-\frac{3}{4} + \left(-\frac{1}{2}\right) + \left(-\frac{7}{8}\right) = \left(-\frac{6}{8}\right) + \left(-\frac{4}{8}\right) + \left(-\frac{7}{8}\right)
$$

$$
= -\frac{17}{8}
$$

Add the sum of the negative numbers and the positive number. To do this find the difference of their absolute values.

$$
\frac{17}{8} - \frac{7}{8} = \frac{10}{8} = \frac{5}{4}
$$

$-\dfrac{3}{4} + \dfrac{7}{8} + \left(-\dfrac{1}{2}\right) + \left(-\dfrac{7}{8}\right) = -\dfrac{5}{4}$ The sum is negative since the negative number has the larger absolute value.

H. $-\dfrac{5}{6} + \dfrac{3}{2} + \left(-\dfrac{8}{9}\right) + \left(-\dfrac{2}{3}\right)$

Answers to warm ups: **F.** -23 **G.** 0.25   **H.** $-\dfrac{8}{9}$

I. ▦ $-63 + 48 + (-61) + (-14)$

I. $-45 + 37 + (-87) + (-45)$

Solution:

ENTER	63	+/−	+	48	+	61

DISPLAY   63.   −63.   −63.   48.   −15.   61.

                               ↑

                       Result of the
                       first addition

ENTER	+/−	+	14	+/−	=

DISPLAY   −61.   −76.   14.   −14.   −90.

           ↑   ↑

        Result of the   Sum
       second addition

So the sum $-63 + 48 + (-61) + (-14)$ is -90.

J. 🌐 John owns stock that is traded on the American Stock Exchange. On Monday the stock gains \$2, on Tuesday it loses \$3, on Wednesday it loses \$2, on Thursday it gains \$5, and on Friday it gains \$2. What is the net change in the price of the stock for the week?

Solution: To find the net change in the price of the stock, write the daily changes as signed numbers and find the sum of these numbers.

Monday	gains \$2	2
Tuesday	loses \$3	−3
Wednesday	loses \$2	−2
Thursday	gains \$5	5
Friday	gains \$2	2

$2 + (-3) + (-2) + 5 + 2 = 9 + (-5)$ Add the positive numbers and add the negative numbers.

$$= 4$$

The stock gains \$4 during the·week.

J.   A second stock that John owns has the following changes for a week: Monday, gains \$1.25; Tuesday, gains \$0.75; Wednesday, loses \$2.625; Thursday, loses \$1.50; Friday, gains \$1.375. What is the net change in the price of the stock for the week?

Answers to warm ups: **I.** −140   **J.** −\$0.75

NAME _____ CLASS _____ DATE _____

EXERCISES 8.2

Add.

A

1. $-6 + 8$ $\quad 2$

2. $-8 + 2$ $\quad -6$

3. $6 + (-7)$ $\quad -1$

4. $9 + (-4)$ $\quad 5$

5. $-8 + (-6)$ $\quad -14$

6. $-5 + (-9)$ $\quad -14$

7. $-10 + (-6)$ $\quad -16$

8. $-12 + (-7)$ $\quad -19$

9. $-7 + 7$ $\quad 0$

10. $11 + (-11)$ $\quad 0$

11. $0 + (-13)$ $\quad -13$

12. $-15 + 0$ $\quad -15$

13. $-17 + (-17)$ $\quad -34$

14. $-21 + (-21)$ $\quad -42$

15. $7 + (-15)$ $\quad -8$

16. $9 + (-18)$ $\quad -9$

17. $-15 + (-12)$ $\quad -27$

18. $-10 + (-17)$ $\quad -27$

19. $23 + (-18)$ $\quad 5$

20. $-13 + 21$ $\quad 8$

B

21. $-3 + (-6) + 5$
-4

22. $-2 + (-5) + (-6)$
-13

23. $-72 + (-72)$
-144

24. $-48 + (-48)$
-96

25. $-40 + (-40)$
-80

26. $56 + (-56)$
0

27. $-72 + 72$
0

28. $48 + (-39)$
9

29. $-18 + 21 + (-3)$
0

30. $-22 + 25 + (-4)$
-1

31. $47 + (-32) + (-14)$
1

32. $-17 + (-12) + (32)$
3

33. $-2.3 + (-4.3)$
-6.6

34. $-8.2 + (-3.2)$
-11.4

35. $6.3 + (-3.7)$
2.6

36. $-7.4 + 4.1$
-3.3

37. $-\dfrac{2}{3} + \dfrac{1}{6}$
$-\dfrac{1}{2}$

38. $\dfrac{5}{6} + \left(-\dfrac{3}{4}\right)$
$\dfrac{1}{12}$

39. $-\dfrac{3}{4} + \left(-\dfrac{7}{8}\right)$
$-\dfrac{13}{8}$

40. $-\dfrac{5}{6} + \left(-\dfrac{1}{3}\right)$
$-\dfrac{7}{6}$

C

41. $-72 + 81 + 53$
62

42. $115 + (-102) + 17$
30

43. $-81 + (-32) + (-76)$
-189

44. $-75 + (-82) + (-71)$
-228

45. $-65 + (-88) + (-92)$
-245

46. $-78 + (-88) + (-98)$
-264

47. $-31 + 28 + (-63) + 36$
-30

48. $-44 + 37 + (-59) + 45$
-21

49. $49 + (-67) + 27 + 72$
81

50. $81 + (-72) + 33 + 49$
91

51. $-27.1 + (-38.5) + 65.6$
0

52. $92.4 + (-53.5) + (-38.9)$
0

53. $0.345 + (-1.203) + (-0.211)$
−1.069

54. $-0.0035 + 0.751 + (-0.111)$
0.6365

55. $-65.52 + 19.51 + (-87.72)$
−133.73

56. $66.49 + 21.98 + (-72.34)$
16.13

57. $-\dfrac{1}{2} + \left(-\dfrac{7}{8}\right) + \left(-\dfrac{5}{6}\right)$
$-\dfrac{53}{24}$

58. $-\dfrac{2}{3} + \left(-\dfrac{5}{8}\right) + \left(-\dfrac{1}{6}\right)$
$-\dfrac{35}{24}$

59. $14\dfrac{2}{3} + \left(-8\dfrac{2}{9}\right)$ $6\dfrac{4}{9}$

60. $-15\dfrac{1}{2} + 24\dfrac{3}{4}$ $9\dfrac{1}{4}$

Applications

61. An airplane is being reloaded; 877 pounds of baggage and mail are removed (−877 pounds) and 764 pounds of baggage and mail are loaded on (+764 pounds). What net change in weight should the cargo master report?   −113 lb

62. At another stop, the plane in Exercise 61 unloads 1842 pounds of baggage and mail and takes on 1974 pounds. What net change should the cargo master report?   +132 lb

63. The change in altitude of a plane in flight is measured every ten minutes. The figures between 3:00 P.M. and 4:00 P.M. are as follows:

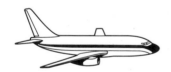

3:00 P.M.	30,000 ft initially	(+30,000)
3:10 P.M.	increase of 220 ft	(+220)
3:20 P.M.	decrease of 200 ft	(−200)
3:30 P.M.	increase of 55 ft	(+55)
3:40 P.M.	decrease of 110 ft	(−110)
3:50 P.M.	decrease of 55 ft	(−55)
4:00 P.M.	decrease of 40 ft	(−40)

What is the altitude of the plane at 4 P.M.? (*Hint:* Find the sum of the initial altitude and the six measured changes between 3 and 4 P.M.)
29,870 ft

64. What is the final altitude of the airplane in Exercise 63 if it is initially flying at 23,000 ft with the following changes in altitude?

3:00 P.M.	23,000 ft initially	(+23,000)
3:10 P.M.	increase of 315 ft	(+315)
3:20 P.M.	decrease of 825 ft	(−825)
3:30 P.M.	increase of 75 ft	(+75)
3:40 P.M.	decrease of 250 ft	(−250)
3:50 P.M.	decrease of 85 ft	(−85)
4:00 P.M.	decrease of 70 ft	(−70)

22,160 ft

NAME _____   CLASS _____ DATE _____

65. The Pacific Northwest Book Depository handles most textbooks for the local schools. On September 1 the inventory is 28,945 volumes. During the month the company makes the following transactions (positive numbers represent volumes received, negative numbers represent shipments): 2386, −497, −924, 475, −997. What is the inventory at the end of the month?   29,388 volumes

66. The Pacific Northwest Book Depository has 12,895 volumes on November 1. During the month the depository has the following transactions: −2478, 514, −877, −213, 97, −482. What is the inventory at the end of the month?   9456 volumes

67. The Buffalo Bills made the following consecutive plays during a recent Monday night football game: 8-yard loss, 10-yard gain, and a 7-yard gain. A first down requires a gain of 10 yards. Did they get a first down?   No; one yard short

68. The Seattle Seahawks have these consecutive plays one Sunday: 12-yard loss, 19-yard gain, and a 4-yard gain. Do they get a first down?   Yes; one yard more

69. Nordstrom stock has the following changes in one week: up $\frac{5}{8}$, down $\frac{1}{2}$, down $1\frac{3}{4}$, up $2\frac{1}{4}$, and up $\frac{5}{8}$. What is the net change for the week?   up $1\frac{1}{4}$

70. If the Nordstrom stock (Exercise 69) starts at $72\frac{7}{8}$ at the beginning of that week, what is the closing price? $74\frac{1}{8}$

71. On a January morning in a small town in upstate New York, the lowest temperature is recorded as 19 degrees below zero. During the following week the daily lowest temperature readings are up 6 degrees, up 8 degrees, down 2 degrees, up 3 degrees, no change, up 1 degree, and down 5 degrees. What is the low temperature reading for the last day?   −8°

72. A new company has the following weekly balances after the first month of business: a loss of $56, a gain of $8, a loss of $95, and a gain of $27. What is their net gain or loss for the month?   −$116

73. Marie decided to play the state lottery for one month. This meant that she played every Wednesday and Saturday for a total of nine times. This is her record: lost $4, won $5, lost $3, lost $8, won $9, lost $6, lost $2, lost $4, won $15. What is the net result of her playing? $2 won

A. $45 - 33$

A. $82 - 76$

Solution: Rewrite as an addition problem by adding -33, which is the opposite of 33.

$$45 - 33 = 45 + (-33)$$
$$= 12 \qquad$$ Add. Since the signs are different, subtract their absolute values and use the sign of the number with the larger absolute value, which is 45.

Since both numbers are positive we can also do the subtraction in the usual manner: $45 - 33 = 12$.

B. $-38 - 41$

B. $-41 - 36$

Solution:

$$-38 - 41 = -38 + (-41)$$
$$= -79 \qquad$$ Add. Since both numbers are negative, add their absolute values and keep the common sign.

C. $-49 - (-24)$

C. $-71 - (-41)$

Solution:

$$-49 - (-24) = -49 + 24$$
$$= -25 \qquad$$ Add.

D. $88 - 107$

D. $67 - 94$

Solution:

$$88 - 107 = 88 + (-107)$$
$$= -19 \qquad$$ Add.

E. $\dfrac{2}{3} - \left(-\dfrac{1}{2}\right)$

E. $\dfrac{3}{4} - \left(-\dfrac{5}{6}\right)$

Solution:

$$\frac{2}{3} - \left(-\frac{1}{2}\right) = \frac{2}{3} + \frac{1}{2}$$
$$= \frac{4}{6} + \frac{3}{6} \qquad$$ Write each fraction with a common denominator and add.
$$= \frac{7}{6}$$

Answers to warm ups: **A.** 6 **B.** -77 **C.** -30 **D.** -27 **E.** $\dfrac{19}{12}$

F. $16 - (-24) - 17$

Solution: Change both subtractions to add the opposite.

$$16 - (-24) - 17 = 16 + 24 + (-17)$$
$$= 40 + (-17) \qquad \text{Add 16 and 24.}$$
$$= 23 \qquad \text{Add.}$$

F. $21 - (-32) - 19$

G. $-0.21 - (-4.2) - (-0.18) - 0.75$

Solution: Change all subtractions to add the opposite and add.

$$-0.21 - (-4.2) - (-0.18) - 0.75 = -0.21 + 4.2 + 0.18 + (-0.75)$$
$$= 3.42$$

G. $-0.67 - 0.76 - (-0.45) - (-1.23)$

H. $-\dfrac{3}{4} - \left(\dfrac{7}{8}\right) - \left(-\dfrac{1}{2}\right) - \left(-\dfrac{1}{8}\right)$

Solution:

$$-\frac{3}{4} - \left(\frac{7}{8}\right) - \left(-\frac{1}{2}\right) - \left(-\frac{1}{8}\right) = -\frac{3}{4} + \left(-\frac{7}{8}\right) + \frac{1}{2} + \frac{1}{8}$$
$$= -\frac{6}{8} + \left(-\frac{7}{8}\right) + \frac{4}{8} + \frac{1}{8}$$
$$= -\frac{8}{8} = -1$$

H. $-\dfrac{3}{5} - \left(-\dfrac{3}{8}\right) - \left(-\dfrac{7}{10}\right) - \left(\dfrac{7}{20}\right)$

I. 🖩 $-481.92 - (-284.7)$

Solution: The calculator does not require you to change subtraction to add the opposite.

ENTER	$\boxed{481.92}$ $\boxed{+/-}$ $\boxed{-}$ $\boxed{284.7}$ $\boxed{+/-}$ $\boxed{=}$
DISPLAY	481.92 -481.92 -481.92 284.7 -284.7 -197.22

So the difference is -197.22.

I. $-346.98 - (-245.82)$

J. 🌐 The highest point in North America is Mount McKinley, a peak in central Alaska, which is approximately 20,300 feet above sea level. The lowest point in North America is Death Valley, a deep desert basin in southeastern California, which is approximately 282 feet below sea level. What is the difference in height between Mount McKinley and Death Valley? (Above sea level is positive and below sea level is negative.)

J. One night last winter the temperature dropped from 18°F to -12°F. What was the difference between the high and the low temperatures?

Answers to warm ups: **F.** 34   **G.** 0.25   **H.** $\dfrac{1}{8}$ **I.** -101.16

C

49. $-18.92 - 14.68$
-33.6

50. $-23.8 - 16.9$
-40.7

51. $-37 - 12.2$
-49.2

52. $-43 - 11.7$
-54.7

53. $-25 - (-11.5)$
-13.5

54. $-37 - (-21.8)$
-15.2

55. $-0.89 - 0.89$
-1.78

56. $-0.43 - 0.43$
-0.86

57. $-0.897 - (-0.897)$
0

58. $-0.092 - (-0.092)$
0

59. $194.82 - (-136.7)$
331.52

60. $289.74 - (-187.7)$
477.44

61. $\dfrac{3}{4} - 1\dfrac{1}{2}$
$-\dfrac{3}{4}$

62. $\dfrac{7}{8} - 1\dfrac{3}{4}$
$-\dfrac{7}{8}$

63. $-\dfrac{5}{8} - \left(-\dfrac{2}{5}\right)$
$-\dfrac{9}{40}$

64. $-\dfrac{6}{7} - \left(-\dfrac{2}{3}\right)$
$-\dfrac{4}{21}$

65. $-61 - (-43) - (-32)$ 14

66. $-91 - (-56) - (-12)$ -23

67. $-\dfrac{5}{8} - \left(-\dfrac{3}{4}\right) - \left(-\dfrac{5}{6}\right)$ $\dfrac{23}{24}$

68. $-\dfrac{2}{15} - \left(-\dfrac{3}{4}\right) - \dfrac{5}{6}$ $-\dfrac{13}{60}$

Applications

69. *Viking II* records high and low temperatures of $-22°C$ and $-107°C$ for one day on the surface of Mars. What is the change in temperature for that day? $-85°C$

70. The surface temperature of one of Jupiter's satellites is measured for one week. The highest temperature recorded is $-75°C$ and the lowest is $-139°C$. What is the difference in the extreme temperatures for the week? $-64°C$

71. At the beginning of the month, Joe's bank account had a balance of $487.52. At the end of the month, the account was overdrawn by $63.34 ($-$63.34). If there were no deposits during the month, what was the total amount of checks Joe wrote? (*Hint:* Subtract the ending balance from the original balance.) $550.86

72. At the beginning of the month Jack's bank account had a balance of $295.72. At the end of the month the balance was $-$8.73. If there were no deposits, find the amount of checks Jack wrote. (Refer to Exercise 71.) $304.45

NAME _____   CLASS _____   DATE _____

73. *Viking II* records a high temperature of 8°C and a low temperature of −51°C. What is the temperature change?   −59°C

74. Carol started school owing her mother $12; by school's end she borrowed $85 more from her mother. How does her account with her mother stand now?   owes $97

75. At the beginning of the month Janna's bank account had a balance of $249.78. At the end of the month the account was overdrawn $2.09. If there were no deposits during the month, what was the total amount of the checks Janna wrote? (*Hint:* Subtract the ending balance from the original balance.) $251.87

76. What is the difference in altitude between the highest point in the world and the lowest point in the United States?

Highest point:	Mount Everest is 29,028 ft above sea level (+29,028)
Lowest point:	Death Valley is 282 ft below sea level (−282)

29,310 ft

77. Marie's bank account had a balance of $195.84. She writes a check for $212.69. What is her account balance now?   −$16.85

78. Thomas started with $75.32 in his account. He writes a check for $92.17. What is his account balance now?   −$16.85

79. On the first sale of the day Gina makes a profit of $125.45. However, on the next sale, Gina loses $245.36 because of another employee's misquote of the price of an item. After these two sales, what is the status of Gina's sales?   −$119.91

80. The temperature at 2 A.M. was 5° below zero. At 6 A.M. it was 12° below zero. What is the difference between the 6 A.M. and the 2 A.M. temperatures?   −7°

81. The New England Patriots started on their 40-yard line. After three plays they were on their 12-yard line. Did they lose or gain yards? Represent this loss or gain with a signed number.   Lost; −28 yd

82. During 1970 the net import of coal was −1.93 quadrillion Btu. In 1980 the net import of coal was −2.39 quadrillion Btu. In 1990 the net import of coal was −2.70 quadrillion Btu. Find the difference in coal imports for each decade and also for the 20-year span.
−0.46 quadrillion Btu; −0.31 quadrillion Btu; −0.77 quadrillion Btu

50. $-0.3(0.05)(-10)(-10)$
-1.5

51. $(-12 + 24)(-2 - 12)$
-168

52. $(9 - 17)(-22 + 7)$
120

53. $-2(-5)(-6)(-4)(-1)$
-240

54. $9(-2)(-5)(-4)(-3)$
1080

55. $\left(-\dfrac{2}{3}\right)\left(-\dfrac{3}{4}\right)\left(-\dfrac{4}{5}\right)\left(-\dfrac{5}{6}\right)$
$\dfrac{1}{3}$

56. $\left(-\dfrac{5}{12}\right)\left(\dfrac{7}{8}\right)\left(\dfrac{3}{14}\right)\left(-\dfrac{8}{15}\right)$
$\dfrac{1}{24}$

57. $\left(\dfrac{4}{9}\right)\left(-\dfrac{3}{8}\right)\left(-\dfrac{1}{5}\right)(9)$
$\dfrac{3}{10}$

58. $\left(-\dfrac{2}{3}\right)\left(-\dfrac{3}{5}\right)\left(-\dfrac{3}{4}\right)(-5)$
$\dfrac{3}{2}$

59. $-24(-18)(-0.5)(-0.25)$
54

60. $-48(25)(-0.4)(-0.125)$
-60

Applications

61. The formula for converting a temperature measurement from Fahrenheit to Celsius is C = $\dfrac{5}{9}$(F − 32). What Celsius measure is equal to −4°F? $-20°C$

62. Use the formula in Exercise 61 to find the Celsius measure that is equal to 68°F. $20°C$

63. While on a diet for eight consecutive weeks Ms. Riles averages a weight loss of 3.5 lb each week. If each loss is represented by −3.5 lb, what is her total weight loss for the eight weeks, expressed as a signed number? -28 lb

64. Mr. Riles goes on a similar diet as his daughter for eight consecutive weeks. He averages a loss of 2.5 lb each week. If each loss is represented by −2.5 lb, what is his total weight loss for the eight weeks, expressed as a signed number? -20 lb

65. The Dow Jones Industrial Average sustains 12 straight days of a 2.83-point decline. What is the total decline during the 12-day period, expressed as a signed number? -33.96

66. The Dow Jones Industrial Average sustains eight straight days of a loss of 1.75 points. What is the total decline in this period, expressed as a signed number? -14

NAME _____ CLASS _____ DATE _____

67. Safeway Inc. offers as a loss leader 10 lb of sugar at a loss of 12¢ per bag (−12¢). If 560 bags are sold during the sale, what is the total loss, expressed as a signed number?   −$67.20

68. Albertsons offers a loss leader of coffee at a loss of 18¢ per can (−18¢). If they sell 235 cans of coffee, find the total loss, expressed as a signed number.
−$42.30

69. Thriftway's loss leader is a soft drink that loses 8¢ per six-pack. They sell 251 of these six-packs. What is Thriftway's total loss expressed as a signed number?   −$20.08

70. Fred Meyer's loss leader is soap powder that loses 12¢ per carton. They sell 326 cartons. What is Fred Meyer's total loss expressed as a signed number?
−$39.12

71. Safeway's loss leader is 1 dozen eggs that lose 14¢ per dozen. The store sells 712 dozen eggs that week. Express Safeway's total loss as a signed number.   −$99.68

72. A scientist is studying the movement, within its web, of a certain spider. Any movement up is considered to be positive, while any movement down is negative. Determine the net movement of a spider that goes up 2 cm five times and down 3 cm twice.   4 cm

73. A certain junk bond trader purchased 850 shares of stock at $8\frac{3}{8}$. When she sold her shares the stock sold for $7\frac{7}{8}$. What did she pay for the stock? How much money did she receive when she sold this stock? How much did she lose or gain? Represent the loss or gain with a signed number.
$7118.75; $6693.75; lost $425; −$425

74. A company bought 300 items at $0.89 each. They tried to sell them for $1.19 and sold only 26. They lowered the price to $1.06 and sold 34 more. The price was lowered a second time to $0.89 and 125 items were sold. Finally they advertised a close-out price of $0.84 and sold the remaining items. Determine the net profit or loss for each price. Did they make a profit or lose money on this item overall?
$7.80 profit; $5.78 profit; 0 profit or loss; $5.75 loss (−$5.75); $7.83 profit overall

State Your Understanding

75. Explain the difference between -3^2 and $(-3)^2$.

76. Write an explanation of how to read the numerical expression $5[-(-3)]$.

D. 🌐 Over a period of 24 weeks, Mr. Rich loses a total of $8736 (−$8736) in his stock market account. What is his average loss per week, expressed as a signed number?

D. Ms. Rich loses $1152 in her stock market account over a period of 24 consecutive weeks. What is her average loss per week, expressed as a signed number?

Solution: To find the average loss per week, divide the total loss by the number of weeks.

$$-8736 \div 24 = -364$$

Mr. Rich has an average loss of $364 (−$364) per week.

How and Why **2** To determine how to divide two negative numbers, we again use the relationship to multiplication that was used to determine how to divide a positive and a negative number.

The expression $-21 \div (-3) = ?$ asks $(-3)(?) = -21$; we know that $-3(7) = -21$, so $-21 \div (-3) = 7$. The expression $-15 \div (-5) = ?$ asks $(-5)(?) = -15$; we know that $-5(3) = -15$, so $-15 \div (-5) = 3$. We see that in each case when dividing a negative number by a negative number, the quotient is positive. These examples lead us to the following rule:

▶ **To divide two negative numbers**

1. Find the quotient of the absolute values.
2. Leave the answer positive.

Examples E–G   **Warm Ups E–G**

Directions: Divide.

Strategy: Find the quotient of the absolute values.

E. $-24 \div (-3)$ **E.** $(-36) \div (-4)$

Solution: The quotient of two negative numbers is positive.

$$-24 \div (-3) = 8$$

F. $-12.5 \div (-0.5)$ **F.** $(-18.6) \div (-0.6)$

Solution: The quotient of two negative numbers is positive.

$$-12.5 \div (-0.5) = 25$$

G. $\left(-\dfrac{3}{4}\right) \div \left(-\dfrac{1}{2}\right)$ **G.** $\left(-\dfrac{5}{6}\right) \div \left(-\dfrac{3}{4}\right)$

Solution:

$$\left(-\frac{3}{4}\right) \div \left(-\frac{1}{2}\right) = \left(-\frac{3}{\overset{}{4}}\right)\left(-\frac{\overset{1}{2}}{1}\right)$$ Invert and multiply. Divide out like factors.

$$= \frac{3}{2}$$

Answers to warm ups: **D.** −$48 **E.** 9 **F.** 31 **G.** $\dfrac{10}{9}$

NAME _____ CLASS _____ DATE _____

EXERCISES 8.5

Divide.

A

1. $-10 \div 5$ -2

2. $10 \div (-2)$ -5

3. $-10 \div (-5)$ 2

4. $-10 \div (-2)$ 5

5. $-16 \div 4$ -4

6. $15 \div (-3)$ -5

7. $18 \div (-2)$ -9

8. $-12 \div (-4)$ 3

9. $-15 \div (3)$ -5

10. $-14 \div (-2)$ 7

11. $14 \div (-2)$ -7

12. $24 \div (-3)$ -8

13. $-28 \div (-4)$ 7

14. $-32 \div (-4)$ 8

15. $-33 \div 11$ -3

16. $-36 \div 9$ -4

17. $48 \div (-6)$ -8

18. $45 \div (-9)$ -5

19. $-54 \div (-9)$ 6

20. $-63 \div (-7)$ 9

B

21. $72 \div (-12)$ -6

22. $84 \div (-12)$ -7

23. $-98 \div (-14)$ 7

24. $-88 \div (-11)$ 8

25. $-75 \div (-15)$ 5

26. $-99 \div (-11)$ 9

27. $6.06 \div (-3)$ -2.02

28. $3.05 \div (-5)$ -0.61

29. $-4.04 \div (-4)$ 1.01

30. $-9.09 \div (-3)$ 3.03

31. $0 \div (-3)$ 0

32. $0 \div (-5)$ 0

33. $-12 \div 0$ Undefined

34. $-18 \div 0$ Undefined

35. $-210 \div 6$ -35

36. $-315 \div 9$ -35

37. $-12.12 \div (-3)$ 4.04

38. $-18.16 \div (-4)$ 4.54

39. $-0.25 \div 100$ -0.0025

40. $-0.32 \div 100$ -0.0032

C

41. $-0.65 \div (-0.13)$ 5

42. $-0.056 \div (-0.4)$ 0.14

43. $-540 \div 12$ −45

44. $-1071 \div 17$ −63

45. $-3364 \div (-29)$ 116

46. $-4872 \div (-48)$ 101.5

47. $\left(-\dfrac{3}{8}\right) \div \left(-\dfrac{3}{4}\right)$ $\dfrac{1}{2}$

48. $\left(-\dfrac{1}{2}\right) \div \left(-\dfrac{5}{8}\right)$ $\dfrac{4}{5}$

49. $\left(-\dfrac{6}{7}\right) \div \dfrac{2}{7}$ −3

50. $\left(-\dfrac{4}{3}\right) \div \dfrac{8}{3}$ $-\dfrac{1}{2}$

51. $0.75 \div (-0.625)$ −1.2

52. $0.125 \div (-0.625)$ −0.2

Simplify.

53. $[-5(-2)] \div (-10)$ −1

54. $-48 \div [-6(-8)]$ −1

55. $(-8 + 4 - 5)(-12)$ 108

56. $(-43 - 65) \div (-36)$ 3

57. $-12(-15) \div (-9)$ −20

58. $-15(-8) \div (-6)$ −20

59. $\left(-\dfrac{2}{3}\right)\left(-\dfrac{3}{4}\right) \div \left(-\dfrac{5}{6}\right)$ $-\dfrac{3}{5}$

60. $\left(-\dfrac{3}{5}\right)\left(-\dfrac{7}{15}\right) \div \left(-\dfrac{1}{30}\right)$ $-\dfrac{42}{5}$

61. $(0.43 - 0.69 - 0.3) \div (-3.5)$ 0.16

62. $(-0.72 - 0.34 + 0.16) \div (-1.5)$ 0.6

Applications

63. The coldest temperatures in Eycee Northland for each of five days are $-13°$, $-9°$, $-8°$, $-2°$, and $-8°$. What is the average of these temperatures?   −8°

64. In northern Norway the daily low temperature is recorded for six days. The temperatures are $-42°$, $-28°$, $-7°$, $-19°$, $-18°$, and $-12°$. What is the average of these temperatures?   −21°

65. A local supermarket reports the following losses from shoplifting for a six-month period: $-\$1896$, $-\$1434$, $-\$1002$, $-\$2016$, $-\$1962$, and $-\$1572$. Find the average loss per month.   −$1647

66. Over a five-day period, a certain stock sustains the following losses: -0.84, -0.52, -1.21, -1.11, and -0.42. What is the average daily loss?   −0.82

NAME _____   CLASS _____ DATE _____

67. The membership of the Burlap Baggers Investment Club takes a loss of $284.22 (−284.22) on the sale of stock. If there are six co-equal members in the club, what is each member's share of the loss, expressed as a signed number?   −$47.37

68. The temperature in Fairbanks, Alaska, drops from 10° above zero (+10°) to 22° below zero (−22°) in an eight-hour period. What is the average drop in temperature per hour, expressed as a signed number?   −4°

69. Mr. Harkness loses a total of 108 pounds in 24 weeks. Express the average weekly loss as a signed number.   −4.5 lb

70. Ms. Harkness loses a total of 60 pounds in 24 weeks. Express the average weekly loss as a signed number.   −2.5 lb

71. A certain stock loses $31\frac{1}{2}$ points in 12 days. Express the average daily loss as a signed number.
−2.625

72. A certain stock loses $30\frac{3}{8}$ points in 9 days. Express the average daily loss as a signed number.
−3.375

73. Determine the population of Los Angeles in 1970, in 1980, and in 1990. Determine the population of Detroit in 1970, in 1980, and in 1990. Find the average yearly loss or gain per decade and also for the 20-year period for each city (written as a signed number). List the possible reasons for these changes.   Answers will vary.

74. A certain company loses $862,200 during one 20-month period. Determine the average monthly loss (written as a signed number). If there are 30 stockholders in this company, determine the total loss per stockholder (written as a signed number).
−$43,110; −$28,740

75. During a 12-month period, the temperature in Ottawa, Canada, ranges from a low of −42° to a high of 102°. Find the average monthly change from the high to the low temperatures. Write your answer as a signed number.   −12°

State Your Understanding

76. When dividing signed numbers, care must be taken not to divide by zero. Why?

77. Explain, in your own words, how to divide two signed numbers.

Challenge

Simplify.

78. $[-|-9|(8 - 12)] \div [(9 - 13)(8 - 7)]$ -9

79. $[(14 - 20)(-5 - 9)] \div [-(-12)(-8 + 7)]$ -7

80. $\left(-\dfrac{5}{6} - \dfrac{1}{2}\right)\left(-\dfrac{2}{3} + \dfrac{1}{6}\right) \div \left(\dfrac{1}{3} - \dfrac{3}{4}\right)$ $-\dfrac{8}{5}$

81. $\left(-\dfrac{1}{3} - \dfrac{1}{4}\right)\left(-\dfrac{1}{3} + \dfrac{1}{6}\right) \div \left(\dfrac{1}{3} - \dfrac{3}{4}\right)$ $-\dfrac{7}{30}$

82. $(-0.82 - 1.28)(1.84 - 2.12) \div [3.14 + (-3.56)]$
-1.4

Group Activity

83. Determine the temperature on the first of each month over a 12-month period in one city in Alaska, one city in Canada, and one city in Hawaii. Find the average change in temperature from January 1 to December 1 for each city. Find the average monthly temperature for each city. Make a chart or graph from these data. Be sure no two groups choose the same cities. Compare the results with your classmates.

Maintain Your Skills (Section 7.7)

84. Find the volume of a cylinder that has a radius of 8 in. and a height of 24 in. (Let $\pi \approx 3.14$.)
4823.04 in.³

85. Find the volume of a sphere with a diameter of 18 cm. (Let $\pi \approx 3.14$.)   3052.08 cm³

86. Find the volume of a cone that has a radius of 12 in. and a height of 9 in. (Let $\pi \approx 3.14$.)
1356.48 in.³

87. Find the volume of a pyramid with a square base of 12 cm on each side and a height of 12 cm, to the nearest cubic centimeter.   576 cm³

88. An underground gasoline storage tank is a cylinder that is 72 in. in diameter and 18 ft long. If there are 231 in.³ in a gallon, how many gallons of gasoline will the tank hold? Round the answer to the nearest gallon. (Let $\pi \approx 3.14$.)   3805 gallons

89. A swimming pool is to be dug and the dirt hauled away. The pool is to be 27 ft long, 16 ft wide, and 6 ft deep. How many cubic *yards* of dirt must be removed?   96 cubic yards

90. To remove the dirt for the swimming pool in Exercise 89, trucks that can haul 8 yd³ per load are used. How many truckloads will there be?
12 truckloads

91. A real estate broker sells a lot that measures 88.75 ft by 180 ft. The sale price is $2 per square foot. If the broker's commission is 8%, how much does she make? $2556

8.6   ORDER OF OPERATIONS: A REVIEW

Objective   Do any combination of operations with signed numbers.

Application   🌐 Hilda keeps the thermostat on her furnace set at 68°F. Her pen pal in Germany says that her thermostat is set at 20°C. They wonder whether the two temperatures are equal. Hilda finds the formula, given below, for changing degrees Celsius to degrees Fahrenheit. Use this formula to find out whether 68°F is equal to 20°C.

$$C = \frac{5}{9}(F - 32)$$

How and Why   The order of operations for signed numbers is the same as that for whole numbers.

▶ **To evaluate expressions with more than one operation**

Order of Operations

Step 1.   **Parentheses** — Do the operations within grouping symbols first (parentheses, fraction bar, etc.), in the order given in steps 2, 3, and 4.

Step 2.   **Exponents** — Do the operations indicated by exponents.

Step 3.   **Multiply** and **divide** — Do only multiplication and division as they appear from left to right.

Step 4.   **Add** and **subtract** — Do addition and subtraction as they appear from left to right.

Examples A–G   **Warm Ups A–G**

Directions: Perform the indicated operations.

Strategy: Follow the order of operations.

A. $-64 + (-22) \div 2$ A. $-36 + (-48) \div 6$

Solution:

$$-64 + (-22) \div 2 = -64 + (-11)$$
$$= -75$$

B. $(-12)(5) - 54 \div (-3)$ B. $(-9)(4) - 24 \div (-6)$

Solution:

$$(-12)(5) - 54 \div (-3) = -60 - (-18)$$
$$= -60 + 18 \qquad \text{Add the opposite of } -18.$$
$$= -42$$

C. $4 \div (-0.8) + 2(-2.4)$ C. $6 \div (-0.5) + 3(-1.7)$

Solution:

$$4 \div (-0.8) + 2(-2.4) = -5 + (-4.8)$$
$$= -9.8$$

Answers to warm ups: **A.** -44 **B.** -32 **C.** -17.1

D. $8 - \left(\dfrac{3}{4}\right)(-4)$

D. $9 - \left(\dfrac{2}{3}\right)(-6)$

Solution:

$$8 - \left(\dfrac{3}{4}\right)(-4) = 8 - (-3)$$

$$= 8 + 3 \qquad \text{Add the opposite of } -3.$$

$$= 11$$

E. $2(-4)^2 - 5^2 + 3(-2)^2$

E. $(-5)(-3)^2 + 32 - (-4)^2$

Solution:

$$2(-4)^2 - 5^2 + 3(-2)^2 = 2(16) - 25 + 3(4)$$

$$= 32 - 25 + 12$$

$$= 19$$

F. ▨ $(-13)(12) - (-42) \div (-7)$

F. $(-18)(11) - 75 \div (-3)$

Solution: If your calculator has algebraic logic,

ENTER	$\boxed{13}$ $\boxed{+/-}$ $\boxed{\times}$ $\boxed{12}$ $\boxed{-}$ $\boxed{42}$

DISPLAY   13. −13. −13. 12. −156. 42.

ENTER	$\boxed{+/-}$ $\boxed{\div}$ $\boxed{7}$ $\boxed{+/-}$ $\boxed{=}$

DISPLAY   −42. −42. 7.   −7.   −162.

The answer is −162.

G. 🌐 Hilda keeps the thermostat on her furnace set at 68°F. Her pen pal in Germany says that her thermostat is set at 20°C. They wonder whether the two temperatures are equal. Hilda finds the formula, given below, for changing degrees Celsius to degrees Fahrenheit. Use this formula to find out whether 68°F is equal to 20°C.

G. How many degrees Celsius is −40°F?

$$C = \dfrac{5}{9}(F - 32)$$

Solution: To find out whether 68°F = 20°C, substitute 68 for F in the formula.

$$C = \dfrac{5}{9}(F - 32)$$

$$C = \dfrac{5}{9}(68 - 32)$$

$$C = \dfrac{5}{9}(36)$$

$$C = 20$$

Therefore 68°F equals 20°C.

Answers to warm ups: **D.** 13   **E.** −29   **F.** −173   **G.** −40°C

NAME _____ CLASS _____ DATE _____

EXERCISES 8.6

Perform the indicated operations.

A

1. $2(-6) - 8$ −20

2. $12 + 3(-4)$ 0

3. $(-3)(-2) + 14$ 20

4. $12 + (-3)(-6)$ 30

5. $2(-8) + 10$ −6

6. $(-3)4 + 9$ −3

7. $-7 + 2(-3)$ −13

8. $-12 + (-3)4$ −24

9. $(-2)10 \div (5)$ −4

10. $(-7)6 \div 3$ −14

11. $(-4)8 \div (-4)$ 8

12. $(-9)12 \div (-6)$ 18

13. $(-6) \div 4(2)$ −3

14. $(-18) \div 3(2)$ −12

15. $3^2 + 2^2$ 13

16. $5^2 - 3^2$ 16

17. $(10 - 2) + (8 - 5)$ 11

18. $(9 - 3) + (12 - 4)$ 14

19. $(4 - 7)(8 - 11)$ 9

20. $(6 - 4)(9 - 14)$ −10

21. $(-2)^2 + 4(2)$ 12

22. $(-3)^2 + 3(5)$ 24

23. $-3 + (3 - 5) - 4(2)$ −13

24. $-5 + (4 - 8) - 3(4)$ −21

B

25. $(-12)(-3) + (-15)2$ 6

26. $(-15)(-4) + (-12)4$ 12

27. $(9 - 7)(-2 - 5) + (15 - 9)(2 + 7)$ 40

28. $(10 - 15)(-4 - 3) + (12 - 7)(3 + 2)$ 60

29. $6(-10 + 4) - 33 \div (-11)$ −33

30. $7(-9 + 4) - 45 \div (-9)$ −30

31. $16(-2) \div (-4) - 12$ −4

32. $(-3)(-8) \div (-6) + 10$ 6

33. $-120 \div (-20) - (9 - 11)$ 8

34. $-135 \div (-15) - (12 - 17)$ 14

35. $-2^3 - (-2)^3$ 0

36. $-4^3 - (-4)^3$ 0

37. $-35 \div (-5)7 - 7^2$ 0

38. $-28 \div (-4)7 - 7^2$ 0

39. $2^2(5 - 4)(7 - 3)^2$ 64

40. $3^2(8 - 6)(6 - 8)^2$ 72

41. $(8 - 12) + (-4)(-2) - (-3)4 - 2^2$ 12

42. $(9 - 14) - (7)(-2) + (-5)(2) - 3^2$ −10

43. $(-2)(-3)(-4) - (-4)(3) - (-2)(-5)$ −22

44. $(-4)(-5)(-1) - (-2)(5) - (-3)(2)$ −4

45. $(-1)(-6)^2(-1) - (-2)^2(-3)^2$ 0

46. $(-1)(-2)^2(-9) - (-3)^2(-2)^2$ 0

C

47. $[(-3)9 + 20](-3) - 25$ −4

48. $[(-4)8 + 30](-4) - 36$ −28

49. $28 \div (-4)(2) - 12 \div 3(-2) + 4(8) \div 4$ 2

50. $36 \div (-4)(3) - 16 \div (2)(-4) + 3(9) \div 3$ 14

51. $4 - 6^2 + (4 - 6)^2 + 4^2 - 6^2$ −48

52. $7 - 5^2 + (7 - 5)^2 + 7^2 - 5^2$ 10

53. $[(-5)6 - 3(8)] \div [6(-3) + 6(6)]$ −3

54. $[(-8)(-6) + 4(11)] \div [7(-8) - (-6)(10)]$ 23

55. $(-6 + 8 - 2)^2 - (9 - 5 - 4)^2 + (-3)^3$ 9

56. $(-12 + 17 - 5)^2 - (16 - 7 - 9)^2 + 2^3$ 8

57. $(4^2 - 3^2)(8) \div (9 - 7)^2$ 14

58. $(7^2 - 5^2)(3) \div (8 - 5)^2$ 8

59. $[128 - 8(-4)^2]^2 - [(-9)(-3) - (-7)(-4)]^2$ −1

60. $[48 - 3(-4)^2]^2 - [(-7)(-1) - (-2)(-3)]^2$ −1

Applications

61. Does 86°F equal 30°C? To check, substitute 86 for F and 30 for C in the formula

$$F = \frac{9}{5}C + 32$$

and tell whether the statement is true.   True

62. The temperature at 5 P.M. is 18°C. If the temperature drops 0.2° every hour until midnight, we can find the midnight temperature by calculating the value of

$$T = 18 + 7(-0.2)$$

What is the temperature at midnight?   16.6°C

63. If the temperature at 7 A.M. is −10°F and rises 3.4°F every hour until 11 A.M., what is the temperature at 11 A.M.?   3.6°F

64. To check whether $x = -6$ is a solution to the equation

$$x^2 - 4x - 7 = 53$$

we substitute −6 for x and find the value of

$$(-6)(-6) - 4(-6) - 7$$

Check whether this expression equals 53.   Yes

65. Check whether $x = 10$ is a solution to the equation in Exercise 64.   Yes

66. Substitute $x = -\dfrac{1}{2}$ in the following equation and check whether it is a solution:

$$\frac{3}{4}\left(x + \frac{2}{3}\right) - \frac{3}{8} = -\frac{1}{4}$$

Yes

67. Check whether $x = \dfrac{1}{2}$ is a solution to the equation in Exercise 66.   No

68. Does $-10°F$ equal $-10°C$? To check, substitute -10 for F and also for C in the formula

$$F = \frac{9}{5}C + 32$$

Tell whether the statement is true.   False

69. On Monday a stock drops 1, Tuesday it rises 2, Wednesday it declines 4, then it rises 8 on Thursday, and it finishes the week by losing 16 on Friday. What is the net result after the week?
Down 11

70. Take your age and square it. Subtract 4. Divide by your age minus 2. Subtract 100. Add your age. Divide by 2. Add seven squared. What is the result?   Your age

71. The Chicago Bears made the following plays during a quarter of a game:

3 plays lost 8 yards each
8 plays lost 5 yards each
1 quarterback sack lost 23 yards
1 pass for 85 yards
5 plays gained 3 yards each
2 plays gained 12 yards each
1 fumble lost 7 yards
2 passes for 10 yards each

Determine the average movement per play during this quarter. Round to the nearest tenth.
2.2 yd gained

72. Find the elevation of each of these places in California: Death Valley, El Centro, Chula Vista, Riverside, Santa Clara, Long Beach, Hollywood, and Oakland. Determine the average elevation of these cities.   Answers will vary.

NAME _____ CLASS _____ DATE _____

73. Consider traveling north and east as positive values and traveling south and west as negative values. A certain trip requires 81 miles north followed by 67 miles west. The next day the trip requires 213 miles south followed by 107 miles west. The last day of the trip takes 210 miles north and 83 miles east. What is the net result of this trip? Determine your position at the end of your trip in relation to your starting point.

−13 mi; 78 mi north and 91 mi west

State Your Understanding

74. Explain the order in which the following problem is worked.

$$(11 - 4 \cdot 3)^2 + 4(8 \cdot 4 \div 2)$$

75. Explain the order in which the following problem is worked.

$$5^2 \cdot 24 \div 6 \cdot 2 \div 10 \cdot 2 - 3^3$$

Challenge

76. Work the problem in Exercise 74.   65

77. Work the problem in Exercise 75.   13

Group Activity

78. Obtain a business summary for a major national company, a local company, and an international company. Chart and graph their net gains and losses (by the quarter) for the previous five years. Determine the average gains and/or losses for each year and over the 20 quarters. Chart and graph these results. Discuss possible reasons for the gain or loss. Compare your results with the class.

Maintain Your Skills (Sections 8.2, 8.3, 8.4, 8.5)

Add.

79. $(-17.2) + (-18.6) + (-2.7) + 9.1$ −29.4

80. $(28.31) + (-8.14) + (-21.26) + (-16)$ −17.09

Subtract.

81. $48 - (-136)$ 184

82. $-62.7 - (-78.8)$
16.1

Multiply.

83. $(-36)(84)(-21)$
63,504

84. $(-62)(-22)(-30)$
-40,920

Divide.

85. $(-800) \div (-32)$ 25

86. $(-25.781) \div (3.5)$
-7.366

87. The four Zapple brothers form a company. The first year the company loses $5832 (-5832). The brothers share equally in the loss. Represent each brother's loss as a signed number.   -$1458

88. The WOW-Smith stock average records the following gains and losses for the week:

Monday	loss 2.25
Tuesday	loss 3.125
Wednesday	gain 4.5
Thursday	gain 2
Friday	loss 1.125

Use signed numbers to find out whether the stock average gains or loses for the week.   No change

8.7 SOLVING EQUATIONS

Objective   Solve equations of the form $ax + b = c$ or $ax - b = c$, where a, b, and c are signed numbers.

Application   🌐 Using the formula $s = v + gt$, find the initial velocity (v) in feet per second of a sky diver if after a time (t) of 3.5 seconds she reaches a speed (s) of 125 feet per second and $g = 32$ feet per sec^2.

Vocabulary   Recall that the **coefficient** of the variable is the number that is multiplied times the variable.

How and Why   The solutions of equations that are of the form $ax + b = c$ and $ax - b = c$, using signed numbers, involve two operations to isolate the variable. To isolate the variable is to get an equation in which the variable is the only symbol on a particular side of the equation.

▶ **To find the solution of an equation of the form $ax + b = c$ or $ax - b = c$**

1. Add (subtract) the constant to (from) each side of the equation to isolate the variable.
2. Divide both sides by the coefficient of the variable.

Examples A–D   **Warm Ups A–D**

Directions: Solve.

Strategy: First, add or subtract the constant to or from both sides of the equation. Second, divide both sides of the equation by the coefficient of the variable.

A. $-5x + 17 = -8$ A. $-6x + 18 = -12$

Solution:

$$-5x + 17 = -8 \qquad \text{Original equation.}$$
$$-5x + 17 - 17 = -8 - 17$$
$$-5x = -25 \qquad \text{Subtract.}$$
$$\frac{-5x}{-5} = \frac{-25}{-5}$$
$$x = 5$$

CHECK: Substitute 5 for x in the original equation.

$$-5(5) + 17 = -8$$
$$-25 + 17 = -8$$
$$-8 = -8$$

The solution is $x = 5$.

B. $-18 = -13x - 44$

Solution:

$$-18 = -13x - 44 \qquad \text{Original equation.}$$

$$-18 + 44 = -13x - 44 + 44$$

$$26 = -13x \qquad \text{Add.}$$

$$\frac{26}{-13} = \frac{-13x}{-13}$$

$$-2 = x$$

CHECK: Substitute -2 in the original equation.

$$-18 = -13(-2) - 44$$

$$-18 = 26 - 44$$

$$-18 = -18$$

The solution is $x = -2$.

B. $9 = -3x - 27$

C. $2x - 4 = 32$

Solution: An alternate format is used to add 4 to both sides of the equation.

$$
\begin{array}{ll}
2x - 4 = 32 & \text{Original equation.} \\
\underline{ 4 \quad 4} & \text{Add 4 to both sides.} \\
2x = 36 &
\end{array}
$$

$$\frac{2x}{2} = \frac{36}{2} \qquad \text{Divide both sides by 2.}$$

$$x = 18 \qquad \text{The check is left for the student.}$$

The solution is $x = 18$.

C. $4x - 5 = 11$

D. ⊕ Using the formula $s = v + gt$, find the initial velocity (v) in feet per second of a sky diver if after a time (t) of 3.5 seconds she reaches a speed (s) of 125 feet per second and $g = 32$ feet per sec^2.

Solution: Substitute into the formula and solve the resulting equation. Recall how to work with units. This was done when units were converted (see Chapter 7).

Formula:
$$s = v + gt$$

Substitute:
$$\frac{125 \text{ ft}}{1 \text{ sec}} = v + \left(\frac{32 \text{ ft}}{\text{sec}^2}\right)(3.5 \text{ sec})$$

$$\frac{125 \text{ ft}}{1 \text{ sec}} = v + \frac{112 \text{ ft}}{1 \text{ sec}} \qquad \begin{array}{l}\text{One factor of seconds} \\ \text{divides out.}\end{array}$$

$$\frac{125 \text{ ft}}{1 \text{ sec}} - \frac{112 \text{ ft}}{1 \text{ sec}} = v + \frac{112 \text{ ft}}{1 \text{ sec}} - \frac{112 \text{ ft}}{1 \text{ sec}} \qquad \begin{array}{l}\text{Subtract 112 feet per} \\ \text{second from both sides.}\end{array}$$

$$\frac{13 \text{ ft}}{1 \text{ sec}} = v \qquad \begin{array}{l}\text{The check is left for} \\ \text{the student.}\end{array}$$

The sky diver's initial velocity was 13 feet per second.

D. Using the formula $s = v + gt$, find the initial velocity (v) in feet per second of a sky diver if after a time (t) of 5 seconds she reaches a speed (s) of 180 feet per second and $g = 32$ feet per sec^2.

Answers to warm ups: **B.** $x = -12$ **C.** $x = 4$ **D.** 20 feet per second

NAME _____ CLASS _____ DATE _____

EXERCISES 8.7

Solve.

A

1. $-3x + 25 = 4$ $\quad x = 7$

2. $-4y + 11 = -9$ $\quad y = 5$

3. $-6 + 3x = 9$ $\quad x = 5$

4. $-11 + 5y = 14$ $\quad y = 5$

5. $4y - 9 = -29$ $\quad y = -5$

6. $3x - 13 = -43$ $\quad x = -10$

7. $2a - 11 = 3$ $\quad a = 7$

8. $5a + 17 = 17$ $\quad a = 0$

9. $-5x + 12 = -23$ $\quad x = 7$

10. $-11y - 32 = -65$ $\quad y = 3$

11. $4x - 12 = 28$ $\quad x = 10$

12. $9y - 14 = 4$ $\quad y = 2$

B

13. $-14 = 2x - 8$ $\quad x = -3$

14. $26 = 3x - 4$ $\quad x = 10$

15. $-40 = 5x - 10$ $\quad x = -6$

16. $-30 = -5x - 10$ $\quad x = 4$

17. $-6 = -8x - 6$ $\quad x = 0$

18. $8 = -5x + 8$ $\quad x = 0$

19. $-10 = -4x + 2$ $\quad x = 3$

20. $20 = -8x + 4$ $\quad x = -2$

21. $-14y - 1 = -99$ $\quad y = 7$

22. $-16x + 5 = -27$ $\quad x = 2$

23. $-3 = -8a - 3$ $\quad a = 0$

24. $-12 = 5b - 12$ $\quad b = 0$

C

25. $-0.6x - 0.15 = 0.15$ $\quad x = -0.5$

26. $-1.05y + 5.08 = 1.72$ $\quad y = 3.2$

27. $0.03x + 2.3 = 1.55$ $\quad x = -25$

28. $0.02x - 2.4 = 1.22$ $\quad x = 181$

29. $-135x - 674 = 1486$ $\quad x = -16$

30. $94y + 307 = -257$ $\quad y = -6$

31. $-102y + 6 = 414$ $\quad y = -4$

32. $-63c + 22 = 400$ $\quad c = -6$

© 1995 Saunders College Publishing.

19. $(-7)(3 - 11)(-2) - 4(-3 - 5)$ −80 [8.6]

20. $\left(-\dfrac{1}{3}\right)\left(\dfrac{6}{7}\right)$ $-\dfrac{2}{7}$ [8.4]

21. $-26 + (-27)$ −53 [8.2]

22. $5(-8) + 44$ 4 [8.6]

23. $-13 = 4x + 7$ $x = -5$ [8.7]

24. The temperature in Chicago ranges from a high of 12°F to a low of −9°F within a 24-hour period. What is the drop in temperature, expressed as a signed number?   −21°F [8.3]

25. A stock on the New York Stock Exchange opens at $6\dfrac{5}{8}$ on Monday. It records the following changes during the week: Monday, $+\dfrac{1}{8}$; Tuesday, $-\dfrac{3}{8}$; Wednesday, $+1\dfrac{1}{4}$; Thursday, $-\dfrac{7}{8}$; Friday, $+\dfrac{1}{4}$. What is its closing price on Friday?   7 [8.2]

26. What Fahrenheit temperature is equal to a reading of −10°C? Use the formula

$$F = \dfrac{9}{5}C + 32$$

14°F [8.6]

Answers to Selected Exercises

Chapter 1

Exercises 1.1

1. ten   **3.** hundred   **5.** thousand   **7.** six hundred twenty-one
9. six thousand, twenty-one   **11.** 3200   **13.** 521   **15.** 2006
17. hundred   **19.** hundred thousand   **21.** ten thousand
23. thirty-four thousand, nine hundred ten
25. three thousand, four hundred ninety-one
27. one million, two hundred thirty-five thousand, nine hundred
fifty-six   **29.** 7   **31.** 7   **33.** 351,006   **35.** 230,429   **37.** 6597
39. ten million   **41.** million   **43.** hundred million   **45.** six
hundred three million, six hundred thirty thousand, sixty-three
47. forty million, forty thousand, four hundred
49. four million, five hundred eighty-nine thousand, three
hundred twenty-four   **51.** 4   **53.** 9   **55.** 561,072,001
57. 15,025,200,002   **59.** 7   **61.** twenty-six thousand, nine
hundred ninety-five   **63.** $92,000   **65.** one hundred fifty-four
thousand, three hundred twenty   **67.** $10,634,750
71. hundred billion   **73.** fifty trillion, fifty billion, fifty
million, fifty thousand

Exercises 1.2

1. $900 + 0 + 1$ **3.** $5000 + 0 + 0 + 7$ **5.** $300 + 20 + 1$
7. 951   **9.** 45,389   **11.** True   **13.** True   **15.** False   **17.** 510
19. 2750   **21.** 600   **23.** $70,000 + 0 + 0 + 0 + 3$
25. $70,000 + 0 + 300 + 0 + 7$
27. $500,000 + 0 + 2000 + 0 + 60 + 5$ **29.** 84,328
31. 45,325   **33.** 54,365   **35.** False   **37.** True   **39.** 240,000
41. 236,890   **43.** 457,200   **45.** 457,250
47. $500,000 + 40,000 + 2000 + 600 + 90 + 9$
49. $2,000,000 + 0 + 30,000 + 4000 + 600 + 50 + 4$
51. 605,241   **53.** 5,342,528   **55.** 7,050,040   **57.** False
59. False   **61.** 456,784,000   **63.** 57,400,000   **65.** 82,579,000
67. $3,600,000   **69.** $4,689,000   **71.** $451,000,000
75. 1145, 1229, 1234, 1243, 1324, 1342, 1423   **77.** Same

Exercises 1.3

1. 48   **3.** 99   **5.** 50   **7.** 92   **9.** 75   **11.** 786   **13.** 502
15. 908   **17.** 91   **19.** 1157   **21.** 151   **23.** 154   **25.** 633
27. 168   **29.** 1761   **31.** 11,819   **33.** 19,000; 19,918
35. 160,000; 159,588   **37.** 201   **39.** 1915   **41.** 3561
43. 4236   **45.** 5320   **47.** 90,000; 95,780   **49.** 60,000; 75,299
51. 3000; 3047   **53.** 30,000; 29,121   **55.** 40,000; 40,883
57. 3589 salmon   **59.** 268,181   **61.** $1043   **63.** 1750 seagulls
65. 2809 miles, no   **69.** seven hundred thousand, nine hundred
71. $165,991

Exercises 1.4

1. 11   **3.** 24   **5.** 12   **7.** 11   **9.** 34   **11.** 38   **13.** 16   **15.** 24
17. 26   **19.** 39   **21.** 302   **23.** 119   **25.** 281   **27.** 389
29. 396   **31.** 500; 469   **33.** 300; 275   **35.** 0; 37

37. 100; 72   **39.** 200; 211   **41.** 163   **43.** 441   **45.** 766
47. 0; 714   **49.** 3000; 2825   **51.** 20,000; 15,163
53. 20,000; 24,268   **55.** 5000; 4378   **57.** 10,000; 17,088
59. 0; 28,233   **61.** 87,762 seats   **63.** 194 lb   **65.** $417,240
67. $22,022   **69.** 407,300 cases   **73.** Two hundred sixty
million, two hundred fifty-nine thousand, nine hundred
sixty-three   **75.** $7,815

Getting Ready for Algebra, p. 37

1. $x = 9$ **3.** $x = 11$ **5.** $z = 7$ **7.** $c = 29$ **9.** $a = 183$
11. $x = 34$ **13.** $y = 47$ **15.** $k = 246$ **17.** $37 = x$
19. $130 = w$ **21.** $393   **23.** 9 meters

Exercises 1.5

1. 124   **3.** 88   **5.** 108   **7.** 441   **9.** 288   **11.** 405   **13.** 0
15. 2100   **17.** 2800   **19.** 936   **21.** 0   **23.** 1856   **25.** 4236
27. 32,400   **29.** 1058   **31.** 8000; 6048   **33.** 56,000; 58,800
35. 20,000; 21,760   **37.** 120,000; 123,600
39. 49,000; 47,101   **41.** 19,278   **43.** 76,038   **45.** 158,270
47. 335,469   **49.** 259,578   **51.** 1,600,000; 1,658,932
53. 700,000; 1,033,112   **55.** 2,500,000; 2,518,521
57. 40,000; 38,880   **59.** 28,000; 34,580   **61.** 4230 dozen
63. 2278 salmon   **65.** 30,375 bacteria   **67.** 9,934,000 gallons
69. $35,100   **73.** Five billion, one hundred thirty million,
three hundred fifty-four thousand, one hundred eighty
75. $23,439,000

Exercises 1.6

1. 12   **3.** 4   **5.** 1   **7.** 71   **9.** 61   **11.** 200   **13.** 2 R 5
15. 3 R 7   **17.** 15   **19.** 30   **21.** 112   **23.** 428   **25.** 3052
27. 206   **29.** 39 R 18   **31.** 58   **33.** 39   **35.** 20; 15 R 30
37. 2000; 2377 R 35   **39.** 3000; 2686 R 15   **41.** 40; 44 R 35
43. 800; 809   **45.** 51   **47.** 125   **49.** 96   **51.** 600; 578 R 68
53. 500; 533 R 153   **55.** 2000; 1790 R 414   **57.** 300; 309
59. 500; 538   **61.** 24,623 packages   **63.** 128 trees
65. $69,575   **67.** 2305 radios; 8 resistors   **69.** 520 hours
73. $45

Getting Ready for Algebra, p. 69

1. $x = 5$ **3.** $c = 18$ **5.** $x = 4$ **7.** $b = 120$ **9.** $x = 12$
11. $y = 312$ **13.** $x = 24$ **15.** $b = 45,414$ **17.** $5 = x$
19. $1278 = w$ **21.** 17 ft   **23.** 2340 lb

Exercises 1.7

1. 18   **3.** 81   **5.** 1   **7.** 1   **9.** 4500   **11.** 70,000   **13.** 12
15. 34   **17.** 64   **19.** 216   **21.** 361   **23.** 1   **25.** 4,350,000
27. 3500   **29.** 35,910,000   **31.** 302   **33.** 6561   **35.** 1024
37. 28,561   **39.** 59,049   **41.** 70,500,000,000   **43.** 9700
45. 348,750   **47.** 976,050   **49.** 12,167   **51.** 38,416
53. 19,487,171   **55.** 387,420,489   **57.** $73,000,000

59. 11,000,000 shares   **61.** 32,768 bacteria
65. $531,441; $797,160   **67.** 9736

Exercises 1.8

1. 53   **3.** 0   **5.** 27   **7.** 15   **9.** 25   **11.** 16   **13.** 0   **15.** 12
17. 39   **19.** 145   **21.** 43   **23.** 31   **25.** 7   **27.** 35   **29.** 217
31. 24   **33.** 28   **35.** 124   **37.** 1   **39.** 45   **41.** 18   **43.** 436
45. 595   **47.** 165   **49.** 1185 cans   **51.** $28,776   **53.** $75
55. $968   **59.** $7 + 3 - 5$; $(7 + 3)^2$; $(7 + 3) \cdot 2$; $(7 + 3) - 2$
61. $154

Getting Ready for Algebra, p. 87

1. $x = 5$ **3.** $y = 24$ **5.** $x = 4$ **7.** $c = 88$ **9.** $x = 6$
11. $c = 12$ **13.** $a = 800$ **15.** $b = 22$ **17.** 7 tickets
19. 6 arrangements

Exercises 1.9

1. 5   **3.** 9   **5.** 7   **7.** 13   **9.** 13   **11.** 9   **13.** 6   **15.** 4
17. 20   **19.** 12   **21.** 28   **23.** 26   **25.** 40   **27.** 18   **29.** 30
31. 36   **33.** 61   **35.** 169   **37.** 110   **39.** 497   **41.** 456
43. 729   **45.** 2104   **47.** 27,458   **49.** 4025 calories   **51.** 86
53. 30 mpg   **55.** 188 lb   **59.** $1200   **61.** 71

Chapter 1 Concept Review

1. False; to write a billion takes 10 digits. [1.1]
2. True [1.1-1]   **3.** True [1.1-4]
4. False; five is less than eighteen. [1.2-3]
5. False; 1345 > 1344 [1.2-3]   **6.** True [1.2-4]
7. True [1.2-4]   **8.** True [1.2-1]
9. False; the sum is 64. [1.3-1]   **10.** True [1.3-1]
11. False; the product is 28. [1.5-1]   **12.** True [1.3-1]
13. True [1.6-1]   **14.** True [1.5-1]
15. False; a number multiplied by 0 is 0. [1.5-1]
16. True [1.6-1]   **17.** False; the quotient is 23. [1.6-1]
18. True [1.6-1]   **19.** True [1.6-1]
20. False; division by zero is undefined. [1.6-1]
21. False; the value is 64. [1.7-1]   **22.** True [1.7-1]
23. True [1.7-2]   **24.** False; the product is 34,000. [1.7-2]
25. True [1.7-2]
26. False; in $(2 + 3)^2$ the addition is done first. [1.8]
27. False; in $(9 - 4) \cdot 5$ subtraction is done first. [1.8]
28. True [1.8]   **29.** True [1.9]   **30.** True [1.9]

Chapter 1 Test

1. 7089 [1.3-1]   **2.** 693,860,000 [1.2-4]   **3.** 17,760 [1.5-1]
4. 1583 [1.9]   **5.** 79 [1.6-1]   **6.** 306 [1.6-1]
7. Four thousand, two hundred five [1.1-4]   **8.** 5600 [1.2-4]
9. 309,963 [1.1-3]
10. One hundred twenty thousand, three hundred fifty-
five [1.1-4]
11. 1300 [1.7-2]   **12.** 43,681 [1.2-2]   **13.** 3527 [1.3-1]
14. 353 R 69 [1.6-1]   **15.** 5230 [1.4-1]   **16.** 256 [1.7-1]
17. 5748 [1.3-1]   **18.** 900 + 30 + 7 [1.2-1]
19. 486,048 [1.5-1]   **20.** 3,006,000 [1.7-2]   **21.** 209 [1.6-1]
22. 16,988 [1.4-1]   **23.** 907 [1.9]   **24.** 20 [1.8]
25. False [1.2-3]   **26.** thousand [1.1-1]   **27.** 89 R 19 [1.6-1]

28. 3373 [1.8]   **29.** 76,000 lb [1.2-4, 1.5-1]
30. $161,440 [1.8]

Chapter 2

Exercises 2.1

1. Yes   **3.** Yes   **5.** Yes   **7.** No   **9.** Yes   **11.** Yes   **13.** Yes
15. No   **17.** Yes   **19.** No   **21.** Yes   **23.** No   **25.** Yes
27. Yes   **29.** Yes   **31.** No   **33.** 2, 3   **35.** 3   **37.** 2, 3, 5
39. 6, 9   **41.** 6, 9, 10   **43.** None   **45.** 2, 3, 5, 6, 9, 10
47. None   **49.** 2, 3, 5, 6, 10   **51.** 2, 5, 10   **53.** 2, 3, 5, 6, 10
55. 3, 9   **57.** 2, 3, 6   **59.** None
61. Yes, 354 is divisible by 3.
63. Yes, 1980 is divisible by 5.
65. 2-lb, 3-lb, 5-lb, 6-lb, and 10-lb since 4560 is divisible by
2, 3, 5, 6, and 10.   **67.** No, 80 is not divisible by 3.
73. Yes; divisible by 3 and 5
75.   **a.** No; the ones-place digit is *not* even.
b. Yes; the sum of the digits is divisible by 3.
c. Yes; the ones-place digit is 5.
d. No; the number is not divisible by 2 and 3.
e. No; the sum of the digits is not divisible by 9.
f. No; the ones-place digit is not 0.   **79.** 87,760
81. 230,000,000   **83.** 37   **85.** 468   **87.** 338 cans

Exercises 2.2

1. 3, 6, 9, 12, 15   **3.** 17, 34, 51, 68, 85
5. 12, 24, 36, 48, 60   **7.** Yes   **9.** Yes   **11.** No   **13.** No
15. No   **17.** No   **19.** 26, 52, 78, 104, 130
21. 41, 82, 123, 164, 205   **23.** 35, 70, 105, 140, 175
25. 40, 80, 120, 160, 200   **27.** Yes   **29.** No   **31.** Yes
33. Yes   **35.** No   **37.** Yes   **39.** 48, 96, 144, 192, 240
41. 44, 88, 132, 176, 220   **43.** 120, 240, 360, 480, 600
45. Multiple of 6 and 9   **47.** Multiple of 6, 9, and 15
49. Multiple of 9 and 15   **51.** No
53. 5, 10, 15, 20, 25, 30, 35, 40, 45, 50, 55, 60, 65, 70, 75
55. Yes   **57.** 810, 825, 840, 855, 870, 885, 900, 915, 930,
945, 960, 975, 990   **59.** 30 boxes
63. Yes   **69.** 43,904
71. 11,128   **73.** 6,336
75. 29,106   **77.** 13 days; 30 cans remain

Exercises 2.3

1. 1, 2, 4, 8, 16   **3.** 1, 23   **5.** 1, 2, 3, 4, 6, 9, 12, 18, 36
7. 1, 2, 4, 7, 14, 28   **9.** 1, 5, 13, 65   **11.** $1 \cdot 18$; $2 \cdot 9$; $3 \cdot 6$
13. $1 \cdot 24$; $2 \cdot 12$; $3 \cdot 8$; $4 \cdot 6$ **15.** $1 \cdot 31$
17. $1 \cdot 50$; $2 \cdot 25$; $5 \cdot 10$ **19.** $1 \cdot 37$
21. 1, 2, 3, 4, 6, 8, 9, 12, 18, 24, 36, 72
23. 1, 2, 4, 23, 46, 92   **25.** 1, 2, 3, 6, 17, 34, 51, 102
27. 1, 2, 61, 122   **29.** 1, 2, 71, 142   **31.** $1 \cdot 98$; $2 \cdot 49$; $7 \cdot 14$
33. $1 \cdot 104$; $2 \cdot 52$, $4 \cdot 26$; $8 \cdot 13$
35. $1 \cdot 105$; $3 \cdot 35$; $5 \cdot 21$; $7 \cdot 15$ **37.** $1 \cdot 212$; $2 \cdot 106$; $4 \cdot 53$
39. $1 \cdot 333$; $3 \cdot 111$; $9 \cdot 37$ **41.** 1, 3, 5, 15, 23, 69, 115, 345
43. 1, 2, 3, 4, 5, 6, 8, 10, 12, 15, 20, 24, 25, 30, 40, 50, 60,
75, 100, 120, 150, 200, 300, 600
45. 1, 2, 4, 5, 10, 20, 23, 46, 92, 115, 230, 460
47. $1 \cdot 345$; $3 \cdot 115$; $5 \cdot 69$; $15 \cdot 23$

49. $1 \cdot 620$; $2 \cdot 310$; $4 \cdot 155$; $5 \cdot 124$; $10 \cdot 62$; $20 \cdot 31$
51. $1 \cdot 550$; $2 \cdot 275$; $5 \cdot 110$; $10 \cdot 55$; $11 \cdot 50$; $22 \cdot 25$

53.

Number of Programs	Length of Each
1	120 min
2	60 min
3	40 min
4	30 min
5	24 min
6	20 min
8	15 min
10	12 min
12	10 min
15	8 min
20	6 min
24	5 min
30	4 min
40	3 min
60	2 min
120	1 min

55.

Number of Programs	Length of Each
1	56 min
2	28 min
4	14 min
7	8 min
8	7 min
14	4 min
28	2 min
56	1 min

57. 1 person, $1230; 2 people, $615; 3 people, $410; 5 people, $246; 6 people, $205; 10 people, $123   **61.** 269   **63.** 257
65. 2499   **67.** 38,016   **69.** 31   **71.** 24 R 40
73. 41 speakers; 16 ft left

Exercises 2.4

1. Composite   **3.** Prime   **5.** Composite   **7.** Prime
9. Composite   **11.** Prime   **13.** Composite   **15.** Prime
17. Composite   **19.** Prime   **21.** Composite   **23.** Composite
25. Prime   **27.** Composite   **29.** Prime   **31.** Composite
33. Prime   **35.** Composite   **37.** Composite   **39.** Composite
41. Composite   **43.** Composite   **45.** Composite   **47.** Prime
49. Prime   **51.** Composite   **53.** Composite   **55.** Composite
57. Composite   **59.** 1997   **61.** 1979   **63.** No; composite
65. Answers will vary.   **67.** Answers will vary.
71. Composite   **73.** Yes; $13 \cdot 17 \cdot 19$ **77.** False   **79.** 15,625
81. 750   **83.** 153   **85.** 38

Exercises 2.5

1. $2^2 \cdot 3$ **3.** 2^4 **5.** $2^2 \cdot 5$ **7.** $2^3 \cdot 3$ **9.** $2^2 \cdot 7$ **11.** 2^5
13. $2^4 \cdot 3$ **15.** $2^3 \cdot 3^2$ **17.** 3^4 **19.** $2 \cdot 3^2 \cdot 5$ **21.** $7 \cdot 13$
23. 2^6 **25.** $2 \cdot 3 \cdot 17$ **27.** $2^2 \cdot 3 \cdot 11$ **29.** $3^2 \cdot 17$

31. $2^2 \cdot 3^2 \cdot 5$ **33.** $2 \cdot 7 \cdot 13$ **35.** $3^2 \cdot 5^2$ **37.** $2 \cdot 3^2 \cdot 17$
39. $2^2 \cdot 3^2 \cdot 11$ **41.** $3 \cdot 101$ **43.** $17 \cdot 19$ **45.** $11 \cdot 29$
47. $7 \cdot 43$ **49.** Prime   **51.** 23^2 **53.** $5^2 \cdot 29$
55. $2^2 \cdot 11 \cdot 19$ **57.** $2^4 \cdot 3 \cdot 19$ **59.** $2 \cdot 3 \cdot 7 \cdot 31$
61. Answers will vary.   **63.** Answers will vary.
67. $2 \cdot 3 \cdot 7 \cdot 71$ **71.** 23, 46, 69, 92, 115, 138, 161
73. Yes   **75.** Yes   **77.** Yes
79. 585, 598, 611, 624, 637, 650, 663, 676

Exercises 2.6

1. 8   **3.** 10   **5.** 10   **7.** 14   **9.** 12   **11.** 24   **13.** 12   **15.** 18
17. 24   **19.** 30   **21.** 30   **23.** 48   **25.** 40   **27.** 48   **29.** 72
31. 120   **33.** 48   **35.** 24   **37.** 200   **39.** 72   **41.** 224
43. 504   **45.** 1,092   **47.** 480   **49.** 750   **51.** 630   **53.** 204
55. 342   **57.** 1,400   **59.** 24   **61.** 240   **63.** 224   **65.** 144
67. Answers will vary.   **69.** $100   **73.** 768   **75.** 18,000
77. 1, 3, 5, 15, 25, 75, 125, 375
79. 1, 2, 4, 8, 61, 122, 244, 488   **81.** Yes   **83.** Yes
85. At least 9

Chapter 2 Concept Review

1. False. Not all multiples of 6 end with the digit 6. For example 12 is a multiple of 6. [2.1-2]   **2.** True [2.1-2]
3. True [2.2-2]   **4.** True [2.2-2]   **5.** True [2.2-2]
6. True [2.2-2]   **7.** False. Only one multiple of 200 is also a factor of 200 — itself. [2.1-1]   **8.** False. The square of 200 is 40,000. One half of 200 is 100. [2.4]   **9.** False. Not all natural numbers ending in 4 are divisible by 4; for example, 54 is not divisible by 4. [2.1-1]   **10.** True [2.2-2]   **11.** False. Not all natural numbers ending in 9 are divisible by 3. For example 19 is not divisible by 3. [2.1-1]   **12.** True [2.1-1]   **13.** False. The number 123,321,234 is *not* divisible by 4. It is divisible by 2, 3, and 6. [2.1-1]   **14.** True [2.1-1]   **15.** False. Two is the only prime number that is not odd. [2.4]   **16.** False. Not all composite numbers end in 1, 3, 7, or 9. All even numbers larger than 2 are composite as are all numbers larger than five that end in 5. [2.4]   **17.** False. Every composite number has three or more factors. [2.4]   **18.** False. Every prime number has exactly two factors. [2.4]   **19.** True [2.4]   **20.** False. All of the prime factors of a composite number are smaller than the number. [2.4]   **21.** True [2.6]   **22.** True [2.5]   **23.** False. The largest divisor of the least common multiple (LCM) of three numbers is not necessarily one of the three numbers. For example the LCM of 4, 6, and 8 is 24. [2.6]   **24.** False. It is not possible for a group of numbers to have two LCM's. [2.6]
25. True [2.6]

Chapter 2 Test

1. Yes [2.2-2]   **2.** 1, 2, 5, 10, 22, 55, 110 [2.3-2]
3. Yes [2.3-2]   **4.** Yes [2.1-1]   **5.** 160 [2.6]
6. $1 \cdot 75$, $3 \cdot 25$, $5 \cdot 15$ [2.3-1]   **7.** $2^2 \cdot 5 \cdot 13$ [2.5]
8. 252 [2.6]   **9.** $2 \cdot 3^2 \cdot 47$ [2.5]
10. 104, 117, 130, 143 [2.2-1]   **11.** No [2.2-2]
12. Prime [2.4]   **13.** Composite [2.4]   **14.** $7 \cdot 11^2$ [2.5]
15. 504 [2.6]

Chapter 3

Exercises 3.1

1. Proper fractions: $\frac{3}{7}, \frac{4}{7}, \frac{5}{7}, \frac{6}{7}$; Improper fractions: $\frac{7}{7}, \frac{8}{7}, \frac{9}{7}$

3. Proper fractions: $\frac{7}{13}, \frac{8}{15}, \frac{10}{13}, \frac{11}{15}, \frac{12}{23}$; Improper fractions: none **5.** Proper fractions: $\frac{10}{11}, \frac{3}{5}$; Improper fractions: $\frac{7}{4}, \frac{13}{13}, \frac{20}{19}$ **7.** $\frac{5}{8}$ **9.** $\frac{4}{7}$ **11.** $\frac{4}{5}$ **13.** $4\frac{3}{4}$

15. $5\frac{1}{2}$ **17.** $5\frac{1}{4}$ **19.** $\frac{39}{7}$ **21.** $\frac{12}{1}$ **23.** $\frac{31}{4}$ **25.** Proper fractions: $\frac{9}{10}, \frac{102}{103}$; Improper fractions: $\frac{5}{5}, \frac{18}{18}, \frac{147}{147}$ **27.** $\frac{5}{3}$

29. $\frac{14}{10}$ **31.** $\frac{4}{10}$ **33.** $42\frac{3}{5}$ **35.** $26\frac{5}{8}$ **37.** $12\frac{4}{9}$ **39.** $\frac{89}{3}$

41. $\frac{77}{6}$ **43.** $\frac{155}{8}$ **45.** $\frac{7}{10}$ **47.** $\frac{11}{8}$ **49.** $\frac{7}{7}, \frac{77}{77}$

51. **53.** $7\frac{7}{13}$

55. $14\frac{21}{22}$ **57.** $22\frac{13}{17}$ **59.** $\frac{547}{11}$ **61.** $\frac{923}{9}$ **63.** $\frac{5364}{101}$

65. $\frac{13}{21}$ **67.** $\frac{45}{68}$ **69.** 150 pounds **71.** $2722\frac{17}{24}$ cases

73. 2130 barriers **77.** $\frac{10}{34}$ are pennies; $\frac{70}{405}$ of the value

79. $2263\frac{2}{30}$ boxes; $90\frac{13}{25}$ cartons; $4050 **83.** 9070

85. 65,536 **87.** 4600 **89.** 935 miles **91.** 8125 revolutions per minute

Exercises 3.2

1. $\frac{1}{2}$ **3.** $\frac{2}{3}$ **5.** $\frac{2}{5}$ **7.** $\frac{3}{5}$ **9.** $\frac{3}{4}$ **11.** $\frac{3}{5}$ **13.** $\frac{4}{5}$ **15.** $\frac{5}{3}$

17. $\frac{7}{9}$ **19.** $\frac{3}{5}$ **21.** 4 **23.** $\frac{7}{3}$ **25.** $\frac{1}{3}$ **27.** $\frac{1}{3}$ **29.** $\frac{3}{4}$

31. $\frac{29}{36}$ **33.** $\frac{2}{3}$ **35.** $\frac{11}{15}$ **37.** $\frac{3}{4}$ **39.** $\frac{9}{16}$ **41.** $\frac{3}{4}$ **43.** 6

45. $\frac{3}{5}$ **47.** $\frac{16}{21}$ **49.** $\frac{3}{4}$ **51.** $\frac{5}{6}$ **53.** $\frac{53}{36}$ **55.** $\frac{16}{45}$ **57.** $\frac{14}{15}$

59. $\frac{54}{85}$ **61.** $\frac{106}{165}$ **63.** $\frac{3}{5}$ **65.** $\frac{2}{11}$ **67.** $\frac{2}{3}$ **69.** $\frac{1}{3}$

71. $\frac{11}{216}$ **73.** $\frac{7}{10}$ **75.** $\frac{23}{79}$ **79.** No **81.** 1906 **83.** 2212

85. 2883 **87.** $2 \cdot 2 \cdot 2 \cdot 2 \cdot 2 \cdot 2 \cdot 5$ or $2^6 \cdot 5$ **89.** 1500 bricks

Exercises 3.3

1. $\frac{2}{25}$ **3.** $\frac{18}{55}$ **5.** $\frac{7}{8}$ **7.** $\frac{1}{6}$ **9.** $\frac{1}{6}$ **11.** $\frac{1}{2}$ **13.** 5 **15.** $\frac{8}{3}$

17. $\frac{1}{5}$ **19.** $\frac{2}{9}$ **21.** $\frac{27}{28}$ **23.** $\frac{3}{8}$ **25.** $\frac{1}{3}$ **27.** $\frac{2}{3}$ **29.** 1

31. $\frac{1}{3}$ **33.** $\frac{2}{3}$ **35.** 1 **37.** $\frac{5}{9}$ **39.** $\frac{8}{9}$ **41.** $\frac{3}{10}$ **43.** $\frac{11}{40}$

45. $\frac{14}{17}$ **47.** $\frac{64}{15}$ **49.** $\frac{3}{4}$ **51.** $\frac{21}{50}$ **53.** $\frac{10}{11}$ **55.** $\frac{1}{4}$

57. $\frac{200}{147}$ **59.** 1 **61.** $\frac{8}{45}$ **63.** $\frac{3}{16}$ **65.** $\frac{1}{2}$ **67.** $\frac{4}{27}$

69. $\frac{1}{15}$ **71.** $\frac{27}{4}$ **73.** $\frac{2}{33}$ **75.** $\frac{5}{21}$ **77.** 3 **79.** $\frac{28}{25}$

81. $\frac{21}{20}$ gal or $1\frac{1}{20}$ gal **83.** 16 pins **85.** $64 **87.** 10 gerbils

89. 150 in. **91.** $\frac{24}{5}$ min or $4\frac{4}{5}$ min **93.** 41 gal **97.** $\frac{2}{99}$

99. 120 **101.** 238,000 **103.** $6\frac{1}{13}$ **105.** No

107. $\frac{5}{9}$ of the class

Exercises 3.4

1. $1\frac{5}{16}$ **3.** 12 **5.** 8 **7.** $22\frac{1}{2}$ **9.** 24 **11.** $3\frac{1}{3}$ **13.** 2

15. $\frac{3}{4}$ **17.** $2\frac{1}{12}$ **19.** $\frac{13}{18}$ **21.** $1\frac{1}{3}$ **23.** $\frac{2}{3}$ **25.** $18\frac{1}{3}$

27. $1\frac{2}{3}$ **29.** $3\frac{1}{16}$ **31.** 0 **33.** 75 **35.** $18\frac{3}{4}$ **37.** $2\frac{2}{3}$

39. $\frac{1}{6}$ **41.** $\frac{7}{30}$ **43.** $\frac{2}{3}$ **45.** $18\frac{1}{3}$ **47.** $8\frac{1}{28}$ **49.** $35\frac{1}{5}$

51. 105 **53.** $69\frac{1}{2}$ **55.** 186 **57.** $14\frac{2}{5}$ **59.** $28\frac{1}{5}$ **61.** $4\frac{2}{3}$

63. 3 **65.** $5\frac{5}{6}$ **67.** $1\frac{5}{49}$ **69.** 77 in.

71. 22 parts per million **73.** 192 glasses **75.** 39 lb per in.^{2}

77. $13\frac{31}{37}$ pieces **79.** 3000 lb **81.** $98\frac{13}{16}$ in.^{2} **85.** $\frac{281}{650}$

89. 15,153 **91.** 41,580 **93.** 360 **95.** $36\frac{13}{15}$ **97.** No

Getting Ready for Algebra, p. 207

1. $x = \frac{3}{4}$ **3.** $y = \frac{16}{15}$ or $y = 1\frac{1}{15}$ **5.** $z = \frac{15}{16}$

7. $\frac{17}{8} = x$ or $2\frac{1}{8} = x$ **9.** $a = \frac{10}{7}$ or $a = 1\frac{3}{7}$

11. $\frac{3}{2} = b$ or $1\frac{1}{2} = b$ **13.** $z = 2$ **15.** $a = \frac{165}{8}$ or $a = 20\frac{5}{8}$

17. $\frac{3}{2}$ mi or $1\frac{1}{2}$ mi **19.** 180 lb

Exercises 3.5

1. $\frac{4}{6}, \frac{6}{9}, \frac{8}{12}, \frac{10}{15}$ **3.** $\frac{14}{16}, \frac{21}{24}, \frac{28}{32}, \frac{35}{40}$ **5.** $\frac{6}{8}, \frac{9}{12}, \frac{12}{16}, \frac{15}{20}$

7. 5 **9.** 10 **11.** 16 **13.** $\frac{7}{9}$ **15.** $\frac{1}{3}$ **17.** $\frac{4}{6}$ **19.** $\frac{3}{7}, \frac{4}{7}, \frac{5}{7}$

21. $\frac{1}{4}, \frac{3}{8}, \frac{1}{2}$ **23.** $\frac{1}{3}, \frac{3}{8}, \frac{1}{2}$ **25.** True **27.** False

29. $\frac{8}{20}, \frac{12}{30}, \frac{16}{40}, \frac{20}{50}$ **31.** $\frac{14}{6}, \frac{21}{9}, \frac{28}{12}, \frac{35}{15}$ **33.** 27

35. 15 **37.** 60 **39.** $\frac{13}{10}$ **41.** $2\frac{3}{8}$ **43.** $\frac{5}{11}$ **45.** $\frac{2}{3}, \frac{3}{4}, \frac{4}{5}$

47. $\frac{4}{5}, \frac{5}{6}, \frac{13}{15}, \frac{9}{10}$ **49.** $2\frac{3}{4}, 2\frac{5}{6}, 2\frac{7}{8}$ **51.** False

53. False **55.** 8 **57.** 46 **59.** 140 **61.** 57 **63.** 120

65. LCM = 24; $\frac{12}{24}, \frac{16}{24}, \frac{4}{24}, \frac{15}{24}$ **67.** $\frac{11}{24}, \frac{17}{36}, \frac{35}{72}$

69. $\frac{6}{14}, \frac{13}{28}, \frac{17}{35}$ **71.** $\frac{11}{30}, \frac{17}{45}, \frac{7}{18}, \frac{2}{5}$

73. $\frac{11}{12}, \frac{14}{15}, \frac{19}{20}, \frac{29}{30}$

75. False **77.** False **79.** True **81.** 32 problems

83. $\frac{3}{32}, \frac{1}{8}, \frac{1}{4}, \frac{5}{16}, \frac{3}{8}, \frac{1}{2}, \frac{9}{16}$

85. Largest, $\frac{3}{4}$ ton; smallest, $\frac{7}{16}$ ton **87.** $5\frac{6}{8}$ in.

89. 90 ounces **93.** $\frac{43}{98}, \frac{12}{25}, \frac{39}{81}, \frac{14}{29}, \frac{29}{60}, \frac{35}{71}$

95. Filipe; Fernando **97.** 13,544

99. 1, 2, 3, 4, 6, 12, 83, 166, 249, 332, 498, 996 **101.** 1575

103. $\frac{221}{8}$ **105.** $3230

Exercises 3.6

1. $\frac{9}{11}$ **3.** $\frac{2}{3}$ **5.** 2 **7.** $\frac{4}{5}$ **9.** $\frac{10}{13}$ **11.** $1\frac{1}{4}$ **13.** $\frac{13}{24}$

15. $\frac{5}{12}$ **17.** $\frac{15}{16}$ **19.** $\frac{19}{30}$ **21.** $\frac{7}{10}$ **23.** $\frac{1}{2}$ **25.** $\frac{5}{16}$ **27.** $\frac{3}{5}$

29. $\frac{7}{8}$ **31.** $\frac{7}{15}$ **33.** $1\frac{7}{60}$ **35.** $1\frac{2}{5}$ **37.** $1\frac{5}{16}$ **39.** $2\frac{5}{8}$

41. $1\frac{77}{144}$ **43.** $2\frac{19}{90}$ **45.** $\frac{3}{5}$ **47.** $\frac{7}{15}$ **49.** $\frac{4}{5}$ **51.** $1\frac{11}{40}$

53. $\frac{281}{432}$ **55.** $\frac{37}{48}$ **57.** $\frac{14}{225}$ **59.** $\frac{87}{100}$ **61.** $1\frac{13}{144}$ **63.** $1\frac{19}{34}$

65. $\frac{57}{80}$ **67.** $1\frac{29}{100}$ **69.** $4\frac{1}{8}$ points **71.** $3\frac{3}{4}$ gallons

73. $1\frac{1}{2}$ in. **75.** $\frac{5}{16}$ point **77.** $\frac{3}{4}$ in. **79.** $\frac{89}{120}$ of income

81. $\frac{31}{45}$ share **85.** Contreras family **89.** 1680 **91.** 1100

93. 78 **95.** 40 **97.** $418\frac{1}{2}$ in. of wire

Exercises 3.7

1. $3\frac{6}{7}$ **3.** $14\frac{2}{5}$ **5.** $8\frac{1}{6}$ **7.** $6\frac{2}{9}$ **9.** $6\frac{5}{14}$ **11.** $15\frac{13}{15}$

13. $15\frac{1}{16}$ **15.** 11 **17.** $26\frac{5}{8}$ **19.** $13\frac{5}{24}$ **21.** $10\frac{1}{6}$

23. $25\frac{43}{80}$ **25.** $49\frac{5}{6}$ **27.** $719\frac{31}{36}$ **29.** $86\frac{11}{30}$ **31.** $60\frac{7}{12}$

33. $118\frac{1}{45}$ **35.** $103\frac{11}{70}$ **37.** $62\frac{3}{20}$ **39.** $12\frac{14}{15}$ **41.** $37\frac{31}{54}$

43. $146\frac{101}{135}$ **45.** $106\frac{5}{72}$ **47.** $87\frac{3}{5}$ **49.** $141\frac{13}{36}$ **51.** $94\frac{7}{72}$

53. $33\frac{47}{72}$ **55.** $139\frac{13}{70}$ **57.** $76\frac{3}{4}$ hr **59.** $2\frac{1}{8}$ in. **61.** 44 ft

63. $61\frac{27}{80}$ mi; $920,000 **67.** No **69.** $39\frac{3}{20}$ in.; yes **71.** $\frac{1}{3}$

73. $\frac{8}{45}$ **75.** $3 \cdot 37$ **77.** $\frac{10}{21}$ **79.** 35; under par

Exercises 3.8

1. $\frac{1}{4}$ **3.** $\frac{1}{4}$ **5.** $\frac{1}{3}$ **7.** $\frac{1}{2}$ **9.** $\frac{7}{16}$ **11.** $\frac{7}{45}$ **13.** $\frac{1}{2}$ **15.** $\frac{5}{18}$

17. $\frac{13}{20}$ **19.** $\frac{9}{20}$ **21.** $\frac{1}{24}$ **23.** $\frac{17}{48}$ **25.** $\frac{4}{21}$ **27.** $\frac{19}{48}$

29. $\frac{1}{18}$ **31.** $\frac{13}{24}$ **33.** $\frac{9}{20}$ **35.** $\frac{5}{36}$ **37.** $\frac{19}{75}$ **39.** $\frac{17}{48}$

41. $\frac{1}{36}$ **43.** $\frac{3}{200}$ **45.** $\frac{7}{30}$ **47.** $\frac{1}{72}$ **49.** $\frac{23}{72}$ **51.** $\frac{19}{108}$

53. $\frac{119}{225}$ **55.** $\frac{4}{63}$ **57.** $\frac{23}{48}$ **59.** $\frac{25}{288}$ **61.** $1\frac{1}{8}$ in.

63. $\frac{5}{12}$ oz

65. Lake Tuscumba, one part per million $\left(\frac{1}{1,000,000}\right)$

67. John, $\frac{1}{24}$ in. **69.** $\frac{3}{16}$ in. **73.** $\frac{835}{4816}$

75. Yes, $\frac{1}{120}$ mi, $44,000 **77.** 22,654 **79.** 2080 R 102

81. $\frac{5}{7}$ **83.** $\frac{9}{28}$ **85.** 11,925 bricks

Exercises 3.9

1. $7\frac{2}{7}$ **3.** $103\frac{1}{5}$ **5.** $5\frac{1}{8}$ **7.** $6\frac{4}{7}$ **9.** $118\frac{1}{6}$ **11.** $2\frac{1}{2}$

13. $15\frac{1}{5}$ **15.** $155\frac{1}{9}$ **17.** $1\frac{5}{8}$ **19.** $9\frac{1}{2}$ **21.** $56\frac{1}{3}$

23. $26\frac{23}{60}$ **25.** $21\frac{3}{4}$ **27.** $7\frac{29}{48}$ **29.** $28\frac{1}{3}$ **31.** $5\frac{25}{32}$

33. $7\frac{11}{36}$ **35.** $22\frac{5}{6}$ **37.** $36\frac{17}{120}$ **39.** $27\frac{31}{36}$ **41.** $26\frac{19}{78}$

43. $10\frac{17}{20}$ **45.** $95\frac{11}{72}$ **47.** $85\frac{17}{48}$ **49.** $8\frac{2}{9}$ **51.** $23\frac{1}{9}$

53. $\frac{1}{2}$ **55.** $1\frac{3}{20}$ **57.** $28\frac{24}{35}$ **59.** $58\frac{19}{36}$ **61.** $1\frac{1}{2}$ lb

63. $18\frac{9}{20}$ tons **65.** $17\frac{7}{10}$ mi **67.** $381\frac{3}{10}$ lb **69.** $74\frac{7}{12}$ gal

73. No **75.** $3\frac{17}{48}$ ft, 6 days **77.** $\frac{13}{17}$ **79.** $6\frac{1}{24}$ **81.** $\frac{2}{15}$

83. $4\frac{1}{2}$ **85.** 28 mi per gal

Getting Ready for Algebra, p. 263

1. $a = \frac{1}{2}$ **3.** $c = \frac{5}{8}$ **5.** $x = \frac{11}{72}$ **7.** $y = 1\frac{38}{63}$ **9.** $a = 1\frac{11}{40}$

11. $c = 4\frac{1}{6}$ **13.** $x = 3\frac{5}{36}$ **15.** $3\frac{1}{6} = w$ **17.** $a = 36\frac{4}{9}$

19. $c = 21\frac{2}{21}$ **21.** $91\frac{5}{8}$ **23.** 46 lb

Exercises 3.10

1. $\frac{2}{9}$ 3. $\frac{1}{7}$ 5. $\frac{1}{2}$ 7. 1 9. 0 11. $1\frac{7}{12}$ 13. $\frac{11}{12}$ 15. $\frac{4}{9}$

17. $\frac{3}{7}$ 19. $\frac{10}{21}$ 21. $\frac{3}{8}$ 23. $\frac{3}{5}$ 25. $\frac{5}{6}$ 27. $\frac{2}{3}$ 29. $\frac{37}{48}$

31. $1\frac{13}{64}$ 33. $\frac{1}{24}$ 35. $\frac{35}{36}$ 37. 4 39. $1\frac{1}{16}$ 41. $1\frac{4}{9}$

43. $1\frac{5}{18}$ 45. 1 47. $2\frac{2}{5}$ 49. $\frac{15}{32}$ 51. $3\frac{37}{54}$ 53. $7\frac{1}{5}$

55. $33\frac{2}{3}$ in. 57. $\frac{7}{10}$ correct 59. $108\frac{1}{4}$ oz, 48¢ per oz

61. $7408 profit 65. $2\frac{57}{1000}$ 67. $19,444 69. $\frac{7}{48}$

71. $1\frac{7}{8}$ 73. $\frac{1}{7}$ 75. $2 \cdot 5^2 \cdot 13$ 77. $1\frac{1}{4}$ in.

Chapter 3 Concept Review

1. False: Use two units with one totally shaded and the other partially shaded. [3.1-1] 2. True [3.1-3] 3. False: The numerator always equals the denominator, so it is improper. [3.1-2] 4. True [3.1-3] 5. True [3.2]

6. False: $\frac{11}{5}$ cannot be reduced. [3.2] 7. True [3.2]

8. True [3.9] 9. True [3.3-2] 10. True [3.3-3]
11. True [3.5-2] 12. True [3.5-2]

13. False: $\frac{3}{11}$ and $\frac{3}{14}$ are unlike fractions. [3.6-1]

14. False: Add the whole numbers and add the fractions. [3.7]
15. True [3.9] 16. True [3.10-1] 17. True [3.10-2]
18. True [3.3-3]

Chapter 3 Test

1. $3\frac{15}{16}$ [3.1-3] 2. $\frac{23}{24}$ [3.6-2] 3. $\frac{79}{8}$ [3.1-4]

4. $\frac{3}{10}, \frac{3}{8}, \frac{2}{5}$ [3.5-3] 5. $\frac{18}{1}$ [3.1-4] 6. 56 [3.5-2]

7. $9\frac{2}{15}$ [3.7] 8. $9\frac{5}{8}$ [3.4-1] 9. $\frac{3}{4}$ [3.10-1] 10. $\frac{2}{3}$ [3.2]

11. $5\frac{3}{8}$ [3.9] 12. $\frac{5}{8}$ [3.3-1] 13. $\frac{12}{35}$ [3.4-2] 14. $\frac{9}{20}$ [3.8]

15. $2\frac{2}{3}$ [3.4-2] 16. $6\frac{13}{20}$ [3.9] 17. $\frac{2}{3}$ [3.2] 18. $\frac{5}{7}$ [3.6-2]

19. $\frac{8}{27}$ [3.3-2] 20. $4\frac{2}{3}$ [3.3-2] 21. $\frac{7}{8}, \frac{7}{9}, \frac{8}{9}$ [3.1-2]

22. $\frac{4}{15}$ [3.3-3] 23. $8\frac{13}{40}$ [3.9] 24. $\frac{7}{12}$ [3.1-1]

25. $5\frac{5}{12}$ [3.9] 26. $\frac{5}{6}$ [3.6-1] 27. $1\frac{3}{8}$ [3.10-2]

28. $\frac{5}{5}, \frac{6}{6}, \frac{7}{7}$ [3.1-2] 29. $\frac{3}{50}$ [3.3-1] 30. False [3.5-4]

31. 22 truckloads [3.4-2] 32. 25 lb [3.4-1]

Chapter 4

Exercises 4.1

1. tenths 3. hundred-thousandths 5. thousandths
7. five tenths 9. sixteen hundredths

11. fifty-eight hundredths 13. seven thousandths 15. 5

17. 0 19. 0.9 21. 0.19 23. 0.444 25. $\frac{3}{10}$

27. $\frac{2}{10} + \frac{3}{100}$ 29. $\frac{1}{10} + \frac{6}{100}$ 31. 0.7 33. 0.23

35. 0.345 37. thousandths 39. one and three tenths
41. six hundredths 43. 0,005 45. 0.0025

47. $\frac{5}{10} + \frac{3}{100} + \frac{2}{1000}$ 49. $\frac{0}{10} + \frac{0}{100} + \frac{4}{1000}$ 51. 0.006

53. 25.801
55. two and three thousand forty-one hundred-thousandths
57. four hundred four and eleven hundred-thousandths

59. 0.233 61. 0.00040 63. $90 + 2 + \frac{4}{10} + \frac{3}{100} + \frac{2}{1000}$

65. $500 + 20 + 4 + \frac{0}{10} + \frac{0}{100} + \frac{4}{1000} + \frac{6}{10,000}$

67. sixty-four and seventy-nine hundredths 69. ten billion

71. 2 75. ten trillion 79. 42 81. $\frac{5}{8}$ 83. $\frac{8}{39}$

85. False 87. $4\frac{5}{8}$ oz

Exercises 4.2

1. $\frac{7}{10}$ 3. $\frac{23}{100}$ 5. $\frac{13}{1000}$ 7. True 9. True 11. True
13. 0.1, 0.6, 0.7 15. 0.05, 0.07, 0.6 17. 4.159, 4.16, 4.161

19. $2\frac{23}{100}$ 21. $6\frac{1}{500}$ 23. $\frac{7}{8}$ 25. False 27. True

29. True 31. 9.59, 9.6, 9.61, 9.62, 9.63
33. 0.87, 0.899, 0.9, 0.904, 0.92

35. 107.05, 107.056, 107.0605, 107.16 37. $21\frac{22}{25}$

39. $700\frac{7}{1000}$ 41. $\frac{321}{2000}$ 43. False 45. True 47. True

49. 0.072, 0.0729, 0.073, 0.073001, 0.073015
51. 0.88579, 0.88799, 0.888, 0.8881

53. 20.004, 20.039, 20.04, 20.093 55. $\frac{1}{8}$ 57. $8\frac{5}{16}$ yd

59. 0.055 61. 98.35 cents 63. more

65. $\frac{11}{25}, \frac{101}{250}, \frac{1011}{25,000}$ 69. $\frac{2}{9}$ 71. $12\frac{8}{25}$ 73. $23\frac{5}{8}$ 75. 4

77. 10

Exercises 4.3

	Unit	Tenth	Hundredth
1.	16	15.9	15.89
3.	448	447.8	447.77
5.	1	0.7	0.74

7. $33.54 9. $513.93

	Ten	Hundredth	Thousandth
11.	10	12.55	12.553
13.	250	245.25	245.245
15.	0	0.55	0.554

17. $57.60 **19.** $246.50 **21.** 700; 654.65
23. 4800; 4809.78 **25.** 650; 654.7 **27.** 10; 7.6
29. 35,000; 34,897.335 **31.** 1000; 976.046 **33.** $11
35. $1129 **37.** 3.8 **39.** 1.62 **41.** 1.6 **43.** $208
45. 371.8 ft **47.** $161.37 **49.** $8450
53. 8.28; 8.28 < 8.282828 **55.** 2.828; 2.828 < 2.828282
57. $3\dfrac{9}{13}$ **59.** $\dfrac{110}{7}$ **61.** 6 **63.** $\dfrac{1}{3}$ **65.** 15 in.

Exercises 4.4

1. 0.6 **3.** 1.8 **5.** 7.7 **7.** 27.7 **9.** 0.677 **11.** 6.87
13. 14.3 **15.** 13.72 **17.** 13.841 **19.** 23.4 **21.** 2.755
23. 9.0797 **25.** 82.593 **27.** 3.34783 **29.** 55.5363
31. 831.267 **33.** 16.2665 **35.** 31.9758 **37.** 470.938
39. 10.8005 **41.** 23.6 **43.** 0.11 **45.** 376.963 **47.** 866
49. 42.06 gal **51.** $132.89 **53.** $11.84 **55.** $348
59. 23 times **61.** 33.7 **65.** $1\dfrac{11}{12}$ **67.** $1\dfrac{19}{36}$ or $\dfrac{55}{36}$
69. $\dfrac{5}{32}$ **71.** $\dfrac{4}{15}$ **73.** $3\dfrac{17}{24}$ in.

Exercises 4.5

1. 0.3 **3.** 0.5 **5.** 0.13 **7.** 6.2 **9.** 11.1 **11.** 1.089
13. 8.09 **15.** 9.277 **17.** 0.457 **19.** 0.948 **21.** 2.89
23. 8.822 **25.** 2.76 **27.** 1.08 **29.** 0.949 **31.** 5.32
33. 5.743 **35.** 105.753 **37.** 24.388 **39.** 4.1971
41. 14.0406 **43.** 74.87 **45.** 0.3 **47.** $31.08 **49.** 2.7 cc
51. $1660.80 **53.** 0.0822 min **55.** 3.874 gal **57.** 0.778 sec
61. 1.5725 **63.** $19\dfrac{23}{24}$ **65.** $7\dfrac{5}{6}$ **67.** 12 **69.** $1\dfrac{5}{16}$ or $\dfrac{21}{16}$
71. $6 per lb

Getting Ready for Algebra, p. 325

1. $11.5 = x$ **3.** $y = 14.98$ **5.** $t = 0.073$ **7.** $x = 12$
9. $2.62 = w$ **11.** $t = 7.23$ **13.** $a = 0.78$ **15.** $x = 6.56$
17. $a = 21.6$ **19.** $s = 6.289$ **21.** $c = 476.02$ **23.** $406.97

Exercises 4.6

1. 2.4 **3.** 4.2 **5.** 1.8 **7.** 0.27 **9.** 0.35 **11.** 0.06 **13.** 0.84
15. 13.5 **17.** 0.015 **19.** 0.01476 **21.** 3.045 **23.** 224.9
25. 4.2488 **27.** 5.576 **29.** 149.4 **31.** 0.3776 **33.** 24.57
35. 0.000352 **37.** 1035.125 **39.** 2995.8741 **41.** 0.084
43. 22.736 **45.** 27.67296 **47.** 852.066 **49.** 10.07232
51. $150.34 **53.** $116.03 **55.** 60.75 yd **57.** $196.41
59. Answers will vary. **63.** 75 **65.** $14\dfrac{17}{42}$ **67.** 70
69. $15\dfrac{39}{40}$ **71.** $1\dfrac{3}{20}$ or $\dfrac{23}{20}$ **73.** $4\dfrac{1}{4}$ ft

Exercises 4.7

1. 4.25 **3.** 183 **5.** 821.4 **7.** 2.76 **9.** 2.14361
11. 1×10^3 **13.** 1×10^{-4} **15.** 10,000 **17.** 0.01
19. 0.003695 **21.** 2,600,000 **23.** 0.12231 **25.** 7×10^2
27. 7.8×10^{-2} **29.** 1.5×10^4 **31.** 60,000 **33.** 0.122
35. 2340 **37.** 21.4 **39.** 0.00832 **41.** 8.216 **43.** 7×10^4
45. 8.16×10^{-3} **47.** 6.27×10^5 **49.** 6,000,000,000
51. 0.0000444 **53.** 785,100 **55.** $2229 **57.** $98,500
59. 12,500 lb **61.** 1.152×10^6 bytes **63.** 3.3×10^{-6} sec

65. 150,000,000 km **67.** 1,245,600,000 Btu **69.** 27.6 gal
73. 6.5×10^{-3} **75.** 4 **77.** $8\dfrac{1}{4}$ or $\dfrac{33}{4}$ **79.** $1\dfrac{5}{6}$ **81.** $7\dfrac{19}{20}$
83. Yes

Exercises 4.8

1. 0.5 **3.** 9.8 **5.** 183.1 **7.** 21.3 **9.** 11 **11.** 2020
13. 2.14 **15.** 3.4 **17.** 12.6 **19.** 0.52 **21.** 0.052 **23.** 0.126
25. 15.555 **27.** 0.221 **29.** 4.510 **31.** 395.349 **33.** 97.06
35. 0.0234 **37.** 8.02 **39.** 7.8 **41.** 358.7 **43.** 17.1 **45.** 25
47. 19 **49.** $1.58 **51.** $2.76 **53.** $44.52 **55.** 19 mi per gal
57. 17.3 hr **59.** 232 ft **61.** 48.7 mph **65.** $\dfrac{3}{2000}$ **67.** $3\dfrac{1}{8}$
69. $11\dfrac{3}{8}$ **71.** $11\dfrac{2}{9}$ **73.** $\dfrac{109}{216}$ **75.** 105 in.

Getting Ready for Algebra, p. 357

1. $x = 6$ **3.** $y = 204$ **5.** $0.06 = t$ **7.** $m = 0.04$
9. $q = 437.5$ **11.** $500 = h$ **13.** $y = 2.673$ **15.** $0.1032 = c$
17. $0.9775 = x$ **19.** $w = 0.0141$ **21.** $z = 30.16$
23. 25 servings **25.** 8.4 amperes

Exercises 4.9

1. 0.125 **3.** 0.375 **5.** 0.6875 **7.** 0.03125 **9.** 0.4375
11. 0.1, 0.11 **13.** 0.6, 0.57 **15.** 0.5, 0.45 **17.** 0.65
19. 0.792 **21.** 0.8, 0.78 **23.** 0.2, 0.15 **25.** 0.9, 0.94
27. 0.5, 0.53 **29.** 3.625 **31.** 15.656 **33.** 0.3, 0.35, 0.349
35. 0.4, 0.39, 0.387 **37.** 11.8, 11.81, 11.810
39. 2.8, 2.78, 2.778 **41.** 21.9, 21.87, 21.865 **43.** 0.75 in.
45. 0.375 in., 1.25 in., 0.5 in. **47.** 0.775 in. **49.** 3.42 yd
51. 24.90 ft **55.** More; 496 **57.** 10.658 **59.** 3890.275
61. 20.17 **63.** 1.66 **65.** 37.5 in.

Exercises 4.10

1. 0.5 **3.** 0.05 **5.** 0.2 **7.** 5.4 **9.** 0.12 **11.** 2.3 **13.** 2.3
15. 3 **17.** 2.42 **19.** 220.1 **21.** 102.4 **23.** 27.67 **25.** 0.06
27. 5.42 **29.** 5.93 **31.** 0.063 **33.** 21 **35.** 7.765
37. 1.738 **39.** 5.6709 **41.** 7.46 **43.** 28.54 **45.** 13.3365
47. 1.92 **49.** $17.33 **51.** $54.38 **53.** 48.7 accidents
55. $10.15 **59.** $3.62 \div (0.02 + 72.3 \cdot 0.2)$ **61.** $(1.4^2 - 0.7)^2$
63. 0.9375 **65.** 0.2125 **67.** $\dfrac{41}{50}$ **69.** $\dfrac{17}{200}$ **71.** $24.79

Getting Ready for Algebra, p. 375

1. $x = 9$ **3.** $x = 0.6$ **5.** $0.1 = t$ **7.** $x = 524$ **9.** $x = 0.32$
11. $m = 67$ **13.** $16.5 = y$ **15.** $p = 3.002$ **17.** $40 = x$
19. $7.28 = h$ **21.** $17.25 = c$ **23.** 2°C **25.** $118.33

Chapter 4 Concept Review

1. False: The word name is "five hundred two thousandths." [4.1-2] **2.** True [4.1-1]
3. False: The expanded form is $\dfrac{7}{10} + \dfrac{5}{100}$. [4.1-3]
4. True [4.2-1] **5.** False: The number at the left is smaller because 821,597 is less than 840,000. [4.2-2] **6.** True [4.2-2]
7. True [4.2-2] **8.** True [4.3] **9.** False: The numeral in the tenths place is 3 followed by 4, so it rounds to 123.3. [4.3]

10. True [4.4]   **11.** False: $8.5 - 0.2 = 8.3$ as we can see when the decimal points are aligned. [4.5]   **12.** False: Not if we leave out the extra zeros in a product such as $0.5(3.02) = 1.51$. [4.6]   **13.** True [4.7-1]   **14.** False: The decimal moves to the left making the dividend smaller. [4.7-2]   **15.** False: Move the decimal left when the exponent is negative. [4.7-2]   **16.** True [4.8]   **17.** False: Most fractions have no exact decimal form. For example, the fractions $\frac{1}{3}, \frac{1}{6}, \frac{1}{7}, \frac{1}{9}$ have no exact decimal equivalents. [4.9]   **18.** False: The rounded value is 0.56. [4.3]   **19.** True [4.10-1]   **20.** True [4.10-2]

Chapter 4 Test

1. 0.040 [4.8]   **2.** 0.7279, 0.728, 0.7299, 0.7308, 0.731 [4.2-2]
3. hundredths [4.1-1]
4. twenty-seven and twenty-seven thousandths [4.1-2]
5. 41.808 [4.6]   **6.** ten-thousandths [4.1-1]   **7.** 0.024 [4.9]

8. 9.00 [4.3]   **9.** 4.211 [4.5]   **10.** $16\frac{37}{40}$ [4.2-1]

11. $700 + 0 + 2 + \frac{3}{10} + \frac{0}{100} + \frac{5}{1000}$ [4.1-3]
12. 2.4×10^{-3} [4.7-2]   **13.** 0.31 [4.9]   **14.** 47,500 [4.3]
15. 15.328 [4.10-1]   **16.** 4.898 [4.5]   **17.** 0.266 [4.7-2]
18. 212.063 [4.1-2]   **19.** 21.6 [4.7-1]   **20.** 25.709 [4.1-3]
21. 3.275×10^4 [4.7-2]   **22.** 7.273 [4.9]   **23.** 0.0008 [4.7-1]
24. 0.01368 [4.6]   **25.** $74.72 [4.10-2]   **26.** 22.989 [4.4]
27. 0.055 [4.8]   **28.** $6.27 [4.10-1]

Chapter 5

Exercises 5.1

1. $\frac{10 \text{ people}}{13 \text{ chairs}}$ **3.** $\frac{5}{6}$ **5.** $\frac{9}{4}$ **7.** $\frac{18 \text{ families}}{47 \text{ children}}$ **9.** $\frac{8 \text{ lb}}{3 \text{ ft}}$

11. $\frac{25 \text{ mi}}{1 \text{ hr}}$ **13.** $\frac{4 \text{ ft}}{1 \text{ sec}}$ **15.** $\frac{4 \text{ ft}}{1 \text{ sec}}$ **17.** $\frac{1}{2}$ **19.** $\frac{2 \text{ trees}}{7 \text{ feet}}$

21. $\frac{2 \text{ books}}{5 \text{ students}}$ **23.** $\frac{20 \text{ mi}}{1 \text{ gal}}$ **25.** $\frac{50 \text{ mi}}{1 \text{ hr}}$ **27.** $\frac{\$3}{1 \text{ pair}}$

29. $\frac{55 \text{ mi}}{1 \text{ hr}}$ **31.** $\frac{3 \text{ cups}}{2 \text{ cakes}}$ **33.** $\frac{15}{17}$ **35.** $\frac{2925 \text{ households}}{2 \text{ cable companies}}$

37. $\frac{37.5 \text{ mi}}{1 \text{ gal}}$ **39.** $\frac{88 \text{ ft}}{1 \text{ sec}}$ **41.** $\frac{42.5 \text{ mi}}{1 \text{ hr}}$ **43.** $\frac{7}{10}; \frac{7}{17}$ **45.** No

47. $\frac{97.6 \text{ people}}{1 \text{ mi}^2}$ **49.** Answers will vary.   **51.** $\frac{7}{12}$ **53.** $\frac{5}{12}$

55. $\frac{1}{3}$ **57.** $\frac{31}{22}$ **59.** **a.** $\frac{7}{20}$ **b.** $\frac{16}{3}$ **c.** $\frac{4}{5}$ **d.** $\frac{8.75}{1}$ gal per

person   **61.** Answers will vary.   **65.** Yes   **67.** $\frac{5}{14}$

69. **a.** $\frac{21}{92}$ **b.** $\frac{24}{89}$ **c.** $\frac{117}{370}$ **d.** $\frac{18}{65}$ **e.** $\frac{243}{482}$ **f.** $\frac{171}{415}$ **g.** $\frac{30}{71}$

h. $\frac{63}{290}$ **71.** four thousand, eight hundred and five thousandths
73. False   **75.** 0.90   **77.** 6.6612   **79.** 2 tens; $8.44

Exercises 5.2

1. True   **3.** True   **5.** False   **7.** 14   **9.** 4   **11.** 10   **13.** 4
15. 18   **17.** 16   **19.** 6   **21.** True   **23.** False   **25.** False

27. $\frac{21}{2}$ or 10.5   **29.** $\frac{22}{5}$ or 4.4   **31.** $\frac{32}{3}$ **33.** $\frac{105}{2}$ or 52.5

35. $\frac{25}{2}$ or 12.5   **37.** 0.6   **39.** 16   **41.** True   **43.** True

45. False   **47.** 225   **49.** 0.01   **51.** 0.25   **53.** 3   **55.** 216
57. 24   **59.** 0.5   **61.** 46.7   **63.** 7.88   **65.** 0.28   **67.** 17.81
69. 1.39   **71.** 300,000 lawn mowers
73. **a.** 245 people   **b.** 102 men   **c.** 70 people   **77.** 5
81. 0.842436   **83.** 2032.056   **85.** 5   **87.** 8.049
89. 55 gal

Exercises 5.3

1. 6   **3.** 15   **5.** $\frac{6}{4} = \frac{15}{x}$ **7.** 30   **9.** x **11.** $\frac{30}{18} = \frac{x}{48}$ **13.** 8

15. x **17.** $\frac{8}{48} = \frac{x}{288}$ **19.** x **21.** $\frac{3}{65} = \frac{x}{910}$

23. 4 teachers   **25.** $180,000   **27.** $\frac{1125}{75,000} = \frac{x}{180,000}$

29.

	Case I	Case II
Games Won	12	x
Games Played	15	30

31. 24 games   **33.** 26 shirts   **35.** 125 hr   **37.** $51   **39.** 50 lb
41. $2.20   **43.** $1.89   **45.** 20 hr   **47.** $49   **49.** 896
51. 7 jobs   **53.** $2025   **55.** $13.50   **57.** 12,800 ft^2
59. No; $1.78   **61.** 0.0075 in.   **63.** 45 boys
65. 28 oz of nuts   **67.** 30 bags   **69.** 3.5 qt   **71.** 114.3 kg
73. $1007   **75.** $5000   **77.** $135   **79.** 51,870 drachma
81. $48   **83.** 1960, 3,752,000 lb; 1970, 3,976,000 lb;
1980, 5,432,000 lb; 1988, 7,336,000 lb   **87.** 193 condors

89. Parisi, $1079; Nguyen, $981   **91.** $\frac{173}{200}$ **93.** 0.547

95. 6.435   **97.** 63.64   **99.** $21.14

Chapter 5 Concept Review

1. False: A ratio is a comparison of two numbers or measures written as a fraction. [5.1-1]   **2.** True [5.2-1]   **3.** False: The cross products of a proportion are equal if the proportion is true. [5.2-1]   **4.** True [5.1-1]   **5.** True [5.2-1]   **6.** True [5.2-2]   **7.** False: The table should look like the following: [5.3]

	First Tree	**Second Tree**
Height	18	x
Shadow	17	25

8. True [5.3]   **9.** True [5.3]   **10.** False: The height of the second tree will be greater than the length of its shadow. [5.3]

Chapter 5 Test

1. $\frac{4}{5}$ [5.1-1]   **2.** 80 correct [5.3]   **3.** $w = 1.2$ [5.2-2]

4. True [5.2-1]   **5.** True [5.2-1]   **6.** $y = 6.5$ [5.2-2]

7. $84.24 [5.3]   **8.** $\frac{1}{12}$ [5.1-1]   **9.** $8.20 [5.3]

10. 17.5 lb [5.3]   **11.** $x = 2.4$ [5.2-2]   **12.** 24 fish [5.3]
13. 20 gal [5.3]   **14.** $a = 5.35$ [5.2-2]

Chapter 6

Exercises 6.1

1. 15%   **3.** 63%   **5.** 17%   **7.** 6%   **9.** 14%   **11.** 40%
13. 48%   **15.** 45%   **17.** 160%   **19.** 100%   **21.** 124%

23. 300%   **25.** 120%   **27.** 130%   **29.** 60%   **31.** $116\frac{1}{4}\%$

33. $10\frac{3}{5}\%$ **35.** $43\frac{3}{4}\%$ **37.** $83\frac{1}{3}\%$ **39.** $87\frac{1}{2}\%$

41. $48\frac{1}{3}\%$ **43.** $66\frac{2}{3}\%$ **45.** $87\frac{1}{2}\%$ **47.** 420%   **49.** 700%

51. 65%   **53.** 62%   **55.** 8%   **57.** $3\frac{1}{4}\%$ **59.** 5%   **61.** 3%

65. $\frac{503}{800}$; $62\frac{7}{8}\%$ or 62.875%   **67.** 0.46875   **69.** 0.94

71. 16.8   **73.** 0.0456003   **75.** Yes

Exercises 6.2

1. 36%   **3.** 476%   **5.** 8%   **7.** 160%   **9.** 1200%   **11.** 0.9%
13. 53.1%   **15.** 29%   **17.** 100%   **19.** 21.4%   **21.** 700%
23. 1321%   **25.** 0.5%   **27.** 70%   **29.** 320%   **31.** 3.17%

33. 284%   **35.** 0.8%   **37.** 575%   **39.** 56.25%   **41.** $74\frac{1}{6}\%$

43. 20.51%   **45.** 10.25% or $10\frac{1}{4}\%$ **47.** 5.2% or $5\frac{1}{5}\%$

49. 0.09%   **51.** 1000%   **53.** 123.4%   **55.** 22%   **57.** 62%

59. 37.5%   **61.** 23.5%   **63.** 6%   **67.** 42.5%; $42\frac{5}{9}\%$

69. 3.872   **71.** 2.6472   **73.** 0.024   **75.** 0.5008
77. $120.15, $30.04

Exercises 6.3

1. 0.16   **3.** 0.82   **5.** 0.73   **7.** 0.0215   **9.** 3.12   **11.** 1.106
13. 0.0004   **15.** 0.0279   **17.** 0.179   **19.** 3.147   **21.** 0.0012
23. 0.005   **25.** 0.0025   **27.** 0.01   **29.** 2   **31.** 0.00058
33. 1.25   **35.** 0.00625   **37.** 0.2975   **39.** 4.755   **41.** 0.00875
43. 0.0125   **45.** 0.014   **47.** 0.7261   **49.** 0.002   **51.** 0.358
53. 0.018   **55.** 0.047   **57.** 0.07   **59.** 0.002   **61.** 0.6
63. 0.04   **67.** 0.6; 0.564   **69.** 0.875   **71.** 1.1875   **73.** 1.8

75. $\frac{143}{200}$ **77.** $206.55

Exercises 6.4

1. 75%   **3.** 22%   **5.** 85%   **7.** 50%   **9.** 28%   **11.** 15%

13. 105%   **15.** 37.5%   **17.** $66\frac{2}{3}\%$ **19.** $116\frac{2}{3}\%$

21. $183\frac{1}{3}\%$ **23.** 5.25%   **25.** 93.3%   **27.** 44.4%   **29.** 83.3%

31. 183.3%   **33.** 8.3%   **35.** 33.3%   **37.** 53.8%   **39.** 142.9%
41. 38.1%   **43.** 0.3%   **45.** 0.4%   **47.** 1.9%   **49.** 1.0%
51. 488.9%   **53.** 80%   **55.** 17.5%   **57.** 1.9%   **59.** 300%
61. 22%   **65.** 0.46%   **67.** 6.96261   **69.** 0.00808   **71.** 15.1
73. 7.74   **75.** $5.35

Exercises 6.5

1. $\frac{1}{20}$ **3.** $\frac{7}{20}$ **5.** $1\frac{1}{4}$ **7.** 4   **9.** $\frac{7}{10}$ **11.** $\frac{14}{25}$ **13.** $\frac{3}{4}$

15. $\frac{9}{10}$ **17.** 1   **19.** $\frac{11}{40}$ **21.** $\frac{63}{1000}$ **23.** $\frac{41}{200}$ **25.** $\frac{1}{300}$

27. $\frac{11}{200}$ **29.** $\frac{21}{200}$ **31.** $\frac{3}{400}$ **33.** $\frac{101}{200}$ **35.** $\frac{117}{700}$ **37.** $\frac{23}{250}$

39. $\frac{2}{45}$ **41.** $\frac{3}{800}$ **43.** $\frac{7}{6}$ **45.** $\frac{1}{6250}$ **47.** $\frac{4}{25}$ **49.** $\frac{7}{20}$

51. $\frac{9}{50}$ **53.** $\frac{1}{8}$ **55.** $\frac{22}{25}$ **59.** $\frac{1}{250,000}$ **61.** $\frac{39}{40,000}$

63. False   **65.** True   **67.** $\frac{\$0.52}{1 \text{ person}}$ **69.** $\frac{147.65 \text{ gal}}{1 \text{ person}}$

71. 2.314 mm

Exercises 6.6

	Fraction	Decimal	Percent
*	$\frac{1}{10}$	0.1	10%
*	$\frac{3}{10}$	0.3	30%
*	$\frac{3}{4}$	0.75	75%
*	$\frac{9}{10}$	0.9	90%
	$1\frac{9}{20}$	1.45	145%
*	$\frac{3}{8}$	0.375	37.5% or $37\frac{1}{2}\%$
	$\frac{1}{1000}$	0.001	0.1%
*	$\frac{1}{1}$ or 1	1	100%
	$2\frac{1}{4}$	2.25	225%
*	$\frac{4}{5}$	0.8	80%
	$\frac{11}{200}$	0.055	$5\frac{1}{2}\%$
*	$\frac{7}{8}$	0.875	87.5% or $87\frac{1}{2}\%$
	$\frac{1}{200}$	0.005	$\frac{1}{2}\%$
*	$\frac{3}{5}$	0.6	60%

53. $\dfrac{33\frac{1}{3}\text{ oz}}{1\text{ in.}}$ **55.** $\dfrac{12\text{ cents}}{1\text{ min}}$ **57.** $\dfrac{9\text{ oz}}{1\text{ in.}^2}$ **59.** $\dfrac{21.25\text{ lb}}{1\text{ min}}$

61. $1\frac{1}{2}$ words per sec **63.** 5 cc **65.** 83.616 kg **67.** $246.40

69. 105 mi; $3\frac{1}{3}$ days **71.** 1.2 oz; $1.50 **73.** $3.50 per piece

77. $\dfrac{5.5\text{ oz}}{\text{in.}^3}$ **79.** $2500 **81.** 80% **83.** $33\frac{1}{3}$% **85.** 87%

87. 27.1% **89.** 15%

Exercises 7.3

1. 22.9 m **3.** 6.6 ℓ **5.** 226.8 kg **7.** 738.2 ft **9.** 10.3 km
11. 10.8 cm **13.** 0.8 lb **15.** 283.9 ℓ **17.** 9.3 in.
19. 17,216.3 m **21.** 0.2 oz **23.** $\dfrac{81,848.6\text{ g}}{1\text{ m}}$ **25.** $\dfrac{46.6\text{ mi}}{1\text{ hr}}$

27. $\dfrac{4.1\text{ g}}{1\text{ cm}^2}$ **29.** $\dfrac{1.1\text{ lb}}{1\text{ qt}}$ **31.** 535.8 g **33.** $\dfrac{19\text{ cents}}{\text{km}}$

35. 133.8 kg **37.** 29.0 m **39.** The Canadian pack
41. 68.1 cm **47.** 22.2 ℓ **51.** 150% **53.** 156.3%

55. $\frac{1}{3}$; $33\frac{1}{3}$% **57.** $36.76

Exercises 7.4

1. 24 in. **3.** 72 in. **5.** 94.2 m **7.** 19 in. **9.** 26 ft
11. 50.24 ft **13.** 32 in. **15.** 32 in. **17.** 36 ft **19.** 54 m
21. 42 in. **23.** 113.39 m **25.** 62.84 in. **27.** 14.28 cm

29. $30\frac{2}{3}$ in. **31.** 54 cm **33.** 70 ft **35.** 67.1 in.

37. 41.68 in. **39.** 38.4 cm **41.** 12 ft **43.** $2880
45. 1261 revolutions **47.** 46 ft; $65.17 **51.** 263.8 ft; 248.1 ft

53.

Fraction	Decimal	Percent
$\dfrac{249}{200}$	1.245	124.5%
$\dfrac{7}{16}$	0.4375	$43\frac{3}{4}$%
$\dfrac{5}{6}$	$0.833\overline{3}$	$83\frac{1}{3}$%
$\dfrac{26}{5}$	5.2	520%

55. 45%

Exercises 7.5

1. 96 in.² **3.** 243 ft² **5.** 169 in.² **7.** 9 km² **9.** 0.785 cm²
11. 20.25 in.² **13.** 119.6 in.² **15.** 552.25 ft² **17.** 484 mm²
19. 7.065 cm² **21.** 144 in.² **23.** 225 yd² **25.** 192 in.²
27. 326.97 m² **29.** 4 rolls **31.** No **33.** 1017.36 in.²
35. 240 oz **37.** 784,080 ft²; 261 parcels; 1080 ft² **43.** 7.5%
45. 37.5% **47.** $7320 **49.** 400 forms **51.** $442.85

Exercises 7.6

1. 30,000 ft² **3.** 255 ft² **5.** 2395 mm² **7.** 418.08 in.²
9. 562.5 cm² **11.** 81.64 cm² **13.** 327.75 in.² **15.** 12.86 ft²

17. 150 m² **19.** 64.94 ft² **21.** 49.60 m² **23.** 50 m²
25. 140 cm² **27.** 10 lb **29.** 21.5 squares of aluminum
31. 538.7 ft² **37.** 90 lb **39.** 20% **41.** 10% **43.** 7 salmon
45. $62.79

Exercises 7.7

1. 525 m³ **3.** 1582.56 in.³ **5.** 125 in.³ **7.** 65.4 cm³
9. 3140 cm³ **11.** 267.9 ft³ **13.** 468 cm³ **15.** 432 in.³
17. 6104.16 in.³ **19.** 1387.5 ft³ **21.** 10,889.5 mm³

23. 69.08 gal **25.** 147,187.5 ft³ **31.** $17\frac{3}{16}$ in. **33.** $2\frac{1}{18}$ yd

35. 6480 sec **37.** 3 mi 5150 ft **39.** 0.0102 in.

Chapter 7 Concept Review

1. False: Equivalent measures are measures of the same object using different units. [7.1] **2.** True [7.1] **3.** True [7.1]
4. False: 1 kiloliter = 1,000,000 milliliters [7.1] **5.** False: Conversions from English to metric are approximate values. [7.2] **6.** True [7.4] **7.** False: The circumference of *every* circle is π (≈ 3.14) times its diameter. [7.4]
8. True [7.4] **9.** True [7.1] **10.** True [7.1] **11.** True [7.7]
12. False: An inch is larger than a centimeter. 1 inch $\approx$ 2.54 cm [7.2] **13.** False: The area of a parallelogram is the same as the area of a rectangle, length times width. [7.5]
14. False: The height of a right triangle can be the length of one of its legs. [7.5]
15. False: A quart is smaller than a liter. 1 qt $\approx$ 0.95 ℓ [7.2]
16. True [7.7] **17.** True [7.5] **18.** True [7.2]
19. False: The area of a *circle* is πr^2. [7.5]
20. False: The radius of a circle is one half its diameter. [7.4]

Chapter 7 Test

1. 7850 mm [7.2] **2.** 13.6 cm [7.4] **3.** $1\frac{7}{8}$ points [7.1]

4. 43.72 ft² [7.6] **5.** 24.8 lb [7.1] **6.** 114.5 g [7.1]
7. 24.28 ft [7.4] **8.** 30 in.² [7.5] **9.** 1 gal 3 qt 1 pt [7.1]
10. 2.5375 gal [7.2] **11.** 152 in. [7.2]
12. 21 gal per min [7.2] **13.** 7.8 ℓ [7.1] **14.** 48 cm² [7.5]
15. 14.13 ft³ [7.7] **16.** 7 cm 2 mm [7.1] **17.** 3.2 kg [7.3]

Chapter 8

Exercises 8.1

1. 4 **3.** −5 **5.** 1.5 **7.** $-\frac{1}{3}$ **9.** $\frac{3}{4}$ **11.** $-\frac{7}{8}$ **13.** 2

15. 12 **17.** 3.4 **19.** $\frac{5}{8}$ **21.** $\frac{4}{5}$ **23.** 42 **25.** 3.21

27. $-3\frac{3}{4}$ **29.** $5\frac{4}{5}$ **31.** −0.45 **33.** 0.25 **35.** −107.3

37. 143.5 **39.** $-\frac{14}{9}$ **41.** 0.027 **43.** 188 **45.** 0.0045

47. $\frac{9}{8}$ **49.** $\frac{19}{29}$ **51.** 4.7 **53.** 15 **55.** 244 **57.** 0.0071

59. $-\frac{4}{9}$ **61.** −46 **63.** $-\frac{5}{8}$ **65.** 12°C **67.** 1875 A.D.

69. +1685 ft, −1246 ft   **71.** −$28.76; $28.76
73. −8 yd, 8 yd   **75.** 97 mi, 152 mi, −72 mi, −18 mi
79. Negative
81. For all numbers greater than or equal to zero.
83. For all numbers less than or equal to zero.   **87.** 13.515 kℓ
89. 18 cm   **91.** 82,000 cg   **93.** 7173 mℓ   **95.** 154.3 g

Exercises 8.2

1. 2   **3.** −1   **5.** −14   **7.** −16   **9.** 0   **11.** −13   **13.** −34
15. −8   **17.** −27   **19.** 5   **21.** −4   **23.** −144   **25.** −80
27. 0   **29.** 0   **31.** 1   **33.** −6.6   **35.** 2.6   **37.** $-\dfrac{1}{2}$
39. $-\dfrac{13}{8}$ **41.** 62   **43.** −189   **45.** −245   **47.** −30   **49.** 81
51. 0   **53.** −1.069   **55.** −133.73   **57.** $-\dfrac{53}{24}$ **59.** $6\dfrac{4}{9}$
61. −113 lb   **63.** 29,870 ft   **65.** 29,388 volumes
67. No; one yard short   **69.** up $1\dfrac{1}{4}$ **71.** −8°   **73.** $2 won
77. −91   **79.** 15   **83.** 660 ft   **85.** 678 ft   **87.** 142 m
89. 72 in.   **91.** $0.65

Exercises 8.3

1. 2   **3.** −10   **5.** −2   **7.** 3   **9.** −17   **11.** −12   **13.** 32
15. −31   **17.** −26   **19.** 1   **21.** 0   **23.** −24   **25.** −60
27. 87   **29.** −138   **31.** 4   **33.** −178   **35.** 182   **37.** 0
39. 0   **41.** 177   **43.** −17.88   **45.** −5.34   **47.** −24.03
49. −33.6   **51.** −49.2   **53.** −13.5   **55.** −1.78   **57.** 0
59. 331.52   **61.** $-\dfrac{3}{4}$ **63.** $-\dfrac{9}{40}$ **65.** 14   **67.** $\dfrac{23}{24}$
69. −85°C   **71.** $550.86   **73.** −59°C   **75.** $251.87
77. −$16.85   **79.** −$119.91   **81.** Lost; −28 yd   **85.** −23.5
87. −24   **89.** 8.3   **91.** 452.16 in.²   **93.** 864 cm²
95. 2.5 words per sec   **97.** 143.06625 km²   **99.** 180 yd²

Exercises 8.4

1. −6   **3.** 18   **5.** −6   **7.** 0   **9.** −48   **11.** 54   **13.** −99
15. −60   **17.** −1   **19.** −1   **21.** 180   **23.** 208   **25.** −315
27. 3.15   **29.** −17.85   **31.** 9   **33.** −120   **35.** 25   **37.** $\dfrac{3}{8}$
39. $\dfrac{3}{10}$ **41.** −49   **43.** −42   **45.** 0.5088   **47.** 0   **49.** −12
51. −168   **53.** −240   **55.** $\dfrac{1}{3}$ **57.** $\dfrac{3}{10}$ **59.** 54   **61.** −20°C
63. −28 lb   **65.** −33.96   **67.** −$67.20   **69.** −$20.08
71. −$99.68   **73.** $7118.75; $6693.75; lost $425; −$425
77. −70   **79.** 56   **83.** 2522 revolutions   **85.** 15 pounds
87. 39.75 ft²   **89.** $\dfrac{\$0.5625}{1\ \text{ft}^2}$

Exercises 8.5

1. −2   **3.** 2   **5.** −4   **7.** −9   **9.** −5   **11.** −7   **13.** 7
15. −3   **17.** −8   **19.** 6   **21.** −6   **23.** 7   **25.** 5   **27.** −2.02
29. 1.01   **31.** 0   **33.** Undefined   **35.** −35   **37.** 4.04

39. −0.0025   **41.** 5   **43.** −45   **45.** 116   **47.** $\dfrac{1}{2}$ **49.** −3
51. −1.2   **53.** −1   **55.** 108   **57.** −20   **59.** $-\dfrac{3}{5}$ **61.** 0.16
63. −8°   **65.** −$1647   **67.** −$47.37   **69.** −4.5 lb
71. −2.625   **73.** Answers will vary.   **75.** −12°   **79.** −7
81. $-\dfrac{7}{30}$ **85.** 3052.08 cm³   **87.** 576 cm³   **89.** 96 yd³
91. $2556

Exercises 8.6

1. −20   **3.** 20   **5.** −6   **7.** −13   **9.** −4   **11.** 8   **13.** −3
15. 13   **17.** 11   **19.** 9   **21.** 12   **23.** −13   **25.** 6   **27.** 40
29. −33   **31.** −4   **33.** 8   **35.** 0   **37.** 0   **39.** 64   **41.** 12
43. −22   **45.** 0   **47.** −4   **49.** 2   **51.** −48   **53.** −3   **55.** 9
57. 14   **59.** −1   **61.** True   **63.** 3.6°F   **65.** Yes   **67.** No
69. Down 11   **71.** 2.2 yd gained   **73.** −13 mi; 78 mi north
and 91 mi west   **77.** 13   **79.** −29.4   **81.** 184   **83.** 63,504
85. 25   **87.** −$1458

Exercises 8.7

1. $x = 7$ **3.** $x = 5$ **5.** $y = -5$ **7.** $a = 7$ **9.** $x = 7$
11. $x = 10$ **13.** $x = -3$ **15.** $x = -6$ **17.** $x = 0$ **19.** $x = 3$
21. $y = 7$ **23.** $a = 0$ **25.** $x = -0.5$ **27.** $x = -25$
29. $x = -16$ **31.** $y = -4$ **33.** $x = 3$ **35.** $b = -7$
37. 22 ft per sec   **39.** 27 rugs   **41.** lots of 50; $45
43. $x = 3$ **45.** $x = -14$

Chapter 8 Concept Review

1. True [8.1-1]   **2.** False: The opposite of a positive number is
negative. [8.1-1]   **3.** False: The absolute value of a nonzero
number is always positive. [8.1-2]   **4.** True [8.1-1]   **5.** False:
The sum of two signed numbers may be positive, negative, or
zero. [8.2]   **6.** False: The sum of a positive signed number
and a negative signed number may be positive, negative, or
zero. [8.2]   **7.** True [8.8-2]   **8.** False: To subtract two signed
numbers, add the opposite of the number to be subtracted. [8.3]
9. True [8.3]   **10.** True [8.4]   **11.** False: The sign of the
product of a positive number and a negative number is
negative. [8.4]   **12.** True [8.5]   **13.** True [8.6]
14. True [8.7]

Chapter 8 Test

1. −14 [8.2]   **2.** 72 [8.6]   **3.** $-\dfrac{5}{4}$ [8.5]   **4.** $\dfrac{2}{15}$ [8.3]
5. −1 [8.6]   **6.** 1.07 [8.2]   **7. a.** 21 [8.1-1]   **b.** 21 [8.1-2]
8. −35 [8.3]   **9.** −2 [8.6]   **10.** 4 [8.5]   **11.** 126 [8.4]
12. −24 [8.4]   **13.** −90.4 [8.3]   **14.** 40 [8.6]
15. −51.1 [8.5]   **16.** $-\dfrac{1}{6}$ [8.2]   **17.** 8 [8.5]   **18.** −43 [8.3]
19. −80 [8.6]   **20.** $-\dfrac{2}{7}$ [8.4]   **21.** −53 [8.2]   **22.** 4 [8.6]
23. $x = -5$ [8.7]   **24.** −21°F [8.3]   **25.** 7 [8.2]
26. 14°F [8.6]

Appendix A

Using a Calculator

The wide availability and economical price of hand-held calculators make them ideal for doing exhausting arithmetic operations. You are encouraged to use a calculator as you work through this text. Calculator examples throughout the text show where the use of a calculator is appropriate. Your calculator will be especially useful for

1. adding, subtracting, multiplying, and dividing whole numbers, fractions, and decimals;
2. checking solutions to equations;
3. checking solutions to problems;
4. finding square roots of numbers;
5. finding powers of numbers; and
6. doing percent problems.

A scientific calculator is recommended for this text. It will perform all of these operations and also has keys that are useful in later mathematics courses. A graphing calculator has many more options than are needed for basic mathematics and is ten to thirty times as expensive. If, however, you have access to a graphing calculator, study its manual. The key strokes differ greatly from those described on page A.2. A typical keyboard for a scientific calculator is shown in Figure A.1.

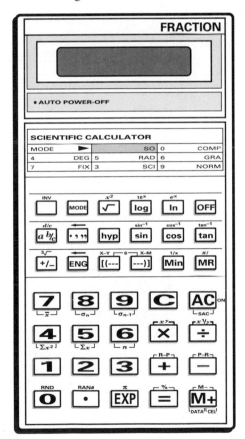

Figure A.1

All scientific (and graphing) calculators have the fundamental order of operations programmed into their circuitry; so, 16 + 24(7) has the value 184.

ENTER | 16 | | + | | 24 | | × | | 7 | | = |

DISPLAY   16.   16.   24.   24.   7.   184.

The calculator has parenthesis keys, which can be used to change the order of operations; so, 7(16 + 24) has the value 280.

ENTER | 7 | | × | | [| | 16 | | + | | 24 | |] | | = |

DISPLAY   7.   7.   0.   16.   16.   24.   40.   280.

Don't forget that both parentheses and fraction bars are used to group operations to show the order.

Expressions	Scientific Calculator Entries	Display
$\dfrac{144}{3} - 7$	| 144 | | ÷ | | 3 | | − | | 7 | | = |	41.
$\dfrac{28 + 40}{16}$	| [| | 28 | | + | | 40 | |] | | ÷ | | 16 | | = |	4.25
$\dfrac{28}{16} + \dfrac{40}{16}$	| 28 | | a$^{b/c}$ | | 16 | | + | | 40 | | a$^{b/c}$ | | 16 | | = |	4⌐1⌐4. $\left(4\dfrac{1}{4}\right)$
$\dfrac{995}{20}$	| 995 | | a$^{b/c}$ | | 20 | | = |	49⌐3⌐4. $\left(49\dfrac{3}{4}\right)$
$\dfrac{995}{20}$	| 995 | | a$^{b/c}$ | | 20 | | = | | INV | | d/c |	199⌐4. $\left(\dfrac{199}{4}\right)$
$13^2 + 14(27)$	| 13 | | x^2 | | + | | 14 | | × | | 27 | | = |	547.
35% of 58	| 35 | | × | | 58 | | % |	20.3
$3\dfrac{7}{8} \div 2\dfrac{1}{3}$	| 3 | | a$^{b/c}$ | | 7 | | a$^{b/c}$ | | 8 | | ÷ | | 2 | | a$^{b/c}$ | | 1 | | a$^{b/c}$ | | 3 | | = |	1⌐37⌐56 $\left(1\dfrac{37}{56}\right)$

Exercises

Practice on your calculator until you can get the results shown in the answer column.

Answers

a. $47 + \dfrac{525}{105}$ 52

b. $\dfrac{45 + 525}{38}$ 15

c. $\dfrac{648}{17 + 15}$ 20.25

d. $\dfrac{140 - 5(6)}{11}$ 10

e. $\dfrac{3870}{9(7) + 23}$ 45

f. $\dfrac{5(73) + 130}{33}$ 15

Answers

g. $\left(1\dfrac{7}{8}\right)\left(\dfrac{5}{9}\right)$ $1\dfrac{1}{24}$

h. $\dfrac{4}{5}\left(\dfrac{6}{11}\right)\left(\dfrac{7}{12}\right)$ $\dfrac{14}{55}$

i. $13\dfrac{1}{2} - 8\dfrac{2}{3} \div 1\dfrac{1}{5}$ $6\dfrac{5}{18}$

j. $5^4 - 16^2$ 369

k. $\left(\dfrac{7}{8}\right)\left(\dfrac{7}{8}\right) - \dfrac{1}{2}$ $\dfrac{17}{64}$

l. 9% of 64   5.76

m. 64% of 9   5.76

n. $\dfrac{19^2 - 7}{32}$ 11.0625 or $11\dfrac{1}{16}$

o. $\dfrac{531}{7^3 - 7^2 + 1}$ 1.8

p. $\dfrac{5^6 - 2^8}{141}$ 109

Round to the nearest hundredth.

q. $\dfrac{388 - 15(4)}{27}$ 12.15

r. $\dfrac{4567}{45(13) - 6(25)}$ 10.50

s. $\dfrac{15^2 - 6^3}{40}$ 0.23

t. $\dfrac{500}{2^{10} - 3^5}$ 0.64

u. $(6.99)(0.72)(\pi)$ 15.81

v. $\sqrt{42}\,(45)\,(1.2)^2$ 419.95

w. $\dfrac{\sqrt{39}}{\pi + 15}$ 0.34

x. $\dfrac{(7.4)(8.2)(4.81^2)}{(1.09)(0.006)(374)}$ 573.97

Additional Study Resources

Bernstein, D. A., and Brkover, T. D. (1973) *Progressive Relaxation Training: A Manual for Helping Professions.* Champaign, IL: Research Press.

Burns, D. D. (1980) *Feeling Good: The New Mood Therapy.* New York: New York American Library.

Davis, Eshelman, and McKay (1988) *The Relaxation and Stress Reduction Workbook.* Oakland, CA: New Harbinger Publications.

Ellis, Albert, and Harper, Robert A. (1975) *A New Guide to Rational Living.* North Hollywood, CA: Wilshire Book Co.

Kogelman, Stanley, and Warren, Joseph (1978) *Mind Over Math.* New York: McGraw-Hill.

Kranzler, B. (1974) *You Can Change How You Feel: A Rational-Emotive Approach.* Eugene, OR: Cascade Press.

Mallow, J. V. (1981) *Science Anxiety: Fear of Science and How to Overcome It.* New York: Van Nostrand Reinhold.

Nolting, Paul D. (1991) *Winning at Math: Your Guide to Learning Mathematics the Quick & Easy Way.* Pompano Beach, FL: Academic Success Press, Inc.

Tobias, Sheila (1987) *Succeed with Math: Every Student's Guide to Conquering Math Anxiety.* Box 886, New York, NY 10101-0886: The College Board.

Tobias, Sheila (1978) *Overcoming Math Anxiety.* Toronto: George J. McLeod Limited.

Progressive Relaxation Tapes

Hopps, Nancy. *Progressive Relaxation/Color Relaxation Cycle*

King, Jim. *Progressive Relaxation*

Miller, Emmett. *Progressive Muscle Relaxation*

Procter, Judith. *Progressive Muscle Relaxation*

CHAPTERS 1 to 4   Midterm Examination

1. Write the place value of the digit 6 in 59,638.   hundred

2. Write the word name for 90,053.
   ninety thousand, fifty-three

3. Add: 1,397
           42
           135
           89,713
           814
           _____
           92,101

4. Add: 786 + 15,382 + 31 + 6   16,205

5. Subtract: 7296
             3759
             _____
             3537

6. Estimate the product and multiply: 307
                                       805
                                       _____
                          240,000; 247,135

7. Multiply: (691)(53)   36,623

8. Divide: 65)8399   129 R 14

9. Divide: 42)5712   136

10. Perform the indicated operations: $7 - 3 \cdot 2 + 10 \div 5$
    3

11. Find the sum of the quotient of 54 and 6 and the product of 11 and 3.   42

12. Find the average of 305, 165, 94, and 100.   166

13. Write the least common multiple (LCM) of 12, 10, and 18.   180

14. Is 107 a prime number or a composite number?
    prime

15. Is 382 a multiple of 9?   No

16. List the first five multiples of 18.   18, 36, 54, 72, 90

17. List all the factors of 204.
    1, 2, 3, 4, 6, 12, 17, 34, 51, 68, 102, 204

18. Write the prime factorization of 192.
    $2 \cdot 2 \cdot 2 \cdot 2 \cdot 2 \cdot 2 \cdot 3 = 2^6 \cdot 3$

19. Change to a mixed number: $\dfrac{41}{9}$ $4\dfrac{5}{9}$

20. Change to an improper fraction: $8\dfrac{3}{4}$ $\dfrac{35}{4}$

21. Which of these fractions are improper?
    $\dfrac{3}{4}, \dfrac{7}{6}, \dfrac{8}{8}, \dfrac{7}{8}, \dfrac{9}{8}, \dfrac{5}{4}, \dfrac{4}{4}$ $\dfrac{7}{6} \dfrac{8}{8} \dfrac{9}{8} \dfrac{5}{4} \dfrac{4}{4}$

22. List these fractions from the smallest to largest:
    $\dfrac{5}{9}, \dfrac{5}{8}, \dfrac{7}{12}, \dfrac{2}{3}$ $\dfrac{5}{9} \dfrac{7}{12} \dfrac{5}{8} \dfrac{2}{3}$

23. Reduce to lowest terms: $\dfrac{48}{72}$ $\dfrac{2}{3}$

24. Multiply and reduce: $\dfrac{5}{8} \cdot \dfrac{2}{25} \cdot \dfrac{6}{5}$ $\dfrac{3}{50}$

25. Multiply. Write the answer as a mixed number:
    $\left(4\dfrac{2}{3}\right)\left(6\dfrac{1}{2}\right)$ $30\dfrac{1}{3}$

26. Divide: $\dfrac{6}{7} \div \dfrac{14}{15}$ $\dfrac{45}{49}$

27. What is the reciprocal of $\dfrac{5}{9}$? $\dfrac{9}{5}$

28. Add: $\dfrac{2}{5} + \dfrac{5}{12}$ $\dfrac{49}{60}$

29. Add: $5\dfrac{2}{3}$

$2\dfrac{5}{7}$ $8\dfrac{8}{21}$

30. Subtract: $9 - 3\dfrac{5}{7}$ $5\dfrac{2}{7}$

31. Subtract: $8\dfrac{3}{5}$

$4\dfrac{7}{9}$ $3\dfrac{37}{45}$

32. Find the average of $2\dfrac{2}{5}$, $1\dfrac{7}{8}$, and $7\dfrac{1}{2}$. $3\dfrac{37}{40}$

33. Perform the indicated operations: $\dfrac{4}{5} - \dfrac{1}{2} \cdot \dfrac{5}{6} \div \dfrac{5}{6}$
$\dfrac{3}{10}$

34. Write the word name for 71.306.   Seventy-one and three hundred six thousandths

35. Write as a decimal: $\dfrac{9}{40}$ 0.225

36. Write as an approximate decimal to the nearest hundredth: $\dfrac{7}{9}$ 0.78

37. What is the place value of the 2 in 39.8972?
ten-thousandths

38. Round to the nearest hundredth: 6.8481
6.85

39. Change to a fraction: 0.2375 $\dfrac{19}{80}$

40. Change to a fraction: $0.16\overline{6}$ $\dfrac{1}{6}$

41. Is the following true or false? 0.4741 < 0.4727
False

42. Add: 2.7 + 12.631 + 3.02 + 6.0032   24.3542

43. Subtract: 23.602
    11.671
    ‾‾‾‾‾‾
    11.931

44. Multiply: 3.603
    5.8
    ‾‾‾‾‾
    20.8974

45. Divide: 28.24 ÷ 10,000   0.002824

46. Divide. Round the answer to the nearest hundredth:
3.5)21.83   6.24

47. Perform the indicated operations:
0.8 − 0.7(0.002) + 0.02   0.8186

48. Letha used 5.2 gallons of gasoline on Monday, 6.2 gallons on Tuesday, 5.9 gallons on Wednesday, 6.7 gallons on Thursday, and 7.4 gallons on Friday. What was the average number of gallons she used per day? (To the nearest tenth.)   6.3 gallons

CHAPTERS 1 to 8   Final Examination

1. Add: $\dfrac{3}{8} + \dfrac{5}{16}$ $\dfrac{11}{16}$

2. Write the LCM (least common multiple) of 12, 14, and 21.   84

3. Subtract: 73.43
   65.45
   7.98

4. Add: $17.09 + 0.095 + 0.21$ 17.395

5. Divide: $\dfrac{3}{4} \div \dfrac{1}{5}$ $\dfrac{15}{4}$ or $3\dfrac{3}{4}$

6. Multiply. Write the result as a mixed number:
   $1\dfrac{5}{6} \cdot 15$ $27\dfrac{1}{2}$

7. Which of these numbers is a prime number? 99, 199, 299, 699   199

8. Divide. Round the answer to the nearest hundredth:
   $0.67\overline{)43.45}$ 64.85

9. Subtract: $10 - 4\dfrac{5}{8}$ $5\dfrac{3}{8}$

10. Multiply: $(0.0098)(10,000)$ 98

11. Round to the nearest thousandth: 79.0068
    79.007

12. Multiply: $(5.6)(8.09)$ 45.304

13. Write as a fraction reduced to the lowest terms:
    70% $\dfrac{7}{10}$

14. Add: $5\dfrac{7}{8}$
    $\dfrac{5}{12}$ $6\dfrac{7}{24}$

15. Solve the proportion: $\dfrac{7}{9} = \dfrac{x}{3}$ $\dfrac{7}{3}$ or $2\dfrac{1}{3}$

16. What is the place value of the 3 in 23.95?   one

17. List these fractions from the smallest to largest:
    $\dfrac{1}{4}, \dfrac{2}{5}, \dfrac{3}{20}$ $\dfrac{3}{20}, \dfrac{1}{4}, \dfrac{2}{5}$

18. Change to percent: $\dfrac{11}{20}$ 55%

19. Divide: $18\overline{)685}$ 38 R 1

20. Write as an approximate decimal to the nearest thousandth: $\dfrac{9}{14}$ 0.643

21. Write the place-value name for "four thousand and four tenths."   4000.4

22. Divide: $0.08\overline{)5}$ 62.5

23. Write as a decimal: $8\dfrac{2}{5}\%$ 0.084

24. Thirty-five percent of what number is 2.1?   6

25. Write as a percent: 2.3   230%

26. Write as a decimal: $\dfrac{33}{200}$ 0.165

27. Sixty-five percent of 32 is what number?   20.8

28. Multiply: $(0.13)(0.2)(0.11)$ 0.00286

E.3

29. If 4 books cost $5.20, how much would 18 books cost? $23.40

30. A CD player set was priced at $400. It is on sale for $335. What is the percent of discount based on the original price?   16.25%

31. List the first five multiples of 13.
13, 26, 39, 52, 65

32. Write the word name for 505.05.
five hundred five and five hundredths

33. Is the following proportion true or false? $\dfrac{1.8}{30} = \dfrac{10}{20}$
False

34. Write the prime factorization of 420.
$2 \cdot 2 \cdot 3 \cdot 5 \cdot 7 = 2^2 \cdot 3 \cdot 5 \cdot 7$

35. Reduce to the lowest terms: $\dfrac{72}{180}$ $\dfrac{2}{5}$

36. Change to a fraction and reduce to the lowest terms: 0.325 $\dfrac{13}{40}$

37. Change to a mixed number: $\dfrac{187}{6}$ $31\dfrac{1}{6}$

38. Multiply and reduce: $\dfrac{4}{21} \cdot \dfrac{28}{64}$ $\dfrac{1}{12}$

39. Change to a fraction: 0.0525 $\dfrac{21}{400}$

40. At a service station 29 out of 50 drivers asked for a ''fill-up.'' What percent of the drivers wanted a full tank of gas?   58%

41. Is 553 a multiple of 3?   No

42. Subtract: $8\dfrac{1}{5} - \dfrac{7}{10}$ $7\dfrac{1}{2}$

43. Change to an improper fraction: $7\dfrac{5}{16}$ $\dfrac{117}{16}$

44. List the following decimals from smallest to largest: 1.32, 1.332, 1.299, 1.322
1.299, 1.32, 1.322, 1.332

45. Divide: $48.73 \div 1000$ 0.04873

46. Divide: $3\dfrac{3}{8} \div 6\dfrac{3}{16}$ $\dfrac{6}{11}$

47. Write a ratio to compare 3 in. to 3 ft (using common units) and reduce. $\dfrac{1}{12}$

48. A woman has calculated that she pays $1.06 for gas and oil to drive 5 miles and that, in addition, it costs her 24¢ for maintenance for each 5 miles she travels. How much will it cost her to drive 5000 miles? $1300

49. Twenty percent of a family's income is spent on food, 8 percent on transportation, 35 percent on housing, 10 percent on heat and utilities, 7 percent on insurance, and the rest on miscellaneous expenses. If the family's income is $1200 per month, how much is spent on miscellaneous expenses? $240

50. In a certain state the gasoline tax is 14 cents per gallon. What is the tax rate (to the nearest tenth of a percent) on gas that costs $1.289 per gallon (not including tax)?   10.9%

51. Perform the indicated operations:
$27 - 4 \cdot 3 + 12 \div 4$ 18

52. Find the average of $\dfrac{7}{12}$, $1\dfrac{5}{8}$, and $4\dfrac{5}{6}$. $2\dfrac{25}{72}$

53. Perform the indicated operations:
$3.4 - 1.8(0.4) \div 3$ 3.16

54. Add: 3 yd 2 ft 9 in.
    3 yd 2 ft 8 in.
    7 yd 2 ft 5 in.

55. Subtract: 4 m 27 cm
    1 m 67 cm
    2 m 60 cm

56. Convert 5¢ per gram to dollars per kilogram.
$50 per kg

NAME _____ _____ CLASS _____ DATE _____

57. Find the perimeter of a trapezoid with bases of $10\frac{1}{2}$ ft and $12\frac{1}{4}$ ft and sides of 3 ft and $5\frac{1}{2}$ ft.

$31\frac{1}{4}$ ft

58. Find the area of a triangle with base 3.3 m and height 1.8 m. 2.97 m^2

59. Find the area of the following geometric figure (let $\pi = 3.14$):

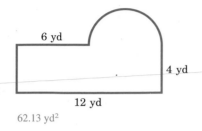

62.13 yd^2

60. Find the volume of a box with length $1\frac{1}{4}$ feet, width 9 inches, and height 6 inches (in cubic inches). 810 in.^3

61. Add: $(-26) + (-18) + 15$ -29

62. Subtract: $(-85) - (-62)$ -23

63. Multiply: $(3)(7)(-6)$ -126

64. Divide: $(-88) \div (-22)$ 4

65. Perform the indicated operations:
$(-6 - 4)(-4) \div (-5) - (-10)$ 2

66. Solve: $12a + 50 = 2$ $a = -4$

Index

Units of Measurement

System-to-System Equivalents

English–Metric Conversions			Metric–English Conversions	
1 inch	=	2.54 centimeters	1 centimeter	= 0.3937 inch
1 foot	=	0.3048 meter	1 meter	= 3.281 feet
1 yard	=	0.9144 meter	1 meter	= 1.094 yards
1 mile	=	1.609 kilometers	1 kilometer	= 0.6214 mile
1 quart	=	0.946 liter	1 liter	= 1.057 quarts
1 gallon	=	3.785 liters	1 liter	= 0.2642 gallon
1 ounce	=	28.35 grams	1 gram	= 0.0353 ounce
1 pound	=	453.59 grams	1 gram	= 0.0022 pound

English Measures and Equivalents

Length	Time
12 inches (in.) = 1 foot (ft)	60 seconds (sec) = 1 minute (min)
3 feet (ft) = 1 yard (yd)	60 minutes (min) = 1 hour (hr)
5280 feet (ft) = 1 mile (mi)	24 hours (hr) = 1 day
	7 days = 1 week

Liquid Volume	Weight
3 teaspoons (tsp) = 1 tablespoon (tbs)	16 ounces (oz) = 1 pound (lb)
2 cups (c) = 1 pint (pt)	2000 pounds (lb) = 1 ton
2 pints (pt) = 1 quart (qt)	
4 quarts (qt) = 1 gallon (gal)	